HAUNTED BY HISTORY

HAUNTED BY HISTORY

Myths in International Relations

Edited by

Cyril Buffet

and

Beatrice Heuser

Berghahn Books
Providence • Oxford

Published in 1998 by

Berghahn Books

Library of Congress Cataloging-in-Publication Data

Haunted by history : myths in international relations / edited by
Cyril Buffet and Beatrice Heuser.
p. cm.
Includes bibliographical references and index.
ISBN 1-57181-940-1 (alk. paper)
1. International relations—History. I. Buffet, Cyril.
II. Heuser, Beatrice, 1961–
JZ1305.H38 1998
327'.09'04—dc 21 97-38353
CIP

British Library Cataloguing in Publication Data

A CIP catalogue record for this book is available from
the British Library.

Printed in the United States on acid-free paper.

Cover illustration: 'European Concert' – private possession of Cyril Buffet, found at Tahune on 20 October 1915 in a German trench.

Contents

List of Tables

Acknowledgements

This research project was supported by the British Council, the Institut Français in Berlin, the Robert Bosch Foundation and the Centre Marc Bloch. We also owe thanks to the Humboldt University in Berlin and to Professor Hartmut Kaelble for permission to use its premises for our conferences.

INTRODUCTION

Of Myths and Men

Beatrice Heuser and Cyril Buffet

Ce qui a été sera, pouvu qu'on s'en souvienne.
Aragon[1]

Hardly a week goes by without historical comparisons being made in contemporary news coverage and political speeches. 'Bosnia, a second Munich?',[2] we read in the papers, followed by suggestions of parallels between the Yugoslav war and the Vietnam war;[3] or a discussion of 'Defence and the Suez factor';[4] in Bosnia-Herzegovina there was a fear of a 'Balkan Yalta',[5] a division of their country between Serbia and Croatia; British journalists alleged that the 'West carves up Europe in a new Yalta'.[6] We see photos of Churchill, Roosevelt and Stalin in the Crimean resort accompanying such articles,[7] or cartoons of a hearse bearing the British-American 'Special Relationship' to its grave.[8] Throughout the Cold War, West German politicians repeatedly reminded each other in public speeches to steer clear of any policies of changing alliances, and to show themselves eternally loyal to the West,

1. 'That what has been will be (again), as long as somebody will remember it.'
2. Hubert de Beaufort and General (CR) Jacques de Zelicourt, 'Bosnie: un deuxième Munich?', *Le Figaro* (30 Dec. 1994).
3. *Ibid.*
4. 'Defence and the Suez factor: John Nott compares the lessons of the Falklands with the fiasco of 1956', *The Times* (6 Nov. 1986).
5. 'Balkanska Yalta', caricature in *Zunanja Politika* (1992).
6. *Observer* (21 April 1996).
7. 'Die großen Drei', *Fränkischer Anzeiger* (11 Feb. 1995).
8. Peter Brooke's cartoon of 30 March 1995, published in the *Independent*.

alluding to the German 'betrayal' of France at Tauroggen, Rapallo, and to the Hitler-Stalin pact.[9] At the time of German reunification, a British historian invoked the need to offset the size and force of the new united Germany through a balance-of-power policy.[10]

What is striking is the way in which historical analogy is used, or indeed, misused. Almost invariably, this is done in the context of recommending a certain policy for the future. Almost invariably, there is the implication that an alternative policy might lead to some negative, perhaps catastrophic development, with the further suggestion that a particularly bleak episode of history would in some way repeat itself. History is used here as a 'myth'.

There are many different and overlapping definitions and usages of the term 'myth'. The following are pertinent to the phenomenon studied in this book: the Pantheist philosopher Friedrich von Schelling called it a 'primitive explanation of the world'. Another philosopher, Ernst Cassirer, pointed to the moral and dynamic dimensions of the myth:

> We fail ... to understand the true character and the full significance of myth if, according to its Greek name, we see in it a mere 'narrative' – a recollection or recital of the memorable deeds of heroes or gods. This *epic* aspect is not the only one and not the decisive one. Myth has always a dramatic character. It conceives the world as a great drama – as a struggle between divine and demonic forces, between light and darkness, between the good and the evil. There is always a negative and a positive pole in mythical thought and imagination. Even the political myths were incomplete so long as they had not introduced a demonic power. The process of deification had to be completed by a process that we may describe as 'devilization'.[11]

Coming closer still to our subject, Edmund Leach defined it as a 'sacred tale about past events which is used to justify ... action in the present'.[12] The German *Brockhaus* encyclopaedia, exploring

9. Heinrich von Brentano, 'Rapallo ist nicht mehr aktuell', *Die Welt* (14 May 1957); Franz Josef Strauss in a Bundestag debate, text in *Frankfurter Abendblatt* (30 Jan. 1958); Manfred Wörner, 'Die Zukunft der Allianz', *Wehrkunde* Vol. 32, No. 3 (Mar. 1983), p. 116.

10. Dr Anne Deighton in a letter to the *Financial Times* (20 July 1990).

11. Ernst Cassirer, 'Judaism and the Modern Political Myths', in Donald Phillip Verene (ed.), *Symbol, Myth, and Culture: Essays and Lectures of Ernst Cassirer, 1935–1945* (New Haven: Yale University Press, 1979), p. 238. See also Ernst Cassirer, *The Myth of the State* (New Haven: Yale University Press, 1946).

12. Edward Leach, 'Anthropological Approaches to the Study of the Bible during the Twentieth Century', in Edward Leach and D. Alan Aycock (eds), *Structuralist*

the myth as 'a vision of the masses which is supposed to trigger political action', pointed out that 'the myth does not give a scientific explanation, but wants to be believed'.

> Like other myths unconsciously, the political myth consciously, in the form of well-aimed propaganda, seeks to give an imaginary explanation of a mission. That which is shown in the image may in the distant past have played a rôle close to reality, but is now supposed to justify present actions through an imaginary duty to the future and make it invulnerable to criticism.[13]

Myth is thus used in this book primarily as a shorthand for a particular interpretation of a historical experience or policy, or a policy with some acknowledged historical antecedents, that is invoked in the present to justify certain policies.[14] There are some contributions in this book that deal with 'myths' both in the sense described above *and* in the sense of 'untrue representation of a past event' (the myth of Yalta as the division of the world, or the myth of Swedish neutrality). It is not our chief purpose to point out that certain parts of history (the conferences of Yalta and Potsdam for example) are commonly misrepresented and look different in the light of historical research. History will always have to be rewritten in the light of new evidence. What is more important, to us, is the political use that is made of particular interpretations of history, which invariably imply that history repeats itself, or that customs and attitudes endure simply because they have – supposedly – been observed since 'time immemorial'.

Our study of this phenomenon is divided into four main subcategories: myths about the international system itself (international order, balance of power, European concert, neutrality); myths about taking sides and betrayal (the Spanish Civil War, Munich, Yalta, Potsdam); myths of special relationships for better or worse (the British-American Special Relationship, Britain and Europe, France's independence, the Franco-German couple, and Islam and Europe), and myths about Germany (the *Sonderweg*, Prussia, Rapallo). This is a loose grouping of these myths, and

---

Interpretations of Biblical Myth (Cambridge: Cambridge University Press, 1983), p. 8. We are very grateful to our co-mythologist Dr Lorna Milne from St Andrews University for this reference.

13. *Brockhaus Enzyklopädie* 17th edn, Vol. 13 (Wiesbaden: Brockhaus Verlag, 1971), p. 143.

14. For other definitions of myths, see particularly pp. 29–31, 117–119, 135 of the present volume.

does not yet reflect a real categorisation which we shall attempt in the last chapter of this book. These myths have been selected by using the following criteria: they are known in *at least* two countries; they are still alive today (as we show through recent references to their use in the media); and they exercise an influence on the debate about foreign policy.

While we consider different myths in this book, and different categories of myths, we make no claim here to comprehensiveness but instead merely endeavour to present a selection of some of the most important. Many important myths have been left out, such as Britain's Splendid Isolation, *Mitteleuropa*, the Monroe Doctrine, the *Entente Cordiale*, Versailles, Prague, the Yellow Peril and the Red Menace, the myth of Brussels, etc. Other conceptual myths, such as bipolarity (with its Manichaean twin, the struggle of Good against Evil) or the mere notion that one can speak of 'international relations' when nations as political actors have at best existed since the American and French revolutions, have been neglected. All these, and indeed a study of the language of myth, thoroughly merit a follow-up research project to the present one, which cannot hope to answer all the questions it raised to begin with, and has moreover given birth to new ones.

To stake a true claim to the international dimension of the subject of our research, the contributors themselves come from seven countries in the Euro-Atlantic region, and thus are mostly familiar with all myths discussed. To demonstrate the interrelation between myth and policy-making, we invited both academics (historians and political scientists, some of whom have been involved in advisory work for politicians, in journalism and in political speech-writing themselves) and practitioners actively involved in policy-making to participate in this project.

The following chapters, then, contain case studies of myths that are rooted in historical experiences. In the final chapter we will draw some general observations about the working of historical myths in international relations, building on the studies presented here. There we shall attempt to categorise the myths we have studied; we shall try to establish how the process of using the historical analogy to defend a particular course of action works, and why it is employed (in preference to other arguments); and we shall try to find out whether this is a rational use of historical evidence.

Part I

Myths of the International System

Chapter 1

Balance of Power, European Concert and Integration

The Myth of a Changing International System

Peter Krüger

In the noisy vestibule of the temple of myths, slogans reign – and close to them, ideology. Myths reduce the complexity of reality to unambiguous, comprehensible, symbolically compressed events, conditions and truths; they also appeal – sometimes more, sometimes less – to the beliefs of people. Balance of power, European concert, integration – three concepts that are fundamental to the modern international system – are some of the less spectacular myths in foreign policy.[1] Confusingly, they are at once scientific terms, concrete relationships and the seeds of myths – only seeds, because they are not fully developed 'myths' in a general sense. Fully developed, effective, spectacular myths are usually those related to historical events such as 'Versailles' and 'Rapallo'; or to perceptions, such as 'the encirclement of Germany', 'hereditary enemies' and 'a people without space'; or to goals, such as 'a place in the sun', 'gaining living space' and 'open door'. Especially in

---

Translated by Michael Juricic

1. For literature on the terms 'balance of power', 'European concert' and 'integration', see the following literature and the accompanying bibliographies: Ernst Kaeber, *Die Idee des europäischen Gleichgewichts in der publizistischen Literatur vom 16. bis zur Mitte des 18. Jahrhunderts* (Berlin, 1907); Carsten Holbraad, *The Concert of Europe: A Study in German and British International Theory, 1815–1914* (London,

foreign policy, such myths are symbols conditioning opinions, wishes and ways of behaving;[2] but they can also create consensus.

The Germans have proved remarkably susceptible to such foreign policy myths. One possible explanation could lie in their inexperience in foreign policy – they often proudly reject the concept of diplomacy (with its compromises) in favour of high principles. Such an approach urges the immediate realisation of wide-ranging goals, theories or ideologies and is frequently based – even if only for propaganda purposes – on myths and oversimplifications. Examples include the 'German people and their right to life' (before 1914 and above all between the two world wars), the myth of the *Reich* and its priority in Eastern Europe,[3] and *Mitteleuropa*,[4] which is repeatedly invoked, but also, in guilt-laden contradiction, a dedication to peace, justice and human rights for the entire world.

The mythical quality of a foreign policy based on ideological slogans and demanding continual ritual statements of support was recognised during the 1920s as a striking contrast to the true requirements of the day, which aimed at balancing interests in a renewed European concert. As Bruno Frank noted in 1928, in Germany 'the masses were bombarded with mystical talk until they began to consider any attainable short-term goal to be beneath contempt'.[5] Here one could well replace mystical by mythical. There was an irrational refusal to pursue interests in dialogue with other governments, even when these interests were limited and amenable to compromise. Especially between the two world wars, there was a widespread refusal to break away from cherished

---

1970); Hans Fenske, 'Gleichgewicht, Balance', in *Geschichtliche Grundbegriffe* Vol. 2 (Stuttgart, 1975), pp. 959–996; Georges Livet, *L'équilibre européen de la fin du XVe à la fin du XVIIIe siècle* (Paris, 1976); Ludolf Herbst, 'Die zeitgenössische Integrationstheorie und die Anfänge der europäischen Einigung, 1947–1950', *Vierteljahrshefte für Zeitgeschichte*, Vol. 34 (1986), pp. 161–205; for an important recent debate see *American Historical Review* Vol. 97, No. 1 (1992), pp. 683–735. For an analysis of myths, see A. Horstmann, 'Mythos, Mythologie', in *Historisches Wörterbuch der Philosophie* Vol. 6 (Darmstadt, 1984), pp. 281–318.

2. See Murray Edelman, *Politik als Ritual: Die symbolische Funktion staatlicher Institutionen und staatlichen Handelns* (Frankfurt/Main, 1976), p. 5.

3. Lothar Kettenacker, 'Der Mythos vom Reich', in Karl Heinz Bohrer (ed.), *Mythos und Moderne: Begriff und Bild einer Rekonstruktion* (Frankfurt/Main, 1983), pp. 261–289.

4. See Sven Papcke and Werner Weidenfeld (eds), *Traumland Mitteleuropa? Beiträge zu einer aktuellen Kontroverse* (Darmstadt, 1988); Richard Plaschka *et al.* (eds), *Mitteleuropa-Konzeptionen in der ersten Hälfte des 20. Jahrhunderts* (Vienna, 1995).

5. Bruno Frank, *Politische Novelle* (orig. 1928, reprinted. Stuttgart: Reclam Universalbibliothek, No. 7830/31, 1956), p. 75.

myths of German supremacy or from a racial, anti-modern, introspective nationalism – even though it was a world of increasing integration. Alternative myths – if myths there had to be – might even at the time have included the ideas of balance of power, European concert and even European integration.

All this tells us something about differences between types of foreign policy myths. 'Balance of power', 'European concert' and to some extent even 'integration' are hardly able to arouse the masses. Instead, they appeal to a smaller group of well-educated people, to politicians, decision-makers and foreign-policy experts. Moreover, they usually concern concepts which, although not unambiguous, are found mainly in the sphere of diplomacy. They belong more within the realm of goals which are neither boundless nor incalculable, but can be achieved by pragmatic means, and are of importance to states whose geographic proximity requires that they must get along with each other. Yet such concepts or myths are often dismissed as inadequate and too unambitious given the vast problems of humankind.

The very term 'international policy goals' can assume mythical qualities when striving towards important goals almost becomes an existential duty and demands unrestricted priority over all other considerations, even though in foreign policy the process, means and methods are decisive. They merit particular attention from researchers.[6] Balance of power, European concert and integration offer good reasons to practise this attention. From a historical as well as a logical perspective they reveal a connection or development that will become more evident from a short discussion of each of the three terms.

Balance of Power

The idea of a balance of power is the oldest of the three terms. It also has the greatest range of meanings, although it is the simplest basic idea. Once turned into a complex system, it virtually effaces itself, giving way to a fundamentally different fabric of the international system, in particular the concert of Europe. Normally, the concert is not seen as something new but as a particular sub-form of balance of power. Such an interpretation would not

6. See Peter Krüger, *Die Außenpolitik der Republik von Weimar* 2nd edn (Darmstadt, 1993), p. 81; and Paul W. Schroeder, *The Transformation of European Politics, 1763–1848* (Oxford, 1994), p. 244.

withstand close scrutiny, yet the reasons for its suitability as a myth may be identified in its venerable age as well as in its adaptability to totally different purposes. While it may be an exaggeration to speak of a continuous historical line of development, the concept of balance of power and its conscious application go at least as far back as fifteenth-century Italy.

The various meanings of balance of power, depending on political and intellectual conditions, interests and points of view, have given the term propagandistic and ideological connotations, thus furthering the creation of the myth. Its lack of focus was also crucial to its complicated relationship with the European concert. In the mid-1920s, this was expressed in Strupp's *Dictionary of International Law and Diplomacy*[7] where for 'balance of power' we find the entry: 'See European concert.' In 1918, Heinrich Meisner characterised the League of Nations as a 'child of equilibrist thought'.[8] This might have been dismissed as a typically biased German approach, rooted in the British-American 'balance of power' designed to contain the German Empire, had Ernst B. Haas not described the United Nations (UN) as the successor of the 'balancing principles' of the European system of states since the Congress of Vienna.[9] Woodrow Wilson, who had conceived his League of Nations almost as a democratic-international antithesis to the rotten system of states of the European balance of power, would not have liked Haas's description.

The already conceptualised system of balance of power in Italy during the second half of the fifteenth century was to receive a major shock as a result of the great power struggles then beginning at the European level. In the sixteenth and seventeenth centuries, conceptions of balance of power first developed quite simply from the global power position of the Habsburgs and their confrontations with the French. It was a configuration with two leading powers on whom other powers depended, giving England (with

7. See the *Wörterbuch des Völkerrechts und der Diplomatie* 3 vols (Berlin and Leipzig, 1924–1929).

8. Heinrich Otto Meisner, 'Vom europäischen Gleichgewicht', *Preußische Jahrbücher* Vol. 176 (1919), p. 245. For the antecedents and the interpretation of the European system as restricting war and regulating international politics until 1914, see Lucien Bély, 'Les trois paradoxes du Congrès d'Utrecht', in Pierre Chaunu (ed.), *Les fondements de la paix* (Paris, 1993), pp. 137–153, and the contributions of Chaunu and Soutou in Pierre Chaunu (ed.), *Les enjeux de la paix: Nous et les autres, XVIIe–XXIe siècles* (Paris, 1995), pp. 18–28, 55–80.

9. Ernst B. Haas, 'The Balance of Power: Prescription, Concept, or Propaganda?' *World Politics* Vol. 5 (1953), p. 473.

the Netherlands soon as a dependent partner) the power of tipping the scales within Europe. These power struggles were rationalised in balancing terms in many propagandistic, theoretical and partisan publications, which attempted to generalise the concept. Soon it was no longer used against the power of the Habsburgs alone, but against the France of Louis XIV and finally for the establishment of a system of balance of power itself. Later, it was promoted further by the rise of other great powers – Russia and Prussia – which geographically expanded the system. The Peace of Utrecht in 1713 introduced the more advanced idea – though hardly the practice – of a just equilibrium (*juste équilibre*) into the *Droit public de l'Europe fondé sur les traités* (Mably).

In addition, balancing ideas were very soon applied to many more areas and in an ever greater variety of ways, thus contributing to an early blurring of their focus. As expected, interpretations depended on interests and predominant opinions about fundamental principles, politics, society, economics and interstate relations on the basis of a sovereignty of states, indispensable for the balance of power. A balance of trade, of religions, of political and societal order with a clear development towards equality were all described as a prerequisite of any balance of power. Several English catchwords were characteristic: liberty, religion, trade and the interest-based links between these various levels. The best example was the British (and Dutch) refusal to support an Austrian company in Ostende (1722–31) specialising in trade in Asia: the reason given was that the weakening of their world trade had to be prevented so that they could maintain their capacity to fulfil duties in preserving Europe's balance of power.

The remaining features of the system of balance of power were also developed early on, including the concept of security (although its dynamics could undermine the balance of power), the sub-systems, barriers, buffer zones of the small states functioning as intermediaries, etc. Finally, there was the realisation that not only the size of one's territory and the strength of one's military were important for a country's position in the system of states, but also one's domestic order, resources and cultural prestige. At the core were the variety of Europe's many states, their *raison d'état* and, especially since the Enlightenment, the belief in a reasonable and predictable organisation of international relations, including the hope that the natural sciences could influence their arrangement.

From the mid-eighteenth until the mid-nineteenth century, one can also find a criticism of balance of power and the development of a counter-myth. On the one hand, it focused on the nature of interstate politics (for example, Justi's *Die Chimäre des Gleichgewichts von Europa* from 1758). On the other hand, it expanded into philosophy and general politics, stressing the ideal of the balance of human passions and motivations (Shaftesbury), or a new vision of the perfect balance of humanity (Herder), whereby any action against humanity would disturb the general balance of things. But it was also expressed in the optimism of Liberalism – in part following Kant – which emphasised the internal balance of a free order as the prerequisite for a dignified international order. The assumption of Kant and his followers was that a Liberal constitution and economic system could reduce the incidence of war and the power-political conflicts inherent in late absolutism and usher in a new era through open co-operation and the peaceful balancing of the interests of sovereign nations.[10] This myth had great influence on the peace programme of Wilson, on the League of Nations and the UN.

The emphatic rejection – although muted in practice – of the concepts of balance of power, concert and the European system of states on the 'Left' had its equivalent on the 'Right' in the hypertrophy of unlimited freedom of action as well as in the rejection of any restricting international order and in the concept of the dynamic 'power state', bloated only by its own interests, where any international order was only an unpleasant obstacle to the powerful state's actions. This anti-myth was legitimised by the exploitation of Hegelian philosophy, which contributed to the brutalisation of foreign policy in post-Bismarckian Germany and in many other parts of Europe, because of a destructive Social Darwinist belief that only the strong had the right to prevail. Influenced by deep social ruptures after 1918, power politics were turned into fascist force and led to a craving for unlimited supremacy freed from the shackles of the rule of law and accountability on the basis of an extreme ideology that emphasised the strongest race and its omnipotence in National Socialism.

Meanwhile, the concept of balance of power had developed in a different direction. The first half of the nineteenth century had above all been the era of the European concert. Only from the middle of the century – due to a growing desire for freedom of action, the establishment of the German Empire, and the growing internal and external problems arising from 'modernisation' –

10. For a comprehensive approach see Reinhard Brandt, 'Europa in der Reflexion der Aufklärung', *Politisches Denken. Jahrbuch 1997*, pp. 1–23.

balance of power once more came to the fore in an increasingly unstable great power system. On the one hand, this was challenged by the growing opposition within the German Empire to the balance of power and ordering principles of the system of states, which culminated in opposition to peace efforts in 1914. Balance of power was denounced as an instrument of English policy aiming to constrain and encircle Germany, giving rise to the slogan that one must trust only in one's own power and follow only one's own goals, if necessary with force.

On the other hand, considerations were under way concerning the formalisation of the European concert in the pursuit of greater humanitarian goals. Nevertheless, these also undermined the old system of the balance of power of the great powers which Ranke and others had wanted to strengthen. In as far as they were still taken seriously between the two world wars, such designs were manifested in the League of Nations, itself the heir of an old myth, together with the new myths of collective security, disarmament and the peaceful arbitration of disputes, as well as Locarno and a few ephemeral attempts to create new forms of European cooperation and integration.[11]

After 1945, the concept of the balance of power experienced a renaissance in its adaptation to the East-West confrontation between the two superpowers and as a scientific research project for the theory and history of international relations. Since 1989, equilibrium and the balancing of security, along with the reconciliation of interests, rights and duties in a regulated framework of power have again become a challenge, above all in the relations between Russia, the rest of Eastern Europe, the European Union (EU) and NATO.

Where could the myth succeed in infiltrating balance-of-power thinking?

- 'Balance of power' has become a myth for a rational code of behaviour and a regulator in international politics.
- The concrete concept of balance has time and again been linked with mystical beliefs. This happened, for example, when the balance of power in itself was regarded as the (self-justifying) aim of an eternal power struggle.

11. See Peter Krüger, 'Der Europagedanke in der Weimarer Republik – Locarno als Kristallisationspunkt und Impuls', in Jac Bosmans (ed.), *Europagedanke, Europabewegung und Europapolitik in den Niederlanden und Deutschland seit dem Ersten Weltkrieg* (Münster, 1996), pp. 15–32.

- From the seventeenth to the nineteenth centuries in particular, 'balance of power' was elevated to a symbol not only of harmony, law, morals, reason and humanity, but also of science and rational accountability.
- The concept attained an even wider, generalising character, and the societal and political balancing which had once taken place only within states was then applied to the system of states and represented a type of ideal, favouring the golden means between the extremes.
- In the twentieth century in particular, a negative mythologisation of balance of power was created: the balance of power as war-generating, favouring the strong, accelerating arms races and resulting in a balance of terror leading to the brink of atomic war in the confrontation between East and West.

One thing stands out: the tendency to transcend or to set aside the importance of the concept of balance of power. Paul Schroeder has argued that although statesmen talk about balance of power, they rarely act according to it.[12] There is hardly a theory of balance of power which actually gets along with that term and its systematisation alone. As a rule, additional assumptions and principles are required. That stands to reason, especially under the current premise that a balance of power is said to be a prerequisite of a certain order, of rules, norms, accountability and security for all participating members. On principle, a pure balance-of-power concept is not suitable for that purpose. Hence the efforts to complement it by additional institutions, theories, treaty arrangements and even such enlargements which come close to myth-making, provided it can influence the conduct of other actors and public opinion. Additional ordering principles must also be adopted which authorise, constrain and legitimise certain actions, such as the embodiment of balance of power in natural and international law, preventive intervention, harmony and balance as hallmarks of a durable, accepted system, and a just European community of states. Such measures remove balance of power, because they mute or suspend its effects of constant restlessness of the whole system resulting from changes within states, their power bases, their constellation and the need to adapt to an ever-changing balance of power (before 1914, the pentarchy of the great powers came close to this exhausting state of affairs). Therefore, a pure

12. See Paul W. Schroeder, 'Historical Reality vs. Neo-realist Theory', *International Security* Vol. 19, No. 1 (Summer 1994), pp. 108–148.

balance of power is very limited in its applications. Consistent application of such a system would presuppose a mechanism for change that was brutal and subjected every actor to continual insecurity and anxiety. Yet this would not create an international order worthy of the name.

As balance of power is such a powerful symbol characterising an international system of sovereign states, it is also the core for all considerations aiming at limiting power. Thus, it requires many supplements, extensions and ties to other concepts and principles if a regulated system of states is to be created[13] – balance of power as a myth of scholarly analysis, too.

The European Concert

One apparent extension, as already noted, is the European concert; of the three concepts, this is the one least accessible to myth-making. Between 1813 and 1815, the concert was conceived as a conscious counter-model to the ruinous balance of power which had rested on territorial compensation but did not address burdens and risks or pass them on to weaker states.[14] The statesmen who led the battle against Napoleon looked for *European* solutions to problems. These solutions were to deal commonly and collectively with dangerous structural problems of the entire system of states; the durability of this arrangement was to be secured through treaties, norms of conduct, mutually accepted borders, zones of influence, inter-regional ties as well as the interdependence of interests between the larger and smaller states, the role and rule of law, buffer zones and noticeable improvements in international law – a political equilibrium instead of a balance of power (Paul Schroeder). A balancing of interests, security, and room for manoeuvre was the accomplishment of the Congress of Vienna. Major conflicts and differences in interests, including the danger of war, persisted, but what changed – and this was decisive – were the methods of handling conflicts: it was accepted that freedom of action had to be restricted.

The European concert in a narrow sense was the contractual obligation of the great powers to deal with the important questions

13. See Peter Krüger (ed.), *Kontinuität und Wandel in der Staatenordnung der Neuzeit: Beiträge zur Geschichte des internationalen Systems* (Marburg, 1991).

14. See especially Schroeder, *The Transformation of European Politics.*

of European politics in co-ordination with each other. This was maintained until the middle of the nineteenth century. But in the consciousness of the leading statesmen it survived until 1914 and revived briefly during the Locarno era. It did not represent an institutionalised balance of power: instead, it meant taking into account fundamental interests in a political equilibrium and almost hierarchical system ranging from the latent hegemons (Britain and Russia) down to the smaller states.[15] This did not mean that the balance of power did not play a role; on the contrary, it was indispensable. Its effectiveness, however, was merely manifested within the security of the prevailing order, especially in the various sub-systems and regional balances of power. It was controlled and restricted by the concert. Above all, balance of power was thus a means for securing the concert, not the reverse as is usually maintained.

The European concert was rarely turned into myth: it was too little known and too concrete. Exceptions include Britain in the second half of the nineteenth century, where there was support for the development of the European concert as an enforcement mechanism for humanitarian goals, self-determination and a peaceful balancing of interests. This was one of the origins of British conceptions of the League of Nations – which did not succeed in 1919 – as a mechanism for consultation and crisis management and opposed to a tight organisation based in mandatory obligations (in 1925, the proximity of the loose British League concept to the concept of the European concert helped to combine the Locarno system with the League). Another exception concerns the European concert as a negative myth, a great power consortium against the pursuit of national interests. On the whole, the concept of a European concert represents the best that Europe has contributed to the regulation of interstate politics. This conception can be of great benefit for the problems encountered in today's Europe, as well as in the 'new world order'.

Integration

Finally, a further important European achievement is the concept of integration. As the specific myth of European integration – older concepts of centralisation, concentration and

15. See Paul W. Schroeder, 'The Nineteenth Century System: Balance of Power or Political Equilibrium?' *Review of International Studies* Vol. 15, No. 2 (April 1989), pp. 135–153.

rationalisation[16] will not be discussed here – this myth is tied to a remarkable change in the meaning of integration. It has been characterised as a union of Europe through supranational institutions based on partial renunciation of national sovereignty ever since the preparation of the European Coal and Steel Community. Under another name (that of European unification) this concept is much older and has been the programme of certain political movements since the First World War. It is a model example of the political myth of securing peace, solidarity, economic prosperity and supranational community in a European federal state.[17]

However, the actual history of European integration was quite different, not with a shared common aim of supranationality. With due mechanisms, nation-states illustrated their ability to change and progress with pragmatic steps toward integration.[18] After 1945, integration became an adequate answer to serious domestic and foreign policy difficulties. The framework of a concert making *ad hoc* agreements was no longer adequate for the complexity of interstate problems. In certain areas suggested by urgent necessities of the time, integration replaced the concert. However, there is a danger that the difference between both methods will be blurred in the future. On the one hand, there is a pragmatic policy of *ad hoc* integration which patiently awaits the creation of a consensus among the participating governments in the best tradition of the concert; on the other hand, there is the construction of a European federal state as an abstract aim. This is a difference which the architects of the European Union have wisely taken into account and which has helped it to survive crises.[19]

Conclusion

The historical approach of my analysis has gone from a weakly defined to an increasingly precise international order in Europe,

16. For two examples, see 'integration' as a generic term for economic union and company mergers, in *Handwörterbuch des Kaufmanns* Vol. 3 (Hamburg and Berlin, 1927), p. 44; and already in the sense of political integration in a discussion of the imperfect integration of the German Empire by Otto Hintze, *Gesammelte Abhandlungen* Vol. 1, 1st edn (Göttingen, 1929), p. 86.

17. David M. Harrison, *The Organisation of Europe* (London, 1994), pp. 1–36.

18. See Alan Milward, *The European Rescue of the Nation-State* (Berkeley, 1992).

19. See Peter Krüger, *Wege und Widersprüche der europäischen Integration im 20. Jahrhundert*, Schriften des Historischen Kollegs, Lecture No. 45 (Munich, 1995).

from balance of power to the European concert to integration, accompanied by their respective myths. But historical experience has shown that neither the balance of power nor the European concert has become obsolete. The states system remains alive even in the new form of integration, and balancing thought is always necessary – even more so are the principles of the European concert. This is the case even for and within the EU, especially when it comes to preparing new tasks and steps towards integration; it is also the case for the EU's external relations, not least as a model for other regions. Even the myths still carry weight. Myths are important precisely in the complicated relationships of contemporary international politics. This is true in so far as they are indisputable key concepts and slogans of general acceptance, but are ambiguous enough to open difficult negotiations on the basis of fundamental agreement about such aims and 'myths' such as 'securing peace' or 'liberalising the international economy'. This was the case with the concepts of balance of power or the European concert in the nineteenth century: then people were convinced of the value of the principles upon which these concepts were based; they limited claims and demands and made them predictable, and yet they created the framework for the pursuit of proper interests.

Chapter 2

MYTHS THAT KEEP SMALL POWERS GOING

Internationalist Idealism in the Netherlands

Jan Willem Honig

The small European powers have lived in a dangerous world for several centuries now. Their imminent demise has been predicted repeatedly. At the turn of the century, the political elites of the major powers generally agreed that the inevitable fate of small powers would be annexation or, at least, exclusive and total economic domination by a great power.[1] Yet, the small powers survived the First World War – if anything, in 1919 there were more of them in Europe than in 1914. At the end of the Second World War, the pre-eminent British Realist, E. H. Carr, wrote, '[t]he conclusion now seems to impose itself on any unbiased observer that the small independent nation-state is obsolete or obsolescent …'.[2] Indeed, the formation of the Soviet East European empire and a string of West European integrationist international organisations, culminating in the European Union, appeared to bring Carr's prediction closer to reality. Yet, by the 1990s the Soviet empire had collapsed and European integration faltered. In the past few years,

1. Fritz Fischer, *Krieg der Illusionen: Die deutsche Politik von 1911 bis 1914* (Düsseldorf: Droste, 1987), pp. 72–73.

2. E. H. Carr, *The Twenty Years' Crisis, 1919–1939: An Introduction to the Study of International Relations*, 2nd edn (New York: Harper and Row, 1964; orig. 1946), p. vii. See also his *Nationalism and After* (New York: Macmillan, 1945).

fourteen new states have emerged in Europe, none of which are indisputably major powers (though, perhaps, some may have the potential). Since 1900 the number of small powers on the continent has more than doubled. If we accept as major European powers Britain, Germany, France and Russia, and in 1900, also Austria-Hungary and Turkey, the number of small powers has gone up from eighteen to forty-two.[3] Still, the old idea that small states are an anomaly dies hard. In June 1991, the Luxembourg foreign minister (as member of the EC foreign ministers' troika sent to Yugoslavia to mediate in the developing crisis) told the Slovenian leadership that independence was not a good idea since their mini-state was hardly viable on its own.[4]

Of course, one could argue that it is the temporary weakness of the major powers which has given small states a chance to survive and multiply. Many still believe that they were and they will remain pawns the great balance of power game. But have not small states existed for rather a long time now? One could equally argue that the idea that great powers have a future is a myth, inspired by the strange belief that the boundless struggle for power, hegemony and survival is innate in states. To expose that myth, however, is not the purpose of this chapter. It proposes to look at the world from the uncommon perspective of the small power. The topic will be approached with the assumption that such a perspective is as prone to myth-making as that of the great powers. However, this chapter will not attempt to make yet another contribution to the growing literature which considers small states as exponents of a mythical idea of nationalism.[5]

3. The following forty-seven states were internationally recognised in 1994: Albania, Armenia, Austria, Azerbaijan, Belarus, Belgium, Bosnia-Herzegovina, Britain, Bulgaria, Croatia, Cyprus, the Czech Republic, Denmark, Estonia, Finland, France, Georgia, Germany, Greece, the Holy See, Hungary, Iceland, Ireland, Italy, Latvia, Liechtenstein, Lithuania, Luxembourg, Macedonia, Malta, Moldova, Monaco, Montenegro, The Netherlands, Norway, Poland, Portugal, Romania, Russia, San Marino, Serbia, Slovakia, Slovenia, Spain, Sweden, Switzerland and Turkey. In 1900 there existed twenty-four states: Austria-Hungary, Belgium, Britain, Bulgaria, Denmark, France, Germany, Greece, the Holy See, Italy, Liechtenstein, Luxembourg, Monaco, Montenegro, The Netherlands, Norway/Sweden, Portugal, Rumania, Russia, San Marino, Serbia, Spain, Switzerland and Turkey (21). Andorra has been excluded from both lists as it is not a state under international law.

4. Peter Hort, quoted in Mark Almond, *Europe's Background War: The War in the Balkans* (London: Heinemann, 1994), p. 33.

5. On the importance of myths to nationalism, see for example Eric Hobsbawm, *Nations and Nationalism Since 1780: Programme, Myth, Reality*, 2nd edn (Cambridge: Cambridge University Press, 1992) and Anthony D. Smith, 'The Ethnic Sources of Nationalism', *Survival* Vol. 35, No. 1 (Spring 1993), pp. 48–62.

Nationalism, at least in small states, often tends to be a self-contained, inward-looking phenomenon that makes states defensive and wary of any international role. This chapter will consider, instead, an example of a second type of small state of which there are a number in Europe too: those that consider themselves non-nationalistic and unselfishly internationalist in outlook.

The Netherlands is such a country. In the words of the writer of a standard work on Dutch foreign policy: 'The Netherlands, geographically one of the smallest states, pursues a worldwide foreign policy as if it were a miniature Super Power.'[6] But this ambitious foreign policy is not inspired by the defence of the national interest and the pursuit of power. The country's population, its Parliament and its government all share the stated common aim of wishing to make the world a better place for all. Many examples can be given of this desire. Let two suffice. In the 1980s the Netherlands was spending around 1 per cent of its gross national product on aid to (or, as it is called officially, on 'co-operation' with) the developing world – a figure surpassed only by Norway. In absolute terms, this made the country the sixth largest donor globally, after the United States, Japan, France, Germany and Italy.[7] The government budgeted 6.6 billion guilders for development co-operation for 1995, in effect an amount equal to almost half the 13.5 billion guilders to be spent on defence.[8] The Dutch contribution to UN peace-keeping operations is also one of the largest in the world. By the middle of 1993, about 3,000 Dutch troops were deployed worldwide under UN auspices – a figure which compared favourably with the 8,700 French and 4,100 British forces so deployed at that time. As a percentage of the Dutch armed forces it was much higher, around 4 per cent, as against 2.1 per cent and 1.5 per cent respectively for the French and the British armed forces. Again, this figure was only surpassed by Norway (and Luxembourg).[9] The Dutch armed forces are presently being reorganised primarily for peace-keeping operations.[10]

6. J. J. C. Voorhoeve, *Peace, Profits and Principles, A Study of Dutch Foreign Policy* (The Hague: Martinus Nijhoff, 1979), p. 3.

7. Wouter Tims, 'Development Cooperation: A Dutch Preoccupation', *Internationale Spectator* Vol. 43 (1989), p. 715. See also *The Economist Pocket World in Figures* (London: Hamish Hamilton, 1993).

8. *NRC/Handelsblad Weekeditie* (27 Sep. 1994), p. 6.

9. Jan Willem Honig, 'The Netherlands and Military Intervention', in Lawrence Freedman (ed.), *Military Intervention in European Conflicts* (Oxford: Blackwell for *The Political Quarterly*, 1994), pp. 144–145.

10. Honig, 'The Netherlands and Military Intervention', pp. 150–151.

Why are the Dutch so keen on military co-operation and peacekeeping? The usual answer points to the strong moral convictions of the Dutch people. The Dutch Foreign Minister, Hans Van Mierlo, advocated the creation of a standing UN brigade, saying 'either we act on the basis of our feelings of horror and indignation, or we suspend our moral judgement'.[11] Development aid and peacekeeping are seen as the foremost expression of a fundamental strand in Dutch foreign policy: internationalist idealism. Dutch foreign policy is traditionally characterised by 'an emphasis on commercial policy, aloofness from regional power-politics, non- or anti-militarism, and internationalism'.[12] All of these characteristics are based on a moral view of international relations, on the idea that foreign policy behaviour needs to be (and, in the case of the Netherlands, is) founded on an active choice of good against evil.

Although trade issues could be considered to clash with the moral foundations of Dutch foreign policy, domestically this is not seen to be the case.[13] The Dutch commonly believe that ever since Hugo Grotius founded his 'new science of morality',[14] the ideas of free trade and international law have been regarded as complementary cornerstones of a policy of true benefit to all humankind.

The 'aloofness from regional power-politics' equally possesses a significant moral dimension. In the period from the Napoleonic wars to the Second World War the Netherlands (like Sweden) avoided alliances and, though not neutral in the strict sense of the word (because the country implicitly relied on a great power – usually Britain – to guarantee its independence), it remained 'aloof' or 'abstained' from participating in the traditional European balance of power politics. Moral distaste as much as the desire not to offend any of the major powers determined this policy. It is hard sometimes to detect which was more important.[15] The fact that strict neutrality à la Switzerland was not chosen indicates that the moral element again may have been

11. Quoted in Sander de Boode, 'Het permanente VN-vredesleger van Van Mierlo', *Transaktie* Vol. 23 (1994), p. 464.

12. Voorhoeve, *Peace, Profits and Principles*, p. 42.

13. Cited in ibid., p. 45.

14. Richard Tuck, 'Grotius and Selden', in J. H. Burns and Mark Goldie (eds), *The Cambridge History of Political Thought, 1450–1700* (Cambridge: Cambridge University Press, 1991), pp. 499 and 520.

15. A. van Staden, 'Historische ontwikkeling van de buitenlandse betrekkingen sinds 1815', in *Compendium voor politiek en samenleving in Nederland* (Alphen aan den Rijn: Samsom, 1986–), II, C0200, p. 11.

more important: a 'Swiss' form of neutrality would have foreclosed exercising the Dutch sense of idealist internationalism. As the international lawyer C. van Vollenhoven wrote in 1913:

> France, the United States, and the Netherlands all have the sense of mission; but in terms of our national development we are superior to France; and in impartiality that is above suspicion we are superior to both. In addition to vocation, these qualities are indispensable. The Lafayette-role now befits us.[16]

Such grand ambitions went unfulfilled and, although the country managed to stay out of the First World War, it quickly succumbed to German aggression during the Second. It henceforth accepted that its ambitions and security had to be pursued in a different way. In 1945, the Netherlands enthusiastically joined the United Nations and, when that organisation became paralysed by the Cold War, transferred its support to the North Atlantic Treaty Organisation (NATO). The appeal of this collective defence organisation, under article 51 of the UN Charter, led by a newly emerging, equally moralistic and idealist superpower, proved irresistible. US behaviour over the years may not have met with full Dutch approval because of the American inability to resist the lure of power politics. NATO nonetheless remained a cornerstone of Dutch foreign policy. Until the recent reemergence of the UN, NATO was perceived to be the only effective platform for an activist Dutch role on the world stage.

Regarding the non- or anti-militarism of the Dutch, the argument generally runs as follows. The precocious Dutch economic development in the early modern period meant that the country could afford an army of foreign mercenaries while its own nationals engaged in more profitable and honourable commercial pursuits. Thus a national military tradition failed to take root.[17] This fortunate state of affairs was reinforced by the Netherlands' non-involvement in European conflicts between 1815 and 1940 (except for a brief, ten-day campaign against Belgium in 1831, which was quite successful – until the French army intervened). In addition to this lack of a military tradition, it is often maintained that the

16. Quoted in J. C. Boogman, 'Achtergronden, tendenties en tradities van het buitenlands beleid van Nederland (eind zestiende eeuw–1940)' in N. C. F. van Sas (ed.), *De kracht van Nederland* (Haarlem: Becht, 1991), p. 31.

17. For example J. Huizinga, *Nederland's beschaving in de 17de eeuw* (Haarlem: Tjeenk Willink, 1956; orig. 1941), pp. 43–44. See also H. L. Zwitzer, *'De militie van den staat', Het leger van de Republiek der Verenigde Nederlanden* (Amsterdam: Van Soeren, 1991), pp. 39–40.

Dutch are also peace-loving as their dependency on trade is best served by peace. Dutch authors much appreciate the saying ascribed to Frederick the Great: 'Holland is peaceful in principle and war-like by accident.'[18] Clearly, it is others that force war upon the Netherlands.

What are the sources of this behaviour? The main one obviously must be the strong Calvinist tradition in the country. Although church membership has declined unabated since the Second World War (around 1980, only 58 per cent of the population belonged to a church[19]), the religious influence has remained strong in politics. The main Christian-Democrat parties (since 1977 unified in the Christian Democratic Appeal, or CDA) were part of every government coalition between 1918 and 1994. Their share of the vote has been stable at about 30 per cent for over twenty years now. However, the socialist PvdA (*Partij van de Arbeid* or Labour Party), which receives another third of the vote, attracts a significant percentage of voters from the main Protestant, Dutch Reformed, church: of the 93 per cent (!) of their number that turned out to vote in the last general election in May 1994, 28 per cent (the largest number) voted socialist.[20] Many of the post-war top party leadership of the PvdA were from a Dutch Reformed (*Nederlands Hervormd*) or from a still more staunchly Calvinist, Reformed (*Gereformeerd*) background. But even the other major parties are not immune to the Calvinist-inspired ethical *mentalité*. Hans Van Mierlo is the founder and long-time leader of the current junior government coalition party, the liberal D'66. Joris Voorhoeve, the writer of the standard work on Dutch foreign policy from which much of the above analysis was drawn, was the leader of the conservative-liberal VVD (*Volkspartij voor Vrijheid en Democratie* or Popular Party for Freedom and Democracy) and is now Minister of Defence.

Everything indicates that the Dutch believe their foreign policy works. Voorhoeve maintains that public opinion (which appears to include himself) believes that the Netherlands is 'small *yet influential*' (his italics).[21] The Netherlands has sought to exercise this influence in two ways: through the exhibition of expertise in

18. Voorhoeve, *Peace, Profits, and Principles*, p. 50.

19. J. P. van Praag, 'Nederland nog een christelijke natie?', in S. W. Couwenberg, *De Nederlandse Natie* (Utrecht/Antwerpen: Het Spectrum, 1981), p. 66.

20. 'Kiezer acht minderhedenkwestie urgent', *NRC/Handelsblad* (16 Sep. 1994). Twenty-six per cent voted CDA and 24 per cent for the conservative-liberal VVD.

21. Voorhoeve, *Peace, Profits, and Principles*, pp. 11–12 and 20.

international organisations and a continuous striving to extend the international legal order. As usual indications of success of the former are taken the relatively large number of Dutch officials in the international organisations that are thought to matter. Particular pride is taken in having supplied two NATO Secretaries-General: Dirk Stikker (1961–1964) and Joseph Luns (1971–1984). The near-misses, especially the failed appointments of former Foreign Minister Max van der Stoel as UN High Commissioner for Refugees in the 1980s and of former Prime Minister Ruud Lubbers as President of the European Commission in 1994 are regarded as tragedies of Dutch foreign policy. Indications of success of the furtherance of international law are the location of the International Court of Justice in The Hague, and the fact that the Netherlands can boast of a comparatively large number of eminent international lawyers, such as Hugo Grotius, the (1911 Peace) Nobel laureate T. M. C. Asser, C. van Vollenhoven and B. V. A. Röling.

It is easy to dismiss these ideas on foreign policy as mythical delusions about how international relations really work and to observe how fortunate, in spite of itself, the Dutch nation has been to survive at all. Realists like Hans Morgenthau, had they had any interest in small nations, no doubt would have expressed their utter amazement at an idealism so utterly devoid of any appreciation of the role of power in international relations. Neorealists, like Kenneth Waltz, would note that no ideological veneer could hide or negate the international system's underlying law that small states either bandwagon, balance or disappear. Had NATO not existed, the Netherlands would quickly have changed their tune.

Being Dutch himself (and having philosophical and historical reservations about Realism as a theory[22]), the present author cannot quite convince himself that the Dutch are completely out of touch with the ways of the world. The Dutch perception of the nature of the international system is based on a myth. If one were an adherent of the Neoliberal-institutionalist school of international relations theory, the Dutch view could be made to appear much more plausible.[23] Is it not true that each and every country's

22. See my 'Totalitarianism and Realism: Hans Morgenthau's German Years', *Security Studies* Vol. 5, No. 2 (Winter 1995/96), pp. 277–306.

23. See Robert O. Keohane, 'Lilliputians' Dilemmas: Small States in International Politics', *International Organisation* Vol. 23, No. 2 (1969); 'The Big Influence of Small Allies', *Foreign Policy* Vol. 1, No. 2 (1971)

(and each and every academic's) perception of the international system rests, to a greater or lesser extent, on a myth? The system is so complicated, if only because it contains so many actors, that there is no single, all-encompassing theory that can adequately explain its reality. In other words, to try to test Dutch perceptions against a theory of international relations is a cumbersome process, fraught with complications and – depending on one's theoretical predilections – it will yield a predictable result.

It appears more fruitful to look at the three elements which can be considered to be fundamental to Dutch foreign policy: the lack of power, the idealist principles underlying its foreign-policy behaviour, and its supposedly influential role in the world. As we will see, the truth of the perception of all three elements can be contested and, though not purely fictitious – what perception is ever wholly fictitious? – they can be shown to contain elements of myth.

The dominant image within the Netherlands is that the nation is a small power and that its nevertheless relatively influential foreign policy is characterised by idealism. (Foreign perceptions rarely go beyond the observation that the country is small and can therefore be ignored.) The Netherlands is small, but not in every respect. In terms of territory the country ranked 120th among 216 states in 1985, and in terms of population it ranked 52nd.[24] Territory and population are regarded as sources of power – the supposed property that to Realists matters most in international relations – yet, they are not the only ones. To the founder of modern Realism, Hans Morgenthau, geography, natural resources and industrial capacity were the constituent elements of the ultimate source of power: military preparedness.[25] For the most prominent Neorealist, Kenneth Waltz, the 'rank' of countries on the league table of power depends on 'how they score on *all* of the following items: size of population and territory, resource endowment, economic capability, military strength, political stability and competence'.[26] According to such benchmarks, the Netherlands scores remarkably well.

In terms of population, territory and natural resources, the country may not do so well (it possesses only gas in abundant

24. *The World in Figures*, Editorial Information Compiled by *The Economist*, 5th edn (London: Hodder and Stoughton, 1987).

25. Hans J. Morgenthau, *Politics among Nations: The Struggle for Power and Peace*, 4th edn (New York: Knopf, 1967), p. 114.

26. Kenneth N. Waltz, *Theory of International Politics* (New York: McGraw-Hill, 1979), p. 131 (italics in original).

quantities, being the fourth largest producer in the world in 1991). But in all other respects, the Netherlands is not badly endowed: geographically it is positioned along one of the great trade arteries in the world (hence Rotterdam is by far the largest port in the world). It possesses the fourteenth largest economy in the world in terms of gross domestic product (seventh in Europe and, globally, it is on a par with numbers twelve and thirteen, Australia and India). In terms of share in world exports, it ranks seventh (fifth in Europe) and it ranks thirteenth in terms of industrial output (sixth in Europe).[27] Perhaps most surprising is Dutch military strength. In the early 1990s its defence budget was the seventh largest in Europe as a whole and the seventh largest in NATO (see Table 2.1). In terms of military hardware it does even better comparatively (see Table 2.2). It is virtually indistinguishable from Spain (and qualitatively arguably much better), and in quantity and quality, it even compares well with Britain and France.

No one can doubt the Netherlands' political stability and competence. Major political scandals are unknown.[28] Centre-Left and Centre-Right coalitions (and, at the moment, the first ever Left-Right coalition) take turns in governing the country without noticeable upheaval in domestic or foreign policy. The political competence of the Dutch is reflected in the already mentioned attainment of high office in international organisations by Dutch nationals. In addition to Stikker and Luns, one can mention Piet Lieftinck (World Bank), H. J. Witteveen (World Bank), Sicco Mansholt (EEC), Max van der Stoel (OSCE) and Hans van den Broek (EU).

National power is a notoriously fuzzy concept. Even if one could carefully define the elements of power regarded as important by such paragons of power analysis as Morgenthau and Waltz, how could one work out their aggregate with mathematical certainty and show how it interrelates with the other national powers in the world? Nevertheless, on the basis of the criteria applied above, one can make a reasonable argument that the Netherlands is not a major power but, as former Foreign Minister Joseph Luns was fond of saying, definitely 'a major power among the small powers'. But is it perceived as such? The answer must be negative: neither at home nor abroad is the country regarded as at all powerful. Why is this?

27. *The Economist Pocket World in Figures, passim.*

28. For the rare defence scandals, see Jan Willem Honig, *Defense Policy in the North Atlantic Alliance: The Case of the Netherlands* (Westport, Ct.: Praeger, 1993), p. 243.

TABLE 2.1 NATO Member States Defence Budgets, 1993–1994 (in billions of dollars, according to the NATO definition; excluding the US and Iceland)

	1993	1994	1994 Ranking
Belgium	3.7	3.9	10
Canada	10.3	9.5	5
Denmark	2.7	2.7	12
France	42.6	43.9	1
Germany	36.5	35.8	2
Greece	4.1	4.3	9
Italy	20.6	21.2	4
Luxembourg	0.1	0.1	14
The Netherlands	7.6	7.1	7
Norway	3.2	3.4	11
Portugal	2.2	2.3	13
Spain	8.3	7.6	6
Turkey	7.1	5.4	8
United Kingdom	35.1	34.8	3

Source: *The Military Balance 1995–1996* (London: Brassey's for the International Institute for Strategic Studies, 1995)

TABLE 2.2 Military Hardware in Selected NATO Member Countries, 1994

	The Netherlands	Canada	France	Germany	Italy	Spain	Britain
MBT	740	114	1,047	2,855	1,210	1,012	921
APC/AIFV	1,975	1,404	4,688	6,480	2,831	1,992	4,187
SP Art.	284	76	431	577	274	186	220
SS	6	3	18	20	9	8	14
FF/DD	18	15	43	12	29	17	38
Cbt ac	196	198+62	868+43	518	368+87	170	586+71

Note: MBT=Main battle tanks; APC/AIFV=Armoured personnel carriers/ Armoured infantry fighting vehicles; SP Art.=Self-propelled artillery; SS= Submarines; FF/DDFrigates/Destroyers; Cbt ac.=Combat aircraft (plus in store)

Source: *The Military Balance 1994–1995* (London: Brassey's for the International Institute for Strategic Studies, 1994)

Internationally, it must be simply because the British, Americans, Germans and French have now long been used to seeing the Netherlands as a small country. This points again to the importance of perception, coloured by tradition and myth, in determining the nature of the international order and the position of individual countries in that order. Indeed, despite their definitions of power, Morgenthau and Waltz treat the actual distinction between great and small powers superficially: the great powers are those we are all used to regarding as great. How long did it take for the United Republic to loose its reputation of greatness? Once lost, the contemporary international institutional framework serves to conserve the old system with its established pecking order.

Domestically, the sources of the perception of the Dutch lack of power are slightly different. A majority believes this to be positive; this view tends to be ascribed to the innate modesty of the Dutch. The pursuit and exercise of power are immoral preoccupations, expressions of that cardinal sin: pride. Those critical of Dutch foreign policy find fault with the moralism of the Dutch people and its elected representatives. In their view, the moralistic approach easily degenerates into pedantic and impractical policies which squander the power which the Dutch nation possesses.[29] Nevertheless, both camps agree that Dutch foreign policy lacks power.

The Dutch may thus not be powerful, but are they perhaps influential? This many believe to be the case. Yet, it is extremely difficult to produce major examples where a moralist, idealist policy has been successfully implemented. Contrary examples, such as the loss of New Guinea to Indonesia in 1962, and now the loss of Srebrenica to the Bosnian Serbs in July 1995, are easier to find.[30] It may be that one is unable to arrive at an informed judgment because neither diplomats nor academics have chosen to provide a list of Dutch post-Second World War foreign-policy successes of a moralist idealist nature. But why not? Dutch diplomats have always maintained that secrecy is the key to successful diplomacy and barely any have written worthwhile memoirs. A reasonable assumption therefore appears to be that these idealist successes have been few and small.

29. Frits Bolkestein, 'Hard knokken voor het nationale belang', *NRC/Handelsblad* (25 Feb. 1995).

30. René Steenhorst and Frits Huis, *Jospeh Luns* (Amsterdam: Teleboek, 1985), p. 69; see also P. B. R. de Geus, *De Nieuw-Guinea Kwestie: Aspecten van buitenlands beleid en militaire macht* (Leiden: Martinus Nijhoff, 1984), p. 211.

No effective power, no clear signs of influence, all idealism, no realism, is that the conclusion at which one arrives? Not necessarily. Recent research into the foreign policy behaviour of Dutch governments in late 1940s and 1950s indicates that they were far more realist – in the sense of being sensitive to the policies and interests of other countries – than they have habitually been given credit for. The process of joining the European integrationist institutions, like the European Defence Community and the Common Market, met with significant scepticism and serious attempts to establish the benefits and drawbacks associated with membership. Little blind idealism can be detected.[31] Even NATO, the supposedly unquestioned cornerstone of Dutch foreign policy throughout the 1950s and 1960s, was seen by Prime Minister Willem Drees (in office from 1948 to 1958) quite simply as 'an insurance premium to keep the Americans in Western Europe for our protection'. Otherwise, he considered it 'really a waste of money'.[32] Early Dutch involvement in the Yugoslav crisis as president of the European Community, was also quite realistic in the sense of being based on principles and ideas shared by the European partners. If it failed to address the Yugoslav problem effectively, that was because the EC as a whole failed to grapple with the real problem.[33] Actual Dutch foreign policy can be more realistic than the declaratory policies and the domestic debates indicate.

Why then this dissonance between the perceptions of foreign policy and its reality? One must distinguish here between the practitioners of foreign policy who feel foreign pressures, and the parliamentarians and public opinion at home who do not. The practice of foreign policy can hardly fail to make one more realistic. Only the most foolhardy and blinkered diplomat can remain totally unaware of his limits.

Nonetheless, the difference between the two groups is often one of degree only. 'Realists' such as Stikker and Luns grew highly dissatisfied with domestic pressures and continued their careers abroad. Undoubtedly, the lure of a grander stage and the prospect of real influence played their role as well. Many policy-makers have not been able to shed the moralistic *mentalité*. The belief that

31. See Richard T. Griffiths (ed.), *The Netherlands and the Integration of Europe, 1945–1957* (Amsterdam: NEHA, 1990), esp. p. xi.

32. Quoted in Honig, *Defense Policy in the North Atlantic Alliance*, p. 35. See also *ibid.*, pp. 25–30, esp. p. 30 on how the 1951–54 defence budget total was arrived at.

33. See Henry Wijnaendts, *L'Engrenage: Chroniques Yougoslaves, Juillet 1991–Août 1992* (Paris: Denoël, 1993).

the country is not powerful, yet influential and moral, is obviously attractive even when it is neither. These are cosy myths, satisfying a Calvinist country's need for self-esteem. They give the nation a positive foreign-policy programme and thus help to define its place in the world. Yet it is a programme that is not often tested. The Dutch sociologist Johan Goudsblom likened it to a one-way mirror effect: the Dutch are open to foreign influences (though they interpret them through their own peculiar mental prism) but, because they are a small country with a specific culture and language, they are neither understood nor noticed abroad.[34] The net result is a sense of collective singularity that is continually reinforced but not corrected.

The Netherlands is not alone in possessing these particular foreign-policy myths. Canada and the Scandinavian countries, for example, share them. Canada in particular also appears as not that small, rather realistic (witness their economic success), but hardly influential. Some Dutch diplomats undoubtedly sympathise with the 'secret thrill of defiance' in Canada's foreign ministry during the 1995 'turbot war' with Spain.[35] They would wish the Netherlands had a positive opportunity like Canada to attract international attention and be taken seriously.

Sadly, when it came to a test with the Serb attack on the Dutch-protected Muslim enclave of Srebrenica in July of the same year, the Dutch failed to meet the challenge. Domestic internationalist idealism had pushed a Dutch government that was tempted to increase its international influence through participation in peacekeeping, into dispatching troops to Bosnia with an extremely risky mission. Here both the realist practitioners of foreign policy and their moralist domestic constituency suffered a moral defeat.[36]

34. Cited in Abram de Swaan, 'Platform Holland: Dutch Society in the Context of Global Cultural Relations', *Internationale Spectator* Vol. 43 (1989), p. 721.

35. Flora Lewis, 'Safety Nets to Snare the Turbot War', *International Herald Tribune* (17 March 1995).

36. See Jan Willem Honig and Norberth Both, *Srebrenica: Record of a War Crime* (Harmondsworth: Penguin, 1996).

Chapter 3

THE MYTH OF SWEDISH NEUTRALITY

Ann-Sofie Dahl

Swedish Myths

Politics, as life in general, is full of myths. In daily life, a myth is often thought of as something which has been believed for a long time but which is no longer thought to be true. This is also true in Sweden, where today one hears about *the myth of the welfare state,* or the subject of this chapter, *the myth of Swedish neutrality.* Only a few years ago, when the concept of the welfare state still had a general following and the idea of Swedish military independence remained unchallenged by facts, such statements would have been unlikely in Swedish society.

The myth of Swedish neutrality refers to the traditional posture of the country as adhering, according to the ever-repeated formulation, to nonalignment in peacetime aiming at neutrality in times of war.[1] According to those dismissing neutrality as a myth, this formulation presents a false picture of Swedish security; Sweden, they would argue, never did, is not today and may never live up to the demanding conditions placed on a truly nonaligned and neutral actor.

Who is right, then? Those who believe in the traditional formulation, or those who claim it is untrue, a myth? Would a profound

1. A brief description of the traditional Swedish policy of nonalignment/neutrality is presented by Sverker Åström, *Sweden's Policy of Neutrality* (Stockholm: Svenska institutet, 1983).

analysis of Swedish security policy – as presented in the official doctrine referred to previously[2] – confirm the view that Swedish 'neutrality' (as this policy is commonly known, despite the fact that neutrality really is a status into which an actor only enters in wartime) is a myth? Or is the myth of Swedish neutrality nothing but a myth? The ambition of this chapter is to test the alleged myth of Swedish neutrality by comparing the content of this policy to a definition of myth on the basis of previous research in the field.

Defining a Myth

The process of definition

Nobody accustomed to the habits of academia will be surprised to hear that consensus is lacking in its literature as to how to define a myth. One thing is, however, agreed: a myth is believed to consist of not one, but several aspects. On the characteristics of these, however, there is little agreement.

A myth is something in which a substantial number of people believe; a common perception of a certain aspect of reality, a shared set of ideas on a specific subject. While also including some additional elements to which we will return later, the psychoanalyst C.G. Jung defined a myth as 'universal beliefs stored in the collective unconscious'.[3] While a belief has been described as 'any simple predisposition, conscious or unconscious, inferred from what a person says or does ...',[4] a belief system is 'a system of empirical and normative ideas about reality'.[5] Let us retain for our purposes the definition of a myth as (A) a collection of universally, collectively or commonly (to a specific community) held *beliefs*, in other words empirical or normative ideas about a certain part of reality (that to which the myth refers).

2. Doctrines may be official or nonofficial; an official doctrine – or the official part of a doctrine – 'consists of signals or arguments conveyed by an actor'. For a more detailed discussion of this problem, see Ann-Sofie Nilsson (now Dahl), *Political Uses of International Law* (Lund: Dialogos, 1987), p. 42 ff.

3. *Nationalencyklopedien* (Höganäs: Bra Böcker, 1994), Vol. 13.

4. Milton Rokeach, 'The Nature of Attitudes', in David Sills (ed.), *International Encyclopedia of the Social Sciences* (New York: Macmillan & Free Press, 1968), p. 450, also cited in Nilsson, *Political Uses*, p. 13, fn 9.

5. Katarina Brodin, *Studiet av utrikespolitiska doktriner* (Stockholm: SSLP, 1982), p. 97, Kjell Goldmann, *International Norms and War between States* (Stockholm: Läromedelsförlagen, 1971), p. 11, and Nilsson, *Political Uses*, p. 13.

In addition, when part of a myth, these beliefs do not come into existence overnight, as beliefs seldom do. Though this aspect is rarely emphasised in theoretical literature, it seems evident that (B) the beliefs of which a myth is made have been collected, established, formulated and repeated (see below) during a prolonged period – *over time*. Some think of myths as the classical legends of ancient Greece and Rome. A myth is a well-known story (a collection of beliefs) from the past; but not limited to the past in the sense that it is still of relevance to peoples' lives. It has the ability to appear as relevant today as it did when it was first formulated in the near or distant past.

Furthermore, a myth, again according to Jung, evokes a certain response or association, or results in a secondary reaction (of a kind which, Jung adds, may seem somewhat unusual for a modern human being).[6] Though it might refer to a historic event, it remains a model from which to interpret and understand our daily life.[7] The Danish poet and literary critic Brian Möller-Jensen considers a myth to be 'a good, strong word, which gives us a world of associations to religion and literature as well as to our daily life'.[8] (With Jung, Möller-Jensen concludes that it is a myth that one can live without a myth.[9]) A myth could also be a traditional story with an extra meaning added on.[10] To conclude, a myth is not a myth unless it is capable (C) of evoking a *certain response or association*. As such, it also requires a public capable of responding.[11] Because of this, in political life a myth may be used as an instrument to unite – or divide.[12]

The way this response is evoked is often by *repetition* (D). A myth is heard and told many times and, in addition, it is heard and told in virtually identical terms, which in turn is a significant factor for the above-mentioned response. A myth is 'a ritualised body of text', according to the sociologist Hans Blumenberg.[13] It includes an undeniable element of familiarity, bringing us back to the universal beliefs in (A). Though the beliefs may be common to a large group, what is essential here is the ritual or similar procedures or words through which a myth is expressed.

6. *Nationalencyklopedien*, Vol. 13 .

7. Jung, quoted in Brian Möller-Jensen, *Myter. Myte og realitet* (Herning: Systime, 1988), p. 7.

8. Möller-Jensen, *Myter*, p. 7. My translation from the Danish text.

9. *Ibid.*

10. Also in Möller-Jensen, *Myter*, p. 15.

11. Hans Blumenberg, *Work on Myth* (Cambridge, Mass.: MIT Press, 1985), p. 274.

12. Cf. *Gyldendals Leksikon* 1978, quoted in Möller-Jensen, *Myter*, p. 13.

13. Blumenberg, *Work on Myth*, p. 150.

It is quite clear that the above parts on their own are not sufficient to create a myth. A myth is not just a set of beliefs, collected and repeated over time and evoking a certain reaction; it also is not altogether – if at all – true. To put it kindly, a myth has a degree of independence from reality. A myth is thus perhaps not entirely true, although the core of a myth consists of a set of beliefs designed to *seem* true and which may have been true in the past. It is a set of beliefs or ideas universally held but not necessarily universally believed to represent reality. A myth is a set of beliefs (etc.) which at some stage may be questioned, scrutinised, criticised, challenged. It is, as Blumenberg notes, a 'collective invention'. Möller-Jensen goes one step further, declaring it to be 'untrue as a matter of principle'.[14] Finally, then, (E) a myth has a loose relation to – or is *detached from* – reality.

Selecting a definition

Having gone through the different components of a myth, as we see it, the interchangeable nature of the various parts that we have discussed becomes evident. For example, (E) is obviously related to (A), (B) to (D), and (C) to (D). All parts hang together, and all are as significant in order to create the whole – a definition of myth. In this chapter and based on the previous discussion: *A myth is a universally held set of beliefs collected and repeated over time which evokes a certain response and which includes a detachment from reality.*

Testing a Myth

A myth of Swedish neutrality?

The second part of this chapter consists of an empirical study of one case of an alleged myth, that of Swedish policy of neutrality, from the perspective of the definition elaborated above. Each part of the definition (A), (B), etc., will be discussed empirically to see if Swedish neutrality actually fulfils our definitions of a myth.

Universal beliefs

BELIEFS The beliefs at the core of the notion of Swedish neutrality are easily identified. They are expressed quite clearly in the official

14. *Ibid.*, p. 149–155, Möller-Jensen, *Myter*, p. 14; see also Rollo May, *Ropet efter myten* (Stockholm: Rabén & Sjögren, 1991), p. 28 ff.

security doctrine previously referred to: *nonalignment* in peace, aiming at *neutrality* in the event of war. With the exception of a slight modification during the last couple of years, when a few words were changed and others added – 'which may lead to neutrality in the event of war in our neighbourhood' – this formulation and doctrine has stayed unchanged for many years. The beginnings of the Swedish policy of neutrality, as it is commonly known despite the legal complications of such vocabulary in peacetime, can be traced all the way back to the end of the Napoleonic wars.[15] Thereafter it was adjusted to the shifting game of power politics which was being played on the Continent. Nevertheless, there can be said to have been a certain failure to modernise as the doctrine still departs conceptually from the bipolar division of Europe – and the world – which existed during the Cold War.

In that bipolar conflict, the Swedish ambition was to stay nonaligned and 'neutral' between the two contending parties. While such an approach was supposed to improve Swedish chances of remaining unaffected by any war, additional political measures were undertaken to further improve that position. An activist, internationalist policy, advocating global disarmament, Third World support and peaceful settlements of conflict, was pursued in parallel to the neutral security policy, in an effort to reduce international tension generally and, thus, as a consequence, also make Northern Europe a safer place to live.[16]

As that bipolarity vanished with the Cold War, the Warsaw Pact, the Berlin Wall and the Soviet Union, many expected the official Swedish doctrine to adjust to changing realities. It did not, or so far has done so only very slightly. Though conceived in its present form in response to a bipolar world which no longer exists, the official Swedish doctrine remains basically intact; the only sign of the new times are the rather limited changes mentioned above, which declare neutrality in the event of war to be an option, no longer the automatic and reflexive response to conflict. These additions, which are somewhat controversial,[17] serve to create some uncertainty as to the Swedish response to a potential conflict in the three Baltic countries.

15. Krister Wahlbäck, *The Roots of Swedish Neutrality* (Stockholm: Svenska institutet, 1986).

16. Ann-Sofie Nilsson (now Dahl), *Den Moraliska Stormakten* (Stockholm: Timbro, 1991), for example, pp. 11ff.

17. *Svenska Dagbladet* (3 May 1995).

The Swedish policy – or myth, as remains to be seen – of neutrality is an expression of the belief (and ambition) that Sweden was and still is capable of defending itself on its own and does so; that Swedish national defence was and still is (though international contacts are now acknowledged) independent and strong. In other words, that Swedish defence is truly 'not aligned', not dependent on foreign forces for the survival of the country. As simple proof of this self-reliance, the fact that Sweden belongs to no alliance is presented; it is, thus, in a formal interpretation of the term, nonaligned. If applied in times of war, this independent attitude would translate into a neutral posture similar to that held by Sweden during the two world wars, neither of which saw Swedish military participation.

UNIVERSAL It is no exaggeration to state that the beliefs presented above – that Sweden manages its own defence – enjoy a wide following among the Swedish people. Swedish neutrality is so much more than a mere (official) doctrine on how to defend and secure the country; just like the *smörgårdsbord* or the traditional celebrations, maypole and all, of that typically Swedish festivity, *midsummer,* neutrality is a crucial part of Swedish national identity. To be a good Swede is to be neutral (that is, believe in neutrality/nonalignment) and never to question the independence of the country's defence.[18] Popular belief in this policy may even have increased as the years – and decades – have gone by as it was apparently this security policy which kept the population out of conflict while wars, particularly the two world wars of this century, raged all around.

Until recently, when the universal support for this interpretation gradually decreased to support by only a large majority,[19] to question Swedish neutrality was tantamount to treason. Swedish authorities looked severely upon such an act, not stopping at efforts to intervene with independent research projects in their ambition to silence nonconformists.[20] Any criticism directed at Swedish neutrality – as not effective, or as not real – was interpreted by them as a sign of lacking reliability and branded as a threat to the credibility of neutral Sweden's defence capacity. Nevertheless, there appears to have been a popular assumption that, regardless of the official eagerness to fight alone, the US (and presumably NATO) would come to Sweden's rescue due to

18. *Ibid.*
19. Due to the revelations discussed in the section below on 'Elements of Untruth'.
20. Ingemar Dörfer, *Nollpunkten* (Stockholm: Timbro, 1991), p. 10.

Sweden's strategic significance, were the country ever attacked (which presupposes an attack not from the West but from the East, and suggests a less than neutral attitude during the Cold War among the Swedish population).

As indicated previously, the Swedish attitude to the hitherto sacred policy of neutrality appears to have changed slightly over the past few years. Nevertheless, a study by Ulf Bjereld suggested that 70 per cent of the population still considers neutrality/nonalignment the best security policy available.[21] The methodology of Bjereld can be criticised for having favoured this outcome; a different set of questions might have provided different figures. Nevertheless, Bjereld's study shows the solid support which neutrality still enjoys in Swedish society.

The policy of nonalignment and neutrality can indeed be characterised as based upon, and formulating, a universal set of beliefs. It is, however, uncertain which definition of the Swedish doctrine, and which beliefs, enjoy this universal adherence. Does it refer to the traditional version cited above, which lacks the modifications produced in 1992? Such an interpretation would seem to be verified by Bjereld's study, which apparently used the unmodified formulation when analysing the security inclinations of the Swedish population.[22] The recent modifications may not be commonly known or understood.

Those who do know and understand the new formulation of 1992, which abandons the automatic, reflexive turn to neutrality, calling it merely an option to pursue neutrality in the event of war 'in the neighbourhood', appear to view it with some scepticism. In elite circles, this scepticism may be less widespread, though expressed daily in Swedish security debate (which, after decades of nonexistence, is quite lively today). The most prominent sceptics are former Prime Minister Carlsson and Defence Minister Petersson, accompanied by representatives from the neutralist Centre Party. Former Prime Minister Carl Bildt (Conservative Party), whose government formulated the modifications in response to instability in the Baltic countries, and members of the Liberal Party are among those advocating a less static approach. To what extent either of these positions finds popular support is difficult to tell. For that, a more extensive survey, with a greater

21. Ulf Bjereld, 'Starkt stöd för neutraliteten', *Dagens Nyheter* (14 Feb. 1995).

22. *Ibid.* A more detailed presentation of the research programme underlying this article, including a more elaborate presentation of method and the exact questions asked in the poll, was still not available at the time of writing.

and more varied set of questions, than that presented by Bjereld is required.

OVER TIME Another part of our definition refers to the time which is required for a myth to come into being. The long history of Swedish neutrality and the long roots of the universal beliefs in nonalignment and neutrality also show clearly the existence of our second element (B) in the Swedish policy of neutrality. Swedish neutrality is almost two centuries old, though adjustments have occurred along the way. The modern version, or interpretation, with its tacit reference to bipolar conflict, was defined from 1949 and was based on the experiences of the Second World War.[23] We have already noted the most recent modifications of 1992, when Baltic security was high on the foreign policy agenda of the government.

REPETITION Yet another element, closely linked to the historic past discussed above, is repetition. Swedish neutrality also easily fulfils requirement (D). The formulation used to express the Swedish official security doctrine has gained a mantra-like quality. The way it has been used over the years, as an automatic one-line response to any inquiry on the policy pursued by the country, almost suggests magical powers – say the words and any problem will go away. At times, it seemed like the sole foreign policy formulation available. Sweden's policy of 'nonalignment in peacetime, neutrality in war' is certainly repeated enough to make it a myth.[24]

CERTAIN RESPONSE A myth is also expected to evoke *a certain response* or association (C). In Möller-Jensens view, a myth is a positive word which assists us in our efforts to interpret our daily lives.[25] In addition, we suggested that a myth often is part of the national identity. In Sweden, neutrality is clearly capable of evoking such positive reactions. To many – perhaps most – the idea of nonalignment/neutrality has comfortable associations of safety and peace, states which the country has enjoyed during the entire period when this official doctrine has been in place. Not surprisingly, many credit neutrality and nonalignment for this happy state of affairs. Sweden's neutrality is usually identified as the

23. K. Wahlbäck, *The Roots of Swedish Neutrality* (Stockholm: The Swedish Institute, 1986), p. 80.

24. To verify this repetition, see *Documents on Swedish Foreign Policy*, published yearly by the Ministry for Foreign Affairs (Stockholm: Aktstycken utgivna av Utrikesdepartementet. Ny serie I:C:15–44, 1965–1994).

25. Möller-Jensen, *Myter*, p. 7.

prime factor responsible for the many years of peace and stability. Without reflecting on the destiny of other, formerly neutral countries (such as Belgium) whose desire to keep out of trouble was proved irrelevant by history, Swedes tend to conclude that their own country managed to stay out of the two world wars because of their country's neutral security doctrine. In times of great international change, with a wider debate on the future direction of Swedish security policy, a nostalgic quality surrounds the belief in neutrality and nonalignment: it is associated with those prosperous days when Sweden topped every statistic of achievement and living standards; when the welfare state was intact and expanding; and when the privileged Swedish way of life promised to continue forever. As Sweden has come to experience the financial and political turmoil which many other countries have long been accustomed to, allusions to those happier and more stable days of the recent past are not uncommon. In the electoral message of the political Left in Sweden, which has grown to sizeable proportions (the former Communists, the Left Party, have repeatedly come in as the third largest party in opinion polls in the mid-1990s), such references make regular and central appearances.

For a response to make sense, a public capable of responding is required, as postulated above. Such a public obviously exists in our Swedish case. Furthermore, it was suggested that, because of the response, a myth may be used as a political instrument to divide or unite a population or section thereof. The ongoing debate on Swedish relations to NATO – the mere idea of such relations is still considered provocative to many, despite the fact that today Sweden is an active participant in the Partnership for Peace programme – indicates an official inclination to use neutrality in such a uniting way.[26] Indeed, it is invoked to suggest that any deviations from traditional formulations (even, sometimes, the present, slightly more extensive, one) are hazardous experiments, likely to have divisive and disastrous consequences for Sweden's harmonious and peaceful society.[27] Anyone proposing a change in the official doctrine is, consequently, implicitly accused of also proposing a change away from the hitherto generally stable political climate of the country.

ELEMENT OF UNTRUTH In order to fulfil the requirements of our definition, a myth also has to include an element of detachment

26. For example, *Svenska Dagbladet* (3 and 4 May 1995).
27. *Ibid.*

from actual reality. A myth might be believed to be true by everyone, but may nonetheless be a distortion or false representation of reality. Is this also the case with the Swedish policy of neutrality and nonalignment?

We have seen that today, neutrality is only one option for Sweden in the case of a conflict in its own neighbourhood. As a statement of potential intention, this part of the official doctrine can neither be true nor false and therefore would need additional elements in order to be seen as a myth. Judging from the Swedish ability to remain outside of war in the past, its neutrality might also be upheld in future conflicts. On the other hand, Swedish membership in the EU has increased foreign demands on Swedish loyalty, as has its observer status in the WEU. We cannot, in either case, pronounce this statement of intention a myth.

Nevertheless, the part of the current doctrine which states that Sweden pursues a policy of nonalignment in peacetime, is a different story. A few years ago, evidence presented by an official investigation revealed extensive Swedish contacts with a number of NATO countries – Norway, Denmark, Great Britain and the US – during the Cold War and ever since the late 1940s.[28] While the Swedish population had been repeatedly told that their country depended on no foreign assistance for its defence, that very same country had established links with one of the military alliances of the time, contacts which were so close as to render the country semi-aligned. Indeed, in a policy document from 1960, the US concluded that relations were so friendly that alliance membership was no longer seen as a necessity to secure close co-operation, as had been the view in previous documents (in 1948 and less so, in 1952).[29]

Owing to the strategic significance of Sweden, the US gradually came to abandon its previous condition for military assistance: alliance membership. The document of 1952 stressed, however, that the NATO alliance members should not be given the impression that Sweden could enjoy all the benefits of membership without any obligations.[30] Nevertheless, intense co-operation – trading intelligence for technical assistance – took place during an extended period between Sweden and the above-mentioned NATO countries. In addition, a Swedish document dating from

28. *Om kriget kommit … Förberedelser för mottagande av militärt bistånd 1949–1969.* (Stockholm: SOU 1994:11).

29. *Ibid.*, chapter 4.

30. *Ibid.*

1949 reveals plans to engage in military planning with the two NATO neighbours, Denmark and Norway.[31] Details of the various aspects of officially neutral Sweden's contacts with NATO over the years are publicly available only until 1969. Former Supreme Commander Bengt Gustafsson, however, known personally to favour Nordic co-operation, has emphasised that such contacts were maintained throughout his years in office (Gustafsson retired in 1994).[32] As a result of these long contacts, Sweden is referred to at NATO HQ in Brussels as 'the 17th member' of the alliance.

NATO accepted these special arrangements with Sweden primarily because of Sweden's strategic significance to both superpowers, but also because there was little alternative, given the profound feelings of the Swedish population about the historically successful policy of nonalignment. That popular sentiment, which as we have seen still appears to prevail, forced this small state, which despite the rhetoric could not have withstood a full-scale Soviet onslaught without US aid, to engage in a complex game of double doctrines – the official one of nonalignment, and the other, unofficial one of crypto-alignment. Yet even today, as Sweden actively engages in the Partnership for Peace (PfP) while preparing for an equally active role as observer to the WEU, the official doctrine remains basically the same.

Thus there is and has been an element of untruth present in the policy of nonalignment. While it may well have been the Swedish intention to pursue a policy of neutrality in war – on this we can only speculate – it would be incorrect to say that, with such extensive contacts with one of the alliances, the peacetime policy was one of true nonalignment.

The Myth of Swedish Neutrality

At this point, we are able to conclude that the Swedish policy of neutrality, which has provided the empirical basis for this study, fulfils all the definition-related requirements of a myth. It consists of a set of core beliefs (A), which are repeated over time (B and D), manage to provoke a certain association among those sharing the beliefs (C), and, finally, contains an element of untruth – that

31. *Ibid.*, chapter 6. See also Wilhelm Agrell, *Den stora lögnen* (Stockholm: Ordfronts förlag, 1991).

32. *Dagens Nyheter* (9 Feb. 1994).

loose relation to reality which, according to our definition, distinguishes a myth from a simple story (E). Apart from being an academic exercise, what is the significance of this conclusion?

From a political point of view, if the Swedish policy of neutrality and nonalignment is indeed a myth, then the official doctrine – and the defence – of the country is founded on a myth, on an incorrect or manipulated (official) interpretation of reality. There is also the question of historical accuracy. The sections of Swedish history books which deal with past security policy during the officially nonaligned years should perhaps be rewritten to present a more accurate description of reality.

After the official group commissioned to investigate the policy of neutrality since the end of the Second World War, *Neutralitetspolitikkommissionen* (NPK) presented its results, many expected Swedish security policy somehow to change in an effort to bring reality and rhetoric closer together. That did not happen, and the Swedish people seemed unimpressed by the revelations brought forward by the Commission. Few Swedes seemed to feel betrayed by the fact that their government had not told them the whole truth on how the country related to the surrounding world in matters of national security and sovereignty (thus, testifying to the strength of the myth). If anything, the reception given to the NPK's report revealed a surprisingly solid lack of popular interest in Sweden in the area of security policy. The popular outrage which might have been expected in a mature democracy when a people has evidence that it has been deliberately kept in the dark or even misinformed by its elected government, never materialised.

Nonalignment aiming at neutrality remains the official Swedish doctrine. What also remains is the intense affection felt for this doctrine by the Swedish people. In this context, it is evidently hard to distinguish the chicken from the egg. The continuation of the official policy of nonalignment is largely a function of the perceived popular sentiments towards this doctrine. As is often the case with myths, this particular one can definitely be said to form an important part of the national identity of the country.

As long as most official foreign policy is carried out secretively, as has been done in previous years, in spite of the results of the *NPK* which one would have thought to have had revolutionary consequences on Swedish domestic and security policy alike, there is also a continued discrepancy between what is said and done; a continuation of a policy of double doctrines, one for public use and one for operational reality, which some might call hypocritical.

Swedish security has for some time now been based on a myth. From this, it is possible to make the observation that yet another characteristic of a myth may be that it is very difficult to dislodge and replace by a new concept. But what will happen in the future? Can the security of a country be for ever based on a myth?

As a member of the EU, a participant in PfP and an active observer in the WEU, the neutral/nonaligned policy of Sweden appears to have entered into a new phase. One option for Sweden to follow is that of a truly nonaligned policy. This would indeed constitute a dramatic break not only with tradition, but also with the present picture. The previous situation in which Sweden was a free rider on NATO generosity, is unlikely to remain an option in the future. Relations today are open, if not exposed, and becoming ever more so as international contacts multiply in complex patterns. In this context, minute but significant steps have been taken to modernise the Swedish doctrine, bringing it up to date with new realities, although the end of the bipolar system in which Sweden was supposedly neutral is only reluctantly accepted and is often, quite paradoxically, seen as an argument for continued neutrality. An optimist might see a new and promising pattern here, in which official and nonofficial/practical doctrine might at some future point converge. If that were to happen, the myth of Swedish nonalignment would, indeed, be nothing but a myth.

Chapter 4

THE GREEN PERIL

Rémy Leveau

Myths in International Relations

Compared with states themselves, interstate relations are still little institutionalised. Apart from the creation first of the League of Nations and then of the United Nations, some concrete progress has been achieved in the economic sphere. Many issues that touch on the sovereignty of states are still jealously defended by them. Their legitimate authority is seen as all the more absolute in interstate relations when it is founded internally upon the principle of popular sovereignty.

Systems of collective beliefs mobilise people. For decision-makers or influencers, converging and strongly motivated behaviour can play a decisive role. Imaginary or subconscious concepts can serve to condition reactions beyond mere obedience to regulations.

Gilbert Durand has defined myth as a 'dynamic system of symbols, of archetypes and dynamic plans'. He sees myth as 'an attempt to rationalise'.[1] The effect of myths is never direct. The legends which accompany them can be ends in themselves, or can serve to explain the world and its changing nature, or

---

Translated by Evelyn Pignatari

1. Gilbert Durand, *Les structures anthropologiques de l'imaginaire* (Paris: Dunod, 1962), p. 64.

both.[2] Myths also can anticipate and try to influence change. An idea, entertained by many, may have a certain influence on collective behaviour.[3] For example, the great Indo-European myths studied by Georges Dumezil, spread through conquest or less violent means, played a part in the internal structuring of these societies on a hierarchical model.[4] Myths have influenced intergroup relations for some time, and there are links between the internal structuring of societies and their external behaviour, their internal values and how they relate to other societies.

Was the creation of the 'Communist Threat' and the division of the world into two blocs between 1947 and 1989 comparable? Based on actual conflict, imaginary conflicts justified new solidarities. This unifying perspective lasted for over half a century if one accepts that it was forecast in the Wilsonian institutions at the end of the First World War.

In the following, I shall argue that such an imaginary view of European identity and the difference of other groups (here, Muslims) has become a myth which is the driving force behind both the defence of state prerogatives in the control of frontiers, and European integration. Politicians and civil servants both on a state level and a supra-state level exploit the fear of Islam if it furthers their aims. This is not a conspiracy, but an unconscious convergence of thinking among decision-makers.

The Green Peril from the *Chanson de Roland* to the Gulf War

Even after the ratification of the Maastricht Treaty, Europeans are still in two minds about the future European Union (EU). They are torn between favouring a European space and a European force, i.e. between a vast free-market area, or the transposed model of the sovereign state. Yet European integration continues to move forward, driven by the fears of rupture and new external dangers. Among these, the Islamic threat holds a particular place as it thrives on the

2. See Marie Moscovici, *Il est arrivé quelque chose* (Paris, 1989), p. 391; Gilbert Grandguillaume, 'Mythes et récits d'origine', *Peuples Méditerranéens* No. 57–58 (July–Dec. 1991).

3. See Robert Ilbert, 'La cohérence et l'informel: Essai pour servir à une histoire de l'Égypte contemporaine', in Christian Decobert (ed.), *Itinéraires d'Égypte: Mélanges offerts au Père Maurice Martin* (Cairo: IFAO, 1992), pp. 323–344.

4. Georges Dumézil, *Mythe et Épopée* I, II, III (Paris: Gallimard, 1995).

collective imagination and the fears, both old and new, which it raises. Dim historic memories of centuries of conflict between Christianity and Islam, from the battle of Poitiers, the Song of Roland, the Crusades, the fall of Constantinople, the *Reconquista*, the battle of Mohac, the sieges of Vienna, Napoleon's use of the *guarda di Mamellucos* in Spain, the wars of Greek independence against the Turks, to clashes with Maghrebine troops of the French army in Germany and Italy in the Second World War have created a fertile soil for today's fears. These are nurtured by the Iranian revolution, the Gulf War and an Islamic revival throughout the Arab world, from Maghreb via Egypt and Palestine to the former Soviet Republics of the south, and Pakistan, Malaysia and Indonesia beyond. European identity is defined in contrast to, as other than, Islam.[5]

These atavistic fears are also fanned by the presence in Europe of nearly six million Muslims who have migrated there mainly since the 1970s. These in turn are obscurely associated with images of illegal immigration, drug smuggling, terrorism, the arms trade, but also of child prostitution and female slavery. Be they cause or effect, these fears manifest themselves in a crisis of identity in Europe. Sectors of society most threatened by economic change tend to express their fears of the future through violent and racist actions towards Islamic minorities.

European governments on the whole have responded with a two-pronged approach: while discouraging racism, they have also tried to address the socio-economic roots of these domestic fears, albeit, arguably, not to an adequate extent, as Damian Sanges d'Abadie has shown in a recent study of immigration into Spain, France and Italy and of national and EU responses over the last decade.[6]

One option which the governments of a limited number of EU member states have pursued (some rather half-heartedly) since 1990 is that of opening up the frontiers within Europe while transferring decisions on immigration from the states to a central EU authority. This became codified in the Schengen agreement which entered into force in 1995, but which was for a long time not fully applied by one of the treaty's signatories, France, and does not, for example, apply to Schiphol airport in the Netherlands.

This agreement nevertheless involved the transfer of a degree of state jurisdiction to authorities whose powers, while not as yet

5. Speech of Cardinal Lustiger in Berlin, *Le Monde* (10 May 1995).

6. Damian Sanges d'Abadie, 'Immigration and government policy in France: Spain and Italy' (M.S. Ph.D.: King's College, University of London, 1995).

federal, are nevertheless above those of the states. Those who opposed this transfer of power to a supra-state level did so by appealing to the fear of increased illegal immigration, smuggling and criminality in general. But paradoxically, those backing the Schengen arrangement equally played on the myth of illegal immigration to justify institutional changes required to implement the agreements, including a strengthening of the Third Pillar of the EU (justice and home affairs), and greater police co-operation across state frontiers within the Schengen area.[7] The myth of the 'green peril' is offset by the myth that a European police-state is in the making.[8]

Reluctance to Expand Further

The admission of Greece, Spain and Portugal in the 1980s and of neutral countries in the 1990s led post-Cold War East European states to dream of similar benefits of economic support and a strengthening of democracy. Further enlargement of the EU would see the need for restructuring the institutions and decision-making apparatus of the Union. But the Inter-Governmental Conference of the European Union which began in Turin in March 1996 and was concluded in Amsterdam in June 1997 has resulted in virtually no further integration.

Meanwhile, there is no support within the EU for any idea of extending its boundaries towards the south. Instead, the EU aspires to a degree of cultural and political unity, which, it is argued, could not be maintained if the EU were to include Russia, Turkey, all the remaining Balkan countries and the Maghreb.[9] Nevertheless, Turkey, for example, has long professed its desire to join the EU. Some of these countries have also, at different times and under different circumstances, been the source of important groups of immigrants who have settled within the EEC/EU. After some years of residence, citizenship is not denied to them by the country to which they have migrated. The problem arises more frequently from the fact that their country of origin will deprive

7. For a factual treatment of this subject, see Roland Bieber and Joerg Monar (eds), *Justice and Home Affairs in the European Union: The Development of the Third Pillar* (Brussels: European Interuniversity Press, 1995).

8. Didier Bigo, *Polices en réseaux: L'expérience européenne* (Paris: PFNSP, 1996).

9. See Francis Gutman, *Le nouveau décor international* (Paris: Julliard, 1994); Zaki Laïdi, *Un monde privé de sens* (Paris: Fayard, 1994).

them of their citizenship if they apply for a new one. Turkey, for example, does not normally recognise dual citizenship; Turks have to choose between acquiring a European citizenship or retaining their Turkish citizenship and thus facing a potential termination of their right to residence within the EU.

The establishment of large groups of Muslim immigrants from the Maghreb, from Turkey or from the Indian sub-continent has created problems in France since 1974, when regulations concerning the status of permanent residence were introduced. Since then, the assimilation of a Muslim minority within has posed a psychological problem. There is no difficulty if immigrants and their descendants agree to conform individually to the norms and values of the recipient culture. The EU and most of its member states offer a variety of models for integration.

Even so, there is a problem inherent in the incompatibility of Islamic thinking and the Western concept of state sovereignty and secularism. There is no equivalent in Islam to the Christian 'render unto Caesar what is Caesar's and unto God what is God's', no concession of a division between the private (or religious) and public spheres. While this does not prevent individuals and groups from coming to an arrangement with themselves and with the states within which they live, this logical tension between the *Umma*, which does not recognise state boundaries or non-Islamic jurisdiction, and the secular duties of citizens in laicistic democracies returns to haunt Muslims in times of international crisis.[10]

Islam can thus be a stumbling block for integration, particularly for those who wish to settle in EU countries without abandoning too many of their customs. In turn, a majority in the population of the host countries often develop fears of losing their own identity in a multicultural society. This conflict, often set against a background of economic crisis, has expressed itself in public debate about the Salman Rushdie affair, in France in debates about whether schoolchildren should be allowed to wear the Islamic veil in school, and throughout Western Europe during the Gulf War.[11] Even if Muslims profess their loyalty towards the secular state, suspicions remain.

10. See Sohail Hashmi, 'Sovereignty and the Umma', in Sohail Hashmi (ed.), *State Sovereignty: Change and Persistence in International Relations* (Philadelphia: Pennsylvania State University Press, 1996).

11. Rémy Leveau, 'A muslim population in France', in Sam Nolutshungu (ed.), *Margins of Insecurity: Minorities and International Security* (Rochester: University of Rochester Press, 1996), pp. 59–73.

This is consciously or unconsciously exploited by all those who try to increase frontier controls. This is no conspiracy, but I think that there is a sort of collective practice of playing on these suspicions in order to retain for whichever organisation (member states, ministries, supra-state organisations, etc.) the control and jurisdiction over frontiers. Certainly, the EU's trade and commerce policy of creating a free economic space within the EU at once involves the application of tariff barriers against products from the south.

Television and Immigration

Meanwhile, the EU projects an external image which attracts immigration. This image is in part the result of conscious attempts to project such images, through the cultivation of *Francophonie*, or television broadcasts across the Mediterranean. Rapid urbanisation results in a large mass of young people, often unemployed, congregating in the outskirts of cities. Still attached to the values and customs of their societies and to their family solidarity, they experience difficulties in becoming truly integrated into the city.[12] They wait for, and dream of, an 'elsewhere'. They form the natural audience for these television broadcasts in French, Spanish and Italian which give them glimpses of prosperity, comfort, sport, cars, as well as the potential ability to observe the political aspects of European public life from election debates to judicial scandals. These youngsters are left frustrated by the impossibility of being a part of this feast of modern life, and begin to resent their own situation.[13] They see the gradual integration of Eastern Europe into this economic and social area, and feel themselves even more discriminated against. Attraction turns into envy, envy into 'sour grapes', and 'sour grapes' into rejection and anti-European feelings.

Meanwhile, perceptions of Europe in the Maghreb become increasingly remote from reality. For example, at the time of the Gulf War, the image of an aggressive Europe was created. The Maghrebine elites felt powerless because the Islamic world needed to turn

12. Mounia Bennani-Chraibi, *Soumis et rebelles: Les jeunes au Maroc* (Paris: CNRS, 1994); Séverine Labat, *Les islamistes algériens entre les urnes et le maquis* (Paris: Le Seuil, 1995).

13. Susan Ossman, *Picturing Casablanca: Portraits of Power in a Modern City* (Berkeley: University of California Press, 1995), pp. 63–79.

to the non-Muslim powers to restore order in the Middle East after Saddam Hussein's attack on Kuwait. Within Arab and Islamic nationalism, there exists both a fascination with and a rejection of the European model. Europe's indifference towards the Arab world was at times seen as more harmful than the aggression against Iraq. Europe is wrongly perceived as strong and united, and its institutions as much more coherent than they are in reality. This image in turn creates fears of Europe in the Maghreb, with the result that the anti-Western arguments of Arab nationalism and the anti-Christian arguments of sectors of Islamic public opinion in parts join forces in a more general anti-European discourse.

Counter-reaction

The northern Mediterranean (southern European) states in turn see this as justification for the creation of a defensive stance towards the Maghreb. In France, this is fuelled above all by the Algerian civil war which holds black memories of the 1950s and early 1960s.[14] But in one way or another, Britain, Italy and Spain have similar memories.

Even if the majority of politicians do not call into question the right of Muslim people to reside in Europe, the reactions of the parties of the extreme Right are less moderate. For example, Jean Marie le Pen during the 1995 presidential election campaign in France declared that he intended to write into the constitution the principle of 'national preference' for immigration, denouncing the presence in France of 'foreign populations that cannot be assimilated', and who are potential allies of the south. To confront this danger, he proposed the redeployment of military force towards the south and the creation of a national guard to fight against the 'internal insecurity created by the presence of foreign elements', this term being taken to mean in the larger sense a reexamination of the conditions of granting French nationality to the 2.5 million foreigners naturalised since 1974.[15] A minority of the electorate in various West European countries would support such measures. In turn, in France and elsewhere, certain politicians who do not wish to leave the way clear for the extreme

14. Rémy Leveau (ed.), *L'Algérie en guerre* (Brussels: Complexe, 1995).
15. *Le Monde*, 6 June 1995.

Right, in order to capture part of the protest vote it represents, exploit its themes.

This political controversy is indirectly sustained by an academic debate on the nature of future conflicts following the collapse of the Communist system and the Gulf War. The controversy surrounding Samuel Huntington's thesis reflects what is at stake. According to him, the fundamental source of future conflicts will no longer be ideological or economic, but cultural: clashes between civilisations will dominate world politics, taking place along cultural (and religious) fault-lines. Drawing on the writings of M.J. Akbar, Huntington foresees greater cohesion among Islamic nations from the Maghreb to Pakistan, which might result in a struggle for a new world order, as Bernard Lewis argues.[16] This thesis is echoed as much by the press as by politicians.

European Security Response

The creation of a European security policy began before the major debates that accompanied the fall of the Berlin Wall and the Gulf Crisis.[17] Initially it aimed at little more than the control of migration, ideas put forward in the multilateral negotiations that led to the Schengen accords (applied in part since 1995) on the free movement of persons. This has created the need for co-operation among customs officials and civil servants from various ministries (Interior, Justice, Finance, Defence). The aim for those members participating in the agreement is to extend it to Union level. Nevertheless, for the time being this agreement is still anchored in intergovernmental and thus interstate relations, just as the Third Pillar (of which the Schengen accord is not a part) is not included in the First Pillar of *Communautaire* affairs.[18]

The opening of borders calls into question the traditional tasks of frontier control which are tied to a precise notion of the role of the state, of the territory within their jurisdiction and of boundaries. It therefore met with strong opposition from all those to whom the preservation of state sovereignty is ultimately more

16. Samuel Huntington, 'The clash of civilisations', *Foreign Affairs* Vol. 72, No. 3 (Summer 1993).

17. See Bigo, *Polices en réseaux*.

18. On the history of the Schengen agreement, see Klaus-Peter Nanz, 'The Schengen agreement: preparing the free movement of persons in the European Union', in Bieber and Monar (eds), *Justice and Home Affairs*, pp. 29–48.

important than European integration. To gain public support for their opposition, they have mobilised myths focusing on the encroachment of Brussels on the national prerogatives of EU member states.[19] Police surveillance of the movement of people is a central feature in this context.

Borders are thus in the focus of attention: are they still the immutable limits of supposed nation-states? Have they lost their role within Europe? Are they seen in both cases as important to keep out alien cultures, such as Islam? In discussing the abolition of its internal borders, Europeans pose with new urgency the question of Europe's identity and of the difference between 'Us' and 'Them'. What should Europe's relationships be with social groups beyond and even within the EU who find themselves outside the dominant culture? The increased influence of the extreme Right in various European countries means that these are not just academic questions. These groups use the fear of Islam to argue for the creation of national police-states. But even transposed to a European level, Islam serves as a focus by offering an anti-identity to define oneself against.

Compared with some of the great constructions of the past, the new myths can seem trivial. They serve to compensate for the weakness and the absence of a shared feeling of identity that could satisfy all of the collective needs. Even so, the risks of negative effects of such a process cannot be denied.

19. See Bigo, *Polices en réseaux*, pp. 266, 341.

Part II

Compromise or Compromised?

Chapter 5

The Spanish Civil War

'Betrayal' by the Bourgeois Democracies

Aline Angoustures

On 15 July 1995 the *Guardian* carried a full-page article by Ed Vulliamy entitled, 'For whom does the bell toll now?' The sub-title read: 'The left buried its differences to fight Fascism directly in the Spanish civil war. Now ... it has a range of reactions to Bosnia – but [it] is mostly agreed that we should keep out.' A Bosnian is quoted as saying, 'Sarajevo is the Madrid of our time'; a Scottish politician as describing Bosnia as 'Spain, Abyssinia and Czechoslovakia rolled into one'.

The illustration of the article by Martin Rowson is even more fascinating. Picasso's painting *Guernica* is shown being white-washed by a man dressed in pinstripes (representing the 'West', presumably a civil servant in view of his clothes) saying, 'Sit still and do bugger allwards!' He is flanked on either side by two men painting Guernica. One, on the right, is labelled 'The spirit of Munich', shouting 'Backwards!'; the other, on the left, is a Spanish soldier shouting 'Forwards'. He carries, besides his paintbrush, a banner with the caption 'The Spirit of Spain'. This article and cartoon, drawing on Picasso's painting, Hemingway's novel on the Spanish Civil War and a rich collection of historical myths and imagery (Sarajevo, Abyssinia, Munich), was not published in

---

Translated by Philippe Boyer and Ian Moore

connection with a historical anniversary or commemoration of the Spanish Civil War, but as an analysis of interstate relations today. Yet *Guardian* readers, mainly to be found on the political Left, were supposed to understand all the references contained in this article and cartoon, which centred around the myth of the Spanish Civil War, testifying to the fact that this myth, paradox as it is, is alive and well.

In this chapter, myth is used as a synonym for a representation or a story, simplified or illusory, which deals with a past event but which has an explanatory value in the present day. It is illusory or simplified, because a myth, although always having an 'objective foundation',[1] differs from them qualitatively by exaggerating or otherwise transforming the facts. By explaining it, myths interpret the past rather than analysing present realities. Pierre Laborie has noted that public opinion is less easily explained as a function of real events 'than by the analysis of mental representations through which these events are perceived, experienced, commented and judged by contemporaries. The truth which decides the attitudes of social actors is not the truth of the event which the historians strive to … reconstitute.' Instead, public opinion is a function solely of subjective perceptions, through the lens of received ideas, myths and previous experiences.[2]

And where is the Spanish Civil War among all this? This chapter will focus first on the myths it engendered in the 1930s, then on the transformation of the war itself into a myth in the 1940s. This particularly affected France, but also to a lesser extent Britain and the United States.

The Spanish Civil War, the 1930s

Metamorphosis into a myth

The participants of the Spanish Civil War themselves created myths. There are two fundamental reasons for this: firstly, the ideological nature of the confrontation, and secondly, the need to internationalise it and to inspire participants from very different cultural backgrounds.[3] From the beginning, therefore, fiction became as important as reality: the Republican government claimed to control the situation when in reality it controlled nothing; and

1. See Raoul Girardet, *Mythes et Mythologies Politiques* (Paris: Seuil, 1986).
2. Pierre Laborie, *L'Opinion française sous Vichy* (Paris: Seuil, 1990), p. 18.
3. Emile Témime, *La guerre d'Espagne commence* (Brussels: Complexe, 1986), p. 101ff.

the Nationalists used bluff instead of conquest. Propaganda became essential in both camps – the Civil War was in addition a war of words.[4]

The mythical construct of the war is based, quite simply, around the opposing poles: on the Nationalist side, we find the Fascist mythology of the Phalanx and of the 'Francoist Crusade',[5] which evokes the image of religious crusades in Spain's past, with Spain as bastion of Christianity. On the Republican side, we find the Revolutionary myth, combined with the theme of democracy attacked by the counter-revolution or Fascism. Both sides' cases are pervaded with conspiracy theories: the Communist conspiracy vs. the Fascist and clerical plot. Glorious and heroic episodes are elevated to myth: the stories of Francisco Franco, José Antonio Primo de Rivera, La Passionaria and Buenaventura Durruti.[6]

There is thus the mythical confrontation between religion and the 'secular religions' (Raymond Aron), i.e. the ideologies,[7] and notably Communism.[8] From this point of view, the Spanish Civil War was an incarnation of the tensions between the political and religious orders, between Revolution and the Golden Age. This war of symbols and representations encouraged and exalted individual and collective sacrifice, and contributed to make all compromise impossible by casting the war in terms of a struggle between good and evil.[9]

The Revolutionary myth

The Spanish Left from the time of the rapid collapse of the state invoked the Revolutionary myth. Workers' organisations took in hand their defence and attempted to turn the conflict into a revolution, using propaganda to set the people against the 'old order'

4. Gema Iglesias Rodriguez, 'La Propaganda politica: fuente para le estudio politico-social de la España republicana durante la guerra civil española', *Bulletin d'Histoire Contemporaine de l'Espagne* No. 19 (June 1994), p. 45ff.

5. Herbert Southworth, *El mito de la cruzada de Franco* (Paris: Ruedo Iberico, 1963).

6. Marc de Smet, 'Pour une métapolitique', *Questions de Mythes et Histoire* No. 59 (Paris: Albin Michel, n.d.).

7. Jean Pierre Sironneau, *Le retour du mythe* (Grenoble: Presse universitaire de Grenoble, 1980).

8. See Mircea Eliade, *Mythes: rêves et mystères* (Paris: Gallimard, 1965)

9. See Pierre-Paul Gregorio, 'Guerre civile et information. Etude contrastive des deux editions du Journal ABC dans le contexte de la guerre civile espagnole (1936–1939)', *Bulletin d'Histoire Contemporaine de l'Espagne* No. 17–18 (June–Dec. 1993), pp. 304–309.

embodied by the clergy or by Francoism. On the Right, the Fascist crusade also presented itself as revolutionary.[10]

On the whole, the revolutionary passion of Spain frightened and divided the democratic countries, even their Left-wing parties. All the fears created by the excesses of the French and Bolshevik revolutions welled up again, but also the controversies surrounding Christianity vs. laicism, nationalism vs. internationalism.[11] The Spanish Civil War thus incarnated the greatest political controversies of the conflicts of the time.

The mythification of the Spanish Civil War began in the summer of 1936.[12] It immediately appealed to the imagination of the French, appealing to France's 'founding' myth of 1789. Yet the French revolutionary period had been one of particularly great hostility between Spain in France. The collective French memory of the Spaniards is one of religious fanatics (memories here of the Inquisition!) and counter-revolutionaries.[13] These connotations, regarded as positive by the Right and as negative by the Left, fitted in with the internal divisions within the French political culture. For the French Left, Spain appeared to have an anti-bourgeois society devoid of capitalism and materialism, a sort of pre-capitalist Middle or Golden Age, both mythic and nostalgic. The Left celebrated the insurrection as one they wished for their own country.

The Right, however, feared it as the harbinger of the collapse of the existing social and moral order throughout Europe.[14] The parallels between Spain in 1936 and Russia in 1917[15] indicate the importance of the stakes: French Socialists saw the revolution of 1917 as heir to that of 1789. The Right cast the Bolshevik revolution

10. Charles-Oliver Carbonell and Jean Rives (eds), *Mythes et Mythologies politiques*, Centre of Studies and Research on the Political Mythologies (Toulouse: Presses de l'institut d'Etudes Politiques de Toulouse, 1991).

11. Cf François Furet, *Le passé d'une illusion: histoire de l'idée communiste* (Paris: Robert Laffont/Calmann-Lévy, 1995).

12. Pierre Laborie, 'Espagnes imaginaires et dérivés pré-vichystes de l'opinion français, 1936–1939', in *Les Français et la guerre d'Espagne* (CREPF-Université de Perpignan, 1990), p. 91.

13. Lucienne Domergue, 'France-Espagne: image de l'autre', publication forthcoming care of the CSIC; Daniel-Henri Pageaux, 'L'Espagne devant la conscience française au 18e siècle' (Doctoral thesis: Paris III, 1975), 2 Volumes; Léon-François Hoffman, *Romantique Espagne* (Paris: Presses Universitaires Françaises 1961).

14. Pierre Laborie, *L'opinion française sous Vichy* (Paris: Seuil, 1990), p. 49.

15. Victor Morales Lezcano, 'La opinión pública en Francia y el frente popular en España', in *Opinion publique et politique extérieure 1915–1940* (Rome: Ecole française de Rome, 1984), pp. 383–428.

as an incarnation of barbarism challenging the values (centring on religion) of the West.[16] Spain for Frenchmen on both sides symbolised a direct confrontation between the ancien régime and the Bolshevik revolution.[17]

Turning our attention to the other side of the Channel, K.W. Watkinson argued that no foreign event 'since the French Revolution had … so bitterly divided the British People.'[18] Here, too, many leading politicians saw a revolutionary threat and not a democratic regime suffering from a Fascist attacks. From 1931 onwards, the British leaders watched the Spanish situation with a growing fear of suddenly seeing a revolution break out at home.[19] In the liberal political culture of Britain, as of the United States, the revolutionary fervour of the kind demonstrated in Spain, especially in the violence of revolutionary trade unions, is quite alien. During the Congressional vote in Washington on an arms embargo against Spain (January 1937), Senator Pittman, speaking in favour of the embargo, described the Spanish Civil War as a war of 'theories from foreign governments' which had nothing to do with democracy.[20]

The revolution and pacifism

All three Western powers were the 'targets' of Spanish Republican propaganda,[21] while the Francoists mainly addressed themselves to Germany and Italy. Both factions used propaganda to persuade the outside world that their interests and values, too, were at stake in this conflict. This stood in stark contrast with the memory of Spanish neutrality in the First World War. The Spanish revolutionary myth could hardly be as powerful as the pacifist myth, which

16. Raoul Girardet, *Mythes et mythologies politiques*, p. 100ff.

17. See D. W. Pike (ed.), *Les français et la guerre d'Espagne* (Paris: PUF, 1975); M. Bertrand de Muñoz, *La guerre civile espagnole et la littérature française* (Paris: Didier, 1972).

18. K. W. Watkins, *Britain Divided: The Effects of the Spanish Civil War on British Political Opinion* (London: Thomas Nelson, 1963), p.11.

19. Juan Carlos Pereira Castañares, 'Las relaciones entre España y Gran Bretaña en la epoca contemporánea', *Bulletin d'Histoire contemporaine de l'Espagne* No. 8–9 (June 1989), pp. 15–28.

20. Hugh Jones Parry, 'The Spanish Civil War, a study in American public opinion: Propaganda and pressure groups' (MS Ph.D., Los Angeles University of Southern California, June 1949; University library photo-duplication service, 1958), p. 92.

21. In France even the extreme Right party uses pacifism as its prime mobilisation theme: E. Gonzalez Calleja, 'Los intellectuales filo Fascistas y la defensa del Occidente', *Revista de Estudios politicos* No. 81 (July–Sept. 1993).

created greater consensus and was paradoxically associated with a revolutionary myth at the time. Pacifism was extremely strong in the three Western powers at this time and had its roots in the horrendous experience of the First World War, which in view of the huge sacrifices made retrospectively seemed pointless. The diplomacy of the Western powers at the time of the Spanish Civil War was concentrating its efforts on the avoidance of another war. From this stemmed the French initiative of nonintervention, decried later as the result of the 'Briandisme' and the 'Pactomania'.[22] The 'Neutrality Act' of 1936 adopted in the United States was ironically described by the New York Herald Tribune as aimed at keeping the United States out of the war of 1914–1918 [*sic*!], which shows this mythical transposition of the Spanish Civil War.[23]

In the United States, there was a post-Versailles belief in the good in humanity, in humankind's opposition to war and its perfectibility, an optimism shared by Franklin D. Roosevelt. In Europe, there was a widespread variant of this concept, according to which people fought wars because they were led into them by selfish governments. The contradictions in the discourses of Léon Blum on the subject of the Spanish Civil War, trapped as he was between his anti-Fascism and his pacifism,[24] stand for the torn feelings harboured by most Left-wing and Liberal western politicians at the time. Both sides in the Spanish Civil War tried to appeal to the outside world to overcome any tendencies towards war-weariness and pacifism, by trying to play upon the general significance of their cause.

The Spanish Civil War in the 1940s

The transformations of the war

Two events served in a crucial way to give the Spanish Civil War its own mythical character: the bombardment of Guernica in 1937, and the Munich agreements of 1938, followed by the invasion of Czechoslovakia in the following year. The bombardment by the German air force of the civilian population of a region perceived as more Catholic and traditional than revolutionary deeply moved the Western powers and changed the image of the war, dimming its

22. Claude Thiebaud, 'Léon Blum. Alexis Leger et la nonintervention en Espagne', in *Les Français et la guerre d'Espagne*, p. 23ff.

23. Hugh Jones Parry, 'The Spanish Civil War', p. 69ff.

24. Juan Avilés Farré, *Pasión Y farsa: franceses y britanicos ante la guerra civil española* (Madrid: Eudema, 1994).

'revolutionary' aspect. The effect was enormous (one need only mention the importance of Picasso's painting); thenceforth, the conflict was more widely seen as a manifestation of the universal conflict between tyranny and democracy. In addition, the agreements of Munich were a sign of the failure of the politics of appeasement, and deprived pacifism of its popularity for decades to come.

The evolution of propaganda accompanied this change: as Franco had relied on the support of National Socialist Germany and Fascist Italy, he became increasingly identified with Fascism. On the other hand, the Republican side was increasingly identified with Communism, eclipsing the other Left-wing movements, Socialists, Anarchists and Republicans. Yet in the light of Munich and the beginning of the Second World War, Republican Spain began to seem more like a besieged democracy and less like a country in the grip of a serious Bolshevik plot.

The shame of the democracies

As early as 1936, it was said that the Western democracies, with their desire for peace, were weak in dealing with the dictatorships whose values dominated in Spain, where the Fascists derided the 'congenial cowardice' of the democratic factions. The longer the Spanish Civil War went on, the more the strength of this idea gained ground. From 1945 onwards this war was explicitly presented as one of the causes of the Second World War, as one of the main capitulations to Fascism, which ultimately prepared the way for general war. While the Western powers with their policy of nonintervention had undoubtedly underestimated the National Socialist threat and undervalued Soviet strength, it is stretching this argument to turn this into a cause of the Second World War. This is a counterpart of the myth of Munich,[25] appealing to the guilty conscience of Left-wingers throughout Europe. This theme is particularly strong in France, a country where nonintervention became a particularly strong guilt complex because of the proximity to Spain and the sympathies which connected the French Left-wing Popular Front Government of Léon Blum with the government of the Spanish Republic.

Of course, the strength of this feeling of guilt came with hindsight.[26] Spanish refugees, during the exodus of 1939, were treated with great suspicion in France before the Second World War.

25. See chapter 6, David Chuter, 'Munich, or the Blood of Others', this volume.

26. See Raymond Aron, *Introduction à la philosophie de l'histoire* (Paris: Gallimard, 1938, repr. 1986), chapter VI.

Afterwards, however, they were celebrated as the first opponents to Hitler, incarnating resistance to oppression.[27] This change of attitude is also reflected in Frédéric Rossif film *Mourir à Madrid.*[28] The central theme of the film is that the battle of Madrid was the last, lost chance of the democracies to prevent a world war. Released in 1963, the film used a mix of archive and contemporary images like a 'documentary' to create the impression of 'objectivity'.[29] The strength of the idea was also a result of the realities of the Cold War world. After the Second World War, the Spanish Civil War could retrospectively be more easily cast in black and white, with the Republican side clearly on the side of the heroic victims, the Fascists on the side of the National Socialist villains.[30] For France, one must also cite the film by André Malraux, made in 1939, but released in 1945, *L'Espoir*.[31] The Gaullist political culture of France presented a particularly favourable soil for this perception, as it could be linked with the mythification of the Resistance, and in the Resistance, of the use of armed force.[32]

This myth that the nonintervention of the democracies in the Spanish Civil War was the cause of the Second World War, summed up as the 'shame of the democracies', had drastic effects. The 'Parliamentary Commission of Enquiry into the events which took place in France between 1933 and 1945' decided in 1946 to devote numerous pages to trying to find those responsible for the war and blamed members of the Quai d'Orsay, notably the diplomat-poet Alexis Léger. Similar phenomena could be observed in Britain and the United States, namely, the pillorying of those responsible for ignominious 'appeasement'. This self-criticism within the democracies assumed mythical

27. See Pike (ed.), *Les Français et la guerre d'Espagne, passim*; Antonio Bechelloni, 'Italiens et Espagnols dans la presse française de septembre 1944 à decembre 1946', in Pierre Milza and Denis Pechansky (eds), *Italiens et Espanols en France* (Paris: L'Harmattan, 1995); Ralph Schor, *L'opinion publique française et les étrangers 1919–1939* (Paris: Publications de la Sorbonne, 1985); Aline Angoustures, 'L'exil espagnol et le statut de réfugié', proceedings of the 40th anniversary meeting France's Application to the Geneva Convention, in the university library of the OFPRA.

28. The film was seen by 191,033 people in eleven weeks in Paris (it was released on 19 April 1963) and was shown on television shortly afterwards.

29. 'La guerre d'Espagne vue par le ciméma', *Cahiers de la Cinémathèque* No. 21. (Jan. 1977); Jean-Marie Tixier, 'Un film de 1963. Mourir à Madrid', *Cahiers de la Cinémathèque* No. 46–47, p. 151ff.

30. Furet, *Le passé d'une illusion*, p. 308.

31. *Ibid.*, p. 309.

32. 'Que reste-t-il de la Résistance?', *Esprit* (Jan. 1994).

proportions.[33] Studies which described Francoism as relatively nondangerous or which try to understand rather than condemn the attachment to peace of the governments of Léon Blum and Neville Chamberlain are comparatively recent.[34]

The myth of the culpability of the democracies could be found in the reactions in France to the war in the former Yugoslavia.[35] It is mentioned to jog our memories and prick our 'consciences' that nonintervention (here the embargo, or abstaining from intervention) had permitted the Fascist uprising and ultimately the war, and that it is this attitude which, in the wake of the 'thaw' in the East, prepared the ground for the reawakening of a Fascist 'dream' which might be the basis of a war to come.

It even serves as a weapon to use against democracy, presented as soft and incapable of decisive action in crisis. Frenchmen nostalgically recall the International Brigades, full of intellectuals; this militancy is contrasted with the weakness of the democracies, their ineffectiveness and their tendency to yield to the dictates of others. This is the international counterpart to the myth of domestic democratic paralysis, the rejection of diplomacy and the problems and shortcomings of parliamentarianism. Yet these only overlap in part with the Spanish myth.

The people betrayed by the bourgeois democracies, or the glory of anti-Fascism

Retrospectively, nonintervention seemed particularly culpable because it contrasted with a characteristic of the Spanish Civil War, 'the nation in arms', the popular war, the bravery of 'all the people fighting', as Roosevelt is quoted as having commented on Joris Ivens's movie, *Spanish Earth*.[36] During the Cold War, this popular view of the myth was stressed. The Spanish Republic became legendary; it could be used as propaganda material by Communist anti-Fascism.[37] The retrospective propagandistic comparison between the behaviour of the democracies and that of the USSR and the sincerity and enthusiasm of the men enrolled in the International Brigades made the Spanish Civil War particularly appealing.

33. See Thiebaud, 'Léon Blum. Alexis Leger'.
34. Avilés Farré, *Pasión y farsa*.
35. Jorge Semprun in *Le Monde* (17 Jan. 1995), p. 15.
36. *Spanish Earth* (1937) was an American film written with the collaboration of Ernest Hemingway. It was used as a court exhibit at the National Society on the debate on Spain.
37. Furet, *Le passé d'une illusion*.

Significantly, Joris Ivens's film was used as a quarry for sequences on Spanish history put together in a film produced in the German Democratic Republic in 1962.[38] The analysis of nonintervention as a cause of the war allows Communist historiography to condemn the bourgeoisie for betraying revolutionary ideals and collaborating with Fascism, abandoning the working classes who had to maintain their own revolutionary, or even democratic, ideal inherited from preceding centuries.

This idea is especially strong in the political and intellectual life of the West where Communism, as a political myth and social idea, survived longer in the political imagination than in the exercise of actual institutional or political power. In France, Marxist ideology was very strong during the 1950s and anti-Communism was marginalised in intellectual circles. The Communist Party is, furthermore, 'the party of guns', symbolising the Resistance of the Second World War,[39] carrying the torch of the clandestine anti-Fascist fight, which is close to the image of the Spanish war.

Furthermore, the democracies were made to feel guilty by the continuing existence of the Francoist government, hardly a presentable ally for the 'free world'.[40] The behaviour of France is typical of the guilty conscience associated with Franco's Spain. Relations between France and Spain from 1946 to 1975 were overshadowed by a desire to hide any visible links. Frenchmen refused to register the actual political character of Spain:[41] instead, they thought of Spain in terms of the valiant Republican people fighting Fascism, fused with the earlier romantic view of the Spaniards as the proud and fierce guerrillas fighting the French. For the Left, this mythical picture fuses anti-capitalist nostalgia and revolutionary passion, while condemning the Francoist government which seemed to mix Fascism with the medieval inquisition.[42] For the Right, this image allows indulgence in nostalgia, pure and simple, for a world moulded from the ancient order, immutable but freed from shameful references to a recent past.

38. *Espagne ardente* by Jeanne and Kurt Stren, produced in the DEFA studios.

39. Pierre Nora, *Les lieux de Mémoire* Vol. III, *Gaullistes et Communistes* (Paris: Gallimard, 1992).

40. Furet, *Le passé d'une illusion*, p. 305.

41. Aline Angoustures, 'L'opinion publique française et l'Espagne, 1945–1975', *Revue d'histoire moderne et contemporaine* (Sep.–Dec. 1990), pp. 672–686.

42. See Aline Angoustures, 'L'Espagne et les espagnols dans le cinéma français de 1945 à 1965', paper presented at the conference in 1991, 'On the emergence of a

An instrument against Fascism and against the democracies of the 'free world', the anti-Fascist myth of the Spanish war progressively detached itself from its object and became a myth with different meanings. The Spanish Civil War is the perfect image of the fight of the poor against the rich, the citizens against the army, the colonised people against their oppressors. The mythical resistance, to which the student movement of the 1960s in France belongs,[43] allowed Spain to remain, despite the protest of Stalinist Communism, the symbol of mobilisation, of all the struggles of the Left against all oppression. The Spanish theme was used more frequently after the war in Algeria. It surfaced during the Chilean coup and allowed an indictment of the United States, the Left's prime target in those times – was not the United States responsible for maintaining Franco as head of Spain? The famous picture of Capa, depicting the death of a Spanish Republican, symbolised, in a general way, guerrilla or colonial resistance.

This use of the myth had a boomerang effect on French-Spanish relations after the death of Franco. The Spanish Civil War became a constant reference during the period from 1963 until 1975, whether in demonstrations, in the media or in cultural life. The death of Franco seemed to revive the country of the Civil War, allowing the European Left at last to discharge their collective shame. French-Spanish relations were very difficult between 1975 and 1986, as though there had been a gap between a historical image and reality, the historical image being more powerful in the minds of Frenchmen than the reality of the new Spain in transition to full democracy.[44]

Conclusion

How is this myth faring today? It was nurtured during the Cold War by the anti-Fascist propaganda of the USSR and its revolutionary

---

European identity in the movie industry' (Political Studies Institute of Paris), directed by Pierre Milza.

43. Alain Monchablon, 'Le mouvement étudiant et sa mémoire: l'UNEF après 1945 entre tradition et oubli', *L'homme et la société. Générations et mémoires* No. 111–112 (1994), pp. 1–2, 113–117

44. See Furet, *Le passé d'une illusion*, and A. Darre, 'Relaciones internacionales y representaciones reciprocas: una aproximation al caso franco-espanol', in *Francia-Espana-Aquitania-Euskadi: 'imagenes reciprocas en los medios de comunicacion social'* (Bilbao: Sociedad editorial del Pais Vasco, 1993).

myth. Can it stay alive without Communism, and without the backing of the USSR? Some myths can adapt themselves to new circumstances. We have already mentioned that the myth of the Spanish Civil War and the abandonment of innocent victims by the democracies was re-activated with respect to the war in the former Yugoslavia. Criticising the inertia of the democracies, a world dominated by material interests (oil justified the Gulf war), and a West hostile to Islam, this myth is useful in an age in which the liberal and bourgeois democracies seem to lack both enemies and power. Myths demonstrate that *Realpolitik* does not arouse enthusiasm. Myths, as carriers of meanings as much as of ideals, can arouse it. This is another lesson of the heritage of the Spanish Civil War.

Chapter 6

MUNICH, OR THE BLOOD OF OTHERS

David Chuter

The myth of Munich is the most powerful and influential political myth of the second half of the twentieth century. There is scarcely a major international crisis of this era where its baleful ghost has not peered in through the windows of conferences and crisis meetings, and scarcely a theme of foreign and security policy which does not show its influence. Even today, the accusation that a given policy amounts to a 'new Munich' is generally regarded as a knock-down argument.

As with most powerful myths, that of Munich has never really been defined, and the 'lessons of Munich' are more readily invoked than they are analysed. Thus, much of the myth has to be inferred from references to it, usually when something else is the ostensible subject of discussion. The Munich myth is generally held to demonstrate the need to 'stand up to aggression', although aggression as such was not offered in 1938, and to avoid 'appeasing dictators', although the British and French governments of the day believed that the policy of appeasement was both necessary and wise.

As is usually the case with myths, that of Munich has become almost completely detached from the circumstances of 1938, when Chamberlain's government believed they had found a magic formula which would promote a system of security in Europe. Moreover, it was backed by discreet threats if the Germans did not do the sensible thing.[1] For some time after the agreement, indeed, the British government saw signs everywhere that these desirable goals were already in the process of being achieved.

Yet history remembers Munich entirely differently. This has to do with the nature of the Munich myth. Its first characteristic is that it is effectively *unanimous*. Although the main Western participants defended their actions, claiming, as my parents used to insist, that Munich had 'bought time' for rearmament, neither this, nor the occasional piece of historical revisionism, has influenced the way in which the myth has been used in the political debate. The disappointment of the policy was so abrupt, so violent and so massive, that there has scarcely been room for real debate about the wisdom of the settlement itself.

The settlement was relatively popular at the time. The political, diplomatic and military classes of France and Britain, businessmen and the stock exchanges, as well as practically all of the media, rejoiced that a needless war had been averted, as did the enthusiastic crowds who turned out to greet Chamberlain and Daladier on their return.

So general was the terror of war, so great the euphoria that a peaceful solution had been found, that nearly all parts of the political spectrum were implicated in what Léon Blum (one of the few to oppose the agreement) described as the 'craven relief' of Munich.[2] Subsequently, governments of the Left were as ready to invoke the 'lessons of Munich' as the mistakes made by the Right. At the time, opposition was generally confined to marginal individuals. As a result, the shame and humiliation which quickly followed was felt by an unprecedented range of actors, many already in positions of power, others coming to prominence in later years. For an entire decision-making and influencing class, the lessons of a policy which had manifestly failed were associated with catastrophe. Much of recent history can be explained as a series of attempts by this class to perform expiation in a series of later crises.

It may seem odd that the anathema pronounced against Munich does not extend to the other great foreign-policy mistakes of the 1930s. A reasonable case can be made, after all, that Western timidity at the demilitarisation of the Rhineland in 1936, and studious disinterest in the plight of the government forces in the

1. See, for example, RAC Parker, *Chamberlain and Appeasement: British Policy and the Coming of the Second World War* (London: Macmillan, 1993).

2. See Jean Lacouture, *Léon Blum* (Paris: Seuil, 1977), pp. 426–432, and see also Marcellin Hodeir's chapter in this book, pp. 107–109.

Spanish Civil War, each contributed to encourage the belief that the democracies were spineless in the face of the increasing threat. But, even if true, neither of these episodes would do as the foundation of a convincing myth. The lesson of the first, after all, would be that one should be prepared to invade sovereign states if they fail to observe the provisions of treaties relating to behaviour on their own territory. The Spanish Civil War is even worse, since there is no common interpretation of events among Left and Right (see Aline Angousture's contribution in this volume). Munich is then obliged to function as a surrogate for all of the mistakes in the 1930s.

The other great characteristic of the Munich myth is that it is *didactic*, to a far greater extent than most myths are. It presents an orderly schema of error and punishment, a cause and effect relationship so obvious as to be universally accepted. The myth incorporates the assumption that Munich-type situations (or at least situations where the 'lessons' are relevant) recur, and, having learnt what to do, one can then act in a more informed way to avoid a repetition of the disaster. Thus, the myth is not only important, it is also useful as a guide to action in the future. As with few other myths, it is possible for pundits to write that 'the lessons of Munich are that we should ...', followed by the appropriate policy recommendation.

This has much to do with the progressive and orderly nature of the myth: *if* something different had been done in 1938, *then* the consequences in later years would have been different. This is essentially a product of *Mein Kampf*, the sacred book which every myth must have. As disappointment with Munich set in, the book was popularly supposed (and the facts here are irrelevant) to be a coherent blueprint for a scheme which Hitler later implemented in detail. Had the West realised this and acted differently at Munich, it was alleged that the later stages of Hitler's game plan, including the dismemberment of Czechoslovakia and the invasions of Western Europe and the Soviet Union, could have been avoided. The implication is that Hitler's was a well-thought-out scheme, progressive in nature and the product of rational analysis of costs and benefits. It is usually assumed that Hitler, confronted in 1938 with a price – the threat of war – which he was unwilling to pay, would have backed down. This was not the perception of the time, when the choice was generally thought to lie between negotiation and war, but again the reality of the situation is largely beside the point.

The progressive, logical nature of the Munich myth is so far removed from what we now know of National Socialist decision-making mechanisms (if that is the word) that it is natural to ask how this interpretation came to be so widely assumed. Part of the reason is that, like most aspects of most myths, it is scarcely ever articulated. Most myths are like icebergs, largely concealed, and this is no exception. But a more powerful reason lies in the fact that history-as-purposive-conspiracy was not a new thought. Since at least the time of the French Revolution, the popular imagination (and thus the political imagination also) had been fed a steady diet of conspiracy theory in lieu of a sensible interpretation of the traumas of the modern world.[3]

Examples of the Influence of Munich

Returning to Munich, I will first mention some examples of direct and acknowledged influence, and then turn to the more indirect and subliminal influences. The sheer number of potential examples is intimidating, and there is room (although not here) for a complete thesis on the subject. The prize for first direct attempt to apply the 'lessons of Munich' probably goes to a relatively obscure, but very influential French naval officer, Admiral Thierry D'Argenlieu. He was sent to Vietnam by de Gaulle in late 1945, together with General Henri Leclerc, to see what could be salvaged from the wreckage there. Although Leclerc managed to negotiate a very favourable agreement with Ho Chi Minh, which would have kept Vietnam in the French Union, D'Argenlieu blocked it, claiming that it represented 'a new Munich', and proclaimed an autonomous republic with a puppet government instead.[4] The rest, of course, is history. One can only speculate how different things would have been if the spectre of Munich had not been in D'Argenlieu's mind.

The Admiral also believed that what was going on in Vietnam was part of a worldwide struggle against Communism. Whilst D'Argenlieu was probably thinking of the traditional fear and hatred expressed by the Right for the Soviet Union ever since 1917, there were others, back in Europe, who were arguing that

3. See Norman Cohn, *Warrant for Genocide: The Myth of the Jewish World-Conspiracy and the Protocols of the Elders of Zion* (London: Eyre and Spottiswoode, 1967).

4. Jean-Pierre Rioux, *The Fourth Republic 1944–1958* (tr. Godfrey Rogers, Cambridge: Cambridge University Press, 1987), p. 93.

the increasingly worrying behaviour of Moscow was no more and no less than a repetition of what had happened under Hitler in the previous decade. This was especially so during the Czech crisis of 1948, where the events of ten years before in the same country were so obviously and blatantly being repeated. A senior French official of the time could not have put it more clearly: 'Communism is simply repeating what Nazism did ten years previously.'[5] This time, however, the West would not be caught napping. The Dunkirk, Brussels and Washington Treaties, as well as their other functions, were specifically designed to repair the omissions of Munich: a mutual security guarantee among Europeans, and in the case of the Washington Treaty, a firm security commitment from the United States.

In 1949 the Soviet Union was seen as a political, rather than a direct military, threat to the West. But the future was again analysed in terms of the past. It was assumed that, following the pattern of the late 1930s, Soviet threats and subversion would break the morale of the Europeans, undermine democracy and intimidate the electorates into voting Communist governments into power. This danger, usually referred to as 'internal aggression' during the Washington Treaty negotiations, was what that Treaty was designed to counter. In the words of Ernest Bevin, its spiritual originator, it was to create a 'spiritual union of the West', steady the nerves of European populations and supply the political glue so conspicuously lacking a decade before.[6] Once again, there were texts to consider. Even if hardly anyone had read *Das Kapital*, there were enough stray statements by Soviet notables which could make it appear that Stalin, just like Hitler, had a carefully worked out plan for world domination which only swift prophylactic action could frustrate. Such fears of course went back to 1917.

One year later came the militarisation of the Atlantic Alliance, largely in response to the outbreak of the Korean War. And once again, it was the Munich myth which provided the interpretative framework: a determined show of strength would avoid war and prevent a creeping take-over of other countries. The despatch of US-led troops to Korea was widely hailed as a triumphant exemplification of the 'lessons of Munich'. When Ambassador Charles Bohlen told Robert Schuman that US troops would be sent to

5. Cited by John Young, *France, the Cold War and the Western Alliance, 1944–49: French Foreign Policy and Post-War Europe* (London: Leicester University Press, 1990), p. 179.

6. The text is in *Foreign Relations of the United States*, 1948, Vol. III, pp. 4–6.

Korea, the latter burst into tears, exclaiming that 'thank God this will not be a repetition of the past'.[7] Korea was to be the first major field upon which the decision-making classes atoned, with the blood of others, for their mistakes of the late 1930s.

Much the same was true of the Algerian war, where French policy, from beginning to end, was soaked in the memory of Munich. The political figures who conducted Algerian policy in its most disastrous phase, between 1954 and 1958, were, as Alfred Grosser notes, haunted by Munich, which was, for them, 'a symbol, a point of reference'.[8] Georges Bidault, a Resistance hero who had been persecuted by the same forces who now threatened military action to keep Algeria French, nevertheless opposed any negotiations with the Algerian national liberation movement (FLN). For Bidault, any form of negotiation or compromise was reminiscent of the progressive slide to disaster between 1936 and 1940, and he contrasted the firmness of purpose shown by Clemenceau in 1917 against German peace offers with Pétain's weakness in 1940. Negotiation might be 'in fashion', from time to time, but it was always wrong.[9] The concept of a progressive conspiracy was there too. In his memoirs, Bidault claimed that, since independence, Algeria had become a 'Communist bridgehead', part of a plot by the UN to spread Communism throughout Africa.[10]

The parallels between the FLN and the Nazis may not seem striking to us, but at the time they were thought to be close. Just as the Sudeten Germans who had agitated for assimilation into Germany were judged at the time to be a subversive element trying to destroy Czechoslovakia, so the FLN could not possibly represent popular Algerian opinion. The FLN were the stooges of the Soviet Union, and Ben Bella was simply a new Henlein, the puppet leader of the Sudeten Germans. Moreover, Algeria had been legally part of France for longer than anything had been part of Czechoslovakia, so Algerian independence would have the same effect on France as the removal of the Sudetenland had on Czechoslovakia. The parallels were not exhausted: just as Munich had been one step in a carefully planned campaign aimed at world domination, so

7. Charles E. Bohlen, *Witness to History 1929–69* (London: Weidenfeld and Nicolson, 1977), pp. 289–290.

8. Alfred Grosser, *Affaires extérieures: La politique de la France 1944–1989* (Paris: Flammarion, 1989), p. 13.

9. Cited by Jacques Dalloz, *Georges Clemenceau: Biographie Politique* (Paris, L'Harmattan, 1992), p. 389.

10. Georges Bidault, *Resistance: The Political Autobiography of Georges Bidault* (tr. Marianne Sinclair, London, Weidenfeld and Nicholson, 1967), pp. 257–258.

ripping Algeria away from France would permit the success of a vast Soviet flanking manoeuvre 'through China, the Far East, the Indies, the Middle East, Egypt and Africa ... to encircle Europe', as the French commander in Algeria put it in a speech to SHAPE in 1957. Only the 'determination of France' to stay in Algeria was preventing the fall of Europe, and, subsequently, Soviet domination of the whole world.[11]

The epitome of such thinking was, of course, the Suez débâcle of 1956, in which the British were also heavily involved. It remains curious, to say the least, that a Socialist, internationalist, government in Paris, should have joined with France's traditional enemy, in an area of the world where their rivalry had always been extreme, in an operation aimed at protecting the financial interests of a private company. It is true that Egypt was providing support to the FLN, it is also true that, at that date, French policy was very pro-Israel. But the main motivation was Munich. Both governments claimed, and appeared to have believed, that the nationalisation of the Suez Canal was only the first step in a campaign by Nasser, the new Hitler, to dominate, if not the world, then at least the North African element of it. Once again there was a text with a masterplan: Nasser's *Philosophy of the Revolution* was held, generally by those who had read neither, to be a 'reissue' of *Mein Kampf*. Such intellectual gymnastics, bizarre as they may seem, still enabled the Socialists and Radicals in the French government 'to liberate themselves from the Munich complex which had troubled them for a quarter of a century'.[12]

The British government was of the same view. Writing in 1971, Harold Macmillan defended the operation staunchly:

> Nasser was determined to throw his weight in favour of revolution and Arab expansion with the help of Communist intrigue and supported by Communist money and arms. With a jealous eye on the oil-bearing countries, he was determined to pursue an aggressive policy on the lines of which we had only too recent and too painful experience.[13]

What is interesting here is the Macmillan saw no need even to mention the word 'Munich', so confident was he that his readership

11. Raoul Girardet, *La Crise militaire française 1945–1962: Aspects sociologiques et idéologiques* (Paris: Armand Colin, 1964), p. 177.

12. Bernard Droz and Evelyne Lever, *Histoire de la guerre d'Algérie, 1954–1962* (Paris: Seuil, 1982), p. 103.

13. Harold Macmillan, *Riding the Storm 1956–1959* (London: Macmillan, 1971), p. 102.

would catch the reference, so obvious were the parallels between Hitler in 1938 and Nasser in 1956. The majority of the British political class felt the same. Hugh Gaitskell, the Leader of the Opposition, had private doubts about the means employed, which he confided to his diary, but supported the government in public. Even though he argued against the use of force, he accepted unquestioningly that Nasser was a dangerous aggressor in the mode of Hitler, haunted as he was by the memory of Munich.[14]

Later, in the 1960s and 1970s, there the spectre of Munich was conjured up to suggest, this time, the possibility of betrayal of Europe by the United States, as previously, Britain and France were seen as having betrayed Czechoslovakia. Might the US reach a 'Munich'-style agreement with the Soviet Union and abandon Western Europe to its fate?[15] Would Europe see an American withdrawal, just as Britain had abandoned France in 1940 through its 'Dunkirk'-operation, in the face of an enemy onslaught?[16]

By the 1980s, repetition of this theme may be becoming wearisome, although in a whole variety of crises, including the Falklands War and up to the Gulf War, the vocabulary and thought-patterns of Munich are abundantly to be found. In a discussion of how to respond to the Argentinian seizure of the Falklands in 1982, for example, Denis Healey, then Shadow Foreign Secretary, explicitly took issue with those who claimed that 'as in 1938', the Falklands was 'a far-away country that is indefensible'. Unless Britain acted,

> ...the next thing we shall see is an invasion of Belize by the brutal dictatorship in Guatemala, a possible invasion of Nicaragua by her neighbours, an invasion of Grenada or Cuba by their neighbours, and, perhaps the invasion of Guyana by Venezuela. Indeed, there could be threats to British overseas colonies such as Gibraltar and Hong Kong.[17]

14. Philip Williams (ed.), *The Diary of Hugh Gaitskell 1945–1956* (London: Jonathan Cape, 1983), pp. 547–622.

15. Editorial (Christian Audejean, Yves Bertherat, Jacques Delpeyrou, Jean Irigaray, André Marissel, Paul Thibaud), 'Le choix', *Esprit* Vol. 31, No. 323 (Dec. 1963), p. 866; General Charles Ailleret: 'Défense "dirigé" ou défense "tous azimuts"', *Revue Défense nationale* Vol. 23, No. 11 (Dec. 1967), p. 1932; see also the former minister Albin Chalandon, 'L'esprit de Munich', *Le Monde* (15 Nov. 1973); Albin Chalandon, 'L'esprit de Munich', *Le Monde* (15 Nov. 1953).

16. General Armengaud, 'La force de frappe indépendante: mélange de réalisme dépassé et d'excessive témérité', *Ecrits de Paris* No. 228 (July–Aug. 1964), p. 28.

17. *Hansard*, House of Commons, 7 April 1982, Col. 965.

Sometimes, the main actors themselves drew attention to the supposed parallels. It has been pointed out, for example, that, at the time of the Gulf War, George Bush:

> ... was influenced most of all by the need to uphold the principle of nonaggression and the analogy with the failure of appeasement in the 1930s.... The President himself tended to describe the crisis in these terms. When he took his decision on doubling forces, he reported that he had been reading Martin Gilbert's lengthy history of the Second World War.[18]

To many political leaders of Bush's generation it must have seemed almost a heaven-sent opportunity for atonement.[19] If they grasped it so readily, it was perhaps because they realised that, during their time in power, they might not get another one. Yet why should expiation have to go on for so long? Surely there comes a point where the original mistake has been redeemed? The answer, perhaps, is that, whilst Munich was a fact, these other episodes, lethal as they may have been for those involved, are only symbols, and, in practice, not even an infinite amount of penance can undo the original sin. The impulse to fight instead of having another 'Munich' carries on, with ever newer and stranger Hitler-figures being discovered. Here, by way of conclusion, is the former Head of the French Secret Service, writing in the mid-1980s:

> In the 1930s the flabby democracies behaved like cowards, letting Hitler grow and grow; and we are doing the same – letting the new Hitlers ... grow and grow. We wait until the last moment, when the sword is upon us, instead of stepping in.[20]

It was, in fact, a plea for military action against Colonel Gadaffi and the Ayatollahs of Iran, to frustrate their Hitler-like designs. But instead of their names, which I have deleted in this quotation, one could put any substitute.

Deterrence

Much of the influence of Munich was thus subliminal. It has underlain not merely Western behaviour in specific cases, but the whole direction of Western security policy after 1945. It may be

18. Lawrence Freedman and Efraim Karsh, *The Gulf Conflict 1990–1991: Diplomacy and the New World Order* (London: Faber, 1993), p. 212.

19. Thierry de Montbrial, 'Nous ne sommes pas à Munich', *Le Figaro* (5 Oct. 1990).

20. Count de Marenches, *The Evil Empire: The Third World War Now*, tr. Simon Lee and Jonathan Mark (London: Sidgwick and Jackson, 1988), pp. 4–5.

useful to begin with the theory of deterrence. The idea that Hitler could have been deterred in 1938, to repeat, is not an interpretation of Munich made at the time, but one made later, when it was assumed that a resolute attitude in 1938 would have avoided war. The first failed test for this view was the Polish crisis of 1939, when a suitably resolute attitude was struck by the West, but was ignored by Hitler. Not a good start for the theory of deterrence. Nevertheless, the theory of deterrence persisted.

For it to work, certain things had to be true. The 'deterree' had first to be aggressive, openly so, and not feel a military threat from the country he was intimidating. Next, there had to be a master-plan for aggression, which could be dislocated by a show of firmness. Mere aggressive thrashing around on an opportunistic basis was far more difficult to deter. Finally, the decision-making process of the aggressor had to be rational enough to affect by resolution. A war started out of fear or through misunderstanding could not be deterred easily, if at all. All of these characteristics were attributed to the Soviet Union in the Cold War. They might have been true, and they might have been false, but they all ultimately derive from the way in which German behaviour in the late 1930s was interpreted subsequently, and not from analysis of the actual situation.

This is true of Western policy from the earliest days: even before NATO was conceived. The doctrine of containment, for example, is manifestly an attempt to apply the 'lessons' of the 1930s. Containment, as interpreted by Clark Clifford, Truman's Special Counsel, assumed that

> [t]he language of military power is the only language which disciples of power politics understand. The United States must use that language in order that Soviet leaders will realise that our government is determined to uphold the interests of its citizens and the rights of small nations. Compromise and concessions are considered, by the Soviets, to be evidence of weakness, and they are encouraged by our 'retreats' to make new and greater demands.[21]

This was written in the summer of 1946. But it becomes clear immediately that it is in fact *German* attitudes of the 1930s, as they were then interpreted, which lie behind this thinking and which are being attributed to the Soviet Union.[22]

21. Reprinted in Thomas H. Etzold and John Lewis Gaddis (eds), *Containment: Documents on American policy and Strategy 1945–50* (New York, Columbia University Press, 1978), p. 66.

22. See Beatrice Heuser, 'Stalin as Hitler's successor', in Beatrice Heuser and Robert O'Neill (eds), *Securing Peace in Europe, 1945–1963* (London: Macmillan, 1992).

Even when explicit parallels were not drawn, memories of the Munich crisis so dominated the imaginations of the decision-making classes that they could not imagine crises unfolding in a different way. An obvious example is the Vietnam war, where much of American policy was predicated on the 'domino theory', which held that, if Chinese aggression were not halted in Vietnam and the country 'fell', the Chinese would move through Thailand, Malaysia and the Philippines and Hawaii, until they splashed ashore on the beaches of California. The decision to escalate the US involvement in Vietnam in 1965 has been comprehensively studied, and it is clear that memories of Munich played a major role. Dean Rusk, for example, defended the policy of escalation thus:

> The principal lesson we learned from World War II is that if a course of aggression is allowed to gather momentum that it continues to build and leads eventually to a general conflict ... Our problem is to prevent World War III.

The appeal to history encourages a search for parallels, and the part of Winston Churchill, staunch foe of appeasement, was here to be played by President Diêm.[23] Whilst Munich was not the only episode to be cited in this way in 1965, it is interesting that the others – Korea, Suez and the French experience in Indo-China, were *themselves* all believed at the time to be echoes of the events of 1938. Richard Nixon was still arguing in the late 1980s that the Soviet Union's '*stated goal* today is a communist world *ruled* from Moscow',[24] and that Afghanistan was 'the most recent step in a *long-term strategy* to win control over the oil resources of the Persian Gulf' (emphases added). The Soviets were compared to a chess player 'who makes a bold but well-studied gambit'.[25] Naturally, the policy recommended is one of increasing firmness: as was Czechoslovakia in 1938, so is Afghanistan fifty years later. It is probably not a coincidence that the book's sub-title – *Victory Without War* – is a summation, in three words, of the Munich myth.

The influence of the myth is exceptionally strong on nuclear policy: indeed, it is not an exaggeration to say that Western and NATO nuclear policy is largely conditioned by memories of Munich. The

23. Yuen Foong Khong, *Analogies at War: Korea, Munich, Dien Bien Phu and the Vietnam Decision of 1965* (Princeton: Princeton University Press, 1992), pp. 177–178.

24. Richard Nixon, *1999: Victory Without War* (London: Sidgwick and Jackson, 1988), p. 72.

25. *Ibid.*, p. 40.

myth of Munich is a myth of weakness, of the democracies giving Hitler what he wanted out of fear. There was an element of fear in the decision to negotiate in 1938, but it was quite specific; it was fear of air attack. Although French and British military potential comfortably outgunned that of Germany, the two governments were scared witless by the bombing potential of the Luftwaffe.[26] One need only recall Chamberlain's famous BBC broadcast of 27 September 1938, in which he said:

> How horrible, fantastic, incredible it is that we should be digging trenches and trying on gas-masks here because of a quarrel in a far-away country between people of whom we know nothing.[27]

It is crucial also that the tidal change in the attitudes of Chamberlain's government came in the Winter of 1938/1939, when there were – unfounded – rumours about a German surprise invasion of the Netherlands, and leading on from this, an airstrike by Germany on Britain.[28] Fear of this more than anything else, underlay early NATO nuclear policy. It continued to underlie fears of nuclear blackmail on the part of the Soviet Union. The INF Treaty of 1987 on the elimination of Intermediate-range nuclear missiles from Europe was called a 'European Munich' by French Defence Minister André Giraud. It has been taken for granted by French security experts ever since that this treaty was the first step towards de-coupling the United States from Europe and finally of American disengagement, so long feared.[29]

Lessons of Munich?

Much of what we think of as 'common sense', or 'the lessons of history' is, in fact an attempt to give one interpretation of the events of

26. For the background, see Uri Bialer, *The Shadow of the Bomber: The Fear of Air Attack and British Politics 1932–1939* (London: Royal Historical Society, 1980), *passim*.

27. Quoted in Sir Alexander Cadogan, *Diaries, 1938–45*, ed. David Dilks (London: Hamish Hamilton, 1971), p. 200.

28. Donald Cameron Watt, *How War Came: The Immediate Origins of the Second World War, 1938–1939* (London: Heinemann, 1989), pp. 101–103.

29. Jean Klein, 'Portée et signification du traité de Washington', *Politique étrangère* Vol. 53, No. 1 (Spring 1988), p. 60; Yves-Marie Laulan, 'Le grand choix à faire pour assurer notre sécurité', *Revue Défense nationale* Vol. 44, No. 3 (Mar. 1988), p. 41; Colonel Roland Lahellec, 'Option triple zéro', *Libres Réflexions sur la Défense* No. 22, in *Armées d'aujourd'hui* No. 129 (Apr. 1988), pp. ii–iii. Nicolas Tenzer, 'La défense européenne et ses mythes', *Revue Défense nationale* Vol. 44, No. 11 (Dec. 1988), p. 47.

1938 universal validity. This is unsurprising for a generation of decision-makers and journalists for whom the trauma of Munich was a formative experience. As a historical analogy, the application of the Munich myth did not, *a priori*, mean that the conclusions would necessarily be unsound, but it did mean that the actual situation was unlikely to be seen clearly, and that two specific dangers arose, which could otherwise have been avoided. First, in whichever way history may be thought to repeat itself, it will never do so exactly. The rush to find points of comparison with 1938 gets in the way of coherent thought and encourages identifications which are at best superficially true. For example, it was widely asserted in 1956 that Nasser's seizure of the Suez Canal was a direct repetition of Hitler's march into the Rhineland in 1936, of the betrayal of Czechoslovakia by Britain and France in 1938,[30] or that it was comparable to 'the rape of Czechoslovakia' by the Communists.[31] Logically, proponents of this view then had to argue that Nasser himself was a new Hitler (the comparison was made both by the British and the French prime ministers[32]), and that the Egyptian panzer divisions would soon be rolling across North Africa if nothing was done. The most dangerous by-product of the Munich myth, indeed, is the need for the demonisation of new opponents, so that they can be cast in the role of the latest Hitler, this time not to be appeased.

Secondly, the Munich myth, especially in its cruder forms, is an argument for always fighting (or threatening to fight) rather than negotiating, and always preferring violent solutions to compromise. The very concept of negotiation can be dismissed as weakness, as was sometimes suggested in the Reagan years. Confrontation and eyeball-to-eyeball posturing, on the other hand, are believed to denote strength and moral virtue and to promise success. This is the more unfortunate since there have always been powerful political reasons for governments the world over to prefer confrontation and war to negotiation and peace anyway. The tendency for weak governments to seek confrontation abroad is proverbial, and many wars have been launched because governments have preferred probable military defeat to certain political oblivion. Yet it is not obvious

30. Gilles Martinet, 'Munich n'est pas sur le Nil', *France Observateur* (2 Aug. 1956).
31. 'Ted Leather flays Dulles', *Daily Mail Commonwealth* (6 Oct. 1956).
32. Sir Anthony Eden, *Memoirs: Full Circle* (London: Cassell, 1960), pp. 430–432. Guy Mollet is quoted in Claude Julien, 'L'Égypte et "son" canal', *Témoignage chrétienne* (3 May 1956).

from history that confrontation is necessarily always an effective policy, let alone a wise one. And sometimes it takes more courage to talk than it does to fight.

Even so, appeal to the Munich myth has always been very popular among West European decision-makers and those who influence them. I would suggest two reasons for this. The first is clarity. The myth portrays the events of 1938 with a cartoon-like simplicity, and so once it is decided that a given situation resembles Munich closely enough for the 'lessons' to apply, many things which were previously complex become black-and-white. In place of a confused and multifaceted problem, a simple pattern emerges: there is an aggressor, there is a victim, there are consequences which will follow if intervention is not performed. For overworked decision-makers, viewing crises in all their actual complexity may be impossible in the time available. But if negotiation or compromise, for example, can be publicly stigmatised as weakness by reference to the lessons of Munich, then the range of alternatives needing to be examined is narrowed, and deciding what to do becomes correspondingly easier.

The second reason is that the rhetoric of Munich is humanitarian and idealistic. Few politicians actually go into politics for entirely mercenary reasons, or consciously to do evil. Most like to think of themselves, at least part of the time, as motivated by moral principle and working for the good of humanity. How attractive, then, to discover a situation where a government can claim to be acting in an avowedly moral and idealistic fashion. There is an unmistakable air of moral luxury about the behaviour of governments applying the 'lessons of Munich'.

Twilight of a Myth

I suggested earlier that there is a generational component to the Munich myth. The generation of leaders who remembered the events of 1938, and even more the events which followed, are now leaving the stage: the Gulf War was their last hurrah. The generation replacing them is, of course influenced by the Munich myth, since they grew up on it, but they lack the sense of sin and the need for expiation which comes from personal experience. Munich is for them primarily a question of rhetoric.[33]

33. Guy Leclerc-Gayrau, 'De Munich à Maastricht', *Le Monde* (22 Jan. 1992).

We can see this most clearly in the debate about intervention in Bosnia. The Munich myth has been mentioned frequently, and there is no doubt that, for some, it has had the useful clarifying function mentioned above. In this way, the fearsome complexities of the situation can be simplified, and the huge burden of Balkan history dismissed as irrelevant. And it is then clear what we should do, and to whom. But Bosnia also demonstrates the limitations of the *Munichois* interpretation of history. If the Serbs (or the Bosnian Serbs, anyway) are the Nazis, and the Muslims (or the Bosnian Muslims) are the Czechs (or the Czech Czechs), then who are the Croats, wherever they may be? The lack of response to reports of Croat atrocities against Muslims, for example, was more for practical than for moral reasons. It was unclear how a three-cornered war could satisfactorily be interpreted by a myth which allows for only two sides: one good, one bad.

Interestingly, however, although these ideas have been common in the debate itself, they played almost no part in the decisions taken by Western governments during the crisis. This may be so partly because the identification with Munich cannot be pushed far: a Bosnian Serb march on Trieste may be thought relatively unlikely. Moreover, there has been a half-hearted quality to much of the *Munichois* analysis, and it is possible that the myth itself is slowly losing its force. Only the 'eleventh hour' argument that the West should have acted earlier has been advanced with any conviction, and this course of action, for practical reasons, was not possible. Different interpretations, such as Bosnia being a test of European will to solve local problems, jostled for space in the op-ed columns of newspapers. But partly also, this is because governments have tended to focus on the problem as it really is, rather than according to the rules of a myth. Insofar as clear thinking and a rational analysis of the situation never hurt anybody, that can be accounted progress.

Chapter 7

YALTA, THE MYTH OF THE DIVISION OF THE WORLD

Reiner Marcowitz

The Myth

'The order which was born fifty years ago at Yalta, that of a bipolar world divided into two antagonistic blocs, has been wiped away five years ago.' This is how a journalist, writing for the Belgian *Le Soir*, typically began his article commemorating the fiftieth anniversary of the Yalta conference.[1] Certainly, 1945 was a turning point. Henceforth, the new superpowers the United States and the USSR decided international politics – just as Alexis de Tocqueville had predicted one hundred years earlier.[2] Europe was divided into two spheres of influence, between which an 'Iron Curtain' was lowered.

While this fact is indisputable, its causes are very much in dispute. Was bipolarity intentionally established? And was it, as the above quotation implied, the intentional creation of a new order, agreed by the two superpowers at the Yalta conference of February

---

Translated by Michael Juricic

1. Pierre Lefèvre, 'La marque de Yalta', *Le Soir* (4/5 Feb. 1995); see also Felix Hartlieb, 'Die Teilung der Welt', *Fränkischer Anzeiger* (11/12 Feb. 1995); John Palmer, 'West carves up Europe in a new Yalta', The *Observer* (21 Apr. 1996).

2. Alexis de Tocqueville, *Oeuvres, papiers et correspondences.* Edition définitive publiée sous la direction de J. P. Mayer, Vol. I, *De la démocratie en Amérique* (Paris: Gallimard, 1951).

1945? Was Yalta just like the other meetings of the 'Big Three' – Franklin D. Roosevelt of the US, Joseph V. Stalin of the Soviet Union and Winston Churchill of Great Britain – such as Tehran in November and December of 1943, or like the following Potsdam meeting in July and August of 1945 (where Harry S. Truman succeeded the deceased Roosevelt, and Churchill gave way to Clement Attlee)? Or did the 'Crimean Conference', as the Russians call the meeting, really represent the 'division of the world',[3] as which it is commonly interpreted?

The Facts

It is useful to begin with the pre-history and agreements of the conference. Since mid-1944, Roosevelt had tried to bring about another summit meeting of the 'Big Three' to deal with unsolved military and political problems associated with ending the Second World War, primarily because of the rapid progress being made by the Allied forces.[4] Initially, there was no agreement on a venue. Meanwhile, in October 1944, Churchill and Eden met Stalin and Molotov in Moscow and, unbeknownst to Roosevelt, concluded a bilateral spheres of influence agreement on the future of Europe: Britain and the USSR should each have certain percentages of interest in the central and south-east European countries (with, for example, Britain accorded 90 per cent for Greece against 10 per cent Soviet interest, with the interests in Rumania exactly the reverse).[5] A secret division of Europe thus took place, but between Britain and the USSR, and emphatically not with the approval of the United States; nor was it a total one: each power insisted on securing at least a little influence on the countries discussed.

3. Arthur Conte, *Yalta ou le Partage du monde* (Neuilly-Sur-Seine: Robert Laffont, 1964). See also Marcellin Hodeir's chapter in this book (ch. 9).

4. On the progress of the conference, see *Foreign Relations of the United States (FRUS). Diplomatic Papers. The Conferences at Malta and Yalta* (Washington: Government Printing Office, 1955); see also Jean Laloy, *Yalta, hier, aujourd'hui, demain* (Paris: Robert Laffont, 1988), pp. 95–122.

5. But even this arrangement only comprised Romania, Greece, Yugoslavia, Hungary, and Bulgaria – thus, by no means the entire 'Eastern bloc'. Cf. Elisabeth Barker, *British Policy in South East Europe during the Second World War* (London: Macmillan, 1976), pp. 140–147; Patrick Holdich, 'A Policy of Percentages? British policy in the Balkans after the Moscow conference of October 1944', *International History Review* Vol. 9, No. 1 (Feb. 1987); Martin Gilbert, *Winston S. Churchill*. Vol. VII, *Road to Victory 1941–1945* (London: Heinemann, 1986), pp. 989ff.

In January 1945, the ailing Roosevelt and a buoyant Churchill finally accepted Stalin's invitation for the tripartite meeting to take place in Yalta in the Crimea between 4 and 11 February 1945. The subjects discussed included Europe, the Far East and a future world peace organisation. The following resolutions were made:

- ***Poland*** The Curzon Line should become the new eastern border of Poland; as an indemnity for its resulting territorial losses, Poland should be compensated with Germany's eastern territories in the north and the west, but the exact extent remained undefined. The Communist Provisional Government of Poland in Lublin should be strengthened with further Polish politicians from inside and outside the country; and crucially, Stalin's agreement was secured that general, free and secret elections should be held as soon as feasible.[6]
- ***Yugoslavia*** The previous agreement of 2 November 1944 between the Communist Partisan leader, Tito, and the head of the exiled royal government, Ivan Šubašić, was confirmed, and a representative parliament was to be set up.[7]
- ***Germany*** At the insistence of Churchill, and in the absence of any French representative, France was granted her own occupation zone in Germany, carved out of the US and British zones, as well as a seat at the 'Allied Control Council'. Germany was to be demilitarised and de-Nazified. A reparations commission would be created to determine the size and means of the payments. Roosevelt provisionally accepted Soviet demands for twenty billion US dollars, half of which should go to the Soviet Union. Moreover, Stalin succeeded in gaining acceptance for his proposal that provisions for the dismemberment of Germany be accepted in the agreement on unconditional surrender which the European Advisory Commission had already worked out.[8]
- ***The Far East*** The Soviet Union promised to enter into the war against Japan within two to three months after Germany's defeat. Japan was to yield the southern half of Sachalin Island as well as the Kuril Islands to the Soviet Union. On Chinese territory, the USSR was to receive special rights in the two trading ports of Dairen and Port Arthur and control of the East China-South Manchuria railway. The

6. Protocol of the Proceedings of the Crimea Conference, *FRUS. Diplomatic Papers. Conferences*, p. 989.
7. *Ibid.*, pp. 980f.
8. *Ibid.*, pp. 978f.

Chinese national government would have to recognise the independence of the Mongolian People's Republic and the Soviet Union's protectorate over it. The USSR announced that it was ready to conclude an agreement of friendship and alliance with China, and help it to expel the Japanese.[9]

- ***United Nations*** With regard to the new world organisation which had been planned for some time, it was agreed that the United States, in the name of the 'Big Three', plus China and France, would extend invitations for a conference, to be held in San Francisco on 25 April 1945, in order to work out the final form of the Charter. In addition, they decided that these five countries should have the right of veto in the future Security Council. Stalin contented himself with three seats in the UN General Assembly – for the USSR, as well as the two sister republics of the Ukraine and Byelorussia.[10]
- ***Declaration on Liberated Europe*** Finally, the 'Big Three' declared formally that the countries which they had freed and subsequently occupied were to regain their full sovereignty, with democratic institutions according to the right of national self-determination, and for this purpose were to hold general, free and democratic elections as soon as possible.[11]

Since 1945, there has been no historiographic controversy about the Conference of Yalta or its agreements, despite other profound differences of opinion concerning the origins of the 'Cold War'.[12] No serious historian or political scientist has identified Yalta with the agreement of the division of the world into spheres of influence and interest.[13] However one explains the

9. *Ibid.*, p. 984.
10. *Ibid.*, pp. 975–977.
11. *Ibid.*, pp. 977f.
12. See Michael Wolffsohn, *Die Debatte über den Kalten Krieg: Politische Konjunkturen – historisch-politische Analysen* (Opladen: Leske & Budrich, 1982); Wilfried Loth, *Die Teilung der Welt: Geschichte des Kalten Krieges 1941–1955*, 3rd edn (Munich: Deutscher Taschenbuch Verlag, 1982), pp. 9–18; and Andreas Hillgruber, *Europa in der Weltpolitik der Nachkriegszeit 1945–1963*, 4th edn (Munich: Oldenbourg, 1993), pp. 121ff.
13. André Fontaine, *Histoire de la guerre froide*, Vol. I, *De la Révolution d'Octobre à la Guerre de Corée 1917–1950* (Paris: Fayard, 1965), pp. 273f.; Alfred Grosser, *Les Occidentaux: Les pays d'Europe et les Etats-Unis depuis la guerre* (Paris: Fayard, 1978), p. 59; and Loth, *Teilung*, pp. 91–94; for Eastern interpretations, see A. A. Gretschko (ed.), *Geschichte des Zweiten Weltkrieges 1939–1945 in zwölf Bänden*. Vol. X, *Die endgültige Zerschlagung des faschistischen Deutschlands* (Berlin: Militärverlag der Deutschen Demokratischen Republik, 1982), p. 170 and Vol. XII, *Die Ergebnisse und*

division of Europe, it was not the Conference of Yalta that triggered it. If anything, Yalta was the high-water mark of the 'anti-Hitler coalition' at the crest of its wave of victory, still united in its aims for the post-war world, or so it seemed: 'Not a single text, not a single agreement (even implicit) predicted that in the East, Marxism-Leninism would rule, and in the West it would be liberal democracy.'[14]

Stalin still hoped to expand Soviet hegemony beyond the existing military demarcation line, and the American-drafted 'Declaration on Liberated Europe' was hardly an expression of classic power politics, reiterating the noble aims of the 'Atlantic Charter' of August 1941 and eloquently expressing Roosevelt's Wilsonian hope for 'one' world.[15] Roosevelt underlined this to Congress after his return to Washington on 29 February 1945: 'The Yalta Conference ought to spell the end of the system of unilateral action, the exclusive alliances, the spheres of influence, the balances of power, and all the other expedients that have been tried for centuries – and have always failed.'[16] Roosevelt accommodated Stalin on many issues at Yalta – especially relating to Poland and China – because he believed that co-operation after the end of the war could be continued and that the joint construction of a 'world organization … in which all peace-loving nations finally have the chance to join together'[17] was possible and indispensable for the maintenance of peace.

In February 1945, Europe was *de facto* divided into two different zones, one occupied by the Red Army, one by Americans, Britons and Canadians. The 'Declaration on Liberated Europe' was an attempt to win back through political means what was already irretrievable militarily: the right of self-determination for the states of East-Central Europe which were 'freed' and occupied

---

Lehren des Zweiten Weltkrieges (Berlin: Militärverlag der Deutschen Demokratischen Republik, 1985), p. 483.

14. Laloy, *Yalta*, p. 121; see also Boris Meissner, 'Jalta und die Teilung Europas', in Dieter Blumenwitz and Boris Meissner (eds), *Die Überwindung der europäischen Teilung und die deutsche Frage* (Cologne: Verlag Wissenschaft und Politik, 1986), pp. 13–32.

15. Laloy, *Yalta*, pp. 92f., 97.

16. Henry Kissinger, *Diplomacy* (Easton Press, 1944; repr. New York: Touchstone, 1995), p. 416.

17. On Roosevelt's policies, see John L. Snell, *Illusionen und Realpolitik: Die diplomatische Geschichte des Zweiten Weltkrieges* (Munich: Oldenbourg, 1966), pp. 140ff.; Daniel Yergin, *Shattered Peace: The Origins of the Cold War and the National Security State* (Boston: Houghton Mifflin, 1977), pp. 48ff. and 66ff.; and Kissinger, *Diplomacy*, p. 387ff.

by the Soviet Union. Thus Yalta did not contribute to the division of Europe, but in contrast represented 'a retarding' element.[18]

Roosevelt's hopes were not fulfilled. Stalin used the favourable military situation at the end of the war to expand considerably the Soviet buffer zone and extend his area of control, explaining to his associates that '[t]his war is not like previous ones; he who controls an area also imposes his own social system on it. Everyone enforces his own system as far as his armies can reach. It cannot be otherwise'.[19] Roosevelt's plan miscarried – but not because he had concluded a Machiavellian deal with Stalin.[20] Roosevelt might be blamed for not having extracted greater concessions from Stalin before the Red Army controlled all of Eastern Europe. But at Yalta, the US President was in no way the accomplice of Stalin or the betrayer of Europe.[21]

De Gaulle, the Mythmaker

The factual events at Yalta are not the stuff that myths are made of. Nevertheless, the myth of Yalta as the 'division of the world' has been used by politicians throughout Europe, including Leonid Brezhnev,[22] François Mitterrand,[23] Helmut Schmidt[24] and Václav Havel.[25] But it is Charles de Gaulle who invented the myth. His request for an invitation to the conference – about which the

18. Andreas Hillgruber, '"Jalta" und die Spaltung Europas', in Andreas Hillgruber (ed.), *Die Zerstörung Europas: Beiträge zur Weltkriegsepoche 1914 bis 1945* (Frankfurt/Main and Berlin: Propyläen, 1988), pp. 355–370, at p. 363.

19. Milovan Djilas, *Conversations with Stalin* (London: Rupert Hart-Davis, 1962), p. 105.

20. Laloy, *Yalta*, p. 122.

21. *Ibid.*, pp. 156–161.

22. The Soviet General Secretary asked the US president, Lyndon B. Johnson, before the crushing of the 'Prague Spring' in August 1968, whether the US would still abide by the resolutions of Yalta and Potsdam, by which he was claiming the Soviet Union's legal right to east-central Europe and thus the right to intervene; Arnulf Baring, *Machtwechsel: Die Ära Brandt-Scheel* (Stuttgart: Deutsche Verlags-Anstalt, 1982), pp. 231f.

23. The French president commented on the implementation of martial law in Poland in 1981 with the words: 'Everything which helps us to leave Yalta is good.' See Timothy Garton Ash, *Im Namen Europas: Deutschland und der geteilte Kontinent* (Munich and Vienna: Hanser, 1993), pp. 14f.

24. See Helmut Schmidt, *Die Deutschen und ihre Nachbarn: Menschen und Mächte*, Vol. II (Berlin: Siedler, 1990), p. 35. See also Hillgruber, 'Jalta', pp. 355ff.

25. Interview with Václav Havel, 'Gefahr eines neuen Jalta', *Der Spiegel* No. 7 (Feb. 1995), pp. 136–138.

'Provisional Government' had found out through the press – was turned down by the Allies.[26] France carried little weight with Roosevelt and Stalin near the end of the Second World War, and even Churchill, who wanted to strengthen France as a possible partner against future Soviet preponderance in Europe, regarded the general as troublesome. In view of Britain's efforts to secure for France a share in the occupation of Germany, de Gaulle could hardly complain about the results of Yalta. Nevertheless, de Gaulle henceforth claimed that together with Stalin, the Anglo-Saxons, whom he disliked in any case, had forced 'the states of Central Europe and the Balkans ... to serve the Soviet Union as satellites',[27] and attributed the occurrence of this division of Europe to France's absence from the Crimean Conference.[28] Both accusations were false, as we have seen. Nevertheless, the myth of Yalta became a constitutive element of Gaullist foreign policy and ideology and a tested means for accusing the Americans and British of betraying Europe and doing under-the-table deals with the Soviet Union, while casting France in the rôle of the true champion of European interests and the chosen leader of a Europe 'between the Soviet and Anglo-Saxon camps'.[29] De Gaulle not merely created the Yalta myth, becoming its most capable and enterprising advocate – he passionately believed in it. In this way, he has also provided us with a case study of the influence of myths on the foreign and security policies of statesmen.

De Gaulle's foreign policy between 1958 and 1969, when he was the first President of the Fifth Republic, was a function of his self-fabricated myth of Yalta; as such, it was an 'anti-Yalta policy',[30] an attempt to push back the 'double hegemony'[31] of the two superpowers, the United States and USSR, to structurally undermine bipolarity, to end the division of the world, especially in Europe and to give more global political weight to the European continent

26. See Caffery to Foreign Minister in *FRUS. Diplomatic Papers. Conferences*, pp. 296f. See also Laloy, *Yalta*, pp. 97f.; John W. Young, *France, the Cold War and the Western Alliance 1944–49: French Foreign Policy and Post-War Europe* (Leicester and London: Leicester University Press, 1990), pp. 40ff.; and Georges-Henri Soutou, 'Le Général de Gaulle et l'URSS, 1943–1945: Idéologie ou équilibre européen?' *Revue d'histoire diplomatique* Vol. 108, No. 4 (1994), pp. 303–355, at pp. 340ff.

27. Charles de Gaulle, *Mémoires de Guerre*. Vol. III, *Le salut* (Paris: Plon, 1959), p. 212.

28. *Ibid.*, pp. 202f.

29. *Ibid.*, pp. 179f. The first reference by de Gaulle to Yalta in this context can be found in 1947, see Laloy, *Yalta*, pp. 149f.; Soutou, 'Le Général de Gaulle', pp. 340ff.

30. Ernst Weisenfeld, *Charles de Gaulle: Der Magier im Elysee* (Munich: Beck, 1990), p. 61.

31. Maurice Couve de Murville, *Une politique étrangère 1958–1969* (Paris: Plon, 1971), p. 193.

again.[32] Thus, de Gaulle's 'anti-hegemonialism'[33] was formally directed against the Americans and the Russians. In moments of tension, as during the Second Berlin Crisis (1958–1962) and the Cuban Missile Crisis (October 1962), the French president took the side of the West, i.e. with the Americans, as French historians and political scientists never cease to stress.[34] Yet his dissociation from military integration in NATO as well as the renationalisation and nuclearisation of France's military defences indicated that while de Gaulle might support Washington *in extremis,* he maintained France's independence *vis-à-vis* US supremacy. He adopted his anti-block policy at the particular expense of NATO solidarity only after he had discharged the burden of the colonial war in Algeria in March 1962, and after the end of the Cuban Missile Crisis seemed to give evidence of an atomic stalemate between the superpowers, which gave their allies greater room for manoeuvre.[35] De Gaulle frustrated John F. Kennedy's 'Grand Design' of an 'Atlantic partnership' by rejecting Britain's entry into the EEC; he torpedoed the US project of a 'Multilateral Nuclear Force' which sought to satisfy West Germany's security needs; but above all, he criticised the role of the US in Vietnam with increasing sharpness.[36] The founder of the Fifth Republic seemed to fear the dependence of Europe on the US more than a Soviet attack: 'Not vodka, but whisky will conquer the world.'[37]

Franco-German Alliance against Yalta?

De Gaulle's 'anti-Yalta policy' blended in well with his nationalism. He was deeply convinced of the 'greatness' of France and her

32. Alfred Grosser, *Affaires Extérieures: La politique de la France 1944–1984* (Paris: Flammarion, 1984), pp. 147–229; Jean Lacouture, *De Gaulle*. Vol. III, *Le souverain 1959–1970* (Paris: Plon, 1986), pp. 287–562; Hans-Dieter Lucas, *Europa vom Atlantik bis zum Ural? Europapolitik and Europadenken im Frankreich der Ära de Gaulle (1958–1969)* (Bonn: Bouvier, 1992); and Frédéric Bozo, *Deux stratégies pour l'Europe: De Gaulle, les Etats-Unis et l'Alliance Atlantique 1958–1969* (Paris: Plon, 1996).

33. Reinhard Kapferer, *Charles de Gaulle: Umrisse einer politischen Biographie* (Stuttgart: Deutsche Verlags-Anstalt, 1985), p. 235.

34. See Bozo, *Stratégies*, pp. 45–101.

35. Eckart Conze, *Die gaullistische Herausforderung: Die deutsch-französischen Beziehungen in der amerikanischen Europapolitik 1958–1963* (Munich: Oldenbourg, 1995), pp. 163–260.

36. Joachim Arenth, *Johnson, Vietnam und der Westen: Transatlantische Belastungen 1963–1969* (Munich: Olzog, 1994), pp. 219–237.

37. Karl Theodor Freiherr zu Guttenberg, *Fußnoten* (Stuttgart: Seewald, 1971), pp. 131f.

European mission. But the French president was realistic enough to see that France could not realise his ambitions of recovering her great-power rôle and reversing the European Europe of 'Yalta' without the support of other powers. Above all, he needed the support of the largest country on the European mainland, the FRG with its economic potential. Its leaders' perpetual feelings of guilt in view of Germany's past history made Bonn supremely pliable to moral pressure. The German population's particular interest in overcoming the division of Europe which was also a division of their country also favoured de Gaulle's scheme. The FRG was thus the ideal junior partner for France.

De Gaulle sought to imbue this unequal relationship with the symbolism of past co-operation between 'Gauls and Germans', who, together with the Franks and the Romans, had once put Attila to flight on the Catalaunic Fields.[38] Conscious of the danger which France had faced over the centuries from the fatal dynamism of its eastern neighbour, de Gaulle feared the potential of the new Germany, hoping that it could be channelled by France into co-operation, rather than renewed antagonism – something of which de Gaulle had already dreamed in the middle of the 1930s.[39] In 1958, this opportunity for all this had finally arrived: the Germans were too weak to represent a threat to France, and they were very keen on co-operation with their Western neighbour, an especial desire of Chancellor Konrad Adenauer.

Adenauer himself also became a propagandist of the Yalta myth, although he at first considered the US dominance in the West to be unalterable.[40] He sympathised with de Gaulle's vision of a Europe as independent player in world politics.[41] But it took a marked deterioration in his relationship with Washington before Adenauer was ready to pursue a policy that risked antagonising the Americans.[42] Between 1958 and 1962, Adenauer gained the

38. De Gaulle at a press conference on 16 Mar. 1950, in Charles de Gaulle, *Discours et Messages*, Vol. II, *Dans l'attente: février 1946–avril 1958* (Paris: Plon, 1970), pp. 344–358, at p. 350.

39. On de Gaulle's conception of Germany, see his 1934 essay, *Vers l'armée de métier*, unedited reprint (repr. Paris: Plon, 1971), pp. 25ff.; and Pierre Maillard, *De Gaulle et l'Allemagne: Le rêve inachevé* (Paris: Plon, 1990).

40. See Konrad Adenauer, *Erinnerungen 1945–1953* (Stuttgart: Deutsche Verlags-Anstalt, 1965), p. 510.

41. See Anneliese Poppinga, *Konrad Adenauer: Geschichtsverständnis, Weltanschauung und politische Praxis* (Stuttgart: Deutsche Verlags-Anstalt, 1975), pp. 63ff.

42. See Horst Osterheld, *'Ich gehe nicht leichten Herzens …' Adenauers letzte Kanzlerjahre: Ein dokumentarischer Bericht*, 2nd edn (Mainz: Matthias Grünewald, 1987),

impression that the Americans and Soviets were intending to come to an agreement on Berlin at the expense of the Germans, thus consolidating their 'Yalta' policy. Adenauer remained convinced of the necessity of a US presence in and protection for Western Europe, but his views converged with those of de Gaulle to the extent that by the middle of 1962 he agreed that Franco-German relations should receive priority, with the aim of winning back for the continent a modicum of the political influence it had lost to the superpowers in the Second World War. This convergence was crowned by the Elysée Treaty of January 1963, intended by both statesmen to be the basis of further bilateral, but also European co-operation.

Yet in view of Adenauer's great age, his control of the Bonn government was declining. He could not create majority support for his policy in the Bundestag, the Federal Parliament. Throughout the political spectrum, there were major fears that, on the one hand, a relationship with de Gaulle's France which was too close would block the longed-for supranational unity which might include Britain, because of the general's confederate and anti-British conception of Europe; on the other hand, there was the fear that de Gaulle's critical attitude towards the United States might provoke its withdrawal from Europe.[43]

Adenauer eventually had to step down in the autumn of 1963 and was succeeded by the Atlanticist Ludwig Erhard, whose main priority was economic prosperity. Erhard's subsequent talks with the French president read like a dialogue of the deaf: while the Frenchman would complain about US hegemony and describe lyrically his ideas of a 'European Europe', stretching perhaps 'from the Atlantic to the Urals', allied to the US but fiercely independent, Erhard repeated over and over that of course the Americans should not be allowed to dominate, but that Western Europe could not do without US protection.[44] Erhard's determination to

---

pp. 127ff.; Hans-Peter Schwarz, *Die Ära Adenauer: Epochenwechsel 1957–1963* (Stuttgart and Wiesbaden: Deutsche Verlag-Anstalt, 1983), pp. 254–261 and 288–296; see also Reiner Marcowitz, *Option für Paris? Unionsparteien, SPD und Charles de Gaulle 1958 bis 1969* (Munich: Oldenbourg, 1996), pp. 64–66 and 71f.

43. *Ibid.*, pp. 72–85 and 93–104.

44. See Erhard's discussions with de Gaulle, Bonn, 3–4 July 1964, in *Akten zur Auswärtigen Politik der Bundesrepublik Deutschland 1964*, Vol. II *1. Juli bis 31. Dezember 1964* (Munich: Oldenbourg, 1995), pp. 713–723, 738–749, and 768–787; Horst Osterheld, *Außenpolitik unter Bandeskanzler Ludwig Erhard 1963–1966: Ein dokumentarischer Bericht aus dem Kanzleramt* (Düsseldorf: Droste, 1992), pp. 94–99; Klaus Hildebrand, *Von Erhard zur Großen Koalition 1963–1969* (Stuttgart and Wiesbaden:

defend the United States against de Gaulle's charges[45] condemned the general's 'anti-Yalta policy' to fail at least in Western Europe. France set out on her *Sonderweg* out of the NATO military integration alone, not followed by the FRG or any other West European power, who came to see de Gaulle's policies as more dangerous for their security than US hegemony.

After his anti-bloc policy had failed in Western Europe, de Gaulle tried to achieve a breakthrough at least in the East. Since 1964, the 'year of the thaw',[46] active reciprocal diplomacy had developed between France and the Eastern bloc states, in the process of which the French president propagated his concept of *détente, entente, coopération*. After the Soviet Union had largely disassociated itself from de Gaulle despite recognition for his critical opinions against the United States, he called upon the peoples of the Soviet satellite states, above all the Poles and Romanians, to defend their national, and therefore European, identities, and to free themselves at least in the long term from Soviet supremacy.[47] But this attempt also failed: the crushing of the Prague Spring spelled an end to any hopes of liberalisation within the Warsaw Pact. De Gaulle conceded bitterly in a speech on 24 August 1968: 'The armed intervention of the Soviet Union in Czechoslovakia shows that the government in Moscow has not dissociated itself from its bloc policy which was imposed on Europe as a result of the Yalta accords, which are incompatible with the right of people to self-determination.'[48] De Gaulle's 'anti-Yalta policy' was at an end. In Western Europe, he could hear the call for a strengthening of the Western bloc through the expansion of the European Community to include Britain, and for France's return to military integration in NATO. In Eastern Europe, there was deadly silence, the Soviet Union, appealing to 'socialist internationalism', having claimed the right with the Brezhnev Doctrine to ignore the sovereignty of individual members of the 'socialist community of states' and to impose their domination with force, if necessary.

Deutsche Verlags-Anstalt, 1984), pp. 99–111 and 170–187; see also Marcowitz, *Option*, pp. 177–222.

45. Fred Luchsinger, *Bericht über Bonn: Politik 1955–1965* (Zurich and Stuttgart, 1966), pp. 343f.

46. Couve de Murville, *Politique*, p. 198.

47. See Lucas, *Europa*, pp. 303–368.

48. Declaration of the French Council of Ministers, in Lacouture, *De Gaulle* Vol. III, p. 548; de Gaulle's press conference on 9 Sep. 1968, in Charles de Gaulle, *Discours et Messages*. Vol. V *Vers le terme: Janvier 1966–avril 1969* (Paris: Plon, 1970), pp. 332ff. See also Lacouture, *De Gaulle* Vol. III, pp. 546–550, and Lucas, *Europa*, pp. 373–380.

The 'End of the Order of Yalta'

Nothing changed the division of Europe for twenty years until people in Poland, Hungary and East Germany went onto the streets and demanded democracy and national self-determination, thus breaking with the Soviet mastery in place since the end of the Second World War, the origins of which so many attributed to the decisions made during the Crimean Conference of February 1945.[49] In vain, Mikhail Gorbachev had first appealed to the validity of 'Yalta'[50] – the last reflex of a myth which arose from a historical misunderstanding which developed an astounding, perhaps at times even constructive, dynamic of its own. We are still living in a period which carries traces of the old bipolar order, but is already displaying signs of a new multipolar system. On the one hand, these signs inspire fear, because they seem to point to a new international anarchy; on the other hand, they augur well for the future, because Europe – wherever its exact boundaries may be – has a new chance to become a determining force in world politics. Therefore, it might correspond increasingly to what de Gaulle had in mind when he once conducted his 'anti-Yalta policy'.

49. Garton Ash, *Namen*, p. 15.
50. This was addressed to Richard von Weizsäcker on 8 July 1987. See Hillgruber, 'Jalta', pp. 355f.

Chapter 8

THE MYTH OF POTSDAM

Marc Trachtenberg

In July 1945 the Second World War was almost over. Germany's defeat this time had been total. The allies now had to decide what to do with the nation they had conquered. When the leaders of the three main allied powers met at Potsdam in July, this problem was naturally at the top of the agenda. And the agreement reached at the conference called for Germany, or at least for the part of that country West of the Oder-Neisse Line, to be treated as an economic unit, and implicitly also for Germany's political unity to be maintained intact. It is commonly assumed that it was decided that Germany was to be treated as a single country.[1] According to the standard interpretation, Potsdam showed that the United States and Britain were from the very beginning of the post-war period committed to a policy of treating Germany as a unified country and pursued this policy at least until early 1946. Only after months of frustration, after it became unmistakably clear that the Soviets were going to hold on to their monopoly of power in the Eastern zone, was the policy of East-West co-operation abandoned as unworkable. Only then – thus the standard interpretation – did Britain and the United States turn slowly and

1. Charles Mee, *Meeting at Potsdam* (New York: M. Evans, 1975); Thomas Paterson, *Soviet-U.S. Confrontation* (Baltimore, MD: Johns Hopkins University Press, 1973); Arthur Frank, *De Yalta à Potsdam – des illusions à la guerre froide* (Bruxelles: Complexe, 1982).

reluctantly to the 'Western strategy' of 'organising' the Western zones first economically and then politically, orienting them to the West ultimately even in a military sense which led to the creation of the Federal Republic and the organisation of a Western security system.

From the start, this interpretation of Potsdam and the policy that flowed from it played a key role in arguments about responsibility for the Cold War and for the division of Germany. Britain and the United States had clean hands. No one, especially in Germany, could doubt that from Potsdam on, their goal had been to run Germany as a unit, but the USSR had sabotaged these efforts. Britain and the US had no choice but to embark upon the policy of 'organising' the Western zones. According to this interpretation, it was the Soviet Union that was to blame for the division of Germany.

These claims were of fundamental political importance. By taking this line in 1946, Britain and the US were telling the German people to look on Russia as the great enemy of German national rights. They were implying that they, on the other hand, were fundamentally in sympathy with German national aspirations, vaguely suggesting that the US and Britain might ultimately support the Germans in an active anti-Soviet policy. The Soviets therefore had an interest in blocking this 'Western strategy'. This conflict over Germany was to lie at the heart of international politics during the entire high Cold War period from 1945 to 1963. And the interpretation of what had happened at Potsdam – and of what British and US policy had been in late 1945 – was a central element in the Cold War mix.

Yet the interpretation of Potsdam just described is essentially a myth. For the real heart of the Potsdam conference was not an agreement to treat Germany as an economic unit. In fact, the real decision was to accept the division of Germany – not a four-way division, but a two-way partition of the country between East and West.

The real makers of US policy – especially Secretary of State James F. Byrnes, who was by far the most important individual on these issues – had built their policy on the assumption that a partition of Germany along East-West lines was unavoidable. Germany would be divided, but this did not imply a hostile relationship with the USSR. Quite the contrary: for Byrnes, a separation of responsibilities, where the Russians would run the show in the part of Germany they occupied and the Western powers would control things in Western Germany, was the way – and indeed essentially the only way – a decent, workable relationship with the Soviet Union would be possible. An attempt to run Germany as a unit would lead to endless bickering among the four occupying powers; relations would be a good deal smoother if each side had a free hand in the part of Germany it controlled. And it was not just Germany that was being divided along East-West lines at Potsdam, it was Europe as a whole. In other words, it was Potsdam, and not Yalta, that was the real 'spheres of influence' conference – the meeting where a basic understanding on the division of Europe was actually reached.

The Byrnes Plan

The great bulk of the evidence for this comes from the documents on Potsdam published by the US State Department in 1960, especially the copious material on the Byrnes plan for German reparation.[2] This plan was the heart of US policy at Potsdam, and the key to understanding that conference is the realisation that in dealing with reparation, the three governments were actually dealing with the most basic questions about Germany as a whole.

The fundamental idea of the Byrnes plan was that each occupying power would have the right to take whatever it wanted by way of reparation from its own zone. The plan itself was a reaction to what the Soviets were doing in Eastern Germany: removing everything of value that could be carted off. While US and British officials disliked what the Soviets were doing, there seemed to be little point in trying to stop them. Was it not simpler to let each side draw off whatever it wanted from the areas it controlled?

Even so, reparations could not be isolated from the broader question of how Germany was to be dealt with. If each side was allowed to take whatever it wanted from its part of Germany, then it was unlikely that that country could be run as an economic unit, and indeed Byrnes did make it clear that the Soviets could take whatever they wished from the Eastern zone without limit. But the other side of this coin was that the Western powers would not be called upon to help finance imports into that zone. Otherwise, as a British official later put it, the Soviets would 'simply milk the

2. United States Department of State, *Foreign Relations of the United States: The Conference of Berlin (The Potsdam Conference)*, 2 vols (Washington, DC: US Govt. Printing Office, 1960). The second volume alone, henceforth cited as *FRUS Potsdam:2*, is over 1,600 pages long.

cow which the US and British are feeding'.[3] 'The US position is clear', Byrnes declared at Potsdam, invoking what was called the 'first charge principle', a long-standing US policy. 'It is the position of the United States that there will be no reparations until imports in the US zone are paid for.... We do not intend, as we did after the last war, to provide the money for the payment of reparations.'[4]

If his reparation plan were adopted, Byrnes declared, the USSR 'would have no interest in exports and imports from our [i.e. the Western] zone. Any difficulty in regard to imports and exports would have to be settled between the British and ourselves'.[5] It was thus clear that Germany's foreign trade would also not be run on a four-power basis.[6] A decision had in fact been made, in the words of one internal US document from the period, to 'give up' on a four-power arrangement not just for reparations but for imports as well.[7]

Nevertheless, the management of foreign trade was the key to the overall economic treatment of Germany. If the country were to be run as a unit, exports and imports would have to be managed on an all-German basis. If there were no common regime for foreign trade, normal commerce between Eastern and Western Germany would be impossible: the two parts of the country would have to relate to each other economically as though they were foreign countries.

All this was not just some sort of arcane economic theory that Byrnes and the others were too obtuse to understand at the time. The United States' representatives at Potsdam were fully aware of the implications of their new policy. The US government scrapped the previous policy of running Germany as a single economic unit. It henceforth assumed that the allies would probably not be able to 'pull together in running Germany'.[8] The top British official concerned with these matters at Potsdam, Sir David Waley, who opposed the new US policy, wrote that '[t]he US plan' was 'based on the belief that it will not be possible to administer Germany as a single economic whole with a common programme of exports and imports, a single Central Bank and the normal interchange of goods between one part of the country

3. Murphy to Byrnes, 11 Dec. 1946, *FRUS 1946* Vol. 5, pp. 650–651.
4. Foreign ministers' meeting, 23 July 1945, *FRUS Potsdam:2*, p. 279.
5. Foreign ministers' meeting, 30 July 1945, *ibid.*, p. 491.
6. See Collado to Thorp and Reinstein, 23 July 1945, *FRUS Potsdam:2*, p. 812.
7. Memorandum for Clayton, 23 July 1945, *FRUS Potsdam:2*, p. 813.
8. Rubin to Oliver, 25 July 1945, *FRUS Potsdam:2*, p. 871.

and another'.[9] And Byrnes's own views can scarcely be clearer. When Soviet foreign minister Molotov incredulously asked him whether his plan really meant that 'each country would have a free hand in their own zones and would act entirely independently of the others', the Secretary of State confirmed that this was so, adding only that some arrangement for the exchange of goods between zones would probably also be necessary.[10]

Under the Byrnes plan, Germany was to be divided into *two* parts – not *four*. In the Potsdam discussions, and even in the Potsdam agreement itself, Western Germany was treated as a bloc. There were in fact frequent references to the 'Western zone' and not 'zones', and Byrnes in fact referred to the Western part of Germany, in the singular, as 'our zone'.[11] The assumption was that the three Western powers – the Americans, the British and even the French, who were not even present at the conference – would be able to work out a common policy among themselves, and that Germany would in all probability be divided along East-West lines.[12]

An Amicable Divorce

What had led Byrnes to this new policy? He simply did not see real co-operation with the Soviet Union as possible. The United States and Russia were just too far apart on basics, he said on 24 July 1945 at Potsdam – that is, the day after the new reparation plan was proposed to the Soviets – for a 'long-term program of co-operation' to be feasible.[13] But that did not mean that serious tension was inevitable. The way to get along was to pull apart. The unitary approach, he argued, would lead in practice to 'endless quarrels and disagreements' among the allies. The attempt to

9. Waley memorandum, 2 Aug. 1945, *Documents on British Policy Overseas*, series 1, vol. 1 (henceforth cited in the form, *DBPO* 1:1), p. 1258. See also *ibid.*, p. 948. On Waley's discussion with Byrnes on 30 July 1945, see *ibid.*, pp. 1050–1051. Waley argued here that the Byrnes Plan, by drawing a 'line across the middle of Europe', had an 'importance far transcending reparations'.

10. Byrnes-Molotov meeting, 27 July 1945, *FRUS Potsdam:2*, p. 450.

11. See, for example, notes of foreign ministers' meeting, 30 July 1945, *FRUS Potsdam:2*, pp. 485, 487, 488, 491; or Clayton to Byrnes, 29 July 1945, *ibid.*, p. 901.

12. See, for example, Collado to Thorp and Reinstein, 23 July 1945, and Clayton and Collado to Thorp, 16 Aug. 1945, *FRUS Potsdam:2*, pp. 812, 829, and Secretary of War Stimson to President Truman, 22 July 1945, *FRUS Potsdam:2*, p. 809.

13. Walter Brown diary, 24 July 1945, quoted in Daniel Yergin, *Shattered Peace: The Origins of the Cold War and the National Security State* (London: André Deutsch, 1978), p. 119.

extract reparation on an all-German basis 'would be a constant source of irritation between us, whereas the United States wanted its relations with the Soviet Union to be cordial and friendly as heretofore'. A clean separation was the best solution, the best way to put an end to the squabbling and lay the basis for decent relations among the allies.[14]

The Byrnes plan provided the basis for the Potsdam agreement, but it was not as though the plan was simply imposed on an unwilling Soviet Union, which was then left feeling cheated.[15] Byrnes's goal was to reach an amicable understanding with the Soviets, and he was willing to go quite far to achieve this objective. The original Byrnes proposal was that each occupying power could take reparations from its own zone. This of course was something each of those states would have been able to do even if no agreement were reached, a point that Molotov himself made during the Potsdam discussions.[16] But to get the Soviets to accept this result (which might have come about anyway in the absence of an agreement) Byrnes was willing to make certain additional concessions to Moscow. He offered to accept the Oder-Neisse line as effectively the Eastern border of Germany – that is, to accept the hitherto unilateral Soviet measure of putting the areas East of that line under Polish administration – if the USSR agreed to his reparation plan. This was a major concession, as Truman pointed out.[17]

After a good deal of haggling, the Americans were also willing to give the Russians a substantial share of the industrial capital in the Western zones that the allies could agree was 'unnecessary for the German peace economy'. Fifteen per cent of this surplus capital would be sent East in exchange for food and certain other raw materials (this again reflected the fundamental assumption that Germany was being divided into two parts), and a further 10 per cent would be transferred free and clear to the Soviets, with no return payment of any kind required.[18] In the US view, the USSR

14. Byrnes-Molotov meeting, 23 July 1945; foreign ministers' meetings, 27 and 30 July 1945; plenary meeting, 28 July 1945; all in *FRUS Potsdam:2*, pp. 274, 430, 474, 487, 491.

15. For the claim that the pushing through of the Byrnes plan reflected a new US toughness resulting from the first successful test of a nuclear weapon, see Gar Alperovitz, *Atomic Diplomacy: Hiroshima and Potsdam* (New York: Vintage Books, 1965), pp. 164ff, 173.

16. Foreign ministers' meeting, 27 July 1945, *FRUS Potsdam:2*, p. 430.

17. Truman-Molotov meeting, 29 July 1945, *ibid.*, p. 472.

18. *Ibid.*, pp. 475, 481, 489, 932.

could justifiably feel it had the right to half of whatever reparations could be extracted from Germany, and drawing them only from its own zone would give it a little less than 50 per cent. The 10 per cent from Western Germany was thus a kind of makeweight. The US goal was to reach an agreement that the USSR could be happy with, and to achieve this Byrnes and Truman were willing to give the Russians a little more than they absolutely had to.

The Soviets grasped the hand that Byrnes had held out. Stalin extended the idea to cover the most liquid, and thus the most readily transferable, German assets – the gold captured by the allied armies in Germany, German holdings abroad and shares in German firms. According to his plan, all this would *not* be pooled and apportioned on an all-German basis. Instead, Stalin proposed a simple rule for dividing those assets: along the East-West line of demarcation, 'the line running from the Baltic to the Adriatic'. Everything East of that line, assets in the Eastern zone and German investments in Eastern Europe, would go to Russia. Everything west of the line, including the German gold that had fallen into the hands of the Western armies, would go to the Western powers. This proposal was accepted by his British and US partners.[19] That this reflected a basic spheres-of-influence orientation is clear from its content and phrasing, and is also suggested by the fact that the British, at first, wanted to keep it secret. As a British Treasury official commented at the time, 'however undesirable it may be to draw a line across the middle of Germany, this is bound to happen and it is unrealistic to make a bargain except on a basis which assumes that it will happen'.[20]

Yet the most important point to note about the arrangement is Stalin's role in pressing for it. He was so taken with the basic idea of a division of Germany, and implicitly of Europe as a whole, that he was willing to abandon any claim to the German gold that had fallen into the hands of the Western armies. A unilateral concession of this sort, which was not at all in keeping with the usual Soviet practice at Potsdam of presenting their allies with one demand after another, was thus a striking demonstration of Stalin's wholehearted acceptance of the basic Byrnes concept. Indeed at the very end of the conference, the Soviet leader took what was for him the very unusual step of expressing his gratitude to Byrnes, 'who has

19. Plenary meeting, 1 Aug. 1945, *FRUS Potsdam:2*, pp. 566–567.

20. *DBPO 1:1*, p. 1258; see also Anne Deighton, *The Impossible Peace: Britain, the Division of Germany and the Origins of the Cold War* (Oxford: Clarendon Press, 1990), p. 34.

worked harder perhaps than any of us to make this conference a success'. It was Byrnes, he said, who 'brought us together in reaching so many important decisions... Those sentiments, Secretary Byrnes, come from my heart'.[21]

The Façade of a Unitary Policy

Although Stalin and Byrnes, supported by Truman, had reached a real understanding at Potsdam based on the idea that each side was essentially to have a free hand in its part of Germany, the Potsdam Protocol was full of passages that called for treating that country as a unit.[22] Even foreign trade, according to the text, was supposed to be managed on an all-German basis. But the all-German language of the final agreement was essentially a fig-leaf. The way the key foreign trade issue was handled again shows the real thrust of US thinking at this time. The Americans who had negotiated the terms of the Potsdam agreement covering foreign trade explained at the time why such 'unitary' language was harmless. The provisions calling for all-German arrangements in this area, they wrote, were subject to the already accepted principle that 'if the Control Council failed to agree', policy would be managed on a zonal basis. And they fully expected the Allied Control Council to deadlock on this issue. The control and financing of foreign trade, they pointed out, would then 'revert to the zonal commanders', in which case the three Western powers would probably be able to devise a common import programme for *Western* Germany as a whole.[23] So the all-German language of the Potsdam agreement was a gloss covering provisions permitting a separate administration of the Eastern and Western parts.

These provisions formed the real basis of the Potsdam understanding. The formal agreement might have given a very different impression, but it is scarcely to be expected that a written accord would provide directly for an overt partition of Germany. As long as the real issues had been settled with the agreement on the Byrnes plan, what harm was there in paying a little lip service to Wilsonian platitudes?

21. Plenary meeting, 1 Aug. 1945, *FRUS Potsdam:2*, p. 601. See also James F. Byrnes, *Speaking Frankly* (London: Heinemann, 1947), p. 80ff.

22. Text in *FRUS Potsdam:2*, pp. 1477–1498.

23. Collado to Thorp and Reinstein, 23 July 1945, and Clayton and Collado to Thorp, 16 Aug. 1945, *FRUS Potsdam:2*, pp. 812, 829–830.

The same general point explains US policy in the immediate post-Potsdam period. Byrnes at this time allowed US officials to press vigorously for unitary arrangements – to let those who still believed in co-operation with the USSR and in running Germany on a four-power basis beat their heads against the hard rocks of political reality. Not only did he expect those efforts to fail, but it even seems (and this is one of the big surprises to emerge from recent archival research) that he took certain steps to make sure it would fail.

The key piece of evidence here is a document from the French archives, a 'very confidential' report of a long conversation that Saint-Hardouin, the French Political Advisor in Germany, had with his US counterpart Robert Murphy in October 1945. The French were blocking the policy of setting up central administrations in Germany, which would have been vital to treating Germany as a unit. But what is not well known is that the US government was secretly encouraging the French in their obstructionism. Generals Clay and Eisenhower, the two top US military officers in Germany, not really knowing Byrnes's innermost thoughts and taking the Potsdam Protocol at face value as their charter, were pressing hard for unitary arrangements and were angry about French vetoes in the Control Council. But Murphy told Saint-Hardouin that the French government should not worry too much about that, as these military officers had their orders and were not in the habit of wondering whether there were any valid reasons for the obstacles they found in their way. Murphy went on to talk about the United States' German policy in broader terms. For the time being, he argued, the United States was stuck with the policy of trying to work with Russia. Until US opinion changed, there was no choice but to pursue that policy. But clearly Murphy was not interested in a unified Germany: he was worried that a united Germany would fall under Soviet control. The current need was to play for time, and time, he said, would perhaps bring 'changes that no one can foresee today'. It might be too late now for the United States to repudiate the four-power regime, but there was no reason, he told the French diplomat, why France had to go along with it. He therefore urged the French to avoid the drawbacks of the Berlin-based Control Council system, and to 'orient your zone towards the West, rather than towards Berlin'.[24]

24. Saint-Hardouin to Bidault, 9 Oct. 1945, Series Y-Internationale (1944–49) Vol. 283, French Foreign Ministry Archives, Paris.

How is this document to be interpreted? Murphy was too experienced, too intelligent and above all too professional a diplomat to have been acting entirely on his own. Is it too much to assume, especially given Byrnes's basic Potsdam policy and also the Secretary's well-known tendency to operate on his own, that Murphy had received certain instructions from Byrnes personally, and that the Americans were playing a double game? It is most likely that Byrnes was engaged in a kind of charade: from Potsdam on he was never really interested in running Germany as a unit (which was probably out of the question in any case, given the Soviet attitude). Byrnes's policy was throughout this period based on the expectation that Germany would be divided. But he was not content to allow events simply to take their own course: the process needed to be given a little push, gently administered by Murphy in his remarks to Saint-Hardouin.

The End of the Potsdam Policy

Whether Byrnes was being deliberately obstructionist or not, by early 1946 something very important had changed. It was not that the Americans had finally come to the conclusion that a partition of Germany along East-West lines was unavoidable, since that had essentially been the assumption from July 1945 onwards. What had disappeared was the idea that the division of Germany was a solution that both sides could accept, that it would provide the basis for an amicable divorce between the Soviet Union and her wartime allies. There was no doubt that Germany was going to be divided. But East-West relations in early and mid-1946 were very different from the sort of relatively friendly 'spheres of influence' settlement which Byrnes, and Stalin, had agreed at Potsdam.

Furthermore, it was the US government that played the key role in bringing about this change. What the Soviets were doing in the Eastern zone, running it as they saw fit, which at Potsdam Byrnes had proposed, was now totally unacceptable. The Soviets, the US government now complained, were blatantly violating the Potsdam agreement. What a nerve they had blocking a common import-export programme for all of Germany! This was in fact the key charge being levelled against them in early 1946. And it was made clear to the Soviets that if they did not accept the Western view and permit foreign trade to be organised on an all-German basis, the West would reclaim its freedom of action and move ahead without them.

The new policy for Western Germany was coming to have a distinct anti-Soviet coloration. The USSR was being stigmatised in the eyes of the German people. As a British official put it toward the end of the year, 'we have to make the Russians appear to the German public as the saboteurs of German unity'.[25] The Western powers, on the other hand, were presenting themselves as the great champions of German national rights.

What was going on here? By early 1946, events, in the Near East especially, had convinced Western leaders that the Soviet Union was an aggressive, expansionist power, and therefore ultimately posed a military threat to Western Europe.[26] A tougher, more militant Western policy was the order of the day to mobilise enough power to counter the Soviet threat; opinion at home had to be stirred up, and the Germans had to be won over to the Western side. To the Soviets, however, it was this new Western policy that was viewed as threatening. Western Germany was being 'organised' not just without them, but against them. The Germans were being told that Russia was their enemy, and the new policy implied that Britain and the United States supported their basic national aspirations. And all this was tightly linked to what the Western governments were saying about Potsdam: the Soviets had promised to run Germany as a unit, but were now reneging on that promise; Britain and the United States had tried hard, at Potsdam and after, to work out arrangements that would preserve German unity; it was the Soviet attitude that had made this impossible.

This, however, was simply a myth, propagated mostly by those who had not been privy to what had really gone on at Potsdam, but promoted even by those – most notably, Secretary Byrnes himself – who knew better, but who in 1946 understood the great political value that this myth had come to have. It was a myth that fed into the general tendency to view the Cold War in meta-historical terms as flowing from the basic nature of the two systems, and not as a secular conflict shaped by specific policies and concrete decisions that could easily have been different. And this is a myth, I should add, that historians – amazingly, given how unambiguous the published Potsdam documents are – have never really taken the trouble to clear up.

25. Hankey note, 25 Oct. 1946, quoted in Deighton, *The Impossible*, p. 108.

26. See Bruce Kuniholm, *The Origins of the Cold War in the Near East: Great Power Conflict and Diplomacy in Iran, Turkey and Greece* (Princeton: Princeton University Press, 1980), chapter 5.

Chapter 9

CLICHÉS OF OUR MEMORY

Marcellin Hodeir

For over a century, photography, progressively replacing other illustrations, together with the written and spoken word has constituted one of the principal means of communication of our culture. Closely associated with the event it illustrates, photography, through its power of suggestion and insinuation rather than description, can appeal to the imagination of people without any intellectual effort.

Paradoxically, photographs can go along with or become myths precisely because they seem to be 'objective sources', supposedly conveying 'facts', not 'interpretations'. In reality, photography can be an even better carrier of myths because it has the *cachet* of truth. In the case of photographs of historical events, it is particularly interesting to study this connection between picture and myth: out of the hands of its creator, the photograph can blend into myth, transcend myth, or turn against myth.

Thus, using the examples of four important episodes of contemporary history, we will try to explain in which circumstances a photograph, or 'mechanical memory', can, or cannot, acquire a symbolic dimension with regard to the event it illustrates. The four examples are:

1. Yalta: the division of the world;
2. Munich: the shame of the democracies;

Translated by Philippe Boyer and Ian Moore

3. The Spanish Civil War: the people's fight against fascism;
4. Diên Biên Phu: the end of the colonial empires.

Image Corresponding to Myth: Yalta

'February 1945: three of the victors over Nazism – excluding France – gather in Yalta. Soviets and Americans divide the world among themselves.' Alongside this statement published in the French weekly *L'Express*,[1] a truncated photograph shows the three Allied leaders, from left to right: Winston Churchill, Franklin D. Roosevelt and Josef Stalin, warmly dressed, seated in individual armchairs. The first of them, smoking a cigar, looks at the other two who seem to be speaking to him. This photograph, which went around the world, is linked in most people's minds to the Yalta conference to the extent that it has become a reference when we speak of a division of the world.

Regardless of whether this is an accurate interpretation of the events of Yalta,[2] the picture of these three seated men facing us, also operates outside its historic and geographic context as a binary, almost 'Pavlovian', association with the myth created after the conference: 'the division of the world'. Like the numerous signposts in our train stations and airports, the 'photograph of Yalta', or the several by-products (cartoons, manipulated photographs), convey the unmistakable message 'conference on the dividing of the world' because of the myth attached to that photograph.

The link, made consciously or subconsciously, between the photograph of Yalta and the division of the world, cannot work without a first step of connecting the picture with the historic event. This correlation survives because readers encounter it time and again in history textbooks, newspapers and magazines, expert literature and so forth. Television documentaries also reinforce the associative mechanism, as they often use photographs.

Reiner Marcowitz has shown that the myth was only generated after the event by Charles de Gaulle. We thus find that the coverage by French daily newspapers the day after the agreements of Yalta carried no trace of it. *L'Humanité* published the photograph of 'the three leaders' on the front page, but without

1. *L'Express* (9 February 1995), pp. 34–35.
2. See chapter 7 in this volume: Reiner Marcowitz, 'Yalta, the Myth of the Division of the World'.

any allusion to a division of the world. *Le Figaro* and *Le Monde* underline the decision of the 'Three' to disarm Nazi Germany and the future role of France in the occupation of Germany and the inter-allied Council of control.[3] The idea of a division of the world is totally absent, the myth is not yet formed.

Once it was born, however, we find even in school textbooks the correlation of 'Yalta' with 'the division of the world'. Effectively, out of eighteen French history textbooks,[4] where the agreements of Yalta are part of the curriculum (sixth formers and fourth formers), the photograph of the three Leaders (black or white, or in colour) is used in direct relation to the text by fourteen of them. Those textbooks which did not contain the Yalta illustration printed photographs on the agreements of Teheran or of Potsdam, which also featured the three statesmen seated in armchairs. Thus there is a kind of continuity in the symbolism that perpetuates the 'reflex-association' of image and nature of the event. The classic books on the history of the Second World War or of contemporary Europe, whether they are American, British or French, follow the same iconographic approach.[5] The researchers of specialised historical journals do not escape this 'established rule' in the choice of their images.[6] But in Yalta, the photographers did not take merely one picture, so why that particular photograph?

The answer is that virtually the same set of pictures was distributed by the official press agencies of the Allied countries. A

3. *L'Humanité* (14 Feb. 1945); *Le Monde* (13 Feb. 1945); *Le Figaro* (13 Feb. 1945).

4. List of the history textbooks used for this section. History for sixth formers: Editions Hatier, 1962, 1991, 1993; Editions Fernand Nathan, 1962, 1992; ABC editions Breal, 1992; Editions Casteilla 'ISTRA', 1989; Editions Berlin, 1983, 1989; Editions Bordas, 1969, 1988; Editions Casteilla 'ISTRA', 1988; Editions Hachette, 1988. History for fourth formers: Editions Bordas, 1984; Editions Belin, 1989, 1993; Editions Nathan, 1990, 1993.

5. Making an exhaustive list on the proposed theme linking images and texts would be leaning towards perfection, therefore we have just listed some usual classics readily available in libraries: Jean Baptiste Duroselle (ed.), *L'Europe: Histoire de ses Peuples* (Paris: Librairie Academique Perrin, 1990); Philippe Masson (ed.), *Dictionnaire de la Seconde Guerre Mondiale* (Paris: Larousse, 1979); Abraham Rothberg, *Eyewitness History of World War Two* (New York: Bantam Books, 1962/63); H. Stuart Hughes, *Contemporary Europe: A History* (New York: Prentice-Hall, 1961); Series *World War Two: The Soviet Juggernaut* (US: Time life Books, 1980); *Fichier sur l'histoire mondiale contemporaine* (Geneva: Edito-Service S.A, 1978); Philippe Masson, *La Seconde Guerre Mondiale en Couleurs* (Paris: Larousse, 1984).

6. Pierre Milza, 'La Vérité sur Yalta', *L'Histoire* No. 75 (February 1985), p.34; Jean Baptiste Duroselle, 'Yalta: Le partage du Monde' *Historia Hors Serie* No. 457 (November 1984), p. 123; Liliane Crete, 'Il n'y a pas eu de partage du Monde a Yalta', *Historia* No. 425 (April 1982), p. 123.

survey of five photograph agencies and of an institutional photograph archive[7] showed that three of these own between naught and six photographs on the conference, the three others between twelve and twenty four. It is striking that the variety is very limited: there are sixty-five photographs in total with a high number of duplicates within the agencies. The main photograph of the 'Big Three', with all its variants,[8] represents close to a quarter of all the photographs consulted and can be found in almost all of the agencies. Secondly, we find two types of images dominating: other than the armchairs photograph, another one also with symbolic meaning (the Three and their advisers around a round table), and the other totally neutral (several views of Palace Lividia where the conference took place).[9] Admittedly, about half the photographs that are left neither depict the 'Big Three' together nor show neutral views of the venue. We find here:

- Stalin and Roosevelt, seated, talking
- Advisers of the Three Leaders
- Stalin talking to Molotov
- Roosevelt and Churchill with a few advisers
- Roosevelt with one or several American advisers
- Roosevelt arriving at Yalta airport with Churchill and Molotov
- Stalin, smiling, looking at Churchill handling a cigar
- Churchill on his own
- Roosevelt, Churchill and Molotov posing

But not one of these is linked to the myth of the division of the world.

The recurrence of the 'Big Three' photograph can be explained by the working habits of the researchers of publishing houses and their counterparts in photographic agencies. The former often work with a long-term collection. Because of the variety and urgency of

7. The following photographic agencies were consulted (name/number of photos of Yalta): ETEVE, eighteen; KEYSTONE, twelve; RAPHO, none; NOVOSTY, six; ROGER et VIOLLET, five; Photo-library BDIC, twenty-four.

8. Some photographs were reframed or retouched, emphasising the importance of the three heads of states and obscuring the background filled with ministers and advisers. One of the most representative images using this method is offered by the NOVOSTY agency: with his brush, the retoucher has illuminated, like an aura, the three people seated – particularly Stalin – the background being obscured by an artistic haze.

9. Sixteen photographs with the 'Three Leaders'; eight photographs with the 'round table'; seven photographs with palace Lividia.

their tasks, they usually create very similar collections of photographs for major themes that come up regularly: the photograph collectors of photographic agencies conclude most of their deals by telephone or through faxes. Their collections are sorted by pre-defined themes and each one has its star photographs which are systematically offered to their contacts. To the question: 'Why that particular photograph rather than another?' I invariably received the answer, 'because it is the photograph they expect'. Things have come full circle.

Finally, the photograph of the 'Big Three' has been used also to illustrate the text of a historian critical to the Yalta myth. For that purpose, the photograph of the Three Leaders is spread in colour across two pages with in caption: 'After the signature of the agreements of Yalta, the leaders of the allied delegations and their foreign ministers ... pose *for the photograph which is still today symbolic of "the splitting of the world."*'[10]

Images Falling Short of the Myth: Munich

If the photograph of the Three Leaders has squeezed out all the other photographs of Yalta, we do not find this extreme limitation in the photographic representation of the next two examples, Munich and the Spanish Civil War.

'It is peace in our time.' 'Peace! Peace! It is peace!'[11] These two immediate reactions captured right after the Munich conference indicate the meaning given at the time of the event: 'Munich = Peace'. The photographs published in the daily papers were of considerable variety, but always illustrate this association:

- Daladier or Chamberlain before their departure to Munich
- Daladier or Chamberlain arriving in Munich, met by German officials
- Daladier and/or Chamberlain with Hitler and Mussolini
- Daladier and/or Chamberlain, Hitler, Mussolini signing the agreement
- Daladier's plane arriving back at Le Bourget greeted by a crowd
- Daladier and Bonnet in a car in Paris cheered by a crowd

10. Milza, 'La vérité sur Yalta', p. 34.
11. The latter are the first lines from J. Prouvost's article in *Paris-Soir* (1 Oct. 1938).

- Chamberlain behind microphones, presenting the peace agreement to a crowd, at a press conference at the airport
- The French or English crowds celebrating the 'saved' peace[12]

Owing to the subsequent historical developments, all these photographs took on a completely different meaning, that of illusion and betrayal. Therefore the picture cannot succeed on its own, it needs a caption to interpret it as 'Munich = The cowardice of the democracies'.[13] Thus, a very neutral photograph such as Daladier's plane greeted by the crowd can be followed with this commentary: 'Daladier returning from Munich, seeing the large crowd at Le Bourget, expected hostile manifestations. Triumphantly welcomed as the saviour of the peace, he is supposed to have murmured: '... the fools! If only they knew....'[14] Accompanied by this sort of comment, the photograph can illustrate the author's interpretation. For example, the photograph of Chamberlain upon his return to Heston can be interpreted as meaning that he does not hold in his hands the peace agreement but the betrayal of Czechoslovakia and/or the seeds of the Second World War.[15]

The researchers choose pictures where the body language and the posture of the characters strengthen or serve the purpose of the caption. One history textbook uses the official photograph of the signatories of Munich straight after the agreement acceptance. The caption runs as follows: 'At the end of the Munich conference: family photograph, three piece suits and uniforms. From left to right: Chamberlain: relieved, Daladier: worried and sullen, Hitler: very confident, Mussolini: jubilant but a touch worried....'[16] The same photograph had been published a few year before by a history magazine about the twentieth century, with quite a different caption: '30th September, 1:00 am. Czechoslovakia's fate had been sealed. Only a faint smile on Hitler's face contrasts with the serious expression of the three other signatories of the agreement....'[17] The magazine *L'Histoire* also published this photograph, with the caption: 'The official photograph of the Munich conference does not

12. *Paris-Soir, Ce Soir, l'Excelsior, Le Jour, L'Echo de Paris, L'Oeuvre, Le Populaire.*

13. KEYSTONE, thirty photographs on Munich; ROGER & VIOLLET, thirty-two photographs; and the BDIC, twelve photographs.

14. Voice 'off' commentary during the first episode of the film *French People: If Only You Knew*, André Harris and Alain de Sedouy (dirs.), France 1972.

15. In the series *World War Two: Prelude to War* (US: Time Life Books Inc., 1980).

16. History textbook 1914/1939, sixth formers, by R. Dubreuil, Y. Trotignon and P. Wagret (SCODEL, 1985).

17. *Historia Magazine 20th Century* No.153 (Tallandier, 1970).

provoke joy. At the centre, most at ease, Hitler has the imperious behaviour of the master of the game. Chamberlain and Daladier, the first two from the left, stand back a bit, not very proud.'[18]

There is no one photograph that encapsulates the myth of Munich in its binary interpretation of 'that picture = the shame of the democracies'. The photographs of Munich help us identify a situation, a sequence of events, rather than having symbolic value in themselves. They have not quite reached the status of myths in themselves. In Britain, however, the newsreel scene of Chamberlain's speech at Heston ('… and I believe it is peace in our time') has attained such symbolic value that Chamberlain's umbrella has become for cartoonists and writers a symbol of Munich and of appeasement in general.

The Image Transcending the Myth: The Spanish Civil War

As a propaganda war, the Spanish Civil War was a war not only of words but also of pictures. The two main agencies consulted (Keystone; Roger & Viollet) each had more than four hundred related photographs. The weekly *L'Illustration* printed more than 325 different photographs on the Spanish Civil War, among them five cover illustrations within the first eight months of the conflict. The event was thus particularly richly documented with a wide range of themes.

Building on chapter 5 in this book on the Spanish Civil War, we can list here a number of myths associated with it: the Revolution, Democracy attacked by the Counter-Revolution, Democracy against Fascism, the Overture of the Second World War. These myths are quite difficult to illustrate with photographs. Thus, the pictures used in this context vary. However, like a *leitmotiv*, two images keep appearing.

The first one is not a photograph, but the Pablo Picasso painting *Guernica*, representing the bombing of a little Basque village by the German legion 'Condor' on a market day of April 1937.[19] Created to arouse the horror of the massacre, the work of Picasso

18. Michel Winock, 'L'esprit de Munich', *L'Histoire* No. 58 (July–Aug. 1983), p. 71.

19. Pablo Picasso's *Guernica* is found in three out of four history manuals for fourth formers, and four out of nine for sixth formers; it also appears in Duroselle, *L'Europe: Histoire de ses peuples*, p. 367, and in the special edition of *Historia* No. 22 on the Spanish Civil War (3:1971), pp. 136, 137.

does not leave room for any other interpretations; the binary association is immediate because it was deliberately created by the artist,[20] in a way in which a photographer, able only to capture 'objective' events, is not free to do.

The second picture is a snapshot: the 'Death of a Republican Soldier' taken by Robert Capa in September 1936.[21] This photograph went around the world: in France, it was published with the caption 'Sergeant, why do you agree to die?', side-by-side with an article by Antoine de Saint-Exupéry.[22] A powerful image, Capa's photograph allows the most lyrical associations: '... the sacrifice of the people for the salvation of the Republic' or 'the chests of the proletariat against the Fascist bullets.' Later, this classic of photo-journalism is accompanied by increasingly synthetic captions, sometimes with symbolic connotation such as 'The Agony of the Spanish Republic',[23] or 'The Death of a Republican Militiaman', 'The Death of a Spanish Republican', 'The Death of the Republican'.[24] The researcher from *Historia Magazine* chose another association: 'Mankind and War'.[25] Jean Lacouture, in an introduction to a book on the work of Capa, went even further:

> The most famous snapshot that a reporter has ever got out of his black box dates from 1936. It is that of the militiaman, dressed in light camouflage, pale as an angel of Cocteau, staggering, struck as by lightning against the background of a mountain-range, his rifle blown away by the wind of death. For a long time yet, when people will no longer remember what this war was and what it signified for the world's future, men look with fascination at this rich picture. If our writing were lost like hieroglyphs after the ban by the emperor Theodore, one could make this picture the ideogram of war.[26]

20. On the influence of Picasso's painting on photography, see Aline Angoustures, *Histoire de l'Espagne du 20ème siècle* (Brussels: Complexes, 1993), p. 173.

21. The official caption given by R. Capa is: 'Spain, near Cerro Muriano around 5 September 1936: Death of a republican soldier.'

22. Antoine de Saint-Exupéry, 'La guerre sur le front de Carabancel', *France-Soir* (28 June 1937). Note the ten-month gap between the time when the photograph was taken and its publication in France.

23. History textbook for sixth formers (Nathan: 1992), p. 339.

24. In the following order: (1) history textbook for sixth formers (Hachette Classiques, 1992), p. 346; (2) history textbook for sixth formers (Belin, 1991), p. 251; (3) history textbook for sixth formers (Hachette Lycées, 1988), p. 308.

25. *Historia Magazine Twentieth Century* No. 150 (Tallandier, 1970).

26. Robert Delpire (ed.) for the National Centre of Photography: *Robert Capa*, intro. by Jean Lacouture (Paris: Photo Poche, 1988).

Pacifist ideologists and propagandists used this picture in the 1970s either as poster with the caption 'WHY?' or on postcards with the commentary: 'Never again this ...' Isolated from its socio-historical context, Capa's picture thus transcended its original subject.[27]

Inadequate Images: Diên Biên Phu

On 7 May 1954, the French, at Diên Biên Phu, lost considerably more than a small position in the remote west of Indochina. By forcing the surrender of the elite troops of the expeditionary corps of the French Union, this defeat announced the fall of a colonial empire, of an order based on force and, by extension, the end of European colonialism. Seen from the other side, it is the symbol of all fights for national liberation.

The campaign which lasted about twenty-two weeks[28] was amply covered by the media, both in word and image. We can distinguish three periods of reporting. The first, which corresponds to the French development and fortification of the site, is richly documented. Civil and military photographers covered the following themes:

- Inspection of the entrenched camp by officers of rank
- Departures of French patrols to inspect the area around Diên Biên Phu
- Vietminh prisoners
- Airdrops of troops and materials on the camp
- Daily life of the troops stationed at Diên Biên Phu (radio operators, infirmary, control post, aircraft mechanics, tanks, artillerists etc.)
- The runway with civil and military cargo aircraft, fighter and liaison aircraft
- Fortified positions, trenches, bunkers, artillery caches
- Aerial views (runway approach, view from above of the entire camp)

These pictures, deliberately optimistic, convey an expression of power by showing the forces and *matériel* deployed. They radiate

27. Michel Bôle-Richard, 'Le républicain espagnol inconnu s'appelait Federico Borrel Garcia', *Le Monde* (6 Sept. 1996).

28. The first airdrops on the Diên Biên Phu site as part of the 'Castor' operation date from 20 Nov. 1953; the camp finally fell on 7 May 1954.

security and order: a high-ranking officers' visit, clean barracks, the smiling faces showing confidence. Admittedly, the censors chose these particular photographs for distribution, but these were the images presenting themselves to the reporters.

Next follows the phase of battle. The few civilian photographers had been evacuated by the last planes that were able to leave the camp, leaving only military reporters. Slowly, as the campaign turned bad for France, the people from the Cinematographic Service of the Armed Forces (SCA)[29] abandoned the propagandist slant on their pictures in favour of glimpses of the horrors surrounding them:

- Soldier with helmets but without shirts, exhausted, huddled up in a bomb crater or clinging to the side of a makeshift trench
- Stretcher bearers running towards a plane under enemy fire
- An injured man carried on the back of a comrade
- A group of legionnaires counter-attacking to regain a lost position
- Charred aircraft frames, destroyed tanks, corpses in the mud
- A group of officers, in a underground control post, exhausted by the fight, taking stock of the situation

Admittedly the published commentaries accompanying the photographs at the time praise the high moral values and fighting spirit of the troops engaged at Diên Biên Phu, but they could not hide the sense of destitution caught by the photographers. Going beyond the partisan analysis, the battle pictures tell us of the hardship and the ferocity of the fights, of the tenacity, of the suffering, of the resignation and of the despair of the combatants. A clear vision of death and Hell are communicated: in the photographic material, simulation yields to bitter reality.

The third stage is the vision of the other side, the enemy, the victor. The existence itself of the photographs of this stage is the direct result of victory. Alain Jaubert has proved that the photographs distributed by the Vietnamese were almost all forged:

> Whether they are showing the transportation of *matériel,* the attacks by Vietminh soldiers, both are photographed in full daylight

29. The SCA, now the ECPA (Army Photographic and Cinematrographic Establishment). Furnishing the only military photographers during the battles, the ECPA has the monopoly on the photographs for that period.

> whereas all these operations took place at night; whether they pretend to have been taken during the final assault against the central fortification (soldiers playing dead and smoke bombs giving a war-like ambience), all those scenes were photographed and filmed well after the battle.[30]

Thus, the 'star' photograph of the victory of the popular forces, where we see the Vietnamese flag brandished on the roof of the control post of the General de Castries, is taken from a film directed by the Soviet cinematographer Roman Karmen more than a week after the end of the battle.[31] Such forgeries were still published recently alongside the original captions,[32] but their propaganda function did not stand up against the analysis of the historians.[33]

Photo-archivists and documentalists have used photographs from these three stages of developments, but none seems to have acquired a symbolic value. For the early period, we often find photographs of the invasion of the Diên Biên Phu basin, where in the foreground, the soldiers already on the ground cover the landing of hundreds of others, still in the sky, only seen by their open parachutes. This does not signal the end of empire. Photographs from the second stage show the intensity of the battle. We find, uniforms excluded, the same visual situation as in the battle of Verdun, faces of men engaged in battle, landscape of trenches, etc. Again, nothing signals the end of empire. The third set of photographs was only temporarily useful as a platform for the myth because of the outrageously propagandist character of the posed photographs.

Thus illustrations of the fall of Diên Biên Phu shown in books, journals and history textbooks only make sense if they are accompanied by a solid commentary which connects them to the myth. This is all the more so because other images convey the French defeat. Paul Colin's poster of 1954 shows the body of a soldier fallen on a cross, with the caption: 'DIÊN BIÊN PHU … they sacrificed themselves for freedom.'[34] Here the defeat of Diên Biên Phu is no longer the symbol of the collapse of the colonial empire but an unfortunate episode of the fight of (Western, Christian) democracy against (Godless) Communism in the Far East.

30. Alain Jaubert, *Le Commissariat aux Archives: les photos qui falsifient l'histoire* (Paris: Barrault, 1986), pp. 138–139.

31. *Ibid.*, p. 138. This photograph was distributed by the AFP.

32. Jean Lacouture, 'La défaite de Diên Biên Phu' in *L'Histoire* No. 12 (May 1979).

33. Special edition on Diên Biên Phu, *Historia* No. 28 (Mar.–Apr. 1994).

34. Paul Colin's poster is displayed in the collections of the *Musée de deux guerres mondiales.* It was published several times in school textbooks, e.g. history for sixth formers (Belin 1989) or in specialised reviews, e.g. Special edition of *Historia* No. 28.

Thus in the case of Diên Biên Phu, no single photograph has been established in the binary function which allows it to symbolise the myth.

Conclusion

Some photographs, thanks to their suggestive power, others simply by their uniqueness or the monopoly they have, are associated in our minds with an event as myths, or have become myths in their own right. But in the large majority, as stated by Pierre Fresnault-Deruelle, 'the image alone, compared with words, is singularly weak when it comes, for instance, to explain a causality; and in order to do so, some alterations (to say the least) are necessary for the icon to have its impact'.[35]

Technical progress increasingly makes computer-generated image possible. Without totally replacing photography, they will assign to them other functions, other significance. These even more artificial images create new possibilities for tampering with and manipulating pictures to a degree still largely unimagined and unexploited. With Henri Hudrisier, we have to admit that one of today's paradoxes would be 'that we are in a world flooded with images, and we still imagine ourselves to be under the power of the word'.[36]

35. Pierre Fesnault-Deruelle, *L'Image manipulée* (Paris: Mediathèque Edilig, 1983).

36. Henri Hudrisier, *L'iconothèque* (Paris: La Documentation Française, INA, 1982), p. 78.

Part III

Special Relationships

Chapter 10

THE 'SPECIAL RELATIONSHIP'

A Diverting British Myth?

John Baylis

> The Government fashions an imaginary world that pleases it, and then comes to believe in the reality of that world and acts as though it were real.
>
> *Hans J. Morgenthau, 18 April 1965*[1]

> The 'Special Relationship' is a fact, but a fact of a rather peculiar kind; for myths are also facts. It would be interesting ... to enquire further into why it has been found psychologically so necessary to dress up a perfectly honourable relationship as though national self-interest were something which should play no part in this branch of international politics.
>
> *Max Beloff ,1966*[2]

The author would like to thank Kerry Longhurst for assistance with the research for this paper.

1. Quoted in M.S. Skidmore (ed.), *World Politics, Essays on Language and Politics* (US, James E Freel and Associates, 1972), p. 81.

2. Max Beloff, 'The Special Relationship: An Anglo-American Myth', in M. Gilbert (ed.), *A Century of Conflict, 1850–1950: Essays for A.J.P. Taylor* (London: Hamish Hamilton, 1966), pp. 151–171.

Introduction

With some notable exceptions, diplomatic historians and political scientists have tended to neglect the role of myths in International Politics.[3] Historical methodology which has traditionally privileged the search for 'exact knowledge' and positivist approaches to international relations which have emphasised 'structure' have tended to direct attention away from the more intangible factors affecting the behaviour of states.[4] When myth and reality have been discussed it has usually been a device designed to emphasise one interpretation at the expense of another.[5] However, with the growing importance of interdisciplinary studies, the wide ranging impact of literary criticism and the renewed debates which have arisen in recent years on the nature of history, it has become increasingly apparent that the relationship between myth and reality is more problematic than many writers have conceded in the past.[6] In particular, there is a growing awareness that myths play an important part in international politics and require serious scholarly attention.

The purpose of this chapter is to consider the relationship between myth and reality in the context of the 'special relationship' between Britain and the United States since World War Two. The main thrust of the argument that follows is that myth and reality, as Max Beloff indicated in his 1966 article, are inextricably intertwined

3. See Keith Thomas, *Religion and the Decline of Magic: Studies in Popular Beliefs in Sixteenth and Seventeenth Century England* (London: Weidenfield and Nicolson, 1971).

4. R. Samuel and P. Thompson have argued that: 'For the historian the idea of myth has been viewed as an impediment or hindrance to the "real" world of history, it would be an offence to protocol if myths or tables were to be cited as primary sources in historical research. Myths have been assigned to "antiquarian interest", rather than scholarly research. When we encounter myth our instinct is to devalue it, to demythologise, to rob it of its power.' See R. Samuel and P. Thompson (eds), *The Myths We Live By* (London: Routledge, 1990). For the debates about 'Positivist' approaches in international politics see Ken Booth and S. Smith (eds), *International Relations Theory Today* (Cambridge: Polity Press, 1995).

5. The author of this paper has been guilty of this in the past. See John Baylis, 'The Development of the British Thermonuclear Capability, 1954–1961. Myth or Reality' in *Contemporary Record* Vol. 8, No. 1 (Summer 1994).

6. The convergence of anthropology and history in recent years has been particularly important in securing a recognition of the importance of myth in historical understanding. See Michael Stanford, *A Companion to the Study of History* (Oxford: Blackwell, 1994) and Roy Porter, *The Myths of the English* (Cambridge: Polity Press, 1992). Porter points to the work of writers like Roland Barthes, Jean Baudrillard and Pierre Bourdieu in helping to develop a greater understanding of the symbolism and varied meanings of myths.

in Anglo-US relations.[7] In contrast to the more sentimental interpretations of the 'special relationship', the contention is that British policy-makers have consciously constructed and manipulated a myth about relations with the United States which they have come to believe in, and which has undoubtedly affected the reality of the relationship which has developed between the two countries. In answer to Max Beloff's question it is argued that the myth (and the accompanying rhetoric) of the 'special relationship' was designed to reinforce British interests and in particular to obscure her declining power. The article also suggests, however, that the 'special relationship' had another diverting effect, that of retarding Britain's adjustment to the rank of a mainly European power.

The Founding of a Myth: The Second World War

According to Daniel Maguire myths consist of 'a complex of feelings, attitudes, symbols, memories and experienced relationships through which reality is refracted, filtered and interpreted'.[8] They often involve 'representations of the past, which although they may be based on real events are distortions of the past'.[9] In laying the foundations for the concept of the 'special relationship', the 'symbols, memories and experienced relationships' associated with the Second World War were (and remain) of crucial importance.

In the period before Pearl Harbor, despite US neutrality, a 'common-law alliance' was established between Britain and the United States. During this period 'a gradual mixing-up process' took place, with wide-ranging co-operation involving such things as lend-lease arrangements; the destroyers-for-bases agreement; the Tizard mission; Joint Staff Talks; and the beginnings of intelligence collaboration; all of which laid the foundations of the 'full-marriage' which was to follow.[10] Once the United States had entered the war, the formation of a joint war machine quickly developed. This began with the 'Arcadia' conference and the confirmation of the 'Germany-first' strategy, followed by the formation of a series

7. Beloff, 'The Special Relationship'.

8. Daniel C. Maguire, 'Myth in Politics' in M. Skidmore (ed.), *World Politics: Essays on Language and Politics* (US: James E. Freel and Associates, 1972), p. 81.

9. Alan Macmillan, 'Strategic Culture' (University of Wales, Ph.D. diss., 1996).

10. For a discussion of the military relationship between Britain and the United States during the Second World War see John Baylis, *Anglo-American Defence Relations, 1939–1984: The Special Relationship* (London: Macmillan, 1984).

of Combined Boards, which together played a crucial role in the direction and co-ordination of the allied war effort. The war against Germany, the war against Japan and the two vital areas of Anglo-US co-operation in the fields of atomic energy and intelligence, together highlighted the remarkable degree of collaboration that was achieved. This is reflected in General George C. Marshall's far-reaching claim in 1945 that the Anglo-US partnership between 1941 and 1945 represented 'the most complete unification of military effort ever achieved by two allied states' in the history of warfare.[11]

Crucial to the successful wartime alliance (and the myth of the 'special relationship' which developed later) was the close personal relationship established between Winston Churchill and Franklin Roosevelt. The nature of this relationship can be summed up in the following (perhaps apocryphal) story. Shortly after the Japanese attack on Pearl Harbor, Churchill arrived in the United States for discussions with the US President. During his visit, the Prime Minister stayed in the White House. According to Robert Sherwood, on one occasion, Roosevelt was wheeled into Churchill's room only to find him emerging from the bath – 'wet, glowing and completely naked'. Somewhat disconcerted, Roosevelt started to leave the room only to be called back by his guest. 'The Prime Minister of Great Britain', he declared, 'has nothing to conceal from the President of the United States.'[12]

Whether this story is true or not remains unclear, but it does illustrate some of the main features of what came to be known as the 'special relationship'. In particular, it reflects the importance of the personal relationship between the leaders of both countries and also the informality, as well as the mutual trust, which is said to characterise the relationship in general.[13] Such qualities, together with a common language and common culture, are often seen as setting the Anglo-US relationship apart from other 'normal' relationships in international politics.

While the post-war rhetoric of Anglo-US relations tended to focus on the close, indeed extra-ordinary, partnership which had undoubtedly existed between the two states during the war, what

11. General George C. Marshall, *The Winning of the War in Europe and the Pacific*, Biennial Report of the Chief of Staff of the US Army, 1 July 1943 to 30 June 1945, to the Secretary of War.

12. Robert Sherwood, *Roosevelt and Hopkins: An Intimate History* (New York: Harper Brothers, 1948), p. 442.

13. Henry Kissinger, *The White House Years* (New York: Weidenfeld and Nicolson, 1979), pp. 90–91.

was rarely alluded to was the friction which was also a feature of the relationship. David Reynolds has shown that major differences existed between Roosevelt and Churchill over colonialism and that the President did not always reciprocate in private the admiration which Churchill had for him.[14] Christopher Thorne in his study of *Allies of a Kind* has also highlighted the major divergences which existed over the conduct of the war against Japan. Thorne sees the Far East as an exception to the traditional generalised picture of close harmony between Britain and the United States during the war. 'Neither militarily nor politically', he argues, 'did there exist as regards the Far East anything like the degree of collaboration between the two States that was achieved elsewhere.' In his view, 'the fact that the relationship between the UK and the US ... was at times a remarkably close one can be established without the need to wander off, however well-meaningly, into mythology'. Thorne's contention is that in the Far East relations were 'extremely poor'.[15]

Both Reynolds and Thorne were reacting, in their respective studies, against a tendency of both post-war politicians and historians to idealise the wartime relationship. The idea of a 'special relationship' between Britain and the United States was launched effectively on the world by the repeated and emphatic use of the term by Churchill in his Fulton Speech on the 5 March 1946. In this speech the former Prime Minister spoke about the vital importance of the wartime partnership which resulted from the 'fraternal association', 'the growing friendship' and the 'mutual understanding' between the two 'kindred systems of society'. This rhetoric was taken up by post-war historians like Sir Dennis Brogan, Arthur Campbell Turner and H. C. Allen who pointed to the 'linguistic and cultural relationship between England and the US' which set it apart from the relationship which either state had with any of its other allies.[16] This emphasis on shared history, culture and language is also a feature of some US interpretations of

14. David Reynolds, 'Roosevelt, Churchill and the wartime Anglo-American alliance, 1935–1945: towards a new synthesis', in Hedley Bull and William Roger Louis (eds), *The 'Special Relationship': Anglo-American Relations Since 1945* (Oxford: Clarendon, 1986).

15. Christopher Thorne, *Allies of a Kind: The United States, Britain and the War against Japan* (London: Hamish Hamilton, 1978), p. 725.

16. See B. Brogan, *American Aspects* (New York: Harper and Row, 1964); A. C. Turner, *The Unique Partnership: Britain and the United States* (New York: Pegasus, 1971); and H. C. Allen, *The Anglo-American Predicament* (London: Macmillan, 1960) and *id., Great Britain and the United States: A History of Anglo-American Relations* (London: Odhams, 1955).

the 'special relationship'. George Ball, a former Under-Secretary of State, pointed out in the late 1960s that:

> ... to an exceptional degree we look out on the world through similarly refracted mental spectacles. We speak variant patois of Shakespeare and Norman Mailer, our institutions spring from the same instincts and traditions and we share the same heritage of law and custom, philosophy and pragmatic Weltanschauung ... starting from similar premises in the same intellectual tradition, we recognise common allusions, share many common prejudices, and can commune on a basis of confidence.[17]

The idea that 'sentiment' rather than 'interest' is at the root of the special relationship that these accounts portray has been the dominant one in the historiography of Anglo-US relations. More recently, however, with the opening up of the archives, a rather different view has begun to appear. While it has long been known that close Anglo-US relations have been a more-or-less continuous objective of British foreign policy for much of the twentieth century, there has been little awareness of the fact that British governments both during and after the Second World War attempted to manipulate the concept of the 'special relationship', sometimes quite cynically, in an attempt to promote British interests.[18]

'Steering the Great Unwieldy Barge'

As an example of the British manipulation of the concept of a 'special relationship', on the 21 March 1944 a major Foreign Office paper was written entitled 'The Essentials of an US Policy'. After commenting on 'the special quality' of the Anglo-US relationship which had developed in the war, the paper emphasised the crucial need for skilful British diplomacy to influence the direction of US foreign policy in the future.

17. George Ball, *The Discipline of Power* (London: Bodley Head, 1968), p. 91

18. A good illustration of this objective in twentieth-century British foreign policy is Lord Robert Cecil's memorandum to the Cabinet in Sept. 1917. He argued that the US was beginning to take part in European affairs and, given the difference between British and Continental views, it would be useful if the US could be made to accept 'our point of view in these matters' because it would mean 'the Dominance of that point of view in international affairs'. PRO, CAB 24/26, GT2074, Cecil memo (18 Sep. 1917). See also David Reynolds, 'A "special relationship"? America, Britain and the international order since the Second World War', *International Affairs*, Vol. 62, No. 1 (Winter 1985/6).

> They have enormous power, but it is the power of the reservoir behind the dam which may overflow uselessly, or be run through pipes to drive turbines. The transmutation of this power into useful forms, and its direction into advantageous channels, is our concern.[19]

It was argued in the paper that after the isolationism of the past the Americans were thinking for the first time about taking part in world affairs. In this context, it was believed that it was important not to pursue the traditional policy of balancing British power against that of the United States, but to make use of US power for purposes which suited the British government. In a highly significant part of the paper it was suggested that:

> If we go about our business in the right way we can help to steer this great unwieldy barge, the United States of the US, into the right harbour. If we don't, it is likely to continue to wallow in the ocean, an isolated menace to navigation.[20]

This emphasis on superior British wisdom in directing the less experienced United States in the right direction, particularly away from isolationism, is a recurrent theme in the years that follow. As such, it suggests that the concept of a 'special relationship' can usefully be seen, in part at least, as a deliberate British creation, or what one writer has described as 'a tradition invented as a tool of diplomacy'.[21] It was a policy, however, which met with mixed success.

The Post-war Development of an 'Entangling Alliance': Money Bags and Brains

In the immediate post-war period there was initially a rapid cooling of the close wartime relationship. This was exemplified by the break-up of the integrated war machine in 1945–1946, with the abrupt cancellation by the United States of the lend-lease arrangements, the winding up of the Combined wartime Boards and the unilateral ending of nuclear co-operation by the United States, despite wartime agreements that it should continue.[22] There were

19. PRO, FO371/38523, 'The Essentials of an American Policy', 21 March 1944. Relations between Britain and the US are described as of a 'domestic' rather than 'external' character.

20. *Ibid.*

21. Reynolds, 'Roosevelt, Churchill', pp. 85–86.

22. Continuing collaboration was agreed in the Quebec Agreement of 1943 and the Hyde Park Agreement in 1944.

also suspicions in the United States of British socialism, which were reflected in the difficulties which arose in post-war negotiations over a loan for Britain to see her through the immediate economic crisis bequeathed by the war. Britain regarded the terms offered by the United States as unnecessarily hard, reflecting a failure by the Truman administration to recognise the effort the British people had put into the war, initially alone. The resentment which this caused, together with the continuing British feeling of superiority, can be seen in a mischievous anonymous verse written by one of the British diplomats involved in the loan negotiations.

> In Washington Lord Halifax
> Once whispered to Lord Keynes
> It's true they have the money bags
> But we have all the brains.[23]

The difficulty of guiding the 'unwieldy barge' in the right direction led the Labour government to take the decision in January 1947 to develop an independent nuclear deterrent. As the Prime Minister, Clement Attlee was to explain later:

> We had to hold up our position *vis-à-vis* the Americans. We couldn't allow ourselves to be wholly in their hands, and their position wasn't awfully clear always. At that time we had to bear in mind that there was always the possibility of their withdrawing and becoming isolationist once again.[24]

Serious thought was also given to the possibility of developing a 'third force', independent of both the United States and the Soviet Union. As the Cold War gathered momentum, however, there was a clear recognition in both military and political circles in Britain that security considerations required a restoration of the close military partnership with the United States. The object of overcoming the traditional policy of isolationism and entangling the US in Western European security became the central tenet of Bevin's foreign policy from January 1948 onwards. The Brussels Pact of March 1948 and the concept of a Western Union were seen by the Foreign Secretary as a 'sprat to catch a whale'.[25] British leadership in Western Europe and a demonstration that the European states were

23. Quoted in Richard N. Gardner, *Sterling-Dollar Diplomacy in Current Perspective* (New York: Columbia University Press, 1980), p. xiii.
24. Quoted in Francis Williams, *A Prime Minister Remembers* (London: Heineman, 1961) pp. 118–119.
25. This phrase was coined by Elisabeth Barker in *Britain between the Superpowers 1945–1950* (London: Macmillan Press, 1983).

prepared to help themselves in the struggle against Communism were perceived to be an essential pre-requisite to US involvement in a North Atlantic Pact.

In March 1949, shortly before the North Atlantic Treaty was signed, a major review was undertaken in the Foreign Office of 'Anglo-US Relations: Present and Future'. Britain, it was argued, had a choice between a 'Third Power' grouping or a close partnership with the United States.[26] It was a choice, the paper said, which should not be dictated by 'ties of common feelings and tradition' but by 'a cold estimate of advantage'. It was decided that the 'Third Power' concept should be rejected because 'the partnership with the United States is essential to our security'.

The best policy for Britain, it was suggested, was to be closely related to the US, but independent enough to influence US policy. This would require Britain to remain a major European and world power and to sustain its own independent military capabilities. Britain must be the partner, not the poor relation, of the United States:

> As a leading European power she will speak with great authority to the US and her influence in Europe is likely to depend both on her own strength, military and economic and on the extent to which she is known to enjoy influence and support in the US.[27]

This reflected the British view at the time that there was no contradiction between a European policy and a 'special relationship' with the United States. Indeed the two were complimentary. Playing a leading role in Europe would reinforce British influence with the US and close ties with the US would strengthen Britain's position on the continent.

The 'Special Relationship' and the Search for Influence, 1950 to 1956

During the 1950s, however, it became increasingly clear that Britain did have to make a choice. With the Coal and Steel Community, the proposals for a European Defence Community, the Messina Talks and the Treaty of Rome, the continental states were moving in a direction that the British disapproved of, but over which they had

26. PRO, FO371/76384, 'Third World Power or Western Preponderance' (23 March 1949).
27. *Ibid.*

little control. The 'special relationship' with the United States provided an alternative policy which would reinforce Britain's great power aspirations, ensure her security in the context of Soviet nuclear weapons and conventional preponderance in Europe, and provide backing for the pursuit of her global interests.

Such a policy, it was believed, rested on demonstrating to the United States that Britain was a worthy partner. Bevin had denied in 1947 that Britain had 'ceased to be a great power'.[28] In line with this, the strategy adopted in the 1950s was designed to show that Britain remained a reliable partner of the US and a power that was 'vital to the peace of the world'. This was demonstrated in Britain's support for the United States in the Korean War, despite the serious long-term effects which this had on the British economy. The transformation of Empire into Commonwealth, also reflected Britain's determination to continue to play a world rôle. As David Reynolds has argued, it is important to remember that Britain's self-image as a global power, at this time, was not unreasonable, even if it did breed some illusions. Britain was still the world's third major state in the 1940s and 1950s – economically, militarily and in nuclear capability. As such, it remained a valuable ally for the United States.[29]

In pursuit of the policy of maintaining her great power status and importance to the United States, Britain exploded her first atomic weapon in October 1952 and took the decision in July 1954 to develop thermonuclear weapons to match those first tested by the United States and the Soviet Union in 1952 and 1953 respectively. One of the interesting features of recently released documents is that despite the frequent rhetorical emphasis of the Churchill government on the 'fraternal association' of the two states, in the early 1950s, one of the main objectives of British policy was to seek influence over US policy-making. This was necessary because there was considerable anxiety in government circles about the failure of the United States to provide Britain with information about nuclear planning even though the presence of US bases in Britain (granted in 1948) made her a major nuclear target for the Soviet Union in the event of war. There was also considerable concern that US rashness and impatience might precipitate a global conflagration. Even the Prime Minister himself was concerned about the worrying trends in US policies. In May 1954 he warned Cabinet colleagues:

28. *Hansard's Parliamentary Debates*, Vol. 437, col. 1965 (16 May 1947).
29. See Reynolds, 'A "special relationship"?'.

> The danger is that the Americans may become impatient. I know their people – they may get in a rage and say... why should we not go it alone? Why wait until Russia overtakes us? They could go to the Kremlin and say: These are our demands. Our fellows have been alerted. You must agree or we shall attack you.[30]

The same view was expressed in July by Lord Salisbury, the Lord President of the Council. He told the Cabinet that he was becoming increasingly worried about the adventurous policies of the US government. There was, he said, the greatest risk that Washington might 'plunge the world into war, either through a misguided intervention in Asia or in order to forestall an attack by Russia'.[31]

From the perspective of the government, therefore, it was imperative for Britain to develop thermonuclear weapons, not only to maintain 'her rightful place as a world power', but also to restrain the United States. This reflected a widespread belief in Britain that it would be dangerous if the US were to retain their present monopoly 'since Britain would be denied any right to influence her policy in the use of this weapon'.[32] A British H-bomb was seen as a device to open up nuclear co-operation with the United States which had been ended in 1946 and to allow Britain to influence and guide US policy in a more responsible direction. Once again we see the belief in Britain's greater wisdom and the importance of using the 'special relationship', especially in the military field, in order to achieve greater influence over US policy-making.

Suez and the Re-establishment of the 'Special Relationship'

The Suez Crisis of 1956, however, was a traumatic shock to Britain's great power pretensions and to its policy of pursuing a 'special relationship' with the United States. Faced with US opposition, the Eden government was forced to back down in humiliating fashion, demonstrating the reality of British dependence on, rather than influence over, the United States. For the French, the lesson of Suez was to seek greater independence and a greater role in Europe. For the British, however, the lesson was that there

30. Lord Moran, *Churchill: Taken from the Diaries of Lord Moran. The Struggle for Survival 1940–1965* (Boston: Houghton and Mifflin Company, 1966), p. 580.
31. PRO, CAB 128/27, CC48 (54) (8 July 1954).
32. PRO, DEFE 4/70, Note by the First Sea Lord (12 May 1954).

was a need to develop even closer interdependence with the United States and to avoid the growing integration that was taking place on the continent at the time.

From 1957 to 1963, the Macmillan government put considerable effort into re-creating an intimate and harmonious relationship with the United States. Reflecting past policy, the Prime Minister believed that Britain could 'play Greece to the US's Rome', 'civilising and guiding the immature giant'.[33] This was particularly important, in Macmillan's view, in the nuclear field. At the Bermuda and Washington Conferences in 1957, he sought to build on his close wartime friendship with Eisenhower to create a climate of trust at the highest level of government. The renewal of the 'special relationship' which resulted was reflected in the deployment of Thor Missiles in Britain, joint strategic planning between the air forces of both countries and the achievement of Britain's long term objective of repealing the 1946 McMahon Act, prohibiting full nuclear co-operation between the two countries. As a result of the last of these agreements, Britain was to receive preferential treatment in the form of information from the United States, on the design and production of nuclear warheads, as well as fissile material. This set the scene for the intimate nuclear relationship which was to follow. When Britain cancelled its Blue Streak intermediate range missile in 1960 on grounds of cost and technological obsolescence, the United States stepped in to offer the air-launched Skybolt missile for use with RAF's V-Bomber force. And when the Kennedy government cancelled Skybolt in late 1962, the Polaris submarine-launched missile was made available to Britain at the Nassau Conference in December at a bargain-basement price.

The 'Special Relationship' in Action

The Nassau Conference in December 1962 provides a good illustration of the way the British were able to manipulate the concept of the 'special relationship' to achieve their objectives. After the cancellation of Skybolt there were those in the State Department who saw the opportunity to get Britain out of the nuclear business. US support for the British nuclear deterrent was seen as an impediment to the pursuit of a non-proliferation policy and US interests in a more united Europe. At the beginning of the conference Kennedy

33. Quoted in John Roper, 'British Perspectives of the United States: Historical and Cultural Bases of the "Special Relationship"', *USA Today* (Sept. 1988).

appeared reluctant to provide Britain with Polaris missiles which the British government regarded as the only suitable substitute for Skybolt. Faced with the possibility of a major diplomatic defeat, Macmillan, as he later admitted, had to pull 'out all the stops'. In a highly emotional speech, he referred back to the halcyon days of the Second World War and the foundation of the 'special relationship' between the two countries. If agreement could not be reached now, after all these years, he argued, then he would prefer not to patch up a compromise. 'Let us part as friends ... if there is to be a parting, let it be done with honour and dignity.' Britain would not welch on her agreements (by implication, as the Americans had done). Switching tack, he then went on to ask the US President if he wished to be responsible for the fall of the British government. He warned that if this happened there would be a wave of anti-US feeling in Britain and even the possibility that an anti-US faction might assume the leadership of the Tory party in an attempt to cling on to power. The result would be the end of the close and harmonious relationship between the two countries. In response to this eloquent and evocative appeal, Kennedy gave in and Britain got the Polaris missiles it wanted.[34]

George Ball, one of the State Department officials advising Kennedy, later argued that the President had been seduced at Nassau by 'the emotional baggage of the special relationship' which, in his view had got in the way of cooler judgement. Nassau, he believed, was an illustration of how the United States 'had yielded to the temptations' of a myth. He argued that:

> US interests in both a strong and united Europe and the prevention of nuclear proliferation have been harmed by the overzealous support for the partnership with Britain, especially in the defence field.[35]

He also suggested, however, that the British themselves had become victims of their own rhetoric. Because they had come to believe in the 'special relationship', they had failed to adjust their foreign and defence policies to the reality of their reduced status in the world. The close ties with the US had encouraged successive governments, Ball argued, 'in the belief that she could by her own efforts' play an 'independent great power role and thus it deflected her from coming to terms with her European destiny'.[36]

34. PRO, PREM 11/4229, Record of a meeting held at Bali-Hai, the Bahamas, at 9.50 a.m. on Wednesday, 19 Dec. 1962.
35. Ball, *The Discipline of Power*, p. 93.
36. *Ibid.*

The 'Special Relationship' and the Search for a European Role

Even when British governments in 1963 and 1967 did attempt to readjust their foreign policy by applying to join the Common Market, the 'special relationship' still remained an impediment. This time it was the use made of the concept by Charles de Gaulle in vetoing the British applications to join the European Community.[37] Whether he believed it or not, the French President rejected British membership on the grounds that she remained wedded to close ties with the United States and was not a truly European power. When things went wrong, either economically or militarily, he argued, Britain would always revert to the Anglo-Saxon partnership.

Whilst the strategic and intelligence links between Britain and the United States remained in the 1960s and 1970s, faced with de Gaulle's opposition, there was a concerted attempt by the Wilson and Heath governments to play down the 'special relationship'. In symbolic fashion, the Wilson government deliberately talked of a 'close', rather than, a 'special' relationship between the two countries.[38] In reality, the relationship also became less special as a result of Britain's withdrawal from East of Suez, eroding the global partnership which had been such an important aspect of Anglo-US relations in the 1940s and 1950s. Britain also refused to participate in the Vietnam war, which further undermined an already tetchy personal relationship between Wilson and Johnson.

Heath made a similar attempt to symbolise the changing nature of British policy in the early 1970s by referring to the 'natural relationship', rather than the 'special relationship'.[39] As a committed European, the Conservative Prime Minister quite deliberately turned his back on many of the conventions which had characterised the 'special relationship' in the past. Kissinger reports in his memoirs that Heath was 'immune to the sentimental elements' of the Anglo-US attachment forged in two world wars. He goes on to say that:

> His commitment to Europe was profound: The United States was a friendly foreign country, entitled to the consideration that reflected its power and importance, but the 'special relationship' was an

37. See Jean Lacoutre, *De Gaulle: The Ruler 1945–70* (London: Harvill, 1993), p. 358.
38. Harold Wilson, *The Labour Government 1964–70* (London: Penguin, 1974), p. 80.
39. See *The Daily Telegraph* (19 and 21 Dec. 1970).

> obstacle to the British vocation in Europe. Heath was content to enjoy no higher status in Washington than any other European Leader. Indeed he came close to insisting on receiving no preferential treatment.[40]

Whether Heath's rejection of the concept of the 'special relationship' was crucial in Britain's successful application to join the European Community in 1973 is doubtful. Nevertheless, it did provide a symbolic indication of a desire to change the direction of British foreign policy.

The 'Special Relationship' Restored

The stark choice between Europe and the United States which characterised Heath's policies was not followed by his successors. In the late 1970s the Labour Prime Minister, James Callaghan sought to maintain Britain's position within the EC, while at the same time fostering close personal links with the Ford and Carter administrations in the United States.[41] It was left to Margaret Thatcher, however, in the 1980s to attempt to resurrect the 'special relationship' after 'the rope had been allowed to go slack' in the 1960s and 1970s. The close personal relationship between Thatcher and Reagan laid the foundations for what the Prime Minister described as the 'extra-ordinary relationship'.[42] Her abrasive and confrontational approach towards the European Community contrasted with her determination to play the rôle of the most loyal of the US's allies.

The restoration of the 'special relationship' during the Thatcher era was symbolised by the Trident agreement of July 1980 and March 1982 and the close military (and intelligence) collaboration during the Falklands War. Despite her misgivings, the Prime Minister was also prepared to face considerable domestic political costs in supporting the deployment of Cruise missiles in Britain and allowing US F111 aircraft to use British bases to bomb Libya in 1986. In the latter case, Mrs Thatcher points out in her memoirs the benefits which support for the United States brought for Britain. Special weight, she says, was given to British views on arms control negotiations with the Russians and the Administration promised to

40. Kissinger, *The White House Years*, p. 933.
41. Callaghan even sent his son-in-law as an ambassador to Washington.
42. See *The Sunday Times* (23 Dec. 1979).

give extra support to the Extradition Treaty which the Government regarded as vital in bringing IRA terrorists back to Britain.[43] The fact that so few had stuck by the United States in her time of trial, she suggests, 'strengthened the "special relationship", which will always be special because of cultural and historical links between our two countries'.[44] Despite this emphasis on the importance of 'the cultural and historical links', it is clear from her discussion of the Libyan crisis and her treatment of Anglo-US relations in general that 'interests' rather than 'sentiment' were the crucial basis of the 'special relationship' as far as the Prime Minister was concerned. This is revealed in her comment: 'I knew that the cost to Britain of not backing US action was unthinkable.'[45] The continuity going back to the Korean War is clear. Whether Mrs Thatcher deliberately used the 'special relationship' as a tool of diplomacy during her period in office to reassert Britain's place on the world stage, will only become known when the archives are opened. It was no surprise to learn, however, that like many of her predecessors she saw the 'special relationship' as a useful device to harness US power in the pursuit of British interests. Neither will it be a surprise if it is revealed that the Prime Minister believed in Britain's superior wisdom in guiding (Ronald Reagan and) the United States in the right direction during the crucial events which took place in the 1980s.

The 'Special Relationship' and the End of the Cold War

With the end of the Cold War and the disappearance of Mrs Thatcher and Ronald Reagan from the political scene, the 'special relationship' has undergone a serious challenge. Accusations over Conservative Party meddling in the US presidential election, continuing difficulties over Bosnia and differences over Irish Sinn Fein President Gerry Adams' visits to the United States, have encouraged a number of commentators to argue that Anglo-US relations are 'special no more'.[46] The growing interest in closer

43. Margaret Thatcher, *The Downing Street Years* (London: Harper Collins, 1993), p. 449.

44. *Ibid.*

45. *Ibid.*, p. 444.

46. See J. Dickie, *'Special' No More: Anglo-American Relations – Rhetoric and Reality* (London: Weidenfeld and Nicolson, 1994). The difficulties over Bosnia in 1994 to

Anglo-French nuclear co-operation and the modifications in the British governments approach towards a closer European defence identity have also led to speculation that a significant reassessment is taking place in Whitehall to reflect the changing geopolitical environment.

Where this reassessment might take Britain, however, is still far from clear. Contemporary British foreign and defence policy reflects a hesitant 'wait and see' quality. The battle between 'Euro-enthusiasts' and 'Euro-sceptics' is far from over and it is clear that in this debate the spectre of the 'special relationship' continues to loom large. Apart from the customary rhetoric at the highest political levels suggesting the continuing importance of the 'special relationship', difficulties in Anglo-US relations during John Major's Prime Ministership produced warnings from his predecessor Margaret Thatcher that close relations with the United States remain a vital British interest.[47] This view seems to be shared fully by Tony Blair's Labour government which came to power in 1997.

In the context of the post-Cold War (and perhaps 'fin de siècle') uncertainty it is of some significance that in May 1995 a new sculpture was unveiled in the West End of London. The work by Lawrence Holofcener depicts Winston Churchill and Franklin Roosevelt in relaxed conversation on a park bench. Entitled 'Allies', the sculpture celebrates the remarkable partnership between the two leaders, who more than anyone else epitomised the 'special relationship' which was developed between Britain and the United States during the war. As such, the sculpture links the past and the present in symbolic form, nostalgically reminding those who see it that Britain was once a great power and that her security in a time of major crisis during the Second World War had been secured through close alliance with the United States, rather than the European allies.[48]

In line with this theme Sir Michael Howard argued at the time of the VE Day celebrations in 1995 that the close relationship with

---

1995 centred on the issue of whether to lift the arms embargo which the Americans felt discriminated against the Muslim forces. Since the 1995 decision by the US government to allow Gerry Adams to visit the United States, the Sinn Fein president has been received in 10, Downing Street.

47. John Major told President Clinton after his election: 'I have no doubt ... that the United States and Great Britain will continue to work together very closely and that the Special Relationship we have had for so many years will be maintained.' See Dickie, *Special No More*, p. xii.

48. According to Samuel and Thompson: 'History as myth pivots on an active relationship between the past and the present ...', *The Myths We Live By*.

the United States in the Second World War had had a continuing influence on British foreign and defence policy, right down to the present day. Although it was Britain's 'finest hour', he argued, the nation 'has continued to re-live it disastrously'.

> Its position at the top table in NATO gave it a sense of superiority to its continental allies – countries which it had either conquered or liberated – who sat below the salt. The significance of their economic recovery was under-rated. Their plans for the creation of a European Community were treated with contempt. The special relationship with the United States prolonged British delusions of grandeur. It took the humiliation of Suez to bring home to the British the reality of their position in the world and to force belated readjustments.[49]

It still remains unclear, whether the readjustments have fully taken place, even in the late 1990s. In large part this reflects the continuing power of the concept of the 'special relationship' on British thinking. The problem is that the concept has what one US official has described as a 'misty quality'. It summons up, consciously or unconsciously, deep-seated feelings that Britain remains an important power on the world stage, that it should maintain wide-ranging international responsibilities, and that it has an Anglo-Saxon identity, superior to, and separate from, its European partners. As such the continuing use of the term tends to encourage a nostalgia for the past, at a time when Britain needs to be thinking positively and creatively about its future role at the heart of Europe. As the former US Ambassador to Britain, Raymond Seitz, argued in a valedictory speech before leaving his post in 1994:

> America's transatlantic policy is European in scope. It is not a series of individual or compartmentalised bilateral policies, and never has been. It is the policy of one continent to another. There is a simple observation that if Britain's voice is less influential in Paris and Bonn it is likely to be less influential in Washington.

If, as this chapter argues, the central purpose of the 'special relationship' for Britain has been to influence US policies, it would seem that continuing to use the term will not only help to divert attention from the key debates about the development of the European Union, but it will also be counter-productive as far as British policy towards the United States is concerned.

49. See Sir Michael Howard, 'Victory that exhausted the Nation', *The Times* (28 May 1994).

Chapter 11

Is Britain Part of Europe?

The Myth of British 'Difference'

Antonio Varsori

Introduction

'In everyday speech, myth is regarded as an amplification of reality, a mirage, an image which has no connection with real events.'[1] To this popular definition we may add a further one: a myth is 'the image of a fictitious event, which expresses the feelings of a community and is useful in stimulating actions'.[2] Without moving towards more complex interpretations, such as the ones of Ernst Cassirer,[3] and focusing on connections between myth and reality (that is the history of actual events), we will assume that myths in international relations can be interpreted as the values, beliefs and perceptions of a society, mainly based on the experiences of its members and on historical realities, which exert some influence on the decision-making process, as well as on the attitude of public opinion towards this society's relations with those of other countries.

1. *Enciclopedia Europea Garzanti* (Milan: Garzanti, 1978), p. 647.

2. Jean Lalande, *Vocabulaire technique et critique de la philosophie* (It. ed. Milan: ISEDI, 1971), p. 529; and see *Enciclopedia Garzanti di filosofia* (Milan: Garzanti, 1985), pp. 603–605.

3. Ernst Cassirer, *Symbols: Myth and Culture. Essays and Lectures of Ernest Cassirer 1935–1945* (New Haven/London: Yale University Press, 1979).

The subject we will address here is whether Britain is a part of Europe. While it may be obvious to some that the British Isles are a part of the 'Old Continent' from a mere geographical viewpoint, 'the notion of Europe, indeed the word "Europe", does not have exactly the same meaning, depending on the person, the groups or the period of history'.[4] And, 'having so long clung to a vision of Great Britain as being at once in Europe and outside it because of Britain's "imperial" destiny, do the British really live in Europe in the same way as their European partners?'[5]

Indeed, geographic reality can differ from subjective perception in the light of history. Until the First World War, and to a certain extent until the Second World War, 'Britain' to almost everybody meant 'the British Empire'. Yet even though Britain was a maritime power with world-wide interests, and although the Channel divided her from the continent,[6] to almost anybody she was also European. For Europe was the core of the international system and the European powers were the main actors in world affairs: Europe *was* the 'world' and, also for a country such as imperial Britain, there was no need to choose between the membership of the European 'club' and that which was outside Europe.[7]

On the contrary, after 1945, Britain's 'difference', as well as her European nature, which had previously appeared to be obvious, began to be questioned. Both the British authorities and public opinion were compelled to choose between their supposed 'difference' and a closer association with their continental partners.[8] Simultaneously, from the mid-1940s onwards, the 'Old Continent' was no longer the 'Concert of Europe' based on the interaction among the traditional European powers. The Western half of the continent was forced to co-operate to defend itself against the Soviet 'threat', as well as to re-assert itself *vis-à-vis* the two superpowers: European integration began to dominate the economic,

4. René Girault, 'Introduction', in René Girault (ed.), *Les Europe des Européens* (Paris: Publications de la Sorbonne, 1993), p. 8; see also Jeremy Black, *Convergence or Divergence? Britain and the Continent* (London: Macmillan, 1994).

5. Girault, 'Conclusion', in Girault (ed.), *Les Europe*, p. 144.

6. Cf. Philip Bell and Peter Morris, 'Les "Europe" des Européens ou la notion d'Europe', in Girault (ed.), *Les Europe*, pp. 67–76.

7. Cf. Paul Kennedy, *The Rise and Fall of British Naval Mastery* (London: Fontana, 1991); Corelli Barnett, *The Collapse of British Power* (London: Alan Sutton, 1972); Andrew DePorte, *Europe between the Super-Powers. The Enduring Balance* (New Haven/London: Yale University Press, 1979), chapters 2 to 4.

8. Cf. Anne Deighton and Geoffrey Warner, 'British Perceptions of Europe in the Postwar Period', in Girault (ed.), *Les Europe*, pp. 51–65.

political and social life of the 'Old Continent'.[9] As at the end of the period of 'Splendid Isolation', when she had been confronted with the dilemma of a 'continental commitment',[10] Britain was compelled to take a stand.

In this period the relations between the United Kingdom and the continent were acrimonious. Even once Britain joined the Common Market, London retained the 'reputation as the Communities' awkward partner'.[11] This was not only the consequence of a clash of objective political, economic and strategic interests between London and its continental partners. It was also the result of psychological reactions, of values and prejudices which led British decision-makers, as well as British opinion, to regard themselves as 'different' from the continent. The myth of Britain's 'difference' thus often shaped the relations between London and continental Europe. This chapter aims at identifying the roots, the main characteristics and the development of this myth. The examples cited must be limited; *pars pro toto,* they are drawn mainly from the statements and attitudes of politicians, military leaders and diplomats, as decision-makers, in particular in the context of a democratic system, usually try to be in tune with the opinions and the more popular feelings of voters.[12] Furthermore, the focus will be on the period from the mid-1940s to the early 1960s, followed by only a brief sketch of the following decades to the present day.[13]

9. D. W. Urwin, *Western Europe Since 1945. A Short Political History* (London/New York: Longman: various editions); Walter Laqueur, *Europe in Our Time* (New York: Viking Press, 1992); John W. Young, *Cold War Europe 1945–1989: A Political History* (London: Edward Arnold, 1991); on the European integration process see Pierre Gerbet, *La construction de l'Europe* (Paris: Imprimerie Nationale, 1994) and Marie Thérèse Bitsch, *Histoire de la construction européenne* (Brussels: Complexe, 1996).

10. Michael Howard, *The Continental Commitment. The Dilemma of British Defence Policy in the Era of the Two World Wars* (London: Penguin Books, 1974).

11. Brian Brivati and Harriet Jones, 'Introduction', in *idem., From Reconstruction to Integration: Britain and Europe since 1945* (Leicester/London: Leicester University Press, 1993), p. 1. See also Stephen George, *An Awkward Partner. Britain in the European Community* (Oxford: Oxford University Press, 1994).

12. Paul Kennedy, *The Realities behind Diplomacy. Background Influences on British External Policy 1865–1980* (London: Fontana, 1981). On British decision-makers' attitudes towards Europe see the articles by Paul Cornish, John W. Young; Anne Deighton and Peter Ludlow in Anne Deighton (ed.), *Building Postwar Europe: National Decision-Makers and European Institutions, 1948–63* (London: Macmillan, 1995).

13. David Reynolds, *Britannia Overruled: British Policy and World Power in the 20th Century* (London/New York: Longman, 1991), pp. 173ff.; David Sanders, *Losing an Empire, Finding a Role: British Foreign Policy since 1945* (London: Macmillan, 1990).

The Strengthening of Britain's 'Superiority Complex'

In July 1945, a few weeks after VE Day, the British public went to the polls. The victory of the Labour Party led to what has been called the '1945 revolution'.[14] In a speech he had delivered in late May at the Blackpool conference of the Labour Party, Ernest Bevin, the future Foreign Secretary, had mapped out the main features of Labour's programme on foreign affairs. His speech focused on Britain's rôle as one of the great powers which was going to win the war and to work out a new world settlement. This London had to work out in co-operation with Moscow and Washington, and perhaps Paris, on the basis, *inter alia*, of the concept that 'Left understands Left'.[15] Bevin's words hardly concealed what may be regarded as an 'imperial' consciousness which filtered through socialist ideals and slogans, a feeling which was strengthened by the fact that Britain was the only European power left largely intact, next to the smouldering ruins of the European mainland.

Once in power, both the Attlee cabinet and the Labour Party had to deal with the emergence of two non-European superpowers and the growing estrangement between East and West. Europe's future was in question, and Winston Churchill, now the leader of the Tory opposition, was quick to grasp that European unity could become a precious instrument in order to counter what was perceived as a Soviet expansionist policy. In his famous Zurich speech, he appealed for close European co-operation and stressed Britain's rôle in such a process. Churchill did not imply, however, that Britain should be part of the United States of Europe that he advocated. London would support European co-operation, in particular a rapprochement between France and Germany, but would itself definitely stay outside as a benevolent sponsor, along with the United States and the Soviet Union.[16] This concept was later developed further by Churchill and was reflected in his

14. For example, William Harrington, *The 1945 Revolution* (London: Davis-Pointer, 1978); Kenneth O. Morgan, *Labour in Power 1945–1951* (Oxford: Clarendon Press, 1984); Ritchie Ovendale (ed.), *The Foreign Policy of the British Labour Governments 1945–51* (Leicester: Leicester University Press, 1984).

15. Archives of the British Labour Party (hereafter ABLP), Pamphlets and leaflets, *Labour Party on Foreign Affairs*, 1945.

16. Quoted in Martin Gilbert, *'Never Despair': Winston S. Churchill 1945–1965* (London: Heinemann, 1988), p. 266.

'three circles' theory.[17] It seems that Churchill, like many other Britons, felt that Britain was more different from Europe in the late 1940s than she had been in the aftermath of the First World War. She had long stood alone against Hitler while all the other traditional European powers had been occupied, such as France and Russia, or defeated, such as Germany and Italy, and she had finally triumphed. So by stressing her 'difference' in comparison with Europe, Britain was also asserting her rôle as sole true victor in Western Europe.[18]

Even if many Britons felt that the United Kingdom was losing ground in the international context in comparison with the US or the Soviet Union, at least towards the 'continent', they felt a reassuring superiority complex.[19] The year 1947 saw a steady worsening in the relations between East and West rapidly leading to the Cold War.[20] Forecast by Churchill, this development favoured the prospect of closer ties among the countries of Western Europe: on one hand the United States strongly backed the idea of European integration, not least through the Marshall Plan. On the other hand Europeanist movements flourished in several European countries.[21] British authorities played a leading rôle in encouraging European co-operation, from the Marshall Plan to the Brussels Treaty, in both of which Britain participated.[22] Later on, however,

17. Cf. Anne Deighton, 'Britain and the Three Interlocking Circles', in Antonio Varsori (ed.), *Europe 1945–1990s: The End of an Era?* (London: Macmillan, 1995), pp. 155–169.

18. R. C. A. Parker, 'British Perceptions of Power. Europe between the Superpowers', in Josef Becker and Franz Knipping (eds), *Power in Europe? Great Britain, France, Italy and Germany in a Postwar World 1945–1950* (Berlin/New York: W. de Gruyter, 1986), pp. 447–459; in the same volume see also the contributions by Anthony Adamthwaite, Geoffrey Warner and Martin Ceadel.

19. ABLP, Series II: Pamphlets and Leaflets: Bevin's speech (12 June 1946), 45th Annual Conference of the Labour Party, Bournemouth; Kenneth O. Morgan, 'The Second World in British Culture', in Brivati and Jones (eds), *From Reconstruction*, pp. 34–46.

20. Cf. Victor Rothwell, *Britain and the Cold War 1941–1947* (London: Jonathan Cape, 1982).

21. Gerbet, *La construction*, pp. 55–100; on US policy see Pierre Melandri, *Les Etats-Unis face à l'unification de l'Europe* (Paris: Pedone, 1980). On the role of the Europeanist movement in Britain see John Pinder, '"Manifesta la verità ai potenti": i federalisti britannici e l'Establishment', in Sergio Pistone (ed.), *I movimenti per l'unità europea 1945–1954* (Milan: Jaca Book, 1992), pp. 113–146.

22. Avi Shlaim, *Britain and the Origins of European Unity 1940–1951* (Reading: Reading University, 1978); John W. Young, *Britain, France and the Unity of Europe 1945–51* (Leicester: Leicester University Press, 1984); John W. Young, *Britain and European Unity, 1945–1992* (London: Macmillan, 1993), pp. 1–27; Michael Hogan,

the British attitude became more cautious and by 1950 Labourite Britain would reject any proposal of London's involvement in the early supranational schemes advocated by Paris.

Leaving aside the political and economic reasons which shaped Britain's rejection of a European 'choice', what part did the notion of British 'difference' play in London's estrangement from the European continent? Of some significance in this context is the Labour Party's 1947 pamphlet, *Cards on the Table*, which sketched the main features and goals of Labour's foreign policy. Most of its pages aimed at explaining why, in spite of her difficulties, Britain had to preserve her rôle as a world power. Such a rôle was described as compatible with the belief in Social democracy, and the Labour Party was cast as the standard bearer of a bloodless Socialist revolution. All this made Britain different from the countries of continental Europe, where Socialist Parties were weaker than in Britain. As for London's policy towards the 'Old Continent', *Cards on the Table* stated:

> ... our dependence on overseas trade makes us a world power by necessity, and we will remain as much part of the Atlantic as well as of the European community. Our interests are too widespread, as our principles are too international, for us to restrict ourselves to the idea of regional *blocs*, however constructed.[23]

So Britain appeared to be compelled, not only by economic interests, but also by history and tradition, to be something different from Europe.

In late 1947 the failure of the London Four Power conference led the Labour Cabinet to develop a clearer stand towards the Soviet Union: Western Europe seemed to be threatened by Moscow and the United States did not yet appear ready to play a leading political and military rôle in the 'Old Continent'. Bevin's January 1948 speech was at the origins of the five power European alliance, the Brussels Treaty, which was signed in March 1948.[24] Britain seemed inclined to associate with Europe. But in reality the co-operation with some continental partners strengthened the prejudices nurtured by most British decision-makers. Even if the Benelux countries and France appeared to them as the most 'decent' European

The Marshall Plan: America, Britain and the Reconstruction of Western Europe 1947–1952 (Cambridge: Cambridge University Press, 1987).

23. ABLP, Series II: Pamphlets and Leaflets: *Cards on the Table*, 1947.

24. On the Brussels Treaty and Britain's attitude towards Europe see Antonio Varsori, *Il Patto di Bruxelles (1948), tra integrazione europea e alleanza atlantica* (Rome: Bonacci, 1988).

partners, they were different, and to a certain extent, 'inferior'. As for Belgium, the Netherlands and Luxembourg, they were too small to be regarded as real partners,[25] so France was the point of reference, the symbol of continental Europe. The psychological attitude many British decision-makers had towards France was a mixture of contempt, frustration and pessimism.[26] Those feelings surfaced for example among the British military leaders in mid-1948, when they faced the prospect of some form of continental commitment and close defence co-operation with France in the context of the Brussels Treaty. On the occasion of a Chiefs of Staff Committee meeting the First Sea Lord, Admiral Sir John Cunningham, stressed

> ... that he had heard most disturbing reports on the prospects of any real degree of security being achieved in France. Communism was rife in the Service Ministries there and throughout the whole defence organisation. It would probably take years to effect any substantial improvement. If this was so it would be very dangerous to integrate our defence machinery with theirs.[27]

These remarks are reminiscent of the lack of confidence the British had developed towards France in the 1930s, resultant British reluctance to enter into joint military planning, fears of a 'fifth columnism' dating from the Second World War, and of defeatism which had led to the fall of France in 1940. Even Field Marshal Montgomery, among the few British military leaders who believed in both the need and the feasibility of a British strategic and political commitment to Europe, had a low opinion of France as Britain's major European ally. In July 1948 Montgomery paid an official visit to Paris and on his coming back to London wrote:

> There appear to be three factors which are influencing France today:
> (a) The Government is unable to govern.
> (b) There is no leader to whom the people will give their confidence, and who can unite the nation to meet the danger which threatens.
> (c) The nation is suffering from a tristesse, a malaise of morale, the result of the disasters of World War II.

25. See Deighton and Warner, 'British', p. 62.

26. Young, *Britain: France*: *passim*: as well as *Id.*: *France: the Cold War and the Western Alliance, 1944–1949: French Foreign Policy and Post-War Europe* (Leicester/London: Leicester University Press, 1990) in particular chapters 8 to 10.

27. Public Record Office (hereafter PRO), DEFE 4/14 COS(48)85th Meeting (23 June 1948) Top Secret. Ironically, only a few weeks earlier Donald Maclean had

And Montgomery's explanation to the first item of his list is of some significance :

> ... this is due to the system of Proportional Representation which obtains in France. The Nation does not subscribe to the principle of majority rule, such as we have in Britain; in consequence no party has a sufficient majority to enable it to govern; there is no political stability and it is impossible to get things done. We soldiers should be thankful that in Britain we have political stability; without it we would have made little progress towards our National Army.[28]

Montgomery's scepticism was not limited to France:

> ... I doubt very much if, today, the continental nations of the West would fight if attacked. The spirit is lacking. There is an appalling state of affairs; it means that the Western Union would collapse like a pricked balloon if war breaks out between the East and the West, unless the British take the matter in hand ourselves, and give the lead, we will have only ourselves to blame if disaster overtakes us.[29]

This British conviction about the weakness of the continental partners, France in particular, appeared to be shared by Bevin at the time.[30]

The belief in Britain's moral and political superiority was so rooted amongst her decision-makers that, when in July 1948 the French Foreign Minister Georges Bidault put forward a project for the creation of a European assembly, Bevin rejected this plan with contempt as a mere device in order to enhance Bidault's

---

been a member of the British delegation on the occasion of the early secret talks destined to lead to the creation of the Atlantic alliance and that the French had been excluded from the talks also as a consequence of the unreliability of their security measures; see Ritchie Ovendale, 'Great Britain and the Atlantic Pact', in Ennio Di Nolfo (ed.), *The Atlantic Pact Forty Years Later A Historica Reappraisal* (Berlin/New York: W. de Gruyter, 1992), p. 76.

28. PRO, FO 800/465, memorandum No. CIGS/BM/31/2488, 'Visit to Paris, 10 to 11 July 1948' by B. Montgomery (14 July 1948) Top Secret. On Montgomery's strategic opinions see for example Nigel Hamilton, *Monty the Field-Marshal 1944–1976* (London: Hamish Hamilton, 1986), pp. 725–778.

29. PRO, FO 800/453, memorandum No. CIGS/BM/31/2542, 'The General World Situation' by B. Montgomery (18 Aug. 1948) private and Top Secret. On the other hand, Montgomery effectively campaigned for an Anglo-American engagement to defend Western Europe on the Rhine; see Beatrice Heuser, 'The Demise of Anglo-Soviet and the Birth of Anglo-German Military Co-operation 1941–1955', in Adolf M. Birke and Hermann Wentker (eds), *Germany and Russia in Britain's Policy towards Europe since 1815* (Munich/New Providence/London/Paris: K. G. Sauer, 1994), pp. 123–143.

30. PRO, FO 800/453, Bevin's minute, 24.8.1948.

political stand: 'I've never heard such rubbish.'[31] In the following months France again tried to take the lead in Western Europe through the exploitation of the Europeanist ideals.[32] And again the British authorities reacted negatively, and their positions were not only the consequence of London's political, military and economic interests, but were influenced by a deep belief in Britain's 'superiority'. Such an attitude shaped the content of *Feet on Ground: A Study of Western Union*, published in September 1948 by the Labour Party. This pamphlet advocated the setting up of Europe as a 'Third World power', tried to outline London's rôle in this connection and aimed at countering the projects for a federal Europe. In spite of an apparent goodwill towards European co-operation, the study stressed Britain's unique position:

> ...in the economic and strategic fields Britain is the sheet-anchor of European recovery. The political and economic stability which Britain owes to her Labour Government provides a marked contrast to the unhealthy conditions of some other European states. Without British participation, it is doubtful whether any of the small countries in Europe would link its future to that of the continent as a whole. Her vast overseas dependencies and her close relations with the Commonwealth make Britain the indispensable basis of any third world power.[33]

But the proposals and the plans developed by the French and the Belgian authorities would not afford Britain a 'special' position. Strong criticism of London's attitude surfaced both in Europe and in the United States. Bevin's reactions did not conceal some disappointment and frustration. In a conversation he had with the US Secretary of State George Marshall in early October 1948, the British Foreign Secretary complained that

> ... it did not facilitate the consolidation and development of Western Union so far as Britain is concerned when speeches made in America ... [use] the threat of holding up appropriations if Europe did not immediately federate herself. It caused bitter reactions in Britain when were treated as a small country of no account and accused of dragging our feet in regard to Western Europe.

31. René Massigli, *Une comédie des erreurs* (Paris: Plon, 1976), p. 156.
32. Pierre Gerbet, *Le relèvement 1944–1949* (Paris: Imprimerie Nationale, 1992).
33. *Feet on Ground. A Study of Western Union* (London: Labour Party, 1948), p. 22. On Labour reaction to the Hague Conference see Antonio Varsori, 'Il Congresso dell'Europa dell'Aja (7–10 maggio 1948)', *Storia contemporanea*, XXI (1990) No. 3, pp. 463–493.

He continued:

> ... a Western European Assembly on a parliamentary basis, which would inevitably include proportional representation for the Communists, would give the latter a platform and would result in attacks on Britain, the only country in Western Europe which had no Communists to speak off.[34]

Like Montgomery, Bevin believed that the British political system was definitely better than the ones of Britain's European partners and London could not risk being corrupted by 'continental' political 'diseases'.

In spite of the signature of the treaty which gave birth to the Council of Europe and of London's participation in the new European body, the British authorities made every effort to avoid the implementation of an effective organisation. They lacked confidence in it, as its creation had been the result of the 'fancies' of London's continental allies as opposed to a healthy, pragmatic, British approach.[35] A Gallup opinion poll in 1949 stressed that 67 per cent of the people questioned had heard or read of the first meeting of the Assembly of the Council of Europe and 18 per cent disapproved of the idea.[36] The influence of cultural and psychological aspects in the attitude British decision-makers developed towards Europe is confirmed by a revealing remark about Attlee's feelings. His biographer wrote that Attlee

> ... was not a Little Englander, but in old age he would frequently half in earnest, half in jest make such remarks as 'can't trust the Europeans – they don't play cricket'. He admired and liked Frenchmen, Germans and Italians, but did not approve of the way they ran their countries.[37]

On the other hand Britain thought she could survive and be prosperous without close ties with Europe owing to the 'special relationship' and the Commonwealth. So it is not surprising that in the Labour Party document 'European Unity', issued in May 1950, it was stated:

34. PRO, FO 371, Z 8447/273/72 (673064), Conversation between the Secretary of State and Mr. Marshall at the US Embassy in Paris (4 Oct. 1948).

35. Cf. Bevin's remark: 'If you open that Pandora's box you never know what Trojen 'orses will jump out', quoted in A. Bullok, *Ernest Bevin Foreign Secretary 1945–51* (London: Heinemann, 1983), p. 659.

36. *The Gallup International Opinion Poll. Great Britain 1937–1965* Vol. 1 (New York: Random House, 1976), pp. 204–205.

37. Keith Harris, *Attlee* (London: Weidenfeld and Nicolson, 1982), p. 315.

> ... the Labour Party cannot see European unity as an overriding end in itself. Britain is not just a small crowded island off the Western coast of continental Europe. She is the nerve centre of a world-wide Commonwealth which extends into every continent. In every respect except distance we in Britain are closer to our kinsmen in Australia and New Zealand on the far side of the world than we are to Europe. We are closer in language and origins, in social habits and institutions, in political outlook and in economic interest.[38]

So, slowly but surely, between 1949 and 1950, Labour Britain distanced herself from the European continent, not only on political, economic and strategic grounds, but also on the basis of a myth, the myth of Britain's 'difference', which meant Britain's political, and one might add, 'moral', superiority, based on the following factors: a sound and healthy political system, an 'Imperial' destiny, a great power rôle confirmed by her wartime experience, and the relevant part she had played in saving the West from the Soviet threat between 1947 and 1950. Of course there was some truth in those myths, but they were largely functions of the past and did not take into account the possibility that the nations of Western Europe might recover from the plights of the Second World War and achieve conditions similar to the ones enjoyed by Britain.

The Swan Song of Britain's 'Difference'

Britain's mental attitude towards Europe did not change after the Tories came back to power in late 1951 as the myths connected to Britain's 'difference' still shaped the way of thinking of most decision-makers, as well as the majority of public opinion. Furthermore, the leading members of the new cabinet embodied some of those myths. Historians have commented on the close resemblance between Churchill's wartime cabinet and those of the 1950s.[39] What would today be called the 'feel good factor' among the population in general was high. The succession of young Queen Elizabeth in 1952 and her coronation in 1953 seemed to usher in a 'second Elizabethan Age', evoking the Golden Age of

38. *European Unity. A Statement by the National Executive Committee of the British Labour Party* (London: Labour Party, 1950), p. 4. Quoted also in Parker, 'British Perceptions', p. 456. For the 'imperial idea' see J. M. MacKenzie, *Propaganda and Empire. The Manipulation of British Public Opinion 1880–1960* (Manchester: Manchester University Press, 1984).

39. Alan Sked and Chris Cook, *Post-War Britain. A Political History* (London: Penguin, 1979), p. 116.

English culture in the sixteenth and early seventeenth centuries. Moreover, 'Churchill's presence as premier served to enhance … hopes of national recovery and glory.'[40]

By contrast continental Europe was, during the first half of the 1950s, mainly regarded by both British decision-makers and public opinion as a source of trouble and the symbol of uncertainty and political crisis: West Germany, in spite of its economic recovery, was still subject to Allied military control, France was weak and trouble-ridden, Italy appeared as a definitely minor and unreliable partner.[41] The attempts to bring about European integration, from ECSC to EDC, were regarded in London with deep scepticism. Britain might help the Western Europeans to solve their problems, but owing to her different – that is 'superior' – characters, she had to carefully avoid any involvement.[42] There was a continuing widespread lack of confidence in London's continental allies, as well as in their initiatives and plans. Sir Oliver Harvey, Her Majesty's Ambassador to Paris, usually sympathetic towards France, wrote in his annual report for 1953 that 'there was a growing awareness that France needs fundamental political, economic and social reforms, but little prospect of a Government capable of carrying them through'.[43]

A further example is Churchill's views of the EDC: '… a sludgy amalgam infinitely less effective than the Grand Alliance of national armies.'[44] As an obvious consequence of the comparison between Britain's position and continental plights, London saw its belief in its own 'superiority' and in its ability to tackle the European problems from the outside confirmed. So it is not surprising that Churchill tried to play a leading rôle in achieving détente between East and West through the creation of a new European settlement which would come out of an agreement among the great victorious powers. Such an aspiration did not disappear after Churchill's resignation in April 1955; Eden also pursued a similar

40. *Ibid.*

41. Britain's 'superiority complex' was evident in the case of London's attitude towards Italy; in this connection see Antonio Varsori, 'Great Britain and Italy 1945–56: The Partnership between a Great Power and a Minor Power?', *Diplomacy and Statecraft* Vol. 3, No. 2 (July 1992), pp. 188–228; see also Deighton and Warner, 'British Perceptions', pp. 60–62.

42. See in particular D. Weigall, 'British Perceptions of the European Defence Community', in P. M. R. Stirk and Dick Willis (eds), *Shaping Postwar Europe. European Unity and Disunity 1945–1957* (London: Pinter, 1991), pp. 90–99.

43. PRO, FO 371, WF 1011/1 (122774), Sir O. Harvey (30 Jan. 1954) Confidential.

44. John Colville, *The Fringes of Power. Downing Street Diaries* Vol. 2 *1941–April 1955* (London: Sceptre, 1987), p. 323.

path and, as in Churchill's case, this policy appeared once again to be a product of Britain's 'superiority complex'. In March 1955 Eden outlined the policy which would lead to the Geneva summit conference, and in order to justify the need for a bold initiative on the part of London, the Foreign Secretary confirmed the views most British decision-makers had developed of London's major European allies: '... the Germans are always awkward allies and are likely to be a more awkward after Dr Adenauer has left the scene; and the French cannot yet be relied on to maintain a consistent policy.'[45]

In such an atmosphere it is not surprising that the Messina Conference and the 'relaunching of Europe' were regarded with deep scepticism by British decision-makers and were largely ignored by both public opinion and the press: continental Europe still seemed very distant and imperial Britain, whose leaders were going to meet the representatives of the two superpowers on an apparently equal footing, could continue in her patronising view of European affairs.[46] Not everybody shared this overevaluation of London's rôle. As early as 1952, Harold Macmillan, at that time Minister of Housing and Local Government, had expressed his concern over any prospect of a 'German-dominated continental system'.[47] One year later, in March 1953, in a further memorandum Macmillan confirmed his worries:

> Are we really sure that we want to see a Six-Power Federal Europe, with a common army, a common iron and steel industry ... ending in a common currency and monetary policy?
>
> ... If such a Federal State comes into being, will it, in the long run, be to our interest as an island and Imperial Power?
>
> ... Will not Germany ultimately control this State, and may we not have created the very situation in Europe to prevent which, in

45. PRO, PREM 11/893, Memorandum C(55)83 by E. Eden (26 Mar. 1955) Secret. On Britain's mediation between East and West, see B. P. Hite, 'The British Contribution to East-West Détente, 1953–1963' in Gustav Schmidt (ed.), *Ost-West Bezienhungen: Konfrontation und Détente 1945–1989* (Bochum: Brockmeyr, 1993), pp. 99–116.

46. J. W. Young, '"Parting the Ways?" Britain: The Messina Conference and the Spaak Committee, June–December 1955', in Michael Dockrill and John W. Young (eds), *British Foreign Policy, 1945–56* (London: Macmillan, 1989), pp. 197–224, and contributions by John W. Young and Miriam Camps in Brivati and Jones (eds), *From Reconstruction*, as well as Young, *Britain*, pp. 43–57; see also Eden quoted in Evelyn Schuckburgh, *Descent to Suez. Diaries 1951–56* (London: Weidenfeld & Nicolson, 1986), p. 284; Wolfram Kaiser, *Using Europe, Abusing the Europeans* (London: Macmillan, 1996); and Piers Ludlow, *Dealing with Britain* (Cambridge: Cambridge University Press, 1997).

47. PRO, CAB 129/50, Memorandum C.(52)56, 'Future of the Council of Europe', by H. Macmillan (29 Feb. 1952) Confidential.

> every century, since the Elizabethan age, we have fought long and bitter wars? It may be argued that the rise of the United States and of Russia have transformed the picture. Yet the inner balance of Europe is essential to the balance of world power.

Macmillan added:

> It is perhaps worth reflecting what would be the position [of Britain] in the unlikely, but not impossible event of an easing of the Russian tension, a corresponding American withdrawal from Europe, and the emergence of a Federal Europe, dominated by Germany.[48]

Even if, at a first glance, Macmillan appeared to have a more realistic view of Britain's rôle, his evaluation of European events was influenced more by memories of an Imperial Britain destined to deal with a German threat, similar to the one of 1914 or of 1939, than by contemporary evidence of British strength or German ambition. But Macmillan's fears were not shared by most of his colleagues and until the Suez Crisis, the British government could believe the United Kingdom could afford to have a detached attitude towards continental Europe. But even after Suez and Macmillan's appointment as Prime Minister, Britain rejected the option of any involvement in European affairs; instead, she sought to recover some of her former strength through a renewed 'special relationship'. After Suez, Macmillan

> … firmly decided that the special relationship could and should be rebuilt. He made a conscious choice to put transatlantic links above relations with Western Europe. His efforts to this end over the next three years were broadly approved by the British public. Doubts concerning American policy in any case were often upset by a higher regard for the Americans as a people.[49]

If by late 1956, British decision-makers and public opinion definitely reconciled themselves with the fact that the United Kingdom was no longer a great power similar to the United States or the Soviet Union, they appeared to content themselves with the rôle of Washington's 'junior partners' and with the Commonwealth link.

48. PRO, CAB 129/60, Memorandum C.(53)108, 'The European Defence Community and European Unity' by H. Macmillan (19 Mar. 1953) Secret.

49. C. J. Bartlett, *The Special Relationship. A Political History of Anglo-American Relations since 1945* (London/New York: Longman, 1992), p. 88. For another broader evaluation of the 'special relationship' see William Roger Louis and Hedley Bull (eds), *The Special Relationship. Anglo-American Relations since 1945* (Oxford: Clarendon Press, 1986); and D. C. Watt, *Succeeding John Bull America in Britain's Place 1900–1975* (Cambridge: Cambridge University Press, 1984).

This attitude sharply contrasted with France's European 'choice' and with the outcome of the Brussels negotiations which led to the signature of the Treaties of Rome. As for the 'relaunching of Europe', most British decision-makers regarded this as purely economic.[50] In this context the myth about Britain's 'superiority' over a messy continent had some part in shaping London's attitude towards European policies as the most relevant continental partners could alternatively be regarded with concern or as patronising: France was experiencing the agony of the Fourth Republic and appeared unable to extricate itself from the Algerian plight,[51] Germany was still a divided nation and Italy remained a minor actor.[52] As for the Common Market, Philip de Zulueta, Macmillan's Private Secretary, stated, 'We really don't think the French and the Germans will ever bury the hatchet to the extent of getting together to make the Common Market work.'[53]

The End of a Myth or Its Opposite? Britain's Decadence and Europe's Renaissance

Only in the early 1960s did Britain begin to realise that the Common Market could work. Meanwhile the Commonwealth ties were weakening and the British economy was definitely losing ground in comparison with those of the 'Six', which were experiencing a major economic improvement; only the 'special relationship' appeared to remain valid. Now London seemed to discover the continent and Britain's connection with Europe. In spite of this growing consciousness, the myth of Britain's 'difference', that

50. Alan Milward, *The European Rescue of the Nation State* (London: Routledge, 1992), pp. 424–434. Regarding Britain's attitude to the Treaties of Rome is concerned see Roger Bullen, 'Great Britain and the Treaty of Rome', in Enrico Serra (ed.), *The Relaunching of Europe and the Treaties of Rome* (Brussels: Bruylant, 1989), pp. 315–338.

51. Cf. Alastair Horne, *Macmillan 1957–1986* Vol. 2 (London: Macmillan, 1989), p. 35; and PRO, FO 371, WF 1202/3 (137300), despatch No. 41, Sir G. Jebb (Paris) to S. Lloyd (11 Mar. 1958) Confidential and WF 1202/6 (137300), memorandum MA/Paris/322/40, 'Views of French Army Officers on the Algerian Question' by Brigadier A. C. F. Jackson (28 Mar. 1958) Confidential.

52. See e.g. the British evaluation about the 'naive' attitude of the Italian authorities towards Middle Eastern problems, PRO, FO 371, Rt 1021/3 (130408), lett., W. Morris (Washington) to E. M. Rose (FO), (8 Oct. 1957) Confidential and RT 1021/4 (136719), despatch, H. A. F. Hohler (Rome) to Sir R. Stevens (FO), (13 Sept. 1958) Secret.

53. Horne, *Macmillan*, p. 35.

is her superiority, still exerted some influence. On this subject, *The Economist* wrote in early July 1960:

> ... the Franco-German rapprochement, though much in Britain's interest appears also a threat to Britain's influence as long as Britain is outside. Democrats could feel more hopeful that these new European institutions would strengthen democracy if the most stable democrat countries – Britain and the Scandinavians – were inside there. Economically and in the defence of, a Europe without Britain is obviously less dynamic, less able to benefit from the advantages of scale, than a Europe with Britain inside.[54]

At the same time the famous Lee Report did not rule out the possibility of a serious political crisis in France which might arise if de Gaulle should die suddenly, as well as of a rapprochement between West Germany and the Soviet Union after Adenauer's disappearance.[55] Of course both *The Economist*'s and the Lee Report's interpretations may appear sensible, but they did not conceal the persisting conviction about Britain's 'superiority', as well as the belief in the weakness of London's continental partners, who, in the eyes of the British, seemed eager to rely on London's contribution to the development of the continent.[56] Those feelings, deeply rooted in Britain's experience, at least to a certain extent explain the attitude of both British decision-makers and public opinion between the late 1950s and the early 1960s.[57] Of course such feelings were even stronger among the opponents of the European choice, who stressed Britain's ties with its past, and for example William Pickles of the LSE could write in 1962, 'The EEC is the wrong international grouping for Britain to join, because it is irrelevant to the principal requirement of the age we live in and destructive of the most effective international grouping in the world today, the Commonwealth.'[58]

54. 'Does Europe Want Us?', *The Economist* (2 July 1960).

55. PRO, CAB 129/102, Report of the Economic Steering Committee (May 1960) Secret.

56. In Jan. 1963, when confronted with the question: 'How much harm will it do to Britain if we do not join the European Common Market – a lot, a little or none at all?', 23 per cent of those questioned replied 'a lot', 26 per cent 'little', 51 per cent 'none at all', *Gallup* Vol. 1, p. 666.

57. A Gallup poll of May 1961 showed that 43 per cent of those asked: 'What do you think should be Britain's trade policy in Europe?' had replied 'don't know', only 8 per cent had showed a positive view of joining the Common Market. See *Gallup* Vol. 1, p. 585. For attitudes of British decision-makers, see Milward, *The European*, p. 432.

58. W. Pickles, *Not with Europe: The Political Case for Staying Out* (London: Fabian International Bureau, 1962), p. 31. I am grateful to Ms Anna Lisa Giachi for this

Now, however, it was the turn of a continental leader to stress Britain's 'difference'. Thus 'revenge', not just the consequence of conflicting political and economic interests, materialised in de Gaulle's rejection of Britain's adhesion to the Common Market. In late May 1962 de Gaulle stated:

> England has become a satellite of the United States. That is the choice Churchill has made after Pearl Harbor, when the United States came into the war.... His successors have prudently clung to this choice, except for Eden when he staged the Suez operation, and he suffered for it. Macmillan quickly got back into line.[59]

As for the Commonwealth, on the occasion of a Council of Ministers held in Paris in early June 1962, the French President stressed how this link still negatively influenced Britain's attitude towards Europe.[60] Interestingly, in de Gaulle's opinion, the elements which had been regarded as part of London's strength were now among the reasons for Britain's weakness, as well as the almost obvious symptoms of her decadence. On the eve of his famous press conference of 14 January 1963, the General confided:

> In reality, England has a broken back. She doesn't know what she wants. She is still hanging on to the dream of the Commonwealth ...
>
> It is evident that England is not ready to accept the rules [of the EEC]. That's not a big deal – neither for her nor for us. But we must face this fact and stop these negotiations. Of course I shall doff my cap to the rôle of England in the Second World War, to my friend Macmillan, etc. But I shall close the door again.[61]

De Gaulle's decision marked a dramatic change in Britain's attitude towards Europe, and Macmillan wrote in his diary, 'All our policies at home and abroad are in ruins ... except our courage and determination.'[62]

Even if this process was a slow one, from the 1960s onwards Britain's 'difference' was no longer the result of her superiority, but rather of her decadence, both from a political and an economic viewpoint: 'decadence', 'decline', 'end of a rôle', 'descent from power', 'retreat from power' not only crept into the titles of

quotation, which appeared in her thesis dissertation 'La Gran Bretagna: l'Europa e il Commonwealth (1960–1963)', supervised by me at the University of Florence.

59. Alain Peyrefitte, *C'était de Gaulle* (Paris: Fayard, 1994), p. 299.

60. *Ibid.*, p. 300.

61. *Ibid.*, p. 355.

62. Quoted in Horne, *Macmillan*, p. 447. On Britain's EEC application, see Richard Griffiths and Stuart Ward (eds), *Courting the Common Market. The First Attempt to enlarge the EEC 1961–63* (London: Lothian Foundation Press, 1996).

history books, but they also caught the mood of the period.[63] It is interesting to note that, following a Gallup opinion poll in June 1972 the majority of the people questioned seemed to think that in Sweden, Holland and Germany the standard of living was better than in Britain.[64] The involvement in the European continent, which appeared more and more prosperous and stable, was by then one of the main goals of London's foreign policy,[65] but such an objective contrasted with the feelings that could be described as a mixture of an inferiority complex, wounded pride and vague attempts to safeguard British uniqueness.[66] Even Britain's adhesion to the European Community in 1972 to 1973 did not alter the widespread conviction about Britain's 'difference'.[67]

The mixed feelings towards continental Europe found expression, for example, in the attitude of the Labour Party which was split over the issue of Britain's rôle in the European Community. While Labour leaders such as Harold Wilson and James Callaghan believed that the United Kingdom's destiny could be strongly tied to that of the continent, Tony Benn, a leading representative of the Labour Left could state in October 1978: '... I don't just regard the EMS (European Monetary System) as being contrary to the interest of the Labour Party, I regard it as being treachery to the country.'[68]

The Thatcher Era or the Revival of Post-war Myths

In the late 1970s, however, some sections of the British society began to wonder about the reasons behind Britain's decadence. Martin Wiener in his *English Culture and the Decline of the Industrial Spirit 1850–1980* identified the lack of interest of the British ruling classes in economic development, in scientific culture and in modernisation as a crucial cause of Britain's decline. Wiener contrasted British 'conservative' attitudes with the more modern approach of some continental partners, such as France and West

63. Alan Marwick, *British Society since 1945* (London: Penguin Books, 1982), pp. 188–273.

64. *Gallup* Vol. 2, pp. 1185–1186; only for France the answer was 20 per cent 'better off' and 20 per cent 'worse off'.

65. See the contributions by J. W. Young and R. Hibbert in Brivati and Jones (eds), *From Reconstruction*; as well as Young, *Britain*, pp. 86–106.

66. See Kennedy, *The Realities*, pp. 382–383.

67. Cf. Reynolds, *Britannia*, pp. 238–255.

68. Tony Benn, *Conflict of Interests. Diaries 1977–80*, ed. by R. Winstone (London: Hutchinson, 1990), p. 363.

Germany. In the last part of his volume, completed in 1980, Wiener stressed that 'English' often meant 'holding back the flood'; remembering J. B. Priestley's remarks following which the modern world was 'alien to English temperament', Wiener argued: '... it may be that Margaret Thatcher will find her most fundamental challenge not in holding down the money supply or in limiting government spending, or even in fighting the shop stewards, but in changing this frame of mind.'[69]

The Thatcher era did mark a radical change, not only in British policies, but also in Britain's myths. British decision-makers and public opinion appeared to rediscover the myth of their 'difference', their 'superiority' compared with her continental European partners. The Prime Minister was the standard-bearer of a social 'revolution' – or 'counter-revolution' – and she appeared to be the inventor of 'Reaganism' before Ronald Reagan had come to power. There was much talk about her Churchillian spirit; the 'special relationship' experienced its 'Indian Summer' and Britain won the Falklands War.[70] In this context, Britain rediscovered her imperial pride and once again 'Britannia ruled the waves'. The impact of the Falklands War on the myth of Britain's 'difference' cannot be underestimated. In her memoirs, Margaret Thatcher wrote:

> Nothing remains more vividly in my mind, looking back on my years in No. 10, than the eleven weeks in the spring 1982 when Britain fought and won the Falklands War. Much was at stake: what we were fighting for eight thousand miles away in the South Atlantic was not only the territory and people of the Falklands important though they were. We were defending our honour as a nation, and principles of fundamental importance to the world.

And she added:

> The significance of the Falklands War was enormous, both for Britain's self-confidence and for her standing in the world. Since the Suez fiasco in 1956, British foreign policy had been one long retreat. The tacit assumption made by British and foreign governments alike was that our world rôle was doomed steadily to diminish. We had come to be seen by both friends and enemies as a nation which lacked the will and the capability to defend its interest in peace let alone in war. Victory in the Falklands changed that.

69. Martin J. Wiener, *English Culture and the Decline of the Industrial Spirit 1850–1980* (London: Penguin, 1985), p. 166.

70. Bartlett, *The Special Relationship*, pp. 148–170; see also chapter 10.

> Everywhere I went after the war, Britain's name meant something more than it had.[71]

The myth of Britain's power found expression in a speech the Prime Minister delivered in early July 1982 at the House of Commons, in which she tried to explain the meaning of the 'Falklands spirit':

> We have ceased to be a nation in retreat. We have instead a new-found confidence – born in the economic battles at home and tested and found true 8,000 miles away ... Britain has rekindled that spirit which has fired her generations past and which today has begun to burn as highly as before. Britain found herself again in the South Atlantic and will not look back from the victory she has won.[72]

It is likely that British public opinion sensed the reserve of some European partners with regard to London's interests and ambitions, indeed, there may have been some satisfaction about a military victory achieved against the most 'European' of the Latin American nations, a 'melting pot' of Italian and Spanish immigrants. So the myths of the post-war era reasserted themselves: Britain's military might, the 'special relationship', the stability of the British political system, the recovery of British economy. Britain was no longer an Empire, but she was still different – and superior – to her continental partners.[73] In 1992 the former Labour Minister, Douglas Jay, stated:

> First do we wish to remain an independent self-governing nation? If we do not, we contemplate a rather bizarre world in which Namibia, Estonia, Sri Lanka, Albania, Croatia, Taiwan – not to mention others – would be independent nations, but the UK would not. Not merely would we then cease to be a permanent member of the Security Council of the UN, but presumably cease to be members of the UN at all.[74]

Jay appeared to imply that Britain still had a world rôle to play, a rôle which she could not give up in favour of Europe. On the other hand, in spite of the achievements produced by European

71. Margaret Thatcher, *The Downing Street Years* (London: HarperCollins, 1995), p. 173.

72. *Ibid.*, p. 235.

73. Reynolds, *Britannia*, pp. 256–292.

74. Douglas Jay, 'The Free Trade Alternative to the EC: A Witness Account', in Brivati and Jones (eds), *From Reconstruction*, p. 129. For Britain's attitude towards the EC see George: *An Awkward*, p. 137ff. and Young, *Britain*, pp. 136–164.

integration, in the late 1980s and early 1990s Britain was still regarded as different by her continental partners, not only by diplomats and politicians, but also by public opinion. In this context it is worth quoting the remarks by an Italian correspondent in London, Beppe Severgini, who in 1990 published a humorous book on the English. Severgini commented on the British attitude towards Europe:

> The problem could be that the liberal pundits, and intellectuals, academics and rock musicians with them, may not want to see what they are afraid of, namely Great Britain excluded from Europe and heading the way Portugal is ... But the man in the street loves his daily diet of 'Frogs', 'Huns' and 'Spaghetti-eaters'. He does not quite know what to make of the channel but is convinced that the EEC is full of robbers, out there ready to trick the naive Englishman.[75]

Furthermore he stated:

> Even those British who like to think that they are good Europeans firmly believe that at Euro-Summits, their leaders are set upon by 'useless, vainglorious, spaghetti-eating no-hopers' to quote *The Guardian* (incidentally they mean us the Italians). A number of educated people, people one would never have thought of, hold the view that the new Europe will spell the end of old England.[76]

Conclusions

In late 1990 Margaret Thatcher was replaced by John Major. Since then, the achievements of the 1980s seem to have been fading. The fall of the Berlin Wall and the 'end' of the Cold War have entailed a new international balance, which, as far as Europe is concerned, was going to stress the rôle played by a unified Germany.[77] The 'special relationship', briefly revived during the Gulf War, paled with the arrival of the Clinton administration, even though the US President was a Rhodes scholar at Oxford. It took an upward turn only when Tony Blair came to 10, Downing Street. In the economic field the debate about European monetary union is exerting its influence throughout Europe and the recession has shaken British

75. Beppe Severgnini, *Inglesi* (London: Coronet Book, 1991), p. 20.
76. *Ibid.*, p. 21.
77. Timothy Garton Ash, *In Europe's Name. Germany and the Divided Continent* (London: Jonathan Cape, 1993).

self-confidence along with the self-confidence of other European nations. Where nuclear weapons are concerned, France seems to be more independent than Britain. From the economic point of view, Germany appears able to outmanoeuvre every other European nation. The United Kingdom enjoys a stable political system, but François Mitterrand ruled France for fourteen years and Helmut Kohl has ruled the Federal Republic for even longer. Social fracture is evident in the United Kingdom as much as in France or elsewhere in a Europe suffering from long-term unemployment and the marginalisation of sizeable sectors of society. As for Britain's traditional institutions, the future of the monarchy – or at least some of its aspects – seems to be questioned more seriously at the end of the 1990s than at any time since the abdication of Edward VIII, if not the restoration of the Stuarts.

Nevertheless, many Britons still feel great pride in their way of life, their values and traditions. Something of the myth of Britain's difference from the continent is still alive, also because many Europeans on the continent still believe it or want to believe it. But how much of this is myth, how much reality? I have no definite answer, but I shall conclude with a quotation from the diary of an Italian visitor to Britain:

> The island ... appears to be completely different from the continent. The sea is an extraordinary feature for it is an ocean and is subject to low and high tides. The Thames water has a different taste from the ones of any other river in the world, the cattle, the fish and the food are different from what we are accustomed to. Also horses are of a different breed and all the inhabitants have a peculiar character, and they feel themselves superior to any other people.[78]

These words were written by the Venetian adventurer, Giacomo Casanova, in 1759. Perhaps because of his cosmopolitan outlook and under the influence of the Enlightenment, Casanova added: 'But this happens in every nation: every nation believes to be the first and every nation is right.'[79] Perhaps every European nation is 'different'. Still, Europe itself is more than a myth or a geographical term, Britain included.

78. Giacomo Casanova, *Storia della mia vita* Vol. 2 (Milan: Mondadori, 1984), p. 1496.
79. *Ibid.*

Chapter 12

Dunkirk, Diên Biên Phu, Suez or Why France Does Not Trust Allies and Has Learnt to Love the Bomb

Beatrice Heuser

While historical myths seem to play a defining rôle in the political identity of many nations, the strength and power of myths seem particularly striking in the case of France. To give just one example of a historical myth in domestic politics, the myth of the elective kingship of the Merovingians was utilised even in the Renaissance to define the king's rôle as the executor of the wishes of the Three Estates by the philosopher François Hotman. During the Age of Enlightenment, the Merovingian myth helped shape concepts of the king as the representative of the general will and of contractual relations between the Monarch and the people. In the twentieth century, the Merovingian myth has been cited as evidence for the inherent Frenchness (and thus suitability) of the elective Presidency of the Fifth Republic.

Central among France's foreign policy myths have been those of war and peace, of enemies and unreliable allies in times of need. They have played a formative, or at least an explanatory, rôle in French policy-making, indeed, they are a crucial framework of reference for France's political and national identity:

> [T]he personality of a nation is forged by becoming conscious of military threats which apply pressure on it, sometimes [also] by the possibility of expansion, particularly by the glory of its weapons.

This is how Michel Debré, Minister of Defence under Pompidou, described the relationship between nationhood and defence when he presented the 1972 French 'Defence White Book' which guided France for twenty-two years.[1]

A whole string of historical myths concerns France's relations with what, in a twentieth century context, would be her natural allies, above all Britain, but also the United States. But before turning to relations with the 'Anglo-Saxon' democracies in particular, it is useful to discuss some French historical myths about Alliances in general. One of the earliest here concerns the alliance between François I and the Ottoman Sultan Süleyman the Magnificent against the (Habsburg) Holy Roman Empire. This is generally invoked to argue that for France, national interest comes above any narrow solidarity with powers sharing her religion, culture or values, or, in the twentieth century, democratic ideals. This historical precedent (of what from the other side could be seen as a French betrayal of her natural allies) was thus used to support de Gaulle's decision to withdraw French forces from NATO's integrated command structure in 1966.[2] But there are further examples of French leaders choosing national interest over religious or ideological bonds, such as Richelieu's alliances with Protestant princes against the Catholic parties in the Thirty Years' War, or to move into the twentieth Century, the late Third Republic's attempts to woo Fascist Italy (admittedly with the aim of preventing the Rome-Berlin Axis) or the authoritarian Turkey of the 1930s.

Besides this 'tradition' which could arguably be described as a balance-of-power policy, France also has a strong tradition of alliance membership. But in successful alliances, from a French point of view, France has to be the leading power. This condition is crucial: France lacks a tradition of being one of two or several equally strong powers that are close in religion or ideology. France is either the leader, or the *cavalier seul*, or the ally of her enemy's enemy, whoever that may be. This is at any rate the myth of France's historical attitude towards alliances.

From the perspective of our age, the age that began with the French Revolution, this may seem surprising. It is much less so if one considers the much older relationships between France and the two greatest among her neighbours over the previous centuries:

1. Michel Debré, 'Défense de l'Europe et sécurité en Europe', *Revue Défense nationale* [henceforth, *RDN*] Vol. 28, No. 11 (Dec. 1972), pp. 1788–1789.

2. André Martel, 'Défense française: la menace et l'ennemi, 1536–1966', *Stratégique* No. 1 (1st Term 1979), pp. 31–50.

England on the one side, and the Holy Roman Empire and both its Habsburg and German successors on the other. The latter forms the subject of a separate contribution in this volume; this chapter is thus mainly concerned with the former, that is, relations between France and England.[3]

Le Perfide Albion

The English see themselves (whether gladly or sadly) as heirs of a Franco-Norman culture which William the Conqueror and his followers imposed on the Anglo-Saxons. Yet ever since, English feelings towards France have contained a strong element of rivalry, at times even blatant xenophobic hatred: in the eighteenth century, a Swiss traveller commented that 'no people on earth hates and despises another people more than the English do the French'.[4]

It seems that French feelings about the English never quite stooped to this base level. This is perhaps because French concepts of patriotism since the enlightened eighteenth century, and nationalism since the French Revolution, have been the least ethnic and racist, and the most civic, among all the nationalisms of Europe. They were built on the notion of 'the fraternal bond between all humans', in the words of Buirette de Belloy, an eighteenth century writer considered as one of the greatest French Anglophobes ever. Crucially, then, the French perception of the English is that of 'rivals more than enemies' (again Buirette de Belloy).[5] Perhaps this rivalry is so particularly vibrant because England is seen as progeny of the French culture, as an equal. This sense of rivalry was certainly already fully developed at the time of Henry II and Louis VII, in the second half of the twelfth century. The Hundred Years' War was so dangerous to the French monarchy and to the identity of the nascent state precisely because the English pretenders to the French throne were most worthy and serious candidates. Descended from the French Royal House through the female line,

3. This rivalry is very specifically one between France and the kingdom of England, not Scotland (France's 'aulde ally' against England) or Wales (as *Pays de Galles* the Gauls' Celtic cousins). To this day, Frenchmen refer to the entire United Kingdom as *'l'Angleterre'*, implicitly denying that they are dealing with anything other than their old rival from the time of the Plantagenet kings or the Hundred Years' War.

4. Linda Colley, *Britons: Forging the Nation, 1707–1837* (New Haven, Ct.: Yale University Press, 1992), p. 36.

5. Both quoted in David Bell, 'Recent Works on Early Modern French National Identity', *The Journal of Modern History* Vol. 68, No. 1 (March 1996), p. 87.

Edward III, the Black Prince and Henry V won ample support from French princes and noblemen. When the final victory went to Charles VII and the male line of the Valois, those who had sided with the English pretenders could be branded as traitors – just as England itself could become the symbol of treachery. The myth of the *perfide Albion* was conceived. The strength of this myth may well lie in the way it externalised the guilt of those 'Frenchmen' who had supported the Plantagenets and Lancasters, projecting the guilt to the other side of the Channel.

A century later, Tudor England and the Habsburg Holy Roman Empire were the two main rivals of Renaissance France, competing for power not only in the Old World but also in the New World. Notwithstanding France's willingness to conclude alliances with the Ottoman Empire to spite Rome and Habsburg, and notwithstanding France's 'Gallicanism' (the assertion of France's ecclesiastical autonomy *vis-à-vis* Rome), England's Protestant Reformation was seen in France as a betrayal of Catholicism. *'L'Angleterre! Ah, la perfide Angleterre'*, the theologian Jacques Bossuet exclaimed in the seventeenth century, not long after the royal husband of French King Henri IV's beautiful daughter had been beheaded, and Catholic Henrietta Maria herself and her children banished from British soil. The religious vacillations of the Stuart monarchs in the seventeenth century had direct consequences for the matrimonial bonds between the Anglo-Scottish and the French Royal houses. From the English Civil War onwards, the tables were turned and France stood for the Catholic faction in the United Kingdom; for British Puritans, France increasingly became coterminous with the 'Popish' enemy. France supplied the Jacobite rebellions with soldiers and gold. The staunchly Protestant Hanoverian kings just about managed to temper their enmity towards the Bourbons with gestures of sympathy when Louis XVI lost crown and head. For Revolutionary France, however, just as for Napoleon, Georgian Britain in supporting the exiled Bourbons neatly fitted the image of the treacherous rival previously assigned to England.

Then, since the Napoleonic Wars, Prussia, first a client-state of France which switched sides at Tauroggen by concluding an agreement with Russia, began to contest England's mythical rôle of arch traitor to France. The myth of the betrayal by Germany was born, as discussed elsewhere in this book.[6]

6. See chapter 16 of this volume, Cyril Buffet, 'Rapallo: Sirens and Phantoms'.

Nevertheless, French folklore continues to refer to the ungentlemanly behaviour of the 'English' (by now a united force of Scotsmen, Englishmen and Welshmen) in this context. Napoleon in 1815 appealed to History to witness that there could be no greater sign of esteem and confidence than that he, England's enemy, who had so long fought against it, should come freely, in his misfortune, to seek asylum: 'But how did one respond in England to such magnanimity? One pretended to extend a hospitable hand to the enemy; and when he had surrendered in good faith, one immolated him.'[7] Ever since Napoleon's exile, Frenchmen have ranted about their betrayal by Prussia and the ungallant way in which the English have celebrated their victories over him – from constructing Trafalgar Square to Waterloo Station, many years after the Emperor's death. (That France commemorated Napoleon's victories with the *place d'Iéna* the *rue d'Ulm* and the *gare d'Austerlitz* somehow seems to French people infinitely less tactless.)

The Crimean War saw Britain and France in an altogether unusual constellation, fighting side-by-side, against Russia. Even then, the question of command arrangements proved to be a thorny one: French officers refused to be subordinated to British commanders (and vice versa). The rivalry between the two powers presented a serious problem in their joint operations.[8]

The shocking defeat of France at the hand of the Prussian-led German alliance and the fall of the Second French and birth of the Second German Empires focused French attention on the East, but the rivalry with Britain lived on. The Fashoda Crisis of 1898, in which Britain and France nearly came to blows, shows that against the background of Darwinist nationalism and colonial expansionism, the enemy was almost interchangeable for all sides on the eve of the First World War. Britain was no more seen as France's natural ally than Germany.

The almost random formation and dissolution of alliances in the following years between the Fashoda Crisis and the Great War aligned Britain with France against Germany. One might have expected the experience of common suffering of 1914–1918 and the struggle against Germany and Austria to have forged bonds between Britain and France which would overcome the past rivalry (particularly as the command arrangements were for

7. Napoleon, on board of Bellérophon, 4 Aug. 1815.

8. Andrew Lambert, *The Crimean War* (Manchester: Manchester University Press, 1990), *passim*.

once resolved to the satisfaction of the French, with the French Marshal Foch as supreme commander).

These bonds, however, seemed to melt like ice under the heat of disagreements over the post-war settlement. The British wanted to do everything possible to avoid shedding their blood once more on the battlefields of France and Flanders. The French, however, were not convinced that war could be avoided, except perhaps if the Germans could be deterred by a show of solidarity between France and Britain, with British forces deployed in large numbers in France. But the British hesitated, and the myth of the perfidious Albion came back in strength. Negotiations dragged on: the French asked for a serious army; the British finally conceded a symbolic deployment – too little, too late. The modest contingent that the British government had indeed deployed in France made a hasty but orderly retreat to the Channel when the German *Blitzkrieg* against France unfolded in 1940, and the British troops were evacuated from Dunkirk. What the British to this day celebrate as a triumph of logistics, from a French perspective was a ghastly, cowardly betrayal. No need any longer to talk vaguely about perfidy. Henceforth, 'Dunkerque' said it all.

The Myth of Dunkirk

The 'most traumatic'[9] of the lessons of French history was that of 1940. The French defeat by Hitler's Wehrmacht was variously attributed to the cowardice of the army, to the Communist or pro-Fascist enemy within, to a failure of leadership within France, but also, not least, to treachery, the treachery of the 'English' (who by now were well and truly integrated into the larger 'British' nation, a word obstinately ignored by the French).

What lesson was to be drawn from this? How could France be defended in future without exposing her to the risk of another collapse like that of 1940? The answer had to be that France, particularly the French government, had to be independent both from a demoralised army and from unreliable allies. The magic wand that provided the answer was the nuclear weapon, in the hands of one sole, determined decision-maker. In the words of one French journalist (writing when the *force de frappe* first came into existence):

9. Claude Imbert, 'The end of French exceptionalism', *Foreign Affairs* Vol. 68, No. 4 (Autumn 1989), p. 49.

> If it was de Gaulle who in … 1940 proclaimed that France had lost a battle but she had not lost the war, he has nevertheless not forgotten that the loss of that battle has cost the country fifty months of occupation, and that more than twenty years later, France still shows the psychic scars of that defeat. He hopes to eliminate the possibility of a similar defeat by giving to the nation a strike-force with nuclear weapons.[10]

In 1964, Prime Minister Georges Pompidou, in a speech to celebrate the liberation of Calais, dwelt on the lessons of 1940, which he attributed to de Gaulle:

> Alliances, as necessary, as strong, as loyal as they may be … alliances can make possible the liberation: but they cannot guarantee the initial success, and, in our day and age, that means that they cannot assure our survival.[11]

In other words, a key lesson of 1940 was that France could not trust her allies, however loyal she herself might be towards them.[12] This is a much-repeated tenet that is linked to France's obsessive quest for independence, and the French rarely hesitated to say this to the faces of those who had fought with them in 1940.[13]

All the things Britain did after 1940 – from giving protection to French exiles (including de Gaulle) to fighting on alone, and even to offering the French a joint nationality – could not totally wipe out the trauma of Dunkirk. In 1947, Dunkirk was chosen very deliberately for the solemn celebration which was designed, but failed, to expunge the French experience of British betrayal. The treaty concluded on this occasion, the Franco-British treaty of mutual defence, was almost entirely a mystical attempt to compensate for a past *acte manqué*. As such, it was perhaps the most fruitful of its kind: one could argue that it was the seed of the subsequent treaties of defence co-operation, the Brussels Treaty of 1948 and the Washington Treaty of 1949. In both, under the catalytic effect of the fear of the Soviet Union and a revived German threat, Franco-British co-operation temporarily achieved a harmony not known since.

10. Guy Ponce de Leon, 'L'espiègle Charlie', *Combat* (17 July 1963).

11. Excerpts from Pompidou's speech in K. Christitch, 'M. Pompidou définit les conditions d'une défense nationale valable', *Le Monde* (29 Sept. 1964).

12. André Fontaine, 'Frankreich und die Atlantische Allianz: Die historischen Wurzeln von Zentralismus und Unabhängigkeit', *Europa-Archiv* Vol. 29, No. 14 (1974), p. 480.

13. See Jacques Champagne, 'France', *RUSI Journal* Vol. 110, No. 637 (Feb. 1965), p. 23.

Even so, this harmony was short-lived. Not only did Britain refuse to become involved in the European Defence Community – which seriously troubled France and contributed to the majority decision in the French National Assembly in 1954 to vote against the EDC's ratification; more importantly, there was the experience of Diên Biên Phu.

Diên Biên Phu

Since the defeat of Japan and the end of the Second World War in Asia, France had struggled to re-assert her control over Indochina. But nationalist forces, inspired by Communism, mounted an increasingly successful resistance. The civil war which resulted took the character of an anti-colonial liberation war from the Communists' and Nationalists' point of view, and a war against Communism from the French point of view. The final crunch came in the spring of 1954, when French forces were besieged in Diên Biên Phu, and it became clear that the ability or failure of the French forces to resist would be tantamount to French victory or defeat in the Indochina war. The French asked the Americans to use nuclear weapons to relieve Diên Biên Phu: had not John Foster Dulles just proclaimed the strategy of massive retaliation as an option even for local wars?

The Eisenhower-Dulles administration were prepared to give France logistic aid, but not, as it turned out, nuclear fire-cover. Dulles's 'massive retaliation' talk was mainly rhetoric, aimed at one specific situation at hand (Korea), and like many other US policy statements, awkwardly packaged as a general principle of US policy. Trying to deter China from resuming the Korean War by hinting at the use of nuclear weapons was one thing; actually using them, quite another.

The British played a rôle in this US decision: Foreign Secretary Anthony Eden refused at the last minute to participate in trilateral talks about the use nuclear weapons in Indochina, thus effectively signalling British opposition.[14] Moreover Britain counselled the Americans against nuclear use – indeed, Eisenhower told the

14. Jacques Dalloz, *La guerre d'Indochine, 1945–1954* (Paris: Eds. du Seuil, 1987), pp. 234–237; Greg Herring and Robert Immerman, 'Le jour où nous ne sommes pas entrés en guerre: la politique américaine au moment de Diên Biên Phu', in Denise Artaud and Lawrence Kaplan (eds), *Diên Biên Phu: L'Alliance atlantique et la défense du Sud-Est asiatique* (Lyon: la manufacture, 1989), pp. 116–127.

French government of his oral agreement with Churchill, whereby he had conceded a veto to Britain over any US nuclear-weapons use. The British government position in turn became generally known through a press statement by Dulles two years later: Dulles claimed that both Britain and France had initially wanted to see China threatened with nuclear reprisals had China become involved in the Indochina War, and that Britain had subsequently pulled back. The whole story was dismissed in a British *dementi*' but the bitter taste remained.[15] Diên Biên Phu fell in May 1954, and Frenchmen saw it as an Anglo-Saxon betrayal, the *perfide Albion* joined now by a perfidious America. The lesson: France could not rely on her allies, France had to be independent, and for that reason, France needed nuclear weapons. At the end of December 1954, a French government paper set out the fundamental need for French atomic arms:

> No country can … in the short term claim a real political *independence* if it does not possess atomic weapons and no doubt thermonuclear ones, and the means to launch them.[16]

The New Treacherous Ally: The United States

The fall of Diên Biên Phu not only confirmed the belief in Britain's treachery. It also poisoned Franco-US relations, constituting an important step in the development of another rivalry, that between France and the United States.

Both nations share with many the idea that they are a chosen people, and that they have a sense of mission in respect of the rest of the world. But the self-invented missions of France and the United States are particularly similar: where Britain sought to export Shakespeare and the Bible, France and the United States sought to export democracy. And almost inevitably, this led them to become rivals, for surely, only one or the other could be the true 'Light of the World' (de Gaulle about France[17]), not both. While Americans took a naïve pride in the *acquis* of the US Revolution, the French were always quick to point out that the majority of the

15. See 'Le Foreign Office fait une mise au point modérée à la suite de l'article de "Life"', *Le Monde* (15 Jan. 1956) and the famous interview with John Foster Dulles, 'On the Brink of War', *Life* (Jan. 1956).

16. Quoted in Georges-Henri Soutou, 'La politique nucléaire de Pierre Mendès France' *Relations Internationales* No. 59 (autumn 1989), p. 326, emphasis added.

17. Alains Peyrefitte, *De Gaulle a dit* Vol. 1 (Paris: Fayard, 1994).

ideas behind it were French export products or were shared by the French revolutionaries. Moreover, did not the independent United States owe its recognition to France, the US's 'oldest ally'? Why then did the United States not acknowledge the debt – intellectual and political – which it owed to its spiritual mother, France? How dare it try to compete with her?

Against this French indignation about insufficient US reverence for France's spiritual and cultural greatness, the great debt owed by France to the United States for her deliverance from the Germans in two world wars seems to pale into insignificance. Not for nothing, said Jean d'Ormesson (a rare French Americanophile), was France the fatherland of M. Perrichon, a literary figure characterised by naïveté and ingratitude.[18]

This indignation of an old and proud nation at being overtaken and largely ignored by a young giant translated itself into petty criticism. One such example, crucial for France's defence policies, concerns the United States' readiness to come to the defence of its allies. There were, of course, throughout the Cold War Frenchmen who expressed their confidence that the US to come to their aid in a nuclear age, as they had done in two world wars previously.[19] But doubts about America's commitment grew early on. General Pierre Gallois reminded his contemporaries that although the United States owed their recognition to France, George Washington had refused to enter into the subsequent Franco-British war on the side of France in 1793.[20] Over a century later, had not the United States waited rather a long time before entering even the Great War on the side of France and Britain? Might much of the senseless bloodshed not have been avoided if only the US had come in earlier? Had it not been the same in the Second World War?[21] In the nuclear age, such a delay would be not only catastrophic, it would be decisive.[22] Cynics could even speculate that

18. Eugène Labiche's *Voyage de M. Perrichon* is alluded to in Jean d'Ormesson, 'Nos amis américains', *Revue des deux mondes* Vol. 145, No. 1 (Jan. 1974), p. 4.

19. Editorial, 'Dissuasion et Prestige', *Esprit* Vol. 31, No. 323 (Dec. 1963), p. 813; General Valluy, 'Réflexions sur le "deterrent"', *RDN* Vol. 19, No. 6 (June 1963), pp. 925–936; J. Lévy-Jacquemin, 'Réponse à M. Sanguinetti: notre défense nucléaire', *Le Monde* (3 Oct. 1963).

20. Pierre M. Gallois, 'Les théories de guerre américaines', *Forces Aériennes Françaises* No. 254 (Jan. 1969), p. 18.

21. René Dabernat, 'La désaméricanisation', *Combat* (18 Jan. 1963).

22. For example, Jean Didisheim; 'L'Amérique et nous', *Le Monde* (2 June 1965); Alain Terrenoire's statements at the NATO young politicians' meeting at University College, Oxford, 1965, 'Can the use of nuclear weapons be decided upon

America had wanted the other great powers to bleed themselves white in the two previous world wars, the more easily to become their heir in world politics.

French concerns about the way in which the United States would be prepared to defend Europe were constant even though the particular cause for this concern became totally transformed. In 1954 P.-A. Bourget expressed his conviction that the United States' preference for 'Peripheral Strategy' meant that the US would 'renounce the defence of the European continent and face the aggressor frontally, and it gives its allies indirect help, by attacking the enemy's air- and naval forces, his territory, his natural resources, his factories, his communications. [This would be] an exclusive air and aero-naval strategy, at least at the beginning'.[23] From a European perspective this would mean an evacuation of the Continent, even if this might later lead to a reconquest. Such a scenario activated the fear of another Dunkirk.[24]

Suspicions that the Americans would prefer to remain on the peripheries of any conflict in Europe, rather than becoming fully involved, continued to thrive.[25] Another label attached to this fear of abandonment was that of Munich,[26] but this time, France and Europe would be the victims, and the United States the appeasers in a nuclear crisis.[27]

Tacitly, the myth of the perfidious Albion was thus transformed into the myth of the dominant United States, willing to betray France in order to step into her shoes. Diên Biên Phu could thus be seen not only as US indifference to the loss of French influence

---

collectively?' *NATO Letter* (Oct. 1965), p. 22; Jean Fabiani, 'Pas d'Alliance pour l'aventure'; Marc Valle, 'Les Yankees et la France', *Combat* (18 Apr. 1966); Captain Sallerin, 'Guerre future et armée de l'air', *Forces Aériennes Françaises* Vol. 3, No. 16 (Jan. 1948), p.511.

23. P.-A. Bourget, 'Stratégie Périphérique', *Politique Etrangère* Vol. 19, No. 1 (Feb.–Mar. 1954), p. 65.

24. David Chuter, *Humanity's Soldier* (Oxford: Berghahn, 1996).

25. General Armengaud, 'La force de frappe indépendante: mélange de réalisme dépassé et d'excessive témérité', *Ecrits de Paris* No. 228 (July–Aug. 1964), p. 28.

26. See chapter 6 of this volume, David Chuter, 'Munich, or the Blood of Others'.

27. Editorial (Christian Audejean, Yves Bertherat, Jacques Delpeyrou, Jean Irigaray, André Marissel, Paul Thibaud), 'Le choix', *Esprit* Vol. 31, No. 323 (Dec. 1963), p. 866; General Charles Ailleret, 'Défense 'dirigée' ou défense 'tous azimuts'', *RDN* Vol. 23, No. 11 (Dec. 1967), p. 1932; see also the former minister Albin Chalandon, 'L'esprit de Munich', *Le Monde* (15 Nov. 1973). Another label that was used was that of the feared 'Finlandisation' of Europe, see Guy de Carmoy, 'Force de frappe et défense européenne', *Revue politique et parlementaire* Vol. 75, No. 847 (Dec. 1973), p. 51.

in Indochina, but also as a welcome opportunity for the United States to replace France as the leading power in South East Asia. Not long after the Geneva conference had imposed a precarious and moribund peace on Indochina, US advisers began to establish themselves there, and from that time onward US involvement increased slowly but steadily. Only against this background can the French maliciousness towards America during the following Vietnam War be understood.

US anti-colonial rhetoric and attempts by Washington to undercut the appeal of Communism to anti-colonial movements through the denunciation of imperialism were bitterly resented in France. The French even more so than the British suffered the side-effects of this US Cold War strategy. The second main area where French policies were thus in sharp conflict with US policies was the Middle East. Here, too, the Americans behaved in a way that could be interpreted from a French perspective as treachery. While over a long period of time Algeria was the focus of this conflict among the two Western Allies, it was the Franco-British Suez campaign which became the next crucial myth in French thinking about international relations.

The Suez Complex

From 1956 there was no longer any need to go back to the trauma of abandonment of Dunkirk, or to the lack of nuclear support at Diên Biên Phu. A new key experience was put in its place, Suez, confirming all the previous myths of betrayal. In Britain, Suez was seen at worst as a US betrayal and at best the hour of truth, when the British had to admit to themselves that they were no longer a first-league power. In France, however, great store is set by the fact that the military operation was within a hair's breadth of achieving its aims, and that it was the lack of political will to carry it through to the end that brought the campaign to its ignominious end. And this failure of political will occurred in London, where the British government gave in to US blackmail, the threat to use US economic leverage to bring down sterling and with it Britain's financial reserves. France had to follow suit because French forces were fighting under British command, in a closely integrated command structure.

For the French, therefore, Suez confirmed the long-held beliefs in Britain's fickleness as an ally – rarely did Britain cave in more weakly to US pressure. In addition, as for the British, Suez for the French represented a betrayal of the highest order by the United States, and Frenchmen asked themselves whether the Americans were 'Allies or Rivals'.[28] The Americans were thought to be either blind to Nasser's Communist connections and thus naïve about international politics, or else cunningly seeking to oust France and Britain from the Middle East.[29]

The key lessons of Suez were never to put too much trust in 'certain countries' (the United States and Britain), to have a rapidly deployable force of one's own (so that again, one would not have to rely excessively on an ally), not to put one's forces under the command of another power (a lesson spelled out particularly by General André Beaufre, one of the highest commanders in the operation and later a famous strategic thinker[30]), and to acquire one's own nuclear weapons with which one could deter the Soviet Union's nuclear blackmail.[31]

Henceforth, French fears of abandonment by the United States in the face of Soviet nuclear threats were a key factor in all French reasoning about nuclear strategy. But on top of that came the fear of US-Soviet collusion.

The Yalta Complex[32]

Throughout the Cold War, France shared with the other Europeans the fear that the United States and the Soviet Union were prepared to come to an agreement over the heads of the Europeans, taking further the myth of the deliberate division of the world into two camps at the Yalta Meeting of January 1945 (to which France had not been invited).[33] As a result, France developed a

28. Maurice Duverger, 'Alliés ou Rivaux?', *Le Monde* (5 Dec. 1956); Pierre Chateauviex, 'L'opinion américaine et anglaise devant la crise de Suez', *RDN* Vol. 12, No. 10 (Oct. 1956), pp. 1240–1251.

29. Robert Buron, 'La France face aux Etats-Unis', *Le Monde* (6 Dec. 1956).

30. Général André Beaufre, *L'Expédition de Suez* (Paris, B. Grasset, 1967), *passim*.

31. Admiral Barjot, Deputy of the British commander of operation MUSKETEER, 'Réflexions sur les opérations de 1956', *RDN* Vol. 22, No. 12. (Dec. 1966), pp. 1913–1924.

32. See chapter 7 of this volume, Reiner Marcowitz, 'Yalta, the Myth of the Division of the World'.

33. Grosser, 'General de Gaulle and the foreign policy of the Fifth Republic', p. 207; occasionally the Franco-Russian Peace of Tilsit is also invoked and applied to the 'hot line' between United States and USSR, see Contre-Amiral Lepotier, 'L'OTAN aprés Cuba et Nassau', *RDN* Vol. 11, No. 8 (Aug.–Sept. 1955), p. 13.

'Yalta Complex'.[34] In the words of one writer, Frenchmen could not understand why the United States which 'in 1945, with one million men in the armed forces and a nuclear monopoly, sacrificed to the USSR all the states bordering the latter (including those over whom the war had begun) and brought the Russian armies into Central Europe: this is called Yalta'.[35]

It was a lasting memory of humiliation for France that de Gaulle had not been invited to Yalta: this ignominy could only be wiped out by the diplomatic effects of the French atom bomb.[36] Yet French political mythology managed to turn this humiliation into a moral triumph, as the French interpretation of Yalta is one of a 'division of the world between Stalin and Roosevelt'[37] in two spheres of influence, and a sacrifice of Eastern Europe to the Soviet Union.[38] Britain's presence is conveniently ignored, and the secret Churchill-Stalin percentages agreement of December 1944 was not widely known about even in Britain before the opening of British diplomatic archives.

Yalta thus came to stand for the nightmare of US-Soviet collusion. The French believed that there had been such collusion to prevent France and Britain from achieving their just aims in Suez.[39] But fears of such collusion predated Suez, showing that the crisis only served later to confirm fears that were already deeply entrenched.[40] Claude Delmas spoke of a 'resurgence of the spirit of Yalta',[41] and critics and supporters of the French nuclear programme alike continued to be haunted by the Yalta myth.[42]

34. Manuel Bridier, 'Le Yalta du pauvre', *Le Monde* (24 Feb. 1970).

35. Gaston Bergery, 'Les Etats-Unis et nous', *Le Monde* (19 Jan. 1957).

36. André Raust's caustic comments in 'De Gaulle desintègre l'OTAN', *La Revue Socialiste* Nouvelle Série No. 179 (Jan. 1965), p. 5.

37. André Fontaine, 'Du faux Yalta au vrai?', *Le Monde* (23 May 1972).

38. Paul Stehlin was one of the few Frenchmen who fought against this deformation of 'historical reality'; see 'Une interview du général Paul Stehlin: La France et la nouvelle stratégie', *Informations et Documents* No. 271 (Jan. 1969), p. 18.

39. Adm. Barjot, 'Réflexions sur les opérations de Suez 1956', *RDN* Vol. 22, No. 12 (Dec. 1966), pp. 1916, 1918; Georges B. Manue, 'La leçon de Suez', *RDN* Vol. 12, No. 10 (Oct. 1956), pp. 1156–1157.

40. 'L'Amérique et nous: ... Russes et Américains, vont-ils se ressembler?... Débat', *Le Figaro* (11 May 1956).

41. Claude Delmas, 'Nous devons passer de l'Alliance à la communauté atlantique', *RDN* Vol. 13, No. 11 (Nov. 1957), p. 1621; *id.*, 'L'Alliance Atlantique: Fondements et Perspectives', *Revue militaire d'information* No. 298 (Oct. 1958), p. 19; Jules Moch, 'Les conséquences stratégiques et politiques des armes nouvelles', *Politique étrangère* Vol. 23, No. 2 (Feb. 1958), p. 163; André Stibio, 'De la rencontre de Gaulle-Eisenhower', *Carrefour* (12 Aug. 1959).

42. Maurice Faure, 'Les choix de la France', *Le Monde* (31 Jan. 1964).

It was thus before the Sputnik and US Secretary of State Christian Herter's ill-judged statement that the United States would rather abandon its allies than risk the nuclear annihilation of New York or Chicago, that Frenchmen began to fear an understanding that might result from a 'nuclear tête-à-tête' between the superpowers.[43] Marshal Juin and Raymond Aron used words reminiscent of the tactful way in which the British would broach this issue – errors or doubts on the part of the enemy[44] – but other French strategists did not hesitate to voice their own doubts more clearly.[45] Raymond Aron himself discerned in the spring of 1962, before the Cuban Missile Crisis, an 'unwritten Russo-US alliance against war'.[46] The installation of a 'red telephone' between the White House and the Kremlin corroborated French suspicions of a secret US-Soviet understanding in times of crisis.[47] Joint US-Soviet efforts to come to some arms control agreements, to ban nuclear tests in the atmosphere, and to contain further nuclear proliferation were variously compared to Yalta, or worse still, to Munich.[48] In 1963, with the Elysée Treaty, de Gaulle was widely seen as having confronted Adenauer with the choice between co-operation with Paris and co-operation with Washington using the argument: who was to know whether the US and the USSR 'will not agree to divide the world' between them, as they had the nuclear monopoly?[49]

Tongue in cheek, *Combat* suspected the US spy-plane pilot who had overflown Pierrelatte to be sharing the photographs with Russian colleagues, while the Russians might be sharing their radio-monitoring of France with the Americans.[50] De Gaulle's decision to

43. Maurice Ferro, 'Entretien Pineau-Dulles sur le new-look soviétique', *Le Temps de Paris* (20 June 1956).

44. Marshal A. Juin, 'Que devons-nous penser de la sécurité française?', *RDN* Vol. 13, No. 1 (Jan. 1957), p. 16; Raymond Aron, 'Un nouveau membre du Club', *Le Figaro* (14 Aug. 1959).

45. Pierre M. Gallois, 'L'Alliance Atlantique et l'évolution de l'armement', *Politique étrangère* Vol. 24, No. 2 (1959), pp. 200–203.

46. Raymond Aron, 'Les relations franco-américaines: le centre du débat', *Le Figaro* (12 May 1962).

47. Paul Norder, 'La guerre atomique n'aura pas lieu', *Revue militaire générale* No. 6 (June 1963), p.121; Paul Pigasse, 'L'illusion de la terreur nucléaire', *Revue militaire d'information* No. 353 (Oct. 1963), p. 65; Schumann, 'The evolution of NATO', *Adelphi Papers* No. 5 (1963), p. 24.

48. Pierre Roustide, 'Après l'accord de Moscou: espoirs ou illusions', *Revue militaire générale* No. 1 (Jan. 1964), pp. 3–9.

49. James Reston, 'What do they think we are?', *New York Times* (21 Jan. 1963).

50. F. Fonvielle-Alquier, 'L'Espion qui venait de Carpentras', *Combat* (28 July 1965).

announce France's withdrawal from NATO's military structure, it was rumoured, came 'shortly after the conclusion of secret American-Soviet accords which are supposedly a ... second Yalta ... concerning a global *modus vivendi* between Moscow and Washington ...'.[51] Gallois speculated that this was an agreement to treat each other's countries as inviolable sanctuaries in case of nuclear war.[52]

All subsequent nonproliferation and nuclear arms-control negotiations, as well as the talks about anti-ballistic missile systems between the United States and the Soviet Union were seen in this light:[53] they were, in the words of Pompidou, 'a means of sharing hegemony... This is a danger not only for France, but for many countries of Western Europe and even of Eastern Europe'.[54] While these and other US policies met with understanding on the part of Atlanticists,[55] they were generally taken as evidence that France, and Europe, had to look to its own defence.[56] The first Strategic Arms Limitations Treaty (SALT) was greeted by the journalist André Fontaine in 1972 as the 'real' Yalta, where the division of the world had hitherto not been quite as formally recognised.[57] Like Chancellor Helmut Schmidt in Germany, some French initiates were concerned about what they saw as the US blindness to the European theatre imbalance of forces created by the SALT agreements, especially when it seemed in 1978 that

51. 'Les communistes ne voteront pas la motion de censure', *Combat* (2 April 1966).

52. 'Après la rupture, serons-nous plus en danger qu'aujourd'hui?', *Paris Match* No. 888 (16 April 1966); see also Pierre M. Gallois, 'L'illusoire défensive des pays atlantiques de l'Europe', *Etudes gauliennes* Vol. 3, No. 9 (Jan.–March 1975), pp. 19–36; *id., La Grande Berne: L'atome et les négociations Est-Ouest* (Paris: Plon, 1975), pp. 7–89 and *id., L'Europe change de maître* (Paris: L'Herne, 1972), pp. 57–112.

53. Georges Andersen, 'Coup de grace à la force de frappe française', *Combat* (25 Sept. 1967); Guy de Carmoy, 'Le traité de L'Atlantique nord', *Revue politique et parlementaire* Vol. 70 (May 1968), p. 25.

54. 'Une présence américaine est encore normale en Europe', *Le Monde* (25 Feb. 1970).

55. François Duchêne, 'SALT, the *Ostpolitik*, and the post-Cold War context', *The World Today* Vol. 26, No. 11 (Nov. 1970), pp. 500–511 (which was also printed in German in *Europa-Archiv*.

56. J.N., 'Les Etats-Unis et la défense de l'Europe', *RDN* Vol. 26, No. 6 (June 1970), pp. 1005–1017.

57. André Fontaine, 'Du faux Yalta au vrai?', *Le Monde* (23 May 1972). See also, 'La Nation reproche au *New York Times* d'être imprégné de l'esprit de Yalta', *Le Monde* (19 July 1972); see also Jean Klein, 'Arms control, désarmement régional et sécurité en Europe', *RDN* Vol. 30, No. 8 (Aug.–Sept. 1974), p. 67; Jean Klein, 'L'Europe et les relations transatlantiques à l'ère de la négociation', *Politique étrangère* Vol. 40, No. 1 (Jan. 1975), pp. 59–83 *passim*.

the United States was prepared to throw Cruise missiles into the bargain, and reinforced the Gaullist conviction that one could not trust allies.[58] Nuclear arms control, giving way in the 1980s to the 'zero option' arms reduction, was thought of as a 'Holy Alliance of the Superpowers against nuclear war'.[59] The stand-off between them on the Strategic Defence Initiative that gradually emerged in the later 1980s, was seen as a 'Space-Yalta'.[60] Even the Conference on Security and Co-operation in Europe was regarded by Frenchmen as a sort of 'bargain' between the superpowers,[61] worked out through their 'rivalry-complicity' (in the words of Couve de Murville, de Gaulle's former Foreign Minister).[62]

The political scientist Pierre Hassner, himself an inveterate Americanophile, pointed out that from a US perspective, the Europeans were seen to agonise over US-Soviet understandings as much as over US-Soviet disagreements, so what *did* the Europeans want? They seemed torn between denouncing another Yalta and fearing the rash initiation by the Americans of a Third World War.[63] But for Europeans, 'It was difficult enough to handle first Reagan and star wars, and then Gorbachev and glasnost; but if they join forces, how much room is left for Europe?'[64]

58. Jean-Louis Gergorin, 'Les négociations SALT et la défense de l'Europe', *RDN* Vol. 34, No. 6 (June 1978), p. 56.

59. Daniel Colard, 'Le dialogue stratégique est-ouest et la maîtrise des armements', *RDN* Vol. 41, No. 6 (June 1985), p. 53.

60. Henri Rossel, 'La "guerre des Etoiles": un défi incontournable', *Revue politique et parlementaire* No. 918 (July–Aug. 1985), p. 44; Jacques Baumel, 'Quelle défense pour l'an 2000?', *Revue des deux mondes* (Oct. 1986), p. 64. For further evaluations of the effects of SDI on international relations, and in particular, on European security, see Pascal Boniface and François Heisbourg, *La puce, les hommes et la bombe* (Paris: Hachete, 1986), pp. 121–136.

61. Pierre Dabezies, 'Sicherheit in Europa aus französischer Sicht', *Wehrkunde* Vol. 25, No. 5 (May 1976), p. 231.

62. Maurice Couve de Murville, 'Le système bi-polaire', *Politique étrangère* Vol. 42, No. 3–4 (special issue 1977), p. 254; Jean Paucot, 'L'équilibre stratégique de l'Europe', *Stratégie et défense* No. 1 (May 1978), p. 38; 'Table Ronde: L'Europe: quelle défense pour quelle attaque?', p. 33; Yves Jeanclose and Raymond Manicacci, 'Sécurité de l'Europe et stratégie nucléaire intégrale', *RDN* Vol. 45, No. 4 (April 1989), pp. 23–35, and *idem.*, 'L'accord de Moscou du 12 juin 1989 ou la prévention des activités militaires dangereuses', *RDN* Vol. 45, No. 11 (Dec. 1989), pp. 61–69.

63. Pierre Hassner, 'L'Europe sans options?', *Politique internationale* No. 37 (Autumn 1987), pp. 97–99.

64. Pierre Hassner, 'Zero options for Europe?', *European Journal of International Affairs* Vol. 1, No. 1 (Summer 1988), p. 9.

The Myth of the Anglo-Saxons

Thus during the Cold War, America clearly surpassed Britain in becoming France's number-one rival, but it also fused with 'England' in French thinking: the imagery of the perfidious Albion gave way to that of the treacherous Anglo-Saxons. The term Anglo-Saxons, as a catch-all for Allies who are rivals and cannot be trusted totally, is in itself another myth which as we have seen plays on the idea of a lesser civilisation (that of pre-Normal Anglo-Saxon England) competing with the higher civilisation (that of France). Such, then, is the French perception of the two powers which would be the most natural allies for France in the late twentieth century: both of them democracies, and generally aiming, like France, to spread democratic norms to the rest of the world and to uphold a world order based on the principles of the UN.

Historical experiences of betrayal and abandonment, and an acute sense of rivalry nursed over centuries, stand in the way of a close and sympathetic co-operation between France and the Anglo-Saxons. These experiences and perceptions played a key part in persuading de Gaulle to pull France out of NATO's integrated military structure in 1966, and have raised Marshal Foch's buzzword of preserving France's 'freedom of action' at all cost to the *raison d'état* of the Fifth Republic. This freedom of action *vis-à-vis* the enemy, the determination not to let the enemy choose the weapons of the duel, has become perverted to a freedom of action *vis-à-vis* France's allies, a staunch resistance to committing oneself to close or even integrated co-operation with them.

The result of these myths and perceptions is that France has a deep-seated aversion to close co-operation within any alliance, where she does not hold the leading rôle herself. Dunkirk, Yalta, Diên Biên Phu, Suez – a mosaic of myths which explain why France does not trust her allies and has a high level of resistance to integration of her armed forces to any military alliance structure that is not headed by a French commander. It also explains why France had to wed herself so firmly to the acquisition of an independent – a *completely* independent, not a NATO-assigned – national nuclear force: because nuclear weapons are, from a French perspective, the only substitute for superior numbers and the allies who might supply them; and because allies, Frenchmen have learnt and continue to remind themselves by invoking the myths of famous betrayals, cannot be trusted.

Chapter 13

MARIANNE AND MICHEL

The Franco-German Couple

Cyril Buffet and Beatrice Heuser

> The history of France and Germany has for centuries been one of continuous efforts to come closer to each other, to understand each other, to unite with one another, and to find fulfilment in each other. It was always impossible for both to be indifferent towards each other, for they either had to love or hate each other, to ally with each other or to wage war against each other. Neither the fate of France nor that of Germany can be isolated from the other, nor can it be safeguarded on its own.
>
> *Ludwig Börne, 1836*[1]

Scenes of a Marriage

In political discourse and in the media, we often read and hear about the Franco-German couple. Often, this refers to pairs of French and German politicians, such as François Mitterrand and Helmut Kohl, Valéry Giscard d'Estaing and Helmut Schmidt, Charles de Gaulle and Konrad Adenauer, indeed Aristide Briand and Gustav Stresemann. But in caricature and word, we often see

1. Quoted in Johannes Willms, 'So nah und doch so fern', *Süddeutsche Zeitung* (22 Jan. 1993).

references to a 'couple', indeed the married couple,[2] as symbols of the two nations, sometimes taking on the guise of the national characters Marianne and Michel.[3] Solidarity, closing ranks,[4] the Community of Destiny are all invoked.[5] Some have written lyrically of the complementarity between Germany, the country of thinkers and poets, and France, the mother of arts, armaments [*sic*!] and law, between the French national love for allusions, spontaneity and vivacity, and German *Tüchtigkeit*, that is professionalism, technical proficiency, creative energy.[6] All agree that Franco-German relations are 'at the heart' of European integration.

Differences between French and German views are deemed important, because '[w]ithout a particularly close link between France and the Federal Republic of Germany, no integration processes in and for Western Europe stand any solid chance'.[7] This is indeed a view that is shared by commentators outside of the two countries.[8] The imagery that is used to describe this relationship shows France and Germany as the Motor of Europe,[9] the Pulse of the Community,[10] the Axis, around which Europe revolves.[11]

2. Josef Joffe, 'Szenen einer Ehe', *Süddeutsche Zeitung* (13 Feb. 1996).

3. Daniel Vernet, 'Le couple franco-allemand malmené', *Le Monde* (21 Jan. 1993); Roger Boyes and Charles Bremner, 'Weakened Paris-Bonn axis thwarts greater European unity', *The Times* (29 June 1993); David Buchan and Quentin Peel, 'Odd couple's testing tiffs', *Financial Times* (18 Mar. 1994); Theo Sommer, 'Wenn Marianne mit Michel hadert', *Die Zeit* (25 Mar. 1994); Pierre Lellouche, 'Europe: le vrai dilemme franco-allemand', *Le Figaro* (13 Oct. 1994); Michel Korinman, 'L'axe Paris-Bonn, tabou de l'après-guerre', *Libération* (14 Oct. 1994); *id.*, 'Europa, Europa!', *Süddeutsche Zeitung* (2 Feb. 1995); (Anonymous), 'Couples franco-allemands', *Le Monde* (18 May 1995).

4. 'Paris und Bonn im engen Schulterschluß für Europa', *Die Welt* (15 Feb. 1992); Pierre Haski, 'Paris et Bonn resserrent les rangs', *Libération* (22 May 1992); Josef Joffe, 'Bombenfreund Frankreich', *Süddeutsche Zeitung* (12 July 1995).

5. Jean-Pierre Brunet, 'France-Allemange: une communauté de destin', *Le Figaro* (14 Feb. 1994).

6. *Ibid.*

7. Wilfried von Bredow, 'Die Friedensbewegungen in Frankreich und der Bundesrepublik Deutschland', *Beiträge zur Konfliktforschung* Vol. 12, No. 3 (Autumn 1982), p. 56.

8. See 'El principio de una gran amistad', *El Pais* (22 Jan. 1993); Haig Simonian, *The Privileged Partnership: Franco-German Relations in the European Community, 1969–1984* (Oxford: Clarendon Press, 1984).

9. Richard von Weizsäcker, 'Europe: l'impératif d'un "moteur" franco-allemand', *Le Figaro* (30 Sept. 1992); Jean-Paul Picaper, 'Un déraillement est impossible', *Le Figaro* (23/24 Jan. 1993); Maurice Duverger, 'Une nouvelle alliance franco-allemande', *Le Figaro* (26 Oct. 1994); Klaus Kinkel and Alain Juppé, 'Deutschland und Frankreich bleiben Motor der europäischen Integration', *Frankfurter Allgemeine Zeitung* (12 Jan. 1995).

10. Roger Boyes and Charles Bremner, 'Weakened Paris-Bonn axis thwarts greater European unity', *The Times* (29 June 1993).

11. Lionel Barber, David Marsh and Christopher Parkes, 'Paris-Bonn axis faces pressure', *Financial Times* (23 Mar. 1993); Rudolph Chimelli, 'Die ächzende Achse',

Significantly, however, this motor is more often seen to stutter than to work well, the axis is more often than not depicted as grinding in its hinges, poorly oiled,[12] the partnership between Paris and Bonn is continually 'relaunched', the ties have to be tautened.[13] Most articles discussing the couple talk about tiffs and quarrels, tensions and marital disputes.[14] The Franco-German relationship perpetually seems to be in crisis,[15] undermined by some slight, some indiscretion, endangered by a third party.

What we see here is a myth at work which conditions how people think about the Franco-German relationship, namely as a specially close, friendly, co-operative one. Yet the way in which the imagery is used betrays that all is not quite so well with this relationship. In the following, we shall try to identify its form, and test its content.

There are several levels on which France and Germany form a special 'couple'. On one level, there are the semantics and images we have just cited. On a second level, there is the long bilateral history, which is intertwined to an extent that it is impossible to write the history of one without constant reference to the other. On a third level, the term 'couple' is associated specifically with

---

Süddeutsche Zeitung (14/15 Aug. 1993); 'Kohl: die bösen Geister sind nicht gebannt', *Die Welt* (14 Oct. 1993); 'Pas de nuage sur le couple franco-allemand', *Le Figaro* (23 Apr. 1994); Dominique Moïsi, 'Insecurities, Old and New, Plague the Paris-Bonn Axis', *The Wall Street Journal Europe* (7 Feb. 1995).

12. Roger Boyes, 'Balladur sets out to repair battered Paris-Bonn axis', *The Times* (24 Aug. 1993); Jean Quatremer, 'L'axe Paris-Bonn à l'épreuve de 1996', *Libération* (9 Jan. 1995).

13. Claire Tréan, 'Vers une relance franco-allemande', *Le Monde* (1 Apr. 1993); Peter Gumbel, 'Divisive issues strain Franco-German ties', *The Wall Street Journal* (23 June 1993); Jacques Barrot and Karl Lamers, 'Pour un renouveau du pacte franco-allemand', *Le Monde* (9 June 1994); Lucas Delattre, 'Bonn s'interroge sur ses liens avec Paris', *Le Monde* (29 Nov. 1994); 'M. Balladur veut renforcer l'entente franco-allemande', *Le Monde* (30 Nov. 1994).

14. Willam Drozdiak, 'Mitterrand and Kohl vow to resolve dispute on European security', *International Herald Tribune* (26 June 1991); Bernt Conrad, 'Bonn und Paris trennen 'Nuancen'', *Die Welt* (23 Apr. 1993); David Buchan and Quentin Peel, 'Odd couple's testing tiffs', *The Financial Times* (18 Mar. 1994); 'Chamailleries franco-allemandes', *Le Monde* (19 Mar. 1994).

15. 'L'alliance franco-allemande à l'épreuve', *Le Monde* (4 Mar. 1992); Brandon Michener, 'Can a Week of talks cure what ails Bonn and Paris?', *International Herald Tribune* (23 Aug. 1993); Roland Dumas, 'Amitié franco-allemande: attention, danger ...', *Le Figaro* (1 Mar. 1994); Quentin Peel, 'French-German EU strains show', *The Financial Times* (17 Mar. 1994); 'Paris and Bonn try to defuse dispute', *International Herald Tribune* (21 Mar. 1994); Lionel Stoleru, 'Mark ou Bismarck', *Le Monde* (13 Apr. 1994); Joseph Fitchett, 'French-German military vision clouds again', *International Herald Tribune* (30 May 1996).

several pairs of statesmen, whose policy aims have been to further Franco-German co-operation and European integration. In the following, we shall sketch the second and third levels.

Thereafter we shall turn to testing the contents, rather than the form and rhetoric of the Franco-German relationship: the first test will be that of mutual confidence; the second, more severe test will be that of defence co-operation, an area generally seen as particularly sensitive, requiring a particularly high degree of mutual trust. From that we will draw some conclusions about the strength and future prospects of the Franco-German couple.

Duality in History and Culture

Empire versus nation-state

The special relationship between France and Germany has its roots in the early Middle Ages. Predecessors of both modern states can trace their ancestry to the one political structure ruled by a (Germanic) Frankish king, Charlemagne, seen as ancestor both of the French kings and of the Holy Roman Emperors of the West. Charlemagne, however, divided his Empire between his heirs; the imperial title was not to claimed again in the West until Henry the Fowler established his reign over Saxons and East Franks in the tenth century. But from this time onward, the West Frankish kings, gradually extending their power base beyond the area around the lower Rhine and the Seine, fought to defend their own reign against the succession of emperors of the Holy Roman Empire to their east. Henceforth, the two Frankish peoples, fusing gradually with the earlier inhabitants of the areas which the Romans had referred to as *Gallia* and *Germania* respectively, grew apart, and their kings gradually developed a sibling rivalry, even an antagonism, towards each other.

The West-Frankish ('French') monarchs claimed their own sovereignty, denying the Holy Roman Emperors the right to meddle in their affairs. The battle of Bouvines in 1214, in which King Philip Augustus beat the Emperor Otto IV, became the symbol of France's defiant independence. France's identity, from the beginning of any statehood under that name, defined itself against the Empire, and was thus inextricably tied to it.

This antagonism continued when the Habsburgs turned the imperial crown into their family heirloom, and was only offset, but never eclipsed, by the French kings' equally antagonistic relationship with their cousin England. While the Empire in the hands of the Habsburgs always remained predominantly Catholic, England posed the principal challenge to France, which postured proudly as oldest daughter of the (Catholic) Church through the baptism of Clovis, Charlemagne's Frankish (and thus Germanic) ancestor, (perhaps) in 496. The *roi très chrétien* who called himself 'emperor in his kingdom' could thus cast himself in a favourable contrast to the Protestant states across the Rhine. Napoleon seemed to conclude the rivalry between France and the Empire by summarily taking the imperial title for himself and his country, dressing himself in imperial robes consciously fashioned on those of Charlemagne and effecting the dissolution of the Holy Roman Empire in 1806. But in 1871 Prussia snatched empire and crown from France, deliberately humiliating the French as Napoleon I had humiliated Prussia three generations earlier. They constituted the Second (German) Empire, now stripped of its universalism, perverted into a nationalist state.

While France never again claimed the imperial title for herself, the humiliation of 1871 ensured that the Franco-German antagonism continued, to result in French triumph, celebrated in 1919 in the very place where Prussia had humiliated France almost five decades earlier by proclaiming the Second (German) Empire: the hall of mirrors in Versailles. Once again, as between 1806 and 1870, it was the thirst for vengeance on the eastern side of the Rhine which dominated the obsessive mutual fixation which the two daughters of Charlemagne, Francia and Germania, had developed with regard to each other. Seen against this history, the Second World War has its place in a series of Franco-German wars. On this level, the Franco-German relationship was one of perennial rivalry between two states obsessed with each other, defining themselves as against each other. Just as the French kings defined their own sovereignty against the Holy Roman Empire, German nationhood defined itself against the Napoleonic Empire and the French occupation. It was Napoleon who deprived the diverse states east of the Rhine of their earlier identity as part of a greater empire which had previously prevented the development of nationalism.

This bitter duality, this antagonism between sovereign kingdom (and later, sovereign nation-state) and empire, are present to this day in the French and the German minds. Even in the late twentieth century, France feared being swallowed up by the Empire.[16] As General Pierre M. Gallois, the maker of French nuclear strategy, explained in 1966:

> That which today fundamentally distinguishes the French view of Europe from the German, Belgian, Dutch and Italian, is that … these countries are naturally closer to the idea of integration, as they have for centuries belonged to the Holy Roman Empire, while the French national consciousness has consolidated itself in the struggle against the Holy Roman Empire.[17]

This explains why Germany was seen as France's 'hereditary enemy', and why France as Germany's.

Even so, the two cultures also had a mutual fixation of a fruitful and largely benign sort. Quantitatively, they contributed greatly to the rich and ever-new harvest of European culture, and springing from the same cultural foundations, they had ever-new variations of common themes to give to each other. From the German *Minne* poetry which reflected the Arthurian legend coming from France, to Napoleon's enthusiasm for Goethe's literature, from Voltaire's influence on the Prussian king Frederick II who defied any Frenchman to speak or write better French than him, to French veneration for Leibniz and Kant, from the love that Heinrich Heine bore for his second country, France, to Madame de Staël's adulation for the German 'culture-nation', from Offenbach's light-hearted triumphs in Paris to Wagner's love-hate for the same capital because it rejected him, from Maurice de Saxe's service for the French king as Maréchal de France to Clausewitz's ingenious interpretation for posterity of the strategic successes of Napoleon's campaigns to Clausewitz's rediscovery and erudite study by Raymond Aron, from the mass exodus of Huguenot refugees from France to Brandenburg to the exodus of refugees from National Socialist Germany to France, with experiences reflected in the films of François Truffaut and Volker Schlöndorff, these two cultures never ceased their mutual artistic, intellectual and human exchange.

Thus there was not only mutual hatred, but also the basis for mutual respect, more still, for recognition of intellectual kinship. From this stemmed the regrets which the bloody wars of 1870–71 and 1914–18 provoked in liberal minds both in France and Germany. The quest for a lasting reconciliation began long before the last Franco-German war broke out.

16. Pierre Dabezies, 'Un débat douteux', *Stratégie et défense* No. 4 (Nov. 1979), p. 29.
17. 'GIs als Geiseln', *Christ und Welt* (11 Mar. 1966).

The Statesmen

The roots of European integration, of the idea of a peaceful order to be installed in Europe, went back to the Vienna settlement following the Napoleonic wars, if not to the settlement of the Thirty Years' War one hundred and seventy years earlier.[18] But the urgency for such solutions became clear every time the order of Europe once again broke down in war. For abstruse idealism to be turned into real politics, into actual proposals put forward by governments, it needed a more general change of mentality, a change that announced itself after the First World War, when in both France and Britain doubts arose as to whether this victory had been worth the cost in blood. It was against this gradual (and by no means universal) mental transformation that the first attempt was made to turn the Franco-German antagonists into partners in the pursuit of joint peace and stability.[19] And the two names that are rightly associated with these policies are those of Aristide Briand and Gustav Stresemann.

Briand – Stresemann: The Spirit of Locarno

The 1920s were a decade bearing a particularly rich crop of ideological movements and mass organisations. Among them were the international Pan-European Union, founded in 1923 by the cosmopolitan Count Richard Coudenhove-Kalergi, and the Association for European Co-operation, founded three years later. The mid-1920s saw a new form of foreign policy undertaken by the German Foreign Minister Gustav Stresemann, in association with his French counterpart, Aristide Briand. Stresemann sought to build a new relationship of trust and co-operation between Paris and Berlin, which he hoped might make limited revisions of the Versailles treaty possible without leading to a vicious circle of distrust, revanchism and war. Crucially, Aristide Briand saw the same answer to Europe's internal rivalry, and together, they constructed the edifice of the Locarno Treaties, engaging, in addition to France and Germany, Britain, Belgium and Italy in a pledge to protect the *status quo* along the Rhine. Both men had enormous opposition to overcome in their own countries, while supporters praised the 'Spirit of Locarno'. The Nobel Prize for

18. See Peter Krüger (ed.), *Kontinuität und Wandel der Staatenordnung der Neuzeit* (Marburg: Hitzeroth, 1991).

19. See Georges Pistorius, *L'image de l'Allemagne dans le roman français entre les deux guerres* (Paris: NED, 1964).

Peace, which they received jointly in 1926, made Briand and Stresemann the first couple symbolising Franco-German reconciliation and co-operation.

Briand developed his ideas of European reconciliation further: in September 1929, he proposed the creation of a Federal European Union in a speech delivered to the League of Nations. But the untimely death of Stresemann less than a month later left Briand without a responsive partner in Germany. Elsewhere, he met mainly with incomprehension. On 30 May 1930 Briand presented a memorandum on the subject to several governments. It explained the aim of economic integration as a function of political rapprochement, which was clearly stated as a priority; paradoxically, however, it argued for the retention of sovereignty by the states. The British government concluded from it that Briand really meant to create a European integration, and that this was totally against the interest of Britain and of its Empire. The Soviets, who had not been invited to join, regarded the entire project as an anti-Soviet scheme. Crucially, the German government under Chancellor Heinrich Brüning and Foreign Minister Curtius was vehemently opposed to the plan, fearing that the result would be a European economy dominated by France, and that the whole scheme was irreconcilable with Germany's 'national opposition' to anything touching its prerogatives. Even in France, there was considerable opposition, both from those who, like the Secretary General of the Quai d'Orsay Berthelot, thought that the construct would be dominated by Germany, and from those who, like the Socialist leader Léon Blum, thought the retention of national sovereignty made the plan unworkable.[20]

It took another catastrophe to shake more Europeans out of their complacency about the perpetual tensions in the heart of Europe. It was mainly thinkers of the Resistance movements against German occupation who took up the idea of European integration. This was paradoxical, because their response to the worst ever crimes committed unilaterally by Germany was to propose a reconciliation that drew on the realisation of mutual guilt in the wars preceding the most recent one, and mutual responsibility for their origins. It is worth noting that the movement towards European integration was by no means limited to France

20. Walter Lipgens, 'Europäische Einigungsidee, 1923–1930, und Briand's Europaplan im Urteil der deutschen Akten', *Historische Zeitschrift* Vol. 203 (1966), pp. 46–89, 316–363; Franz Knipping, *Deutschland, Frankreich und das Ende der Locarno-Ära* (Munich: Oldenbourg, 1987).

and Germany, but also encompassed the Benelux countries and Italy, many of whose politicians made crucial contributions to European integration. Promoted by the French Foreign Minister Robert Schuman and, behind the scenes, by the *spiritus rector* of European integration, Jean Monnet, this was built on the European Coal and Steel Community (ECSC), the first truly supranational integration, this time including the newly founded FRG as well as France, the Benelux countries and Italy. Through this organisation, Schuman wanted to control Germany and frame it in economic structures which would make it impossible for it unilaterally to pursue a policy of rearmament and aggression. This has remained the aim of French policy ever since. Schuman's plan for a corresponding multilateral European Defence Community (EDC) was aborted after four years of wrangling; but the European Economic Community (EEC), created in the Rome Treaties of 1957 together with Euratom, complemented the ECSC and took economic integration further. Even though Robert Schuman can be seen as the crucial initiator of Franco-German reconciliation, none of these initiatives were exclusively bilaterally Franco-German; indeed, the Franco-German bilateral relationship was not stressed unduly in the rhetoric surrounding these plans.[21] It was the emergence of a new 'couple' of French and German leaders which revived the myth of the special relationship.

De Gaulle – Adenauer: the marriage of the geriatrics

On both sides of the Rhine, the late 1940s and the early 1950s saw the growth of the determination to end for good 'those civil wars in Europe', which had arisen from the century-old 'Franco-German dispute'.[22] The first Chancellor of the Federal Republic of Germany, Konrad Adenauer (1949–1963), made the integration of his state into the Western political, cultural, economic and defence sphere his priority. But initially, this meant an orientation towards Britain and the US just as much as towards France. Indeed, when Adenauer was a minor politician of the Weimar Republic, he had been thoroughly sceptical of Stresemann's policies towards France.[23] But the French Fourth Republic soon proved to be the most important

21. Ulrich Lappenknüpfer, 'Der Schuman-Plan', *Vierteljahrshefte für Zeitgeschichte* Vol. 42 (1994), pp. 403–445.

22. Fritz Erler at the fifth annual conference of the ISS, 'The Evolution of NATO', *Adelphi Papers* No. 5 (Sept. 1963), p. 26.

23. Andreas Röder, 'Der Mythos von der frühen Westbindung', *Vierteljahrshefte für Zeitgeschichte* Vol. 41 (1993), pp. 543–573.

partner of the FRG in pursuing European integration. Adenauer in turn was usually credited with honesty and reliability by the French, even if they were less sure that his people had undergone a lasting change of heart.[24]

When de Gaulle returned in 1958 to become the first President of the new Fifth Republic, the relationship between him and Adenauer was important for both sides. Even then, de Gaulle's master-plan was in the making. He wanted a return for France to great power status, recognised as such by the United States, Britain and Russia. De Gaulle had a two-pronged approach: either Eisenhower and Macmillan would accept him into their 'special relationship' in a formal tripartite directorate, or else he would seek to persuade the other EEC members under France's leadership to oppose American domination of the Atlantic Alliance, demanding its fundamental restructuring or threatening withdrawal. It was crucial that the FRG should be with France in this enterprise, as de Gaulle explained to Adenauer. De Gaulle did not hide from him even in 1958 that he was prepared to break with the United States, if necessary.[25]

Adenauer, meanwhile, was grateful for the Franco-German reconciliation which de Gaulle offered in return for German support in his endeavours. Like de Gaulle, the West German Chancellor felt that Europe's dependence on the US for its defence was excessive, particularly in view of the vagaries of US nuclear strategy from 1956 until 1963.[26] But Adenauer was solidly opposed to any measure that might endanger the coherence of NATO.[27] Moreover, like the other leaders of the EEC bar de Gaulle, Adenauer wanted to take European integration further, with the aim of true supranationality. This initiative resulted in the Fouchet Plan of 1961, which was ultimately quashed by de Gaulle with his firm opposition to any form of supranationality.

By 1959, having failed to gain for France a generally recognised special position in a joint directorate with the United States and Britain, de Gaulle began to assert France's independence *vis-à-vis* the United States. He sought to persuade Adenauer to become his

24. Ponce de Léon, 'L'espiègle Charlie', *Combat* (17 July 1963).

25. Conversations between Adenauer and de Gaulle, Colombey-Les-Deux-Églises, 14 Sept. 1958. *Documents diplomatiques français*, 1958, Vol. 2, No. 155 (Paris: Imprimerie Nationale, 1993), pp. 341–345.

26. See Beatrice Heuser, *Nuclear Strategies in Europe: NATO, the UK, France and the FRG* (London: Macmillan, 1997), chapters 1 and 5.

27. Conversations between de Gaulle and Adenauer, Château de Rambouillet, 29 July 1960, *Documents Diplomatiques Français*.

partner in this enterprise. He even proposed to Adenauer, at a meeting in Rambouillet in July 1960, the creation of a 'union between France and Germany', without specifying what the content of such a union would be. Yet he claimed to be surprised that Adenauer was unhappy at de Gaulle's request to be admitted to a three-power directorate with the US and Britain, and he showed no sympathy towards Adenauer's concern about Germany's nuclear protection.[28] The Elysée Treaty, concluded between de Gaulle and Adenauer in January 1963, confirmed the inequality between France and the FRG, one a new nuclear power, the other not. De Gaulle hoped that the Treaty would serve as a basis for a defence realignment for the FRG behind France's leadership, to be followed by the alignment of the other four EEC members. In this way, France could have challenged the US as leader of Europe.

De Gaulle, however, offered only oblique promises of nuclear co-operation to replace the American NATO shield. To de Gaulle's great disappointment, Bonn therefore did not risk severing the ties with the nuclear protector in Washington in exchange for vague promises of defence talks with France. A preamble was attached to the Treaty expressing the FRG's loyalty to the Atlantic Alliance, thus arguably frustrating de Gaulle's master-plan. Bitterly, de Gaulle quipped that, treaties 'are like young girls and roses: they last as long as they last. If the Franco-German Treaty is not applied, it would not be the first time in history'.[29] De Gaulle claimed that Bonn had opted against a European Europe and in favour of continuing American satellisation.[30]

The Adenauer-de Gaulle 'couple', the two 'mythical figures' whose 'marriage of the two geriatrics' in the Elysée Treaty is popularly seen as the consummation of Franco-German reconciliation,[31] thus had greatly diverging intentions. Further European integration was systematically obstructed by de Gaulle, while Adenauer desired it. De Gaulle sought to keep the FRG on a level militarily inferior to that of France, while Adenauer sought the rehabilitation of his state and 'equal security' to that of the other West European states.[32] The long-term result was that European

28. Pierre Maillard, *De Gaulle et l'Allemagne, Le rêve inachevé* (Paris: Plon, 1990), p. 187.

29. Quoted in John Newhouse, *De Gaulle and the Anglo-Saxons* (New York: Viking Press, 1970), p. 243.

30. 'De Gaulle va dénoncer la "trahison" de la RFA', *Combat* (20 Nov. 1964).

31. Pierre Servent, 'Il y a trente ans: De Gaulle et Adenauer signent le traité de l'Elysée', *Le Monde* (24–25 Jan. 1993).

32. André François-Poncet, 'Un noeud qui se délie', *Le Figaro* (30 Apr. 1964); *idem*, 'Amertumes allemandes', *Le Figaro* (29 Dec. 1965).

integration made little progress until the Maastricht Treaty of 1991, and even then, the degree of political integration it entailed went nowhere near the provisions proposed in the Fouchet Plan of 1961. Nevertheless, under de Gaulle and Adenauer, the spirit of Franco-German reconciliation was reborn and has remained associated with their names ever since.

Giscard d'Estaing – Schmidt: Cher Helmut, Lieber Valéry

Relations between Bonn and Paris slumped markedly after Adenauer's retirement from politics in 1963. The non-Rhenish Chancellors Ludwig Erhard, Hans-Georg Kiesinger and Willy Brandt were less concerned about Germany's special ties with France. They only brightened up under Helmut Schmidt and Valéry Giscard d'Estaing in the mid-1970s. Schmidt, who as a Protestant from Hamburg was culturally predisposed to like Anglo-Saxons and in the early 1960s showed much sympathy for US strategic preferences, during his time in office, first as Minister of Defence, Finance Minister and finally as Federal Chancellor, became disappointed with US leadership.[33] Giscard d'Estaing gradually showed more sympathy than his predecessors for the Alliance's concerns, and in particular, for those of West Germany.[34] The two statesmen developed a friendship, and it was they who restarted the engine of European integration, creating regular summits among the heads of state and government of EEC members. It was also they who in 1978 launched the European Monetary System and the European Exchange Rate Mechanism, and under whose auspices the direct elections to the European Parliament were introduced. Their reminiscences bear witness to truly good personal relations (through the medium of English).[35] Little if any progress, however, was made in bilateral defence relations.

Schmidt had high hopes for the subsequent Presidency of Mitterrand, who like Schmidt was known as a moderate Socialist.[36] It is of deep significance that Schmidt asked Mitterrand to give the German Bundestag moral advice on how to vote on the Euromissiles: here was the representative of a sister Socialist Party, the

33. 'Entspannung: "Warum denn so eilig?"', *Der Spiegel* (2 June 1975), p. 21.

34. John Goshko, 'Schmidt, Ford to emphasize oil, economy', *Washington Post* (5 Dec. 1974).

35. Valéry Giscard d'Estaing, *Le pouvoir et la vie* Vol. 1 (Paris: Cie 12, 1988), pp. 124–161; Helmut Schmidt, 'Arm in Arm mit den Franzosen', *Die Zeit* (29 May 1987).

36. Maurice Delarue, 'Double accord franco-allemand: pour la défense du franc et sur les euromissiles', *Le Monde* (26 May 1981); Maurice Delarue, 'M. Genscher', *Le Monde* (4 June 1981).

representative of a country that had suffered at the hands of German militarism three times within a century, appealing to the West Germans not to allow themselves to be moved by excessive pacifism to refuse the stationing of the US missiles on their soil for their own protection! The French President was thus called in as the ultimate moral advisor, as Germany's conscience. But it was only after Schmidt's replacement by Helmut Kohl that the myth of the Franco-German couple came back into fashion.

Mitterrand – Kohl: the gesture of Verdun

Immediately upon coming to office, Helmut Kohl, the self-styled 'grandson' of Adenauer, like him a Rhinelander and a Catholic, tried to re-launch the defence co-operation foreseen in the Elysée Treaty of 1963. Konrad Seitz, head of the Planning Staff of the West German Foreign Office, went to Paris to test the waters with a provocative address given at a French research institute less than a month after the change in Bonn. What were France's vital interests, he asked, and how could France be brought to co-operate more closely with NATO on all levels?[37] Neither of these questions received an answer, but the formal contacts which the Elysée Treaty had sought to create were revived.

It was one of Helmut Kohl's chief goals, mapped out in the mid-1960s by Franz Josef Strauss (and frustrated by de Gaulle),[38] to take West European integration further, based on ever-closer Franco-German co-operation, thus strengthening the European pillar of NATO, and from this solid Western base to conduct his *Ostpolitik*.[39] Jointly, Mitterrand and Kohl backed the formulation of the Single European Act, the Western European Union (WEU) Platform, and took their countries through the Maastricht Treaty negotiations. On the twenty-fifth anniversary of the Elysée Treaty,[40] they created a Franco-German Defence Council (although there is little evidence that it has done much to improve bilateral defence relations).[41]

37. Konrad Seitz, 'La coopération franco-allemande dans le domaine de la politique de sécurité', *Politique étrangère* Vol. 47, No. 4 (Dec. 1982), p. 980f.

38. Franz Josef Strauss, *The Grand Design: A European Solution to German Reunification* (New York: Frederick Praeger, 1966), pp. 11–19.

39. Helmut Kohl, 'Deutsche Sicherheitspolitik vor neuen Aufgaben', *Bulletin* No. 21 (23 Feb. 1984), p. 183f.; 'Wörner betont verstärkte Zusammenarbeit mit Frankreich', *Passauer Neue Presse* (19 Apr. 1984).

40. Joseph Fitchett, 'French-German Defense Council: 2 Sides Move a Step Closer', *International Herald Tribune* (22 Jan. 1988).

41. Peter Schmidt, 'Der Deutsch-Französische Rat für Verteidigung und Sicherheit', *Aussenpolitik* Vol. 40, No. 4 (4th Quarter 1989), pp. 370–381.

Mitterrand occasionally wobbled in his determination to pursue Franco-German and European integration: the need to suppress initiatives merely because they had been put forward by his 'Cohabitation' Prime Minister and rival, Jacques Chirac, and, more importantly, the uncertainties provoked in his mind by the prospect of imminent German reunification caused him to swerve off course several times.[42] But it is also striking how much Mitterrand did from 1992 to make up for his ambiguous policies towards German reunification, up to the inclusion of German soldiers in the parade on the Champs Elysées on 14 July 1994.[43] It was under Mitterrand and Kohl that European defence integration was revived and that a Franco-German television channel, Arte, was created.[44]

But the memory that has remained is captured best in the photograph of Helmut Kohl and François Mitterrand at Verdun, holding hands in a moving gesture of reassurance over the graves of the lost generation of French and German soldiers who fell there. The photographs of this gesture have become part of the collection of images that are almost universally known and have become a symbol in themselves. The farewell between the ailing French President and the massive German Chancellor, both at their last summit in November 1994[45] and in the address given by Mitterrand in Berlin on the occasion of the fiftieth anniversary of the end of the Second World War in May 1995,[46] has left an impression of reconciliation that transcends the (limited) practical measures taken jointly by the two leaders.

What is it that made these duos of leaders stand out as special partners? It was the rhetoric they themselves employed about their countries, but very importantly, it was also the deliberate acceptance of the imagery thus created in the press. The relationships between de Gaulle and Adenauer, and Mitterrand and Kohl in particular, were commemorated regularly through photographs and cartoons. Most famous were the photographs of de Gaulle and Adenauer embracing upon the signing of the Elysée Treaty on 22 January 1963 and of Mitterrand and Kohl at Verdun on 22

42. François Mitterrand's apologia with regard to his behaviour towards the two German states in 1989/1990 can be found in *De L'Allemagne, de la France* (Paris: Eds. Odile Jacob, 1996).

43. Jacques Isnard, 'Le défilé du 14 juillet illustre "l'identité européenne de défense"', *Le Monde* (14 July 1994).

44. Pierre Haski, 'Paris et Bonn resserrent les rangs', *Libération* (22 May 1992).

45. 'Mitterrand: l'adieu à 'l'ami Helmut'', *Le Figaro* (29 Nov. 1994).

46. Luc Rosenzweig, 'M. Mitterrand célèbre la 'victoire' de l'Europe contre elle-même', *Le Monde* (10 May 1995).

September 1984.[47] Both were reprinted frequently,[48] both inspired cartoons. With considerable sympathy for Franco-German reconciliation, *Le Monde*'s chief cartoonist Pancho repeatedly used this motif.[49]

Mutual Trust?

The form, imagery and the rhetoric is one of solidarity, of the will to co-operate, to overcome obstacles in order to bring about mutual understanding. But beneath the symbolism, beneath the myth of union, the substance is one of continuing mutual distrust and of French fears of Germany.

Jealousy

Typically for any close relationship, there is jealousy of any third party in the Franco-German couple. It has been a continuous nightmare for the French since the 1960s that West Germany might become the United States' 'privileged ally' on the European mainland. Jean Lecanuet, leader of the French Christian Democrats, warned France of this dreadful consequence when de Gaulle turned his back on NATO in 1966.[50] General Gallois accused the Germans of consciously trying to create such a special relationship with Washington by posing as Washington's prize pupils, in order to get nuclear weapons and US commitment to a revision to the German-Polish border: '... there are more bonds between Germany and the USA than between Germany and France.'[51]

Throughout, both governments have exploited their relations with each other to put pressure on third parties to further their own interest: for example, both tried to persuade the US to be more generous with regard to the sharing of nuclear arms by ostensibly working on the alternative of a purely European nuclear

47. For example, Jochen Thies, 'Franzosen und Deutsche – eine Beziehung kommt in die Jahre', *Die Welt* (19 Jan. 1993); Jonathan Eyal, 'We need not fear the giant', *The Independent* (15 July 1993); August von Kageneck, 'Un point de vue allemand', *Le Figaro* (23 Mar. 1994).

48. For example, *Süddeutsche Zeitung* (22 Jan. 1993), *Le Monde* (24/25 Jan. 1993).

49. For example, *Le Monde* (10 and 22 May 1992).

50. 'L'opposition centriste dénonce la politique atlantique gaulliste', *Combat* (9 March 1966); 'La position française sur l'OTAN renforce la RFA dans son rôle de partenaire privilégié des USA', *Combat* (11 March 1966).

51. 'Würde Frankreich uns verteidigen?', *Christ und Welt* (11 March 1966).

force.[52] Yet the French, while criticising the West Germans for having made their defence relationship with Washington their 'priority' as opposed to their relationship with France, immediately saw a spectre of German neutralism or worse, whenever some Germans voiced criticism of Washington, and would call for greater US leadership.[53] In 1981, one strategist close to the government advocated strengthening the 'Franco-German alliance': faced with US decoupling, Bonn might otherwise be 'looking for a solution in the East' which could lead to reunification and a denuclearisation of Germany. But, he went on, France should of course not 'risk her existence in order to save Germany': after all, 'France could survive the conquest of Germany', and for France, sharing the fate of Finland would be more bearable than either nuclear annihilation or Soviet occupation.[54] It took the stature of somebody like Raymond Aron to argue that 'France is about to adopt, with regard to the Federal Republic, the attitude that the United States and Britain adopted ten years ago with regard to France'.[55]

While German-American understanding made France jealous, German-Russian contacts conjured up just about every French nightmare of the past. Were they the prelude to another Rapallo?[56] Maurice Schumann thought Khrushchev wanted to forge a German-Soviet pact, and that the only way to counter this was an ever-closer integration of West Germany into a European confederation of states.[57] Khrushchev himself tried to tease de Gaulle

52. Leopoldo Nuti, 'Italy and the Nuclear Choices of the Atlantic Alliance, 1955–63', in Beatrice Heuser and Robert O'Neill (eds), *Securing Peace in Europe, 1945–1962: Thoughts for the Post-Cold War Era* (London: Macmillan, 1991), pp. 222–245; Maurice Vaïsse, 'La coopération nucléaire en Europe (1955–1958)', *Storia delle Relazioni internazionali* Vol. 8, No. 1–2, 1992, pp. 201–214; Catherine M. Kelleher, *Germany and the Politics of Nuclear Weapons* (New York: Columbia University Press, 1975), p. 132f.

53. Pierre Lellouche, 'La France et la politique américaine à l'égard de la sécurité de l'Europe', *Politique étrangère* Vol. 44, No. 3 (Dec. 1979), p. 493.

54. Pierre Eylau-Wagram, 'Proposition pour une stratégie française de 1980 à 1990', *Politique étrangère* Vol. 46, No. 1 (March 1981), p. 128.

55. Raymond Aron, 'Force nucléaire nationale et Alliance atlantique', *Le Figaro* (22 Sept. 1966).

56. See chapter 16 of this volume, Cyril Buffet, 'Rapallo: Sirens and Phantoms'; Léo Hamon, 'Le sanctuaire désenclavé? Réflexions sur la stratégie militaire française', *Revue défense nationale* Vol. 39, No. 3 (March 1982), p. 75. Ernst Weisenfeld, 'Les grandes lignes de la Politique Etrangère de la France', *Politique étrangère* Vol. 40, No. 1 (Jan. 1975), p. 10. David S. Yost, 'France in the new Europe', *Foreign Affairs* Vol. 69 (Winter 1990/1991), p. 114.

57. Maurice Schumann, 'The evolution of NATO', *Adelphi Papers* No. 5 (London: Sept. 1963), p. 20f.

with the danger of such a German-Soviet alliance.[58] The Brandt and Bahr-led *Ostpolitik* confirmed many Gaullist Frenchmen's suspicion that Germany put reunification before West-integration, with terrible consequences.[59] 'Far from consecrating the permanent division of Germany', the political scientist Alfred Grosser commented, the *Ostverträge* or treaties between the Federal Republic and her Eastern neighbours seemed to the French to 'constitute the first step towards the creation of a new united and dominating *Reich*'.[60] The Americans were in turn accused of closing their eyes to the danger of neo-Nazism in an explosive combination with nuclear weapons, they were favouring 'the tendency, so far timid but real, of the *Reich* to reconquer the lost territories in the East'.[61] Therefore Germany must never gain access, directly or indirectly, to nuclear weapons, Michel Debré stated openly.[62]

Guy de Carmoy described the French view of Germany's *Ostpolitik* as coloured by the fear that Moscow would hold out to Bonn the promise of reunification in return for neutralisation (as Stalin had done in his note of 1952), and that this 'fear of Germany through the USSR' would lead to 'the fear of Germany as such'. But there was also a hint of pure jealousy: one distinguished foreign policy expert commented that the French were particularly hurt when the Federal Republic 'renewed its traditional vocation as privileged partner of Eastern Europe' in 1970 to 1972 because '*détente* no longer belongs to France!'[63]

Yet West German neutralism was in itself frightening enough for the French.[64] Oddly enough, while the French feared frequently that Germany might turn to Russia, de Gaulle inspired precisely the same fear in Germans. From 1967 to 1968, de Gaulle's

58. PRO, PREM 11/3334, Extract of Conversation Macmillan de Gaulle, 28 Jan. 1961.

59. Centre d'Etudes de Politique Etrangère, 'La France, l'Allemagne et l'avenir de l'Europe', *Politique étrangère* Vol. 38, No. 6 (Autumn 1973), pp. 718, 722.

60. Alfred Grosser, 'Les complexes allemands de la politique française', *Le Monde* (22 Aug. 1973).

61. Pierre Paraf, 'L'Amérique et nous', *Combat* (26 March 1966); Jean Fabiani, 'Pas d'alliance pour l'aventure', *Combat* (12 March 1966).

62. Michel Debré, 'Défense de l'Europe et sécurité en Europe', *Revue défense nationale* Vol. 28, No. 11 (Dec. 1972), pp. 1790–1791.

63. Philippe Moreau Defarges, 'La France et l'Europe: le rêve ambigu ou la mesure du rang', *Politique étrangère* Vol. 51, No. 1 (Spring 1986), p. 212.

64. Jacques Chirac, 'Le rôle de la France dans les relations est-ouest', *Politique étrangère* Vol. 49, No. 3 (Autumn 1984), p. 676.

policies deliberately (and effectively) conjured up the spectre of a Franco-Russian alliance,[65] regardless of ideology.[66]

For Bonn, mixed feelings about France's relationship with Britain entered the picture in the mid-1990s. Some welcomed the possibility of a *ménage à trois*, of a tripartite relationship between London, Paris and Bonn, which might actually help overcome problems between Frenchmen and Germans.[67] Others feared that John Major's Euro-sceptical influence on President Chirac would lead to a strengthening of Gaullists' opposition against supranationality in European integration,[68] fears that subsided somewhat when the very unequal Socialists Tony Blair and Lionel Jospin were elected to govern their respective countries.

Mutual suspicions

More dangerous, because more deeply felt, however, is the resilient fear Frenchmen still have of the Germans. Throughout the Cold War, unease about Germany exceeded fear of the Soviet Union in France. The Germans were seen as 'reassuring *petits bourgeois*, but sensitive to the powers of darkness'.[69] As one French historian noted in 1979, the only thing that could shake the French, protected from any Russian onslaught by the German *glacis*, out of their feeling of relative security would be the reunification of Germany.[70] Indeed, this is what happened. Even if a large majority of Frenchmen professed themselves to be in favour of German reunification,[71] this development conjured all the 'demons' or 'ghosts' of the past that have haunted Franco-German relations since 1870–71.[72] The continual publications of articles saying that there

65. (Anonymous), 'Sperrvertrag unvereinbar mit NATO-Pakt', *Die Welt* (11 Feb. 1967).

66. Uwe Nerlich, 'Die nuklearen Dilemmas der Bundesrepublik Deutschland', *Europa Archiv* Vol. 20, No. 17 (1965), p. 650.

67. Michael Stürmer, 'An open relationship', *Financial Times* (27 Jan. 1995); Jonathan Eyal, 'Will Kohl start to woo Britain?', *The Times* (11 July 1995).

68. Jean-Louis Bourlanges, 'Et si on disait oui aux Allemands?', *Le Monde* (29 Sept. 1994); Lucas Delattre, 'Bonn s'interroge sur ses liens avec Paris', *Le Monde* (29 Nov. 1994); Charles Lambroschini, 'Un signal fort', *Le Figaro* (19 May 1995).

69. Claude Le Borgne, 'Stratégies pour l'Europe', *Revue défense nationale* Vol. 41, No. 2 (Feb. 1985), p. 35.

70. André Martel, 'Défense française: la menace et l'ennemi 1536–1966', *Stratégique* No. 1 (1st term, 1979), pp. 49–50.

71. Sixty-one per cent of Frenchmen asked supported German unification according to *The Economist* (26 Jan. 1990), 73 per cent according to *L'Expansion* (22 Feb. 1990).

72. Lothar Rühl, 'Paris und die Dämonen', *Die Welt* (4 Sept. 1992); Éric le Boucher, 'Bonn: l'exploitation de la peur de l'Allemagne dans la campagne irrite beaucoup …',

is no reason to be afraid of Germany show merely that such a fear continues to lurk in the recesses of the French mind.[73]

But Helmut Kohl directed his campaign for Franco-German entente and European integration precisely against those 'evil spirits of the past, which have not been banished for ever', explaining that only deeper integration can make the return of national rivalry impossible.[74] But the ghosts of the past can serve to make the Franco-German relationship merely a spectre of the promises held out by the myth of a special entente.[75]

The mutual suspicions also concern the respective policies of the two governments towards European integration. As Alfred Grosser has noted, the Germans suspect that 'the French see in the European Union only the means to control, limit and to exploit German resources'. Meanwhile the French suspect that 'if Germany calls herself European, it is because she wants to dominate her partners; if the Germans want a more distinctive Germany, this reflects the aspirations of Germany to be the only one to dominate the entire continent'.[76]

Indeed, while the European policies of the French Fourth Republic and of the FRG converged, the policies of Paris and Bonn have been following quite separate philosophies since the return of de Gaulle: 'Germany thinks of a truly supranational and federal Europe; the French want a much more sovereignty-oriented approach.'[77] In other words, Germans want to lose themselves in the greater whole of Europe, in a concept that is untarnished by the crimes of the German past, while Gaullists want France to be the leader of a Europe that is a force-multiplier for France, but will not swallow it up. The differences are

Le Monde (4 Sept. 1992); Claus Gennrich, 'In Paris regt sich leises Mißtrauen gegen den größeren deutschen Nachbarn', *Frankfurter Allgemeine Zeitung* (16 Mar. 1994).

73. Gilles Martinet, 'Faut-il avoir peur de l'Allemagne', *Le Monde* (15 Jan. 1992); Interview with Jean-Pierre Chevènement, 'Keine Angst vor Deutschland', *Der Spiegel* 46th year, No. 12 (16 Mar. 1992); Pierre M. Gallois, 'Vers une prédominance allemande', *Le Monde* (16 July 1993); Thankmar von Münchhausen, 'Zwischen Unbehagen und Verständnis', *Frankfurter Allgemeine Zeitung* (31 Mar. 1994).

74. 'Kohl: Die bösen Geister sind nicht gebannt', *Die Welt* (14 Oct. 1993).

75. Dominique Moïsi, 'The ghost of a relationship', *Financial Times* (19 Jan. 1996).

76. Alfred Grosser, 'La France et l'Allemagne dans les crises', *Le Monde* (18 Nov. 1993).

77. Axel Sauder, 'Jeux sans frontières', *The Guardian* (27 Sept. 1995); for a brilliant summary of the clashing French and German approaches towards and historical experiences of sovereignty and federalism, see also Norbert J. Prill, 'L'Europe, la souveraineté et le fédéralisme', *Le Monde* (17 Aug. 1996).

also noticeable in the rôle which both powers wish to play in the world: France that of a major actor on the international stage; the FRG more hesitant, still constrained by Germany's historical baggage to tread carefully, with a domestic opinion that is only gradually learning that the use of force might be the lesser of two evils.[78]

Joint Defence?

Let us finally apply the ultimate test to the substance of Franco-German defence relations. Intimate co-operation in defence planning and defence procurement is the hard core of the British-US relationship. Is the Franco-German relationship comparable?[79] The publicist Marc Ullmann has called Franco-German defence relations the greatest contradiction of all French policies:

> France's foreign policy is based on an attitude of trust towards West Germany, whereas her defence policy reflects an attitude of distrust of that country. This contradiction in turn affects her European policy: the French Government aims at maintaining co-operation with West Germany, but at the same time wants to keep its hands free in case this co-operation should break down. By the same token it also blocks the path that could lead to the creation of a truly European government.[80]

A survey of the literature on the subject shows that defence-related issues certainly are among the Franco-German topics most frequently debated. From 1950, when West German rearmament began to be discussed seriously, a majority even in France felt that it was needed to deter (or fend off) Soviet aggression. But a significant minority thought it dangerous:[81] many doubted that it was in France's interest to see West Germany rearmed in any

78. Rudolf von Thadden, 'Français et Allemands: deux conceptions opposées de l'Europe', *Le Monde* (26 Nov. 1991).

79. Karl Kaiser and Pierre Lellouche (eds), *Le couple franco-allemand et la défense de l'Europe* (Paris: IFRI, 1986). Simultaneously published in Germany, *Deutsch-französische Sicherheitspolitik: Auf dem Wege zur Gemeinsamkeit?* (Bonn: Europa Union Verlag, 1986).

80. Marc Ullmann, 'Security Aspects in French Foreign Policy', *Survival* Vol. 15, No. 6 (Nov./Dec. 1973), p. 263.

81. François Goguel, 'L'Enchaînement belliqueux du XXe siècle vu par Raymond Aron', *Revue française de Science politique* Vol. 1, No. 4 (Oct.–Dec. 1951), p. 554.

form.[82] Old fears of the Germans, and not so old fears of German militarism lingered on.[83]

In French policy towards West Germany throughout the Cold War, *le nucléaire* always played an important, often a major part. While the leaders of the late Fourth Republic had been prepared to develop, together with the FRG and Italy, a nuclear force which should have become the force of a united Europe,[84] for de Gaulle and his Fifth Republic, nuclear weapons were the 'symbol of independence in Paris, of dependence in Bonn'.[85] The very decision independently to develop a French nuclear force was inspired, at least in part, by the wish to retain an enduring, qualitative difference between defeated Germany and victorious France.[86] It became clear to German observers that the leaders of Fifth Republic feared nothing more than German military equality, against which the French nuclear force was the ultimate insurance.[87] Not only did Frenchmen fear an abandonment of France/Europe by the US in a war against the USSR, but also an abandonment of France by both superpowers in a war, it was implied, against a renascent German aggressor. Only her own nuclear arsenal would save her in such a situation.[88]

From the mid-1960s, German politicians felt that de Gaulle was treating the FRG with contempt in all defence-related matters.[89]

82. Jules Moch, *Alerte! Le problème crucial de la Communauté Européenne de Défense* (Paris, Laffont, 1954); *idem*, 'Les conséquences stratégiques et politiques des armes nouvelles', *Politique étrangère* Vol. 23, No. 2 (1958), p. 153; Jacques Vernant, 'La logique de Nassau', *Politique étrangère* Vol. 27, No. 6 (1962), p. 508.

83. General Tony Albord, 'La pensée militaire française', *Revue défense nationale* Vol. 16, No. 9 (Oct. 1960), pp. 1583–1585.

84. See Beatrice Heuser, *NATO, the UK, France and the FRG: Nuclear Strategies and Forces for Europe, 1949–2000* (London: Macmillan, 1997), chapter 6.

85. Pascal Boniface, 'Le traité de Washington: victoire dans les faits, défaite dans les textes?', *Revue défense nationale* Vol. 44, No. 5 (May 1988), p. 36.

86. Jean-Yves Haine, 'Les premières décisions nucléaires en France et en Grande-Bretagne: une étude comparative' (Mémoire de D.E.A., Paris-IV Sorbonne, December 1992), p. 124.

87. Christoph Bertram, 'Un point de vue allemand', *Politique étrangère* Vol. 49, No. 4 (Winter 1984/85), pp. 933–941; Josef Joffe, 'Europe's American Pacifier', *Survival* Vol. 26, No. 4 (July–Aug. 1984), p. 178ff.; Thomas Enders and Peter Siebenmorgen, 'Überlegungen zu einem sicherheitspolitischen Gesamptkonzept der Bundesrepublik Deutschland', *Europa-Archiv* Vol. 43, No. 14 (July 1988), p. 388.

88. Colonel E.-J. Debeau, 'Les armes atomiques et la défense nationale', *Revue défense nationale* Vol. 11, No. 7 (July 1955), p. 5; P.G., 'Pouvons-nous réaliser une force de frappe?', *Perspectives* No. 817 (17 Nov. 1962), p.1.

89. 'Guttenberg verteidigt de Gaulle', *Die Welt* (23 Jan. 1964); (Anonymous), 'Die Doktrin des Generals Ailleret: Mit der Auflösung der NATO gleichbedeutend',

They felt that de Gaulle used his nuclear force as trump card not only *vis-à-vis* the Soviet Union, but also with regard to the FRG,[90] and to construct a French hegemony in Europe.[91] When France withdrew from NATO's integration, West German strategists were painfully aware of the loss of the logistic hinterland which West Germany so badly needed, not having access to the Atlantic Coast itself.[92] To most German strategists, it was clear throughout the rule of de Gaulle that French and German defence interests were largely incompatible.[93] In October 1962, 61 per cent of the West Germans asked in an opinion poll thought de Gaulle's policies detrimental for Germany.

With the *Wirtschaftswunder* in the FRG, France's nuclear weight also seemed to represent the counter-balance to Germany's economic might. Pompidou attempted to balance the relations between Bonn and Moscow at the time of *Ostpolitik*, as Jacques Vernant, a prominent foreign policy expert, noted:

> France knows that the Federal Republic weighs more economically than she does. But France represents more than just her economic potential. Her special responsibilities with regard to questions which are the prerogative of the Four [Occupying] Powers in Europe, her permanent membership of the Security Council, her nuclear weapons, the rôle which for historical reasons she continues to play from the Far East to the Middle East, and the privileged nature of her links with Africa, make her a political partner which the Soviet Union has to take into account.[94]

Echoes of this reasoning, which sees the French nuclear force as offsetting the Deutsche Mark, continue until this day,[95] even though

Christ und Welt (21 Aug. 1964); Franz Rodens, 'Die französische Strategie', *Echo der Zeit* (30 Aug. 1964); Carl Damm and Philip Goodhart, 'Die Euro-Gruppe im Atlantischen Bündnis', *Europa-Archiv* Vol. 28, No. 4 (1973), p. 142f. See also Reiner Marcowitz, *Option für Paris?* (Munich, Oldenbourg, 1996).

90. Erwin Janik, 'Atomares Dilemma', *Passauer Neue Presse* (15 Oct. 1965).

91. Hagen Graf Lambsdorff, 'Die nukleare Frage', *Handelsblatt* (2 Dec. 1965).

92. Rainer Mennel, 'Zur logistischen und verkehrsgeographischen Bedeutung des französischen Raumes für die NATO', *Wehrkunde* Vol. 24, No. 6 (June 1975), pp. 313–318.

93. Gen. Johannes Steinhoff, 'Militärische Probleme des westlichen Verteidigungsbündnisses im Schatten der NATO-Krise', *Europa-Archiv* Vol. 21, No. 15 (1966), pp. 537–546; Konrad Kraske, 'Deutschlands Sicherheit in den Siebziger Jahren', *Wehrkunde* Vol. 17, No. 5 (May 1968), p. 228f.; Admiral F. Ruge, 'Die Lage im Bündnis und die deutsche Verteigigungspolitik', *Revue militaire générale* No. 1 (Jan. 1968), pp. 81–96.

94. Jacques Vernant, 'Progrès de la coopération franco-soviétique', *Revue défense nationale* Vol. 26, No. 10 (Nov. 1970), p. 1683.

95. Dominique Moïsi, 'Insecurities, Old and New, Plague the Paris-Bonn Axis', *The Wall Street Journal Europe* (7 Feb. 1995); Lucas Delattre, 'L'Allemagne s'interroge sur le profil européen de Jacques Chirac', *Le Monde* (12 July 1995).

the nuclear force of France, less salient in the post-Cold War world, is now to some extent replaced by France's new commitment to a strong conventional force that can project France's great power status and give it a leading rôle as world policeman, alongside the other permanent members of the UN Security Council (which significantly excludes Germany). Even today, France's military rôle is unmatched by that of Germany and arguably offsets Germany's greater economic power. But how long will this continue to be the case? Helmut Kohl has made it clear that he would like to see German military action only in a NATO or European framework. By forestalling any significant conventional defence integration between France and Germany, by putting greater emphasis on France's rôle as independent actor, the Chirac presidency is positively driving Germany towards becoming a military power capable of force projection in its own right – just what European integration since Robert Schuman sought to avoid.

Nuclear guarantee for Germany?

The touchstone of this paradoxical relationship was arguably always Paris' nuclear policy towards Bonn: before being the instrument of security or death, nuclear weapons proved themselves in this respect to be 'instruments of truth', the touchstones of the true quality of the Franco-German relationship.[96] Increasingly, the contradictory attitudes of France towards the Federal Republic were recognised in Bonn.

It became clear from 1965 that France's tactical nuclear forces would be aimed at targets in the Federal Republic.[97] The story reached public consciousness when *Pluton* missiles was first deployed in 1974, and provoked a crisis of confidence between the two neighbours. France's policy of insisting that there was no 'automaticity' in French engagement alongside her allies was bad enough: it meant that the FRG could not count on France to come to her defence. But the strategy for tactical nuclear employment of *Pluton* against targets on FRG territory (rather than from positions in the FRG against Warsaw Pact territory) meant that France would indirectly be helping Warsaw Pact forces obliterate the FRG.[98]

96. Claude Le Borgne, 'Stratégies pour l'Europe', *Revue défense nationale* Vol. 41, No. 2 (Feb. 1985), p. 36.

97. 'Nationale Atomwaffen geben keine Sicherheit', *Kölnische Rundschau* (6 Dec. 1965); 'Strauss: Französische Atombomben auf Ziele in Deutschland?', *Frankfurter Allgemeine Zeitung* (6 Dec. 1965).

98. Adelbert Weinstein, 'Die atomare "Aufklärung" in Deutschland', *Frankfurter Allgemeine Zeitung* (22 Jan. 1975); Wolfram von Raven, 'Inspektion eines Vorfeldes',

With all the tolerance that a repentant West Germany had for the nationalism of French leaders, tolerated in compensation for her humiliation through German occupation, and with all the German determination that the two countries should henceforth be eternal friends, France's nuclear strategy was a bitter pill to swallow. The concern about the possible employment of French short-range nuclear forces (SNF) cast a perpetual shadow over Franco-German relations until 1991, when France's newest missiles of this category were mothballed, if not until 1996, when President Chirac decided to scrap them all together. From at least the mid-1970s, when the *Pluton* missiles were deployed, the Germans tried to persuade the French to come to some agreement with Bonn on the use of these weapons and on advance consultation. The West German White Paper on defence of 1975/1976 reflects German hopes: French nuclear weapons were singled out as enhancing deterrence; those of the UK were not even mentioned.[99]

The issue was hotly debated in France, where strategists saw the Federal Republic as France's main bulwark of defence.[100] There were two possible approaches: to hope that this *glacis* would keep away invaders (if not, France would try to cut herself off from the European 'defence space' by threatening nuclear use); or to seek to fight the defence of France on German soil, making defensive coordination advisable. In the mid-1970s, President Giscard d'Estaing, his Chief of Staff General Guy Méry, and Prime Minister Jacques Chirac sought to follow the second course.[101] Indeed, the only times when French strategists or journalists ever contemplated extending deterrence to any other power, they spoke of West Germany.[102] Invariably, this was linked to the consideration

---

Die Welt (24 Apr. 1975); Klaus Huwe, 'Raketen am Rhein?', *Deutsche Zeitung* (6 June 1975); August Count of Kageneck, 'Enge Grenzen für deutsch-französische Verteigigungspolitik', *Die Welt* (20 June 1975); 'Atomraketen bringen Giscard in Verlegenheit', *Stuttgarter Zeitung* (8 July 1975); 'Atomziel Württemberg?', *Der Spiegel* (21 July 1975); Heinz Brill, 'Frankreichs taktisch-nukleares Waffensystem Pluton', *Wehrkunde* Vol. 24, No. 9 (Sept. 1975), pp. 441–448; Theo Sommer, 'Le système bipolaire', *Politique étrangère* Vol. 42, No. 3–4 (1977), pp. 268–269.

99. *Weissbuch 1975/1976* (Bonn: Bundesminister der Verteidigung, 1976), p. 51.

100. Vice-Admiral Jacques Bonnemaison, 'Un modèle français de la dissuasion', *Revue défense nationale* Vol. 38, No. 2 (Feb. 1982), p. 72f.

101. Hans-Hagen Bremer, 'Frankreichs Atomraketen sind auf den Nachbarn gerichtet', *Stuttgarter Zeitung* (21 Oct. 1982), and *idem*, 'Die Hades-Rakete soll den Vormarsch stoppen', *Hannoversche Allgemeine* (20 Dec. 1982); 'Chirac's pledge to Bonn', *International Herald Tribune* (14 Dec. 1987).

102. 'Würde Frankreich uns verteidigen?', *Christ und Welt* (11 March 1966).

that it would be the lesser evil, compared with autonomous German development of a nuclear arsenal.[103]

Yet the reaction of 'orthodox opinion' in France to the proposal that France might extend nuclear deterrence to the FRG was strong enough to force Giscard d'Estaing and Jacques Chirac to abandon the pursuit of this policy in the late 1970s. No significant progress was made in this question until well towards the end of the Cold War, when in 1986 the French government agreed to consult Bonn (time and circumstances permitting) on SNF use on German territory, and when in 1988 the Franco-German Defence Council was created. In this context, some Gaullists, including Jacques Chirac, again Prime Minister under Mitterrand, and André Giraud, Defence Minister in 1986, departed from Charles de Gaulle's nuclear policies towards Germany.[104] There was also strong support for extended deterrence in the Socialist Party.

Mitterrand, however, remained opposed to any steps that would formally extend a French nuclear umbrella to cover West Germany. Only towards the end of his presidency, under the Gaullist government of Edouard Balladur, with Alain Juppé (who later became the first Prime Minister under the Presidency of Jacques Chirac) as Foreign Minister, was the issue of nuclear co-ordination tackled. While France had been concerting nuclear strategy and many related issues with Britain since 1992, insisting explicitly that no Germans should attend their talks, it was only in 1995 that French leaders offered the FRG 'nuclear concertation'. But coinciding with the (very welcome) scrapping of the remaining French SNF, this gesture was greeted with polite disinterest among Kohl's government.[105] Defence Minister Rühe explained that Germany had a perfectly good nuclear shield in NATO,[106] and everybody else in Germany was more agitated about the French resumption of nuclear testing in 1995 (which was grist to the mills of the strong anti-nuclear lobby on Germany's political Left).[107]

103. André Fontaine, 'Rebus sic stantibus', *Le Monde* (19 Oct. 1965).

104. Pierre Lellouche, 'La France et la politique américaine à l'égard de la sécurité de l'Europe', *Politique étrangère* Vol. 44, No. 3 (Nouvelle série, Dec. 1979); *id.*, 'A convinced defender of Franco-German co-operation', *Military Technology* No. 11 (Nov. 1986), p. 65.

105. Jean-Paul Picaper, 'Chirac et Kohl cherchent un nouveau départ', *Le Figaro* (26 Oct. 1995).

106. Cäcilie Rohwedder, 'Kohl's Party lists frictions with France', *The Wall Street Journal* (11 Oct. 1995).

107. For French complaints, see: 'Weniger Herz, mehr Verstand: Interview mit Joseph Rovan', *Der Spiegel* No. 36 (1995); letter from Alfred Grosser, *Der Spiegel* No. 36 (1995); André Glucksmann, 'Chers Allemands', *L'Express* (5 Oct. 1995).

French public opinion is very reluctant to extend nuclear deterrence to cover Germany. A minority of French people would be prepared to fight with any weapons if West Germany were attacked.[108] Yet Franco-German conventional military co-operation seems to be a less problematic issue for the French. In 1985, more than half of the French consulted in an opinion poll declared themselves ready to defend the FRG.[109] When the Franco-German brigade was decided upon in 1987, this was a popular idea in France: 60 per cent approved (only 24 per cent disapproved), 58 per cent thought the command should rotate between French and German officers, 53 per cent would have welcomed this as first step on the way to union of the French armed forces and the Bundeswehr, 71 per cent favoured the eventual creation of a single European Army.[110]

Franco-German defence initiatives

Summing up, one can say that between the beginning of the Fifth Republic and the end of the Cold War, France's policy towards European defence integration was paradoxical, if not outright obstructive. From Bonn's perspective, no French government from the EDC to the revived WEU in the late 1980s put forward a European defence option which could credibly rival the gains West Germany derived from the Atlantic Alliance.[111] Seen from Paris, the FRG never gave France the chance with the Elysée and WEU treaties to build up a credible European alternative to an American-dominated NATO. It was as late as in 1987, that President Mitterrand and Chancellor Kohl developed some initiative by creating first a Franco-German brigade, and later, in 1991, the idea to expand it to a Franco-German and then a European corps. It was stated repeatedly on both sides that this might be developed into a 'European Army': once more there was the dream of a nucleus of European defence co-operation.[112]

108. August Graf Kageneck, 'Der Atomschirm soll nicht bis über den Rhein reichen', *Die Welt* (14 June 1980); Pierre Lellouche, 'France and the Euromissiles: the limits of immunity', *Foreign Affairs* Vol. 62, No. 2 (Winter 1983/84), p. 323; Bernard Guillerez, 'En stratégie, l'opinion publique existe-t-elle?', *Revue défense nationale* Vol. 44, No. 4 (April 1988), pp. 157–159.

109. Ernst Weisenfeld, *Quelle Allemagne pour la France?* (Paris: Colin, 1989), p. 160.

110. Poll of *Le Parisien Libéré* of 24 June 1987, printed in Christian Millotat and Hartmut Brühl, 'Kooperation zwischen Paris und Bonn: Partnerschaft zum Nutzen der Allianz', *Europäische Wehrkunde* Vol. 37, No. 2 (Feb. 1988), p. 73.

111. Dominique Moïsi, 'Mitterrand's Foreign Policy: The limits of continuity', *Foreign Affairs* Vol. 60, No. 2 (Winter 1981/82), p. 356.

112. 'Volker Rühe: "La France est notre partenaire naturel"', *Le Figaro* (13 July 1994); Jacques Isnard, 'Le défilé du 14 juillet illustre "l'identité européenne de défense"', *Le Monde* (14 July 1994).

But when Jacques Chirac succeeded François Mitterrand at the Elysée, he decided to abandon conscription, without consulting Bonn on this issue. This negated the concept of a mixed European conscript army, as which both Mitterrand and Kohl had seen the Franco-German brigade and the Eurocorps. Bonn's response was one of disappointment. Kohl and Chirac had agreed only a few months earlier, at their summit in December 1995, on the joint financing of two new satellites, the Helios II and Horus;[113] in the summer of 1996, the German government claimed that for financial reasons, this sharing of production costs might no longer be possible for the FRG .

France, in turn, extended her defence cuts to the NH 90 and Tiger helicopters projects, which in turn angered the German government which felt it had gone out on a limb in committing itself to them.[114] Major joint procurement is undertaken not between France and Germany, but between France and Britain (e.g. the jointly built frigates). All joint defence initiatives which might have paved the way for France and Germany towards a common European defence identity and finally, towards the sort of defence co-operation which one might have expected ever since the Elysée Treaty of 1963, but which never materialised, thus seemed devoid of substance by 1996. The rapprochement between France and NATO obviated another reason often cited in Germany for Franco-German defence co-operation in the Eurocorps: to build a bridge between France and NATO. To sum up, one could say that Franco-German defence relations, even where they aimed at creating a basis for a European defence identity, achieved little of lasting value.

Conclusions: Images of the Myth

The myth of the Franco-German couple is a potent one. It was created by Adenauer and de Gaulle and has been perpetuated by statesmen and journalists ever since. It is built on the unquestionable wish, ubiquitously held in both countries, that any further war between them must be avoided, and that therefore, all profound

113. Jacques Isnard, 'Vers un pôle européen du renseignement militaire', *Le Monde* (20 Dec. 1995).

114. Joseph Fitchett, 'French-German Military Vision Clouds Again', *International Herald Tribune* (30 May 1996); Daniel Vernet, 'Couacs franco-allemands sur la défense', *Le Monde* (12 July 1996).

differences between them must be overcome. This conviction, and with it the imperative of co-operation, has become the basis of Franco-German relations; all governments must at least try to make gestures of goodwill towards it. This is reflected in ceremonious visits to the other capital as the first foreign visit of any new Chancellor, Prime Minister or President, and in statements of deep commitment to Franco-German friendship and co-operation featuring prominently in any FRG government statement on a security-related subject.[115] Indeed, the myth has created its own dynamic. Crucially, the myth is believed outside of France and Germany, and it is carried by the media throughout Europe.

There are some aspects where the myth is not quite as devoid of substance as in the area of defence. Economic integration, from the ECSC to the Treaty on European Union, has been dramatic. Since 1955, each of the two has been the other country's main trading partner. The close alignment of the French Franc and the German Mark since 1988 is a major reflection of this.[116] Popular perceptions of the Germans in France have also improved somewhat since the Second World War. In 1983, 48 per cent of the French thought that the Germans were 'the best friends of France'; in the following year, 57 per cent regarded them as likeable.[117]

If this is the way on which the French now think about yesterday's 'hereditary enemy', the myth of the Franco-German couple cannot be a malignant myth.[118] It is certainly furthering the cause of peace, of European understanding and co-operation. But it is also a myth in the sense that it is misleading: the constant invocation of the Franco-German couple makes it tempting to believe that there is great substance, where at best, there is merely a certain – limited – amount of good will.

For the myth is also hollow.[119] If the test of mutual confidence and even of the willingness to organise a common defence is

115. For example, Kiesinger's first government declaration of 13 Dec. 1966, text in *Survival* Vol. 9, No. 2 (Feb. 1967), p. 48f. For critics of France, see Lt. Gen. Wolf Graf Baudissin, 'Europäische Sicherheit: Kriterien und Anforderungen', *Europa Archiv* Vol. 24, No. 1 (1969), p. 16; Ludwig Freund, 'Gibt es eine französische Alternative?', *Wehrkunde* Vol. 18, No. 4 (Apr. 1969), pp. 186–190.

116. Hartmut Kaelble, *Nachbarn am Rhein, Entfremdung und Annäherung der französischen und deutschen Gesellschaft seit 1880* (Munich: Beck, 1991), pp. 131–145.

117. Ernst Weisenfeld, *Quelle Allemagne pour la France?* (Paris: Colin, 1989), pp. 158–160.

118. Jonathan Eyal, 'The Folly of the Franco-German Entente', *The Wall Street Journal Europe* (23/24 July 1993).

119. See Gilbert Ziebura, *Die deutsch-französischen Beziehungen seit 1945. Mythen und Realitäten* (Pfullingen: Neske, 1970).

applied, it becomes apparent that the relationship glories in symbolism: while the hard facts of operational and doctrinal nuclear concertation are worked out with Britain or even the US, Franco-German defence relations revolve around symbolic parades and the creation of goodwill-furthering joint brigades which are operationally useless, and are stripped even of their symbolism with the abandonment of conscription in France.[120] Meanwhile, it was only the end of the Cold War which showed French leaders the way out of the doctrinal corner into which they had manoeuvred themselves, by designating their 'special partner' Germany as the chief nuclear battlefield for the defence of France. If anything, the force of the myth of Franco-German entente was proved by the Germans when they refused to let go of it despite this cynical French solipsism.

On the French side, fears of Germany continue to exist. The demons of the German past and the imperatives of the Gaullist Presidential heritage are so strong that even a man such as François Mitterrand, who had gone some way towards European integration, was thrown off course by the shock of German reunification: even he feared that once unified, Germany would again fall prey to the temptations of its past. Shortly before his death, Mitterrand told Jean-Pierre Chevènement in December 1995: 'Germany still distrusts itself. But it will do so less and less.'[121] In this context, one should be aware just how easy it is to trigger French reflexes of retrenchment, or to fuel the age-old French obsession with the need to preserve French sovereignty *vis-à-vis* its trans-Rhenish neighbour (whether this be the Holy Roman Empire or a united Germany) by campaigning against further European integration.[122]

On the German side, however, Kohl's generation of leaders is still so guilt-ridden because of Germany's past that it allows itself to be manipulated by France into the semblance of ever new Franco-German initiatives which constitute greater departures from German preferences than from those of the French. But it is questionable whether this attitude will survive his generation, or his replacement by a politician less imbued with the Catholic belief in guilt and redemption through one's own good acts, or less conscious of the common historical roots of France and Germany, or

120. Elisabeth Guigou, 'France-Allemagne: ni rejet ni soumission', *Le Monde* (3 Nov. 1994).

121. Chevènement on *Europe 1* (French Radio), 29 Jan. 1996.

122. Charles Lambroschini, 'Un signal fort', *Le Figaro* (19 May 1996).

the historical depth of Franco-German rivalry. Germany is thus unlikely ten or twenty years hence to be as compliant to France as it has been hitherto, and to make as many concessions as before for the sake of keeping the Franco-German myth alive.

Even now, the deep divergences between French Gaullist views and the views of successive governments of Bonn, particularly with regard to European integration, make the Franco-German couple a brittle alliance: Bonn and Paris want different Europes, Bonn an integrated one, France one she can benefit from or even lead, with a minimal loss of sovereignty to herself. So far, the force of the myth has driven diplomats in both capitals to find ever-more artificial compromises, where the process of reaching them seems more important than the substance. The basic contradiction is thus not resolved, but its resolution is constantly postponed, from the Fouchet Plan to the Single European Act, from Maastricht to Amsterdam. Made pliable by their feelings of Second World War guilt *vis-à-vis* France, the Germans have accepted these repeated postponements. But as the past recedes, perhaps the young generations will have a new confidence, and one day may ask themselves why it is always they who should make concessions. They might not again accept the 'Maastricht broth', brewed for them by the French, which contained 'a spoonful of federalism and a ladle full of inter-governmentalism', as one observer commented.[123]

The future path for the Franco-German couple will be rocky. While the existing level of West European integration arguably suffices amply to forestall any return to nineteenth century national rivalries which might slide into outright hostilities, the force of myths is such that it would destabilise Europe as a whole if the benign myth of Franco-German co-operation were to founder. It is thus in the interests of all sides – including the United States, Britain, the Benelux countries and Italy – not to allow the divergence between form and content in Franco-German relations to become any greater, but to prevail upon both sides to continue to seek agreement. If not, Germany is likely to be driven to ever greater foreign political independence from France, which, although not pernicious *objectively*, would be likely to revitalise the malignant myths rooted in Germany's recent past. Europe had a painful warning of what this could feel like in the crisis over the recognition of Croatia and Slovenia in the winter of 1991 to 1992. A

123. Jean Quatremer, 'L'axe Paris-Bonn à l'épreuve de 1996', *Libération* (9 Jan. 1995).

serious common foreign and security policy for the European Union, or at least for the hard core of Western Europe, would be an obvious solution. For the Franco-German couple is, ultimately, not a bilateral affair – it is the recognition that behind the notion of the nation, there is the variety, and yet the common historical heritage of Charlemagne's Europe. As a comic hero of one of Raymond Queneau's novels explained,

> After all, what is France? ... It is the country of the Franks. Who were the Franks? Germans. Deep down, the word 'France' is a synonym for the word 'Germany'.... What is the most beautiful product of French art? Gothic architecture, obviously. Who were the Goths? Once again, Germans.

One can only conclude, with him, 'Bizarre, eh?'[124]

124. Raymond Queneau, *Un Rude hiver* (Paris: Gallimard, 1939), pp. 164–165.

Part IV

Myths of Germany

Chapter 14

THE MYTH OF THE GERMAN *SONDERWEG*

A.J. Nicholls

The very use of the term *Sonderweg* is by now a red rag to many academic bulls. It is positively out of fashion, doubtless because it was overplayed by historians in the 1960s and 1970s. The difficulty with the term is that it seems to presuppose a 'normal' path of Western development towards a civic culture based on pluralism, individual rights and parliamentary democracy. This ideal system was connected with a social group referred to as the middle class. It was implied – by Marxist and non-Marxist scholars alike – that, by the end of the nineteenth century, 'normal' Western societies would have experienced the assumption of political power and social predominance by the bourgeoisie – as was supposedly the case in France, even though such a class was as difficult to define there as was the *Bürgertum* in Germany.

But Germans have rarely sought to imitate the French. Anglo-Saxon societies, on the other hand, were often seen as ideal examples of pragmatic pluralism to which German liberals might have aspired. When Ralf Dahrendorf posed the question 'why is it that so few in Germany embraced the principle of liberal democracy?'[1] he noted that 'John Locke was no German, neither was Adam Smith nor John Stuart Mill. The *Federalist Papers* were not written

1. Ralf Dahrendorf, *Society and Democracy in Germany* (New York: 1967), p. 14. This is a modified version of the German original *Gesellschaft und Demokratie in Deutschland* (Munich: 1965), translated by Dahrendorf himself.

in Germany …'. So Anglo-Saxon liberalism seemed to be the yardstick against which societies were to be measured for liberal 'normality'.[2] Yet Anglo-Saxon societies are not very helpful when considering the problems facing the German Empire, 1871–1918. The United States of America had a democratic presidential system with a clear-cut division of powers and genuinely federal institutions. None of this was easily transportable to Europe. Britain, on the other hand, boasted a long-established parliamentary system, but was far from being a democracy, nor could its political system be regarded as particularly 'middle class'. It was not until 1911 that the Parliament Act punctured the veto power of the House of Lords. Even then, the hereditary peers retained considerable room for obstruction, and the House of Commons did not rest on anything like equal, universal suffrage until after the First World War. Britain may have been 'liberal' in the sense described by Dahrendorf, but it was not democratic.

Another aspect of the *Sonderweg* theory which has aroused criticism is the view that Germany came late to the comity of nations, and was thus imbued with some sort of national inferiority complex.[3] It might be pointed out that Britain was – and still is – beset with problems relating to national minorities, whilst France is by no means the homogenous national community presented in Jacobin mythology. Most modern 'nation-states' are more or less artificial constructs established since the eighteenth century.

Nevertheless, in this chapter I make a plea for the retention of the concept of the German *Sonderweg*, but in a strictly limited area. It certainly does not refer to national character, nor to deep-seated socio-economic differences between Germany and her Western neighbours in the years before 1914. Rather it concentrates – in a very conventional manner – on the constitutional and political peculiarities of the German Empire as it was established in 1871, and the effects these had on German political culture.

The arguments about the validity of the German *Sonderweg* really date from after the Second World War. At that time it was clear that a major question had to be put to historians of Germany: how was it possible that a society which had exhibited so many signs of 'modernisation', including a high level of industrialisation and urbanisation, very high levels of literacy and

2. Dahrendorf himself points to the impossibility of making generalisations about the West or even Western Europe. See *Society and Democracy*, p. 10.

3. See, for example, the suitably titled study by H. Plessner, *Die verspätete Nation* (Stuttgart 1959).

educational attainment, a bureaucracy which prided itself on incorruptible efficiency and a constitution which apparently combined monarchical authority with parliamentary influence at *Land* and Reich level, how could such a society have blundered into two world wars and a Nazi dictatorship? Was this due to inherent weaknesses in the system of the German Reich as established by Bismarck? Was it a matter of cultural incompatibility between the Germans and their neighbours? Was it the result of deep-seated social characteristics? Was it caused by geo-political factors which impelled Germany into conflicts with other states? Or was it due to exogenous pressures for which the Germans themselves could not be held responsible?

I will begin by looking at the geo-political argument, one which has been presented since the beginnings of the second German Empire and which reappeared with considerable force in the 1980s.

The Second and Third Empires

Primacy of foreign policy?

In January 1871 the German national liberal historian Heinrich von Sybel sought to inform the readers of a liberal British journal about the nature of German unification and the benefits this would bring to European civilisation.[4] He pointed out that in the new, united Germany, the people would not just have one, but two, votes – for the national parliament, the Reichstag, and for the diet of their own *Land*. He admitted that parliamentary control over the executive would not be as rigorous as in Britain, for example, and that there would certainly not be a responsible ministry supported by a majority in the Reichstag. Partly this could be explained by the Germans' lack of political experience and the absence of a two-party system. Sybel made it clear, however, that he feared a rapid democratisation of the political process would undermine the German system. Government required technical expertise. Hence even if Reichstag leaders were to form a government – which of course did not happen until the collapse of the Empire in the autumn of 1918 – they would have to rely on men like Bismarck and Roon to run German foreign policy and ensure the effectiveness of the army respectively. Germany's exposed

4. Heinrich von Sybel, 'The German Empire' in *The Fortnightly Review* Vol. IX, New Series (Vol. XV old series), 1 January– June 1871 (London: 1871), pp. 1–16.

position in Europe meant that no risks could be taken in the sphere of diplomacy or defence.

This was an early and eloquent statement of what became known in German historiography as the *Primat der Außenpolitik* (primacy of foreign policy). According to this argument, Germany's position at the heart of Europe, and her history of division and victimisation at the hands of her numerous neighbours, meant that she had to give absolute priority to the security of state. Popularly elected government was all right for countries like Britain, which was an island protected by her fleet, or for the United States, a continent impervious to invasion. For a nation state occupying Germany's middle position in Europe, democratic experiments would be too dangerous. Hence authoritarian rule could be justified, even if in other respects Germany seemed to enjoy a more 'modern' economic and social development than countries like France or Italy.

Versailles and German apologists

From 1918 until the end of the 1950s, explanations of the second Reich's defeat in the First World War usually tended to concentrate on Germany's diplomatic problems: the collapse of the Bismarckian alliance system, the unfavourable position of a late-comer in the race for imperial possessions, the weakness of the Austro-Hungarian and Ottoman Empires, the revanchism of the French and the expansionist Pan-Slavism of the Russians. It was generally believed in Germany that the Imperial government itself had had no reason to enter the First World War except to protect its ally, Austria-Hungary. When the victorious powers deliberating at the Paris Peace Conference produced Article 231 of the Versailles Treaty, which placed responsibility for the war on the Germans, their Foreign Office set up a special department to refute this so-called war guilt lie, and many distinguished scholars bent their energies to the production of the magnificent multivolume source publication, *Die Große Politik der Europäischen Kabinette*,[5] proving to their satisfaction, though not to that of all their neighbours, that Germany had been guiltless for the outbreak of hostilities in 1914.

5. Albrecht Mendelssohn Bartholdy, Johannes Lepsius and Friedrich Thimme (eds), *Die Große Politik der Europäischen Kabinette 1871–1914. Sammlung der Diplomatischen Akten des Auswärtigen Amtes*, 40 Vols (Berlin: 1925–27). See also Immanuel Geiss, 'The Outbreak of the First World War and German War Aims', in *The Journal of Contemporary History* Vol. 1, No. 3 (1966).

The Versailles Treaty itself seemed to reinforce the arguments of those who saw Germany as occupying a special position in Europe, constantly threatened by malevolent forces aiming at the destruction of its recently won unity. In a country whose identity as a nation-state had only taken concrete form within living memory, fear of national disintegration was peculiarly intense. To this argument one should perhaps immediately respond that nation-states everywhere were largely inventions of the nineteenth century, and that some of them did not finally emerge until after the defeat of the central powers in the World War had made this possible. What is undeniable is that, in the absence of well-defined ethnic and geographical boundaries in Central Europe, an international climate characterised by exaggerated and irrational national feeling would place Germany at the centre of European tensions. In that sense the Germans were bound to have a problem, though whether it was a more serious one than that faced by the Poles or the Czechs, for example, is open to doubt.[6]

Even so, Versailles certainly aroused universal condemnation in Germany, not only on the nationalist right but, and perhaps with more justification, on the democratic left. Social Democrats, Roman Catholic Centrists and left-liberals denounced the treaty as unfair and unworkable. It became one of the standard explanations for the failure of parliamentary Republicanism in Germany between 1919 and 1933. When Otto Braun, the Social Democratic prime minister of Prussia and a staunch supporter of the Weimar constitution, came to write his memoirs, he claimed that the failure of German democracy could be explained in two words, Versailles and Moscow – the latter being a reference to the machinations of the Communist Third International.[7] Both these reasons were, of course, exogenous to Germany.

The same factors could then explain the rise of Hitler and the Second World War – a conflict for which National Socialism was indeed generally held responsible. The nastier developments in the twentieth century, such as the Bolshevik revolution and the rise of fascism, could be regarded as diseases picked up by urban masses and alien to any German tradition. So there was not seen

6. 'The Germans, whatever their history lessons at school, have always found it difficult to forget that being in the centre has its price.' Michael Stürmer, 'A Nation State against History and Geography' in Gregor Schöllgen (ed.), *Escape into War? The Foreign Policy of Imperial Germany* (Oxford: 1990), p. 66.

7. Otto Braun, *Von Weimar zu Hitler* (Hamburg: 1949), p. 5.

to be a continuity between the Germany of Bismarck and William II and that of the Third Reich, except in so far as the need for security inclined Germans towards authoritarian solutions to problems forced upon them from outside.

Critical history in West Germany

As is well known, such comforting interpretations were soon placed under critical scrutiny. In 1946 the most prestigious historian in Germany, Friedrich Meinecke, explained the rise of National Socialism with relatively little reference to Germany's geo-political position or the problems imposed from outside. He argued that it was time for German middle-class citizens, like himself, who had formed the backbone of the nation-state, to look inside themselves (*vor der eigenen Tür zu kehren*[8]) and consider their own responsibility for the German catastrophe, which he saw as the result of a deterioration in spiritual values. Meinecke's views were not widely shared by his peers but, as a new generation of historians began to appear in the 1960s, awkward questions began to be asked about Germany's failure to adapt herself to the European community of nations before 1945, and about the possibility that the legacy of Bismarck's Empire had had something to do with the tribulations which beset Germany in the twentieth century.

The researches of Fritz Fischer and his pupils demonstrated to German readers that the Imperial government had actually harboured extensive ambitions for European hegemony during the First World War. Furthermore, its rôle in the events leading up to the outbreak of the conflict had not been at all passive; on the contrary, it could be seen as managing the crisis for its own ends. It was suggested that to regard Germany's disastrous involvement in the war as an 'works' accident' (*Betriebsunfall*) was excessively indulgent, especially in view of the alacrity with which it subsequently plunged into the Second World War.[9] This began to suggest that there might be something wrong with the 'works'. The decision-making process in the Wilhelmine Empire began to be scrutinised more critically, a process

8. Friedrich Meinecke, *Die deutsche Katastrophe. Betrachtungen und Erinnerungen* 4th edn (Wiesbaden: 1949), p. 6.

9. See Fritz Fischer, *Hitler war kein Betriebsunfall: Aufsätze* 3rd edn (Munich: 1993). This point was raised at the German *Historikertag* in 1964 by the American historian Fritz Stern. See Dahrendorf, *Society and Democracy, p.* 20, citing *Der Spiegel* Vol. 18, No. 43 (1964).

which is by no means over today, as readers of the on-going and magisterial biography of Kaiser William II by John Röhl will appreciate.[10]

At the same time other questions began to be asked about the apparently anachronistic character of German society before 1918. We have already mentioned Ralf Dahrendorf's enquiry into the apparent ineffectiveness of liberalism in Germany by comparison with other Western countries. Although liberalism had apparently flowered in Germany in the middle of the nineteenth century it had proved incapable of informing Germany's political culture. Outsiders, such as the British historians A. J. P. Taylor and Lewis Namier, adopted a critical attitude to German liberals, presenting them as feeble or dominated by national prejudices.[11] Even a more detached and sympathetic historian, James Sheehan, pointed to the dependence of liberalism in Germany on a relatively limited university-educated elite, many of whom were reliant on the public purse for their livelihoods.[12] In both Britain and Germany, liberalism had stood for civic rights, equality before the law, and the control of government by the educated, propertied citizenry. In Britain these objectives had arguably been achieved during the third quarter of the nineteenth century; in Germany liberals were prevented from exercising as much control over the executive as they would have wished, and their political position was undermined by the introduction of manhood suffrage, which gave other – and from their point of view illiberal – elements representation in parliament. For many liberals the achievement of national unity came to overshadow their previous domestic agenda, and strident nationalism became as important as domestic reform.[13]

One explanation presented for the apparent feebleness of German liberalism was that in Germany pre-industrial elites,

10. John C. G. Röhl, *Wilhelm II, Die Jugend des Kaisers, 1858–1888* (Munich: 1993). For a recent and helpful survey of literature relating to the outbreak of war see Gregor Schöllgen, 'The Theme Reflected in Recent German Research' in Schöllgen, *Escape into War?*, pp. 1–17.

11. A. J. P. Taylor, *The Course of German History* 2nd edn (London: 1945) and Lewis Namier, *1848. The Revolution of the Intellectuals* (London: 1944).

12. James J. Sheehan, *German Liberalism in the Nineteenth Century* (Chicago: 1978), especially chapters 1–3.

13. For example, Friedrich Naumann, a forerunner of democratic liberalism, was also a supporter – albeit not excessively nationalistic – of German *Weltpolitik*. See Peter Thiener, *Sozialer Liberalismus und deutsche Weltpolitik. Friedrich Naumann im Wilhelminischen Deutschland (1860–1919)* (Baden-Baden: 1983), pp. 48–52; 70–78, 217–223.

such as the so-called Junkers in the East Elbian provinces of Prussia, had retained far too much power, despite the superficial modernisation of German society as the result of national unification and rapid industrialisation. The middle class, or *Bürgertum*, had failed to fulfil its historic task of breaking the power of the old 'feudal' elites, despite its efforts to overthrow the *ancien régime* in the revolutions of 1848–49 and again in the constitutional conflict in Prussia in the early 1860s. The victory in these struggles had, so it was claimed, gone to reaction in the shape of the Prussian King Frederick William IV and Otto von Bismarck respectively.[14]

As a result, the liberal nationalism associated with emancipatory movements after the French Revolution was overshadowed by a militaristic, state-worshipping form of liberalism which could adapt itself easily to the authoritarian tendencies of the former elites. This was the famous 'feudalisation of the German bourgeoisie', already identified by Eckart Kehr in the Weimar period, but seized upon with enthusiasm by a later generation of historians in the Federal Republic in the 1960s and 1970s.[15] The judgement passed on Wilhelmine Germany was usually negative, and its impact on international relations was perceived to have been disastrous. According to this view, agrarian conservatives and nationalist liberals had been united in their fear of the masses, which were becoming increasingly vocal and well organised towards the turn of the century. The pre-industrial and bourgeois elites therefore sought to manipulate popular opinion by stressing Germany's rôle as a world power – a rôle exemplified by the expansion of the Kaiser's battle fleet by Admiral Tirpitz and strident demands for colonial expansion, demands which yielded little in the way of concrete results. German society, in which the tone was set by a Prussian ruling caste wedded to military values more suited to the age of Frederick the Great than that of William II, became increasingly belligerent in tone at a time when Germany's economic power was growing so fast that a period of calm might have ensured her a virtual continental hegemony without a shot having to be fired. Hence the social

14. Eckart Kehr, *Der Primat der Innenpolitik* edited by Hans-Ulrich Wehler (Berlin: 1965). Cf. Also Hans Ulrich Wehler, *Das deutsche Kaiserreich 1871–1918* (Göttingen: 1973), pp. 33–40 and *idem*, *Deutsche Gesellschaftsgeschichte: Von der 'Deutschen Doppelrevolution' bis zum Beginn des ersten Weltkrieges* (Munich: 1995), p. 194.

15. For a useful brief survey of this controversy, see Gerhard A. Ritter, *The New Social History in the Federal Republic of Germany* (London: 1991), pp. 21–34.

backwardness of the Second Reich was seen as influencing its foreign policy in a fateful way. Even after Germany's defeat in the First World War, the legacy of this backwardness was seen to have had a baneful impact on the Weimar Republic, with much of the middle class alienated from the democratic parliamentary system, and an anti-Republican East Elbian Prussian clique exercising influence through President Hindenburg and the Reichswehr leadership. Although German conservatives were not usually National Socialists themselves, they helped Hitler into power, thereby ensuring a second and even more disastrous attempt by Germany to dominate Europe by force. The result was German defeat and national division which at one time threatened to become permanent.[16]

Was there a more 'normal' way?

The socio-economic interpretation of Germany's disruptive rôle in international affairs was perhaps the most extreme statement of the *Sonderweg* thesis, and one which produced a great deal of fruitful historical discussion. However, it also aroused trenchant opposition. Critics stressed the point that the 'normal' liberal path from which Germany was supposed to have strayed in the late nineteenth century was itself largely a myth. Geoff Eley pointed out that the bourgeois revolution German liberals were accused of failing to achieve had not actually taken place anywhere else; it was unrealistic to think that 'the bourgeoisie triumphantly realises its class interests in a programme of heroic liberal democracy'. Actually the German bourgeoisie had been able to achieve its objectives through the 'revolution from above' spear-headed by Bismarck, and this was 'just as capable of ensuring bourgeois predominance as the different developmental trajectories of Britain and the United States, or France'.[17]

On the other hand the Wilhelmine Empire possessed many of the characteristics of a 'bourgeois' state. Certainly Germany presented, on the eve of the First World War, an apparently admirable example of a middle-class civic society – with law courts, public amenities and a flourishing market economy. In the words

16. This is obviously a very oversimplified account of complicated arguments. For a judicious retrospective view, see Jürgen Kocka, 'German History Before Hitler: The Debate about the German Sonderweg' in *Journal of Contemporary History* Vol. 23 (London: 1988), pp. 3–16.

17. David Blackbourne and Geoff Eley, *The Peculiarities of German History: Bourgeois Society and Politics in Nineteenth-Century Germany* (Oxford: 1984), p. 144.

of David Blackbourn: 'Germany was much more the intensified version of the norm than the exception.'[18]

As for other countries, those in Western Europe possessed either fragmented and politically insecure middle classes – as in France – or powerful and self-confident aristocracies – as in Britain. Indeed, the liberal yardstick against which Germany was often measured, Britain, with a government at the turn of the century led by the patrician figure of Lord Salisbury, whose fastidious distaste for the masses was barely concealed, seemed decidedly inappropriate as a democratic paradigm nor a very convincing model of bourgeois triumphalism. Nor did the propensity of British manufacturers to educate their sons at expensive private schools and encourage them to retire into the lives of country gentlemen suggest that the cultural predominance of the British middle class was so much greater than that of its German counterpart. Certainly Britain had been fortunate in adapting itself relatively painlessly to the stresses of population growth, industrialisation and the limited popular emancipation which had occurred in the nineteenth century, but might that not have been due to precisely those geographical advantages to which German liberals had pointed in the 1870s? The security of Britain, protected by her navy and given economic advantages by her Empire, spared her the fears which plagued continental societies, which is why the British reacted in such neuralgic fashion to the threat from the German battle fleet.

The return of geo-politics

In recent years there has been a renewed interest in diplomatic and even geopolitical aspects of the history of Germany in the nineteenth and twentieth centuries. Seen from such viewpoints Germany's behaviour in international affairs, from 1871 to 1933, is not particularly special, although its situation as a late-comer did cause it to face some problems. It was unfortunate that Germany's unification was rapidly followed by a period in which colonial possessions came to be seen as essential symbols of great power status.

Bismarck was the most successful German statesman in the colonial race, picking up substantial African territories in the 1880s, but he always had a refreshingly pragmatic – not to say cynical – attitude towards such overseas adventures. When visited by one

18. *Ibid.*, p. 292, and see Wehler, *Deutsche Gesellschaftsgeschichte* III, pp. 765, 771.

importunate German colonial enthusiast, he told him: 'Your map of Africa is very pretty, but my map of Africa lies in Europe. Here is where Russia lies, and there lies France, and we are in the middle; that is my map of Africa.'[19]

Unfortunately his successors were not so circumspect. They plunged with greater enthusiasm, but far less success, into the game of imperial rivalry, thus weakening their power position in Europe. Just as they jettisoned Bismarck's reinsurance treaty with Russia, so they gambled away his generally good relations with Britain, assuming that British isolation from France and Russia would be a permanent feature of the international scene.

Looked at from this viewpoint, it can be argued that the German problem in international relations was not caused by any *Sonderweg* or by the inherent weaknesses of Imperial Germany. It was simply the outcome of mistakes in foreign policy made by individual statesmen who overestimated Germany's strength and underestimated the resilience of her neighbours.

This view has a long tradition and is strongly represented today by highly respected German historians. In his recently published lecture 'Reich – Großmacht – Nation', Klaus Hildebrand argues that the Wilhelmine Empire collapsed above all as a result of its 'international relations and its foreign policy decisions, and not because of its domestic circumstances or its social imperfections'.[20] The implication of such an argument is that subsequent foreign policy disasters were the result of quite different problems – the pressures under which the Weimar Republic found itself, or the racist ideology of National Socialism, which was not rooted in Bismarck's Germany.

German Reunification: A New *Sonderweg*?

The flawed structure of the Second Reich

For my part I am neither a committed believer in the extreme versions of the *Sonderweg* theory, nor do I think that it is entirely a myth. Geopolitics, one of the less happy inventions of British

19. Quoted in Klaus Hildebrand, 'Opportunities and Limits of German Foreign Policy in the Bismarckian Era, 1871–1890: "A System of Stopgaps"?' in Gregor Schöllgen (ed.), *Escape into War?*, p. 82.

20. Klaus Hildebrand, 'Reich – Großmacht – Nation. Betrachtungen zur Geschichte der deutschen Außenpolitik 1871–1945', *Schriften des Historischen Kollegs. Vortrag 42* (Munich: 1995), p. 25.

scholarship, does not carry much conviction as a fundamental explanation for international conflicts. Wars are made by people, not by geography. The vast length of the undefended and peaceful frontier between the United States and Canada is a demonstration of the fact that even nations of widely different military potential can live side by side in harmony for generations, provided that they share a level of common socio-economic development and political emancipation, as well as a commitment to the maintenance of international law. For this reason I have no qualms about the international rôle of the recently enlarged Federal Republic of Germany, and I find it extraordinary that some respected German scholars seem to imagine that for Germans to understand their new situation they ought to be thinking themselves back into Bismarck's Reich of 1871.[21] That Reich did represent a *Sonderweg*, and one which was conditioned at least partly by the unsatisfactory manner in which Germany was united. We do not need to postulate peculiar sociological backwardness or sinister traits in the German character to notice that the political structures of the German Reich contained awkward anomalies which were almost bound to lead to political fragmentation and infelicitous decision-making.

The Reich was apparently a federal union or *Bundesstaat*, but its federal character was lop-sided and irrational. Prussia made up half the geographical area and more than half of the population, and could block constitutional change. The uneasy mixture of democracy and oligarchy represented in the German system created political tensions which were bound to be reflected in foreign policy. This situation was particularly difficult in the case of the Reich Chancellor, who had to juggle the tasks of chief Reich executive, government spokesman in the Reichstag, foreign minister – and usually prime minister – of Prussia and, above all, political servant of the Kaiser. Once the founder of this system, Bismarck, had been dismissed in 1890, its weaknesses became apparent. The combination of feudal loyalty to an erratic monarch, progressive nationalism needed to please the Reichstag and social conservatism required for the Prussian Landtag made a coherent policy impossible, even for such a dextrous politician as Bernhard von Bülow, described by one of his most perceptive biographers as 'the Chancellor as Courtier'.[22]

21. See Arnulf Baring's thought-provoking remarks in 'Germany, what now?' in A. Baring (ed.), *Germany's New Position in Europe: Problems and Perspectives* (Oxford: 1994), p. 9.

22. K. Lerman, *The Chancellor As Courtier: Bernhard von Bülow and the Governance of Germany 1900–1909* (Cambridge:1990).

The deep-seated hostility, not only to socialism and democracy but also to parliamentary government, was indeed a 'peculiarity' of the German ruling elite before 1914. To take one not unimportant example, on 1 July 1911 the German Chancellor, Bethmann Hollweg, wrote to the Conservative Count Hans von Schwerin-Löwitz, saying that the German Conservative Party should not lower itself to fish for votes like other parties. Such behaviour might be suitable '... if we were steering toward the parliamentary system of government'. But such a system was 'constitutionally impossible' for both Prussia and the Reich. For the Conservatives to adopt populist campaign tactics would have dangerous consequences: 'The end result would be the weakening of the conservative principle and thereby the acceleration of democratisation. I am watching this unhealthy process with growing concern.'[23] There seemed little likelihood, therefore, that the system would be reformed from within.

German liberalism and nationalism

Here the limitations of German liberalism did manifest themselves in a deleterious way. Denied responsibility, and faced with rival parties such as the Centre and the SPD which seemed better able to mobilise mass support, the liberals' nationalism became ever more strident. Had the parliamentary system developed in such a manner that men like Bassermann or Stresemann, successive leaders of the National Liberals, had been forced to take responsibility for Germany's foreign policy, there is little doubt that far more pragmatism and moderation would have been shown. This was demonstrated in the Weimar Republic, when Stresemann, who started off by rejecting the Republican system, took over the reins of government in 1923 and remained foreign minister until his death in 1929. The result was a policy which combined concern for Germany's national interests with sensible compromises and a successful *Westpolitik*.

The lack of such a conciliatory policy aimed at France had been a marked feature of Imperial Germany's diplomacy before 1914 and a major reason for its failure. If German statesmen and politicians thought of improving relations with the West, they usually looked for some illusory communion of interests with Britain, a

23. Quoted in James Retallack, 'The Road to Philippi: The Conservative Party and Bethmann Hollweg's "Politics of the Diagonal", 1909–14', in L. E. Jones and J. N. Retallack (eds), *Between Reform, Reaction and Resistance: Studies in the History of German Conservatism from 1789 to 1945* (Providence and Oxford: 1993), p. 280.

country without much commitment to continental Europe. Yet in pre-1914 France a rapprochement with Germany would have been conceivable, had the Reich not exhibited militaristic and bombastic characteristics which were themselves inextricably linked to the manner in which Germany had been united. In this respect it is worth remembering von Sybel's fear of democracy and distrust of the masses. German liberal thought concentrated on inculcating the population with a peculiarly intolerant and almost mystical form of nationalism, designed as an antidote to divisiveness created by class distinctions and confessional differences. It was this denial of pluralism which had such a baneful effect on middle class politics in Germany before 1933 and encouraged otherwise rational people to accept totalitarian ideologies.

The Federal Republic of Germany after unification

All this is in complete contrast to the Federal Republic – whether that of 1949 to 1990 or thereafter. Today there is no sign of a German *Sonderweg* in international affairs, although that does not mean that there are no German national interests which Federal governments, with perfect propriety, may be expected to further by diplomatic means. The big difference between the *Sonderweg* of the nineteenth and the early twentieth Centuries and the cautious path mapped out by Adenauer, Brandt, Schmidt and Kohl is that Germany now seeks fulfilment of its international interests in partnership with its neighbours rather than by dominating them. Above all, relations with France have been transformed. German statesmen have cemented the Franco-German axis rather than yearning for an unrealistic *Bündnis* with Britain. German policy is not legitimated by royal prerogative, or by self-appointed arbiters of national interest such as the officer corps or the Protestant intelligentsia of Prussian universities, but rests on the favour of the German electorate, a body which has repeatedly demonstrated its cautious resolution and common sense.

Chapter 15

The Myth of Prussia

Robert Cooper

The Abolition of Prussia

If Generals are accused of refighting the last war, can diplomats also be accused of remaking the last peace?[1] Let us reflect on this tantalising proposition in the context of the abolition of the state of Prussia.

Allied Directive No. 46 of 25 February 1947 begins:

> *Abolition of the State of Prussia*
> The Prussian state, which from early days has been a bearer of militarism and reaction in Germany, has de facto ceased to exist. Guided by the interests of preservation of peace and security of peoples and with the desire to ensure further reconstruction of the political life of Germany on a democratic basis, the Control Council enacts as follows:
> Article 1: The Prussian state, together with its central Government and all its Agencies, is abolished.[2]

Golo Mann commented: '... as the victors were wedded to the erroneous view that Prussia bore the main guilt for Germany's

1. The opinions expressed in this chapter are the author's own and should not be taken as an expression of official government policy or analysis. The author wishes to acknowledge the help of the staff of the Public Records Office and the Foreign Office Research Library.
2. Public Records Office [henceforth PRO] C3690/2877/18.

historical errors and crimes, they ceremoniously carried out a posthumous execution of the dead kingdom.'[3]

The Allied draft is indeed curiously ambiguous.[4] The preamble notes that Prussia has already disappeared; the main text then abolishes it and goes on to draw the administrative consequences. If Prussia had already disappeared when did it happen? This theme has attracted many historians and a number of answers are possible: 1871, when it became a part of Germany; 1918, when the last of the Hohenzollerns left the scene; 1932, when von Papen ousted Otto Braun; 1933, when Hitler put an end to any autonomous government in Prussia; 1945, when Stalin moved the Polish border westwards to the Oder-Neisse Line; or 1947, with the final stroke of the pen from the Allies. The best answer is, probably, that death came in stages. The year 1947 registered the death and distributed what remained of the inheritance. If Prussia was long since gone, why then this 'kick from a victorious donkey to a long dead lion'?[5] The answer, for want of a better word, is the myth of Prussia.

Prussia from British Perspectives

The myth is, or was, to be found on a number of levels. It still exists in the cartoons which restore to German leaders the Pickelhaube and the monocle. And Prussia still remains a slightly humorous byword for the military virtues of discipline, planning and punctuality. At the time of the Second World War, however, the word had a more sinister ring. The Lord Chancellor, Lord Simon, feared that 'Hitler would go but that Prussianism would remain'. He noted: 'Our Allies as well as ourselves are pledged to exterminate this horrible and hateful system from the world. By that system I mean not only Hitler but the whole Prussian regime.' Lord Simon and the US Vice-President Wallace agreed that a 'new war in the future is certain if we allow Prussia to re-arm, either materially or psychologically'.[6]

3. Golo Mann, *The History of Germany since 1789* (London: Chatto & Windus, 1968). See also Giles MacDonogh, *Prussia: The Perversion of an Idea* (London: Sinclair Stevenson, 1994).

4. 'Allied Control Authority', 22 Feb. 1947. PRO C3551/2877/18.

5. Golo Mann, 'Das Ende Preussens', in O. Busch and W. Neugebauer (eds), *Moderne Preussische Geschichte 1648–1947, Eine Anthologie* (Berlin and New York: de Gruyter, 1985), p. 167. Quoted in MacDonogh, *Prussia*.

6. 'House of Lords Debates', 10 Mar. 1943. PRO C2692/279/18.

Or Clement Attlee – not a man given to excesses of emotion or hatred – in a minute to the War Cabinet: 'After the last War the Kaiser was made the scapegoat for Germany and at a later stage the democratic parties were made the scapegoats for Versailles, while all the time the real aggressive elements were left untouched to raise their heads again when a favourable opportunity occurred. What were these? Primarily, the Prussian Junker class with its strong roots in the Reichswehr and the Civil Service.' Later in the same document: 'The Prussian virus has spread very widely through the German Reich. It will take very strong action to eradicate it.'[7] And then Churchill himself speaking in September 1943: 'The core of Germany is Prussia.... (cheers) ... Nazi tyranny and Prussian militarism are the two main elements in German life which must be absolutely destroyed.'[8]

These examples could be multiplied. But they illustrate sufficiently that the idea of Prussian responsibility in the Second World War was widespread among the British political class of whatever party. Of the three, Churchill is the most striking and interesting. First, his condemnation of Prussia is the most frequent and the most colourful. But second, far from wishing to eliminate Prussia, Churchill, if anything, wanted to revive it. In 1940 he was talking of a Europe of five great powers: Britain, France, Italy, Spain and Prussia, together with four confederations: Northern, Middle European, Danubean and Balkan.[9]

Indeed, Churchill's plans to simultaneously revive and punish Prussia runs through the war-time Summit Conferences. In Teheran, for example (1943), in reply to an American proposal to split Germany into five states, Churchill said 'he had two clear ideas in his mind. First was the isolation of Prussia. What was to be done to Prussia after that was only secondary. Then he would like to detach Bavaria, Württemberg, Palatinate, Saxony and Baden. Whereas he would treat Prussia harshly, he would make things easier for the second group ... southern Germans were not going to start another war and we would make it worth their while to forget Prussia'.[10]

7. 'Post-War Settlement-Policy in Respect of Germany Memorandum by the Deputy Prime Minister', 19 July 1943 PRO C10653/279/18.

8. *The Times*, 22 Sept. 1943, p. 6.

9. Gordon Craig, 'Churchill and Germany', in Robert Blake and Wm. Roger Louis (eds), *Churchill: A Major New Assessment of His Life in Peace and War* (Oxford: Oxford University Press, 1993), p 37.

10. Martin Gilbert, *Winston S. Churchill* Vol. VII *Road to Victory 1941–1945* (London: Heinemann, 1986), p. 592.

The idea occurs again in a meeting with Stalin in Moscow in October 1944: 'Prussia is the root of the evil and the Prussia military caste. Prussia must, therefore, be isolated.'[11] Churchill was still expounding this idea as late as spring 1945.[12]

This was, however, never Government policy. After Teheran, Attlee had drawn Churchill's attention to the fact that agreed policy was to decentralise but not to dismember Germany. Nor was the idea any more practical than Roosevelt's five-fold division of Germany. It is notable that at these Summit Conferences Churchill was the only participant to mention Prussia. Stalin, in particular, does not seem to have been a believer in the myth of Prussia – to him all Germans were the same.[13]

Three Myths of Prussia

All historiography, even the best and most thorough academic work, involves some simplification. At the popular level – and this the level at which history meets policy-making – the simplification can be very drastic indeed. Our images of countries are for the most part formed from oversimplified pictures of the past that can make it difficult to see the present at all, even in a simplified version. In the case of Prussia, we have the advantage that there is no present; even so, the past is more complicated than we normally allow. At the very least there are three Prussias, or rather three separate Prussian myths.

First there is the Prussia of Frederick the Great, encapsulated by the motto *Brandenburgische Toleranz*: a rational state rather than a national state, welcoming the Huguenots and the persecuted Jacobites, tolerant of religions and national diversity, yet authoritarian or paternalistic, characterised by Frederick the Great's remark that people could believe what they liked so long as they did what they were told. This image of enlightened Prussia can be overdone; the military element in the state was already very substantial. Frederick the Great himself was, as Maria Theresa said, 'sans foi et sans loi'. Nevertheless, in many respects, Frederick's Prussia was as enlightened as any in Europe at the time.

This Prussia was challenged and defeated by France at Jena. The military reforms that followed this defeat led to a further

11. *Ibid.*, p. 1024.
12. *Ibid.*, p. 1179.
13. *Ibid.*, pp. 643, 592.

militarisation of Prussian society. The national principle that began to establish itself was more powerful than that of the dynastic state. This unhealthy blend of German nationalism and Prussia authoritarianism had, by the end of the nineteenth century, created a deeply troubled and aggressive society.

Thirdly, and more briefly, was the Prussia of Otto Braun and the Weimar Republic, at its heart the swinging Berlin of the supposedly golden 1920s. Here, for the first time, democratic principles enabled the majority working class population to make its interests felt. But the legacy of authoritarianism was not altogether buried: civil service, police, and the army remained essentially as they had been before. Socialism was still-born; liberalism was not even conceived. The transition back to an authoritarian system was an easy one.

It was, of course, the Prussia of 1866 to 1918 that exercised the strongest grip on the popular imagination. Apart from his British grandmother, Queen Victoria, and his British mother, the Princess Royal, Emperor William II had been Prussian and he, in the popular imagination, had been responsible for the Great War. In any case Prussia was known in Britain mostly for wars, and its image was one of officers with monocles and duelling scars.

The Myth of the Other, Good Germany

The myth of another, a 'good' Germany, complements that of Prussian militarism and authoritarianism. This other Germany is Western or Southern, romantic, peace-loving, it conjures up jolly Bavarians with beer, lederhosen and eccentric head gear, or the romantic ruins of castles and the vineyards on the Rhine – so popular with British tourists in the nineteenth and early twentieth century. According to this myth, most of Germany was populated by harmless romantics whose main interests were drinking, singing, and writing lyric poetry. In 1848 the liberal romantics tried to unify Germany but failed, the revolution being put down with Prussian assistance. Later, Bismarck, an evil genius and lineal ancestor of Hitler, unified Germany employing blood and iron. Thereafter, Prussian authoritarianism, militarism and aggression was imposed on Germany leading to the First, and then the Second, World Wars. Refugees from National Socialist Germany, such as Dr Ruth Andreas Friedrich,[14] or Emil Ludwig did

14. Edgar Stern-Rubarth, *Exit Prussia: A Plan for Europe* (London: Duckworth 1940).

much to spread this myth. The latter wrote, 'Everything that honours the name of the German in the world comes from the non-Prussian; the danger however, the brutality and threat, come exclusively from Prussia.'[15]

Another (Catholic) school of anti-Prussianism is represented by G.K. Chesterton. The editor of his book *The End of the Armistice* (published posthumously in 1940 but dating from the mid-1930s) summarises his argument: 'There is a reality called Europe, which makes sense when you see it as Christendom. To this reality Germany belongs but Prussia does not belong. The problem for Europe is the healing of Germany by the exorcising of Prussianism.'[16] Chesterton's chapters have titles such as 'Prussia, The Enemy of Germany'. Throughout his book, Chesterton portrays Prussia as a godless barbarism destroying the Catholic Christian tradition of Germany represented by Austria.[17] Many of these themes can also be found in A. J. P. Taylor's *The Course of German History*.[18] Or in the words of Alfred Zimmern: 'There have always been two Germanys, different in history, in temper, in ideals, and in the stages of development in civilisation. There has been Prussia, or North-East Germany; and there has been the real Germany, the Germany of the South and West.'[19]

The myth of Prussia contains a kernel of truth: Prussia was deeply militaristic; for its survival it had to be. Since the eighteenth century Prussian society was unusually militarised, and had a disproportionately large army. Nevertheless, France was even more militarised during the French Revolutionary and Napoleonic Wars, which resulted in her thorough defeat of Prussia. It was in response to this that Prussia introduced conscription. And it was also true that from 1871 Prussia dominated Germany: only one Chancellor in this period (Hohenlohe) was a non-Prussian and he complained of the complete impossibility of doing anything against the wishes of the Prussian Government.

15. Emil Ludwig, 'Krieg gegen Preussen', *Das Neue Tagebuch* Vol. 8, No. 6 (1940), pp. 134f., 185.

16. G.K. Chesterton, *The End of the Armistice* (London: Sheet & Ward, 1940).

17. *Ibid.*

18. A. J. P. Taylor, *The Course of German History* (London: Routledge, 1945, repr. 1993), pp. 93, 131.

19. Hugh Seton Watson, Dover Wilson, Alfred Zimmern and Arthur Greenwood, *The War and Democracy* (London: Macmillan, 1914), p. 90.

The Counter-Myth

Yet there were defenders also of the other two, the benign myths of Prussia, of the Brandenburg of Kleist's *Prince of Homburg* and of Weimar democracy. These include Sebastian Haffner and Christian von Krockow.[20] Taken together, these two myths are popularised as follows: Prussia can hardly be accused of the nationalist excesses of twentieth-century Germany since Prussia was not itself a nation-state, but a dynastic state, a survivor of a previous order. Its history of tolerance, its incorporation of Huguenots, Scots and Slavs speak for themselves. In the nineteenth century facilities were still available in schools, for example, for the teaching of Polish language and culture. Up to a point at least, it was even tolerant of the Jews – and there were many Jews who were deeply attached to it, such as Walter Rathenau (Jewish Foreign Minister in the Weimar Republic, assassinated by an anti-Semite). In 1870 the last truly Prussian army included sixty Jewish officers; in 1914 the German army had not one (though during the war they were readmitted).[21]

At least some of the elements of German policy in the run-up to the First World War were distinctly un-Prussian. The naval building programme was one: Prussia would never have dreamed of being either a *Weltmacht* or a naval power. In fact, one of the earlier proposals for a German Navy and for a German Empire came from the Paulskirche Assembly, of the 1848 revolutionary liberals – a German, liberal, and anti-Prussian gathering. The naval programme itself was driven by a (rather un-Prussian) mass movement, fuelled by (un-Prussian) industrial interests and officered from the German bourgeoisie. The army, of course, remained the domain of the Prussian aristocracy who resisted its expansion since that would have meant diluting its class basis.[22]

Finally, the resistance to Hitler came out of Prussia more than anywhere else. First, Prussia was the stronghold of social

20. For example, Sebastian Haffner and Wolfgang Venohr (eds), *Preussische Profile* (Frankfurt: Ullstein, 1990); Sebastian Haffner, *The Rise and Fall of Prussia*, trans. Ewald Osers (London: Weidenfeld & Nicolson, 1980); Christian Graf von Krockow, *Preussen – Eine Bilanz* (Stuttgart: Deutsche Verlags Anstalt, 1993). In the English-speaking world MacDonogh also belong to this school.

21. Emilio Willems, *A Way of Life and Death: Three Centuries of Prussian-German Militarism* (Nashville Tennessee: Vanderbilt University Press, 1986).

22. See Sebastian Haffner, *Von Bismarck zu Hitler* (Munich: Kindler, 1987), p. 11. Engl. translation by Jean Steinberg, *Germany's Self-Destruction: Germany from Bismarck to Hitler* (London: Simon & Schuster, 1989).

democracy. Until the administrative coup against the Prussian administration and *Landtag* (1932 and 1933) it had been the most solidly Socialist and democratic of all the *Länder*. The Prussian Minister President, Otto Braun, believed that strengthening Prussia as a bastion against the National-Socialist party was the best way to save Germany. Yet August Bebel, one of the founders of German Social Democracy, called Prussia 'the deadly enemy of all democracy'. Another of the founding fathers of the SPD, Wilhelm Liebknecht, regarded Prussia's abolition as a priority.[23] And Bismarck, the arch Prussian, was also the scourge of the Social Democrats. Still, it is striking how many Social Democrat leaders were Prussian.

And how few 'Nazis'. Prussia remained relatively untouched by National Socialism until after 1928. In the elections in 1928 the NSDAP scored less than 3 per cent. Christian von Krockow calculates that there were disproportionately few Prussians associated with the leadership of the National Socialist Party – only 3.4 per cent; in proportion to the population it should have been 60 or 70 per cent.[24]

Most famously, the majority of those in the 20 July bomb plot were Prussian officers. For all that their numbers were limited and that for some the shift to active resistance came late in the war after defeat had become inevitable, they nevertheless represented an honourable part of the Prussian tradition.

Myth and Decision-Making

How, in view of all these myths, did those who were ultimately responsible for its abolition think of Prussia? The people concerned were mostly to be found in the British Foreign Office (FO). Among other war-time Allies, only the Poles – for rather different reasons – seem to have attached any importance to breaking up Prussia.

Thinking in the Foreign Office was more sober than among the pamphleteers and rather more balanced historically.[25] The FO view on Prussia is developed in a number of different papers. From the start, a nonpolemical view was taken. An FO

23. Gordon Craig, *The End of Prussia* (Madison: University of Wisconsin Press, 1984), p. 70.

24. Von Krockow, *Preussen – Eine Bilanz*, p. 6.

25. 'Views of Allied Governments on Policy towards Germany'. PRO C14672/279/18.

paper of February 1943, discussing the future of Germany after the war, says,

> After this War the blame for the disastrous policy pursued will rest on the National Socialists, whose regime is not based on the power of Prussia. Its foundations are ideological not local, and all parts of the Reich have been in varying degrees affected by it. In fact, National Socialism was at one stage the strongest in Bavaria and Thüringia and weakest in Prussia itself.[26]

A further paper by J. S. Troutbeck, Counsellor in the FO argued that the choice for Germany will be between a unitary state (*Einheitsstaat)* and a federal state (*Bundesstaat)*. Prussia is intimately connected with the former: '... the very structure of the "Einheitsstaat" reflects historic efforts of Prussia during the last 200 years to impose its will first on the German nation and then on the entire world.' Yet

> ... it is also possible to exaggerate the influence which Prussia now has on other parts of Germany, seeing that the Nazi revolution, which undoubtedly welded Germans together as nothing had ever done before, was not founded uniquely on the Prussian tradition, though historically, and to some extent in practice, it expanded and developed the role and mission of Prussia. In any case Prussia still remains, and it is possible that if we could achieve the dissolution of that entity, it would be a step in the right direction.[27]

In June of the same year we find a paper by John Wheeler-Bennett. He argued against the Prussian myth (pan-Germanism began in Mainz, Leipzig and Munich, not in Prussia; National Socialism began in Bavaria and a good deal of the German High Command came from the South, etc.). He then argued against those non-Prussian German émigrés who support breaking Germany up and finally concluded – as did many other FO papers at the time – that the best solution for Germany in the future would be federalism:

> British influence should be directed towards maintaining the Reich as such, while encouraging a separatist tendency within its framework, with particular emphasis on the weakening of Prussia not only in influence but in territorial extent. The federal capital of such a state should certainly be removed from Berlin, and those parts of the Prussian state in which separatist activities exist – such

26. 'Possible Developments in Germany before, during and after a Military Collapse', 17 Feb. 1943. PRO C1818/279/18.
27. 'Some Thoughts on the Future of Germany', Mar. 1943. PRO C2863/279/18.

> as Hanover, Schleswig-Holstein, Westphalia, Hesse, etc. – should be stimulated to secede and apply for autonomous membership in the federal Reich.[28]

This approach to Prussia was widely shared in the FO. For example, in a Research Department memorandum on the dismemberment of Germany (August 1943):

> When one turns to the large state solution there are certain preliminary principles which can be laid down. First, Prussia must be divided. This is necessary for psychological reasons since the history of Prussia is the history of the unification of Germany and the existence of Prussia in its present or pre-war form was the main obstacle to the working of any decentralised system of government.[29]

Llewellyn Woodward, a historian turned FO official, noted that 'the view that Prussian militarism is the outstanding danger to Europe looks too much to the past' and that Prussia was by no means responsible for National Socialism: 'Hitler is not merely Austrian by birth, he owes his doctrine to Vienna and not to Potsdam.'[30] Attempting to prevent German unity would be futile in the long run. T.H. Marshall of the Research Department agreed: '... it is the dismemberment of Prussia, not of Germany, that is needed.'[31] By the end of 1943, this stream of thought had become the orthodoxy so that late in 1944 Anthony Eden, the Foreign Secretary minuted the need 'to secure what appears to me a vital point viz. the dissolution of Prussia whether into federal states or into administrative areas'.[32]

The FO consensus was thus not that Prussia, nor the Prussian tradition were bad; rather, that the abolition of Prussia was necessary for essentially practical reasons – that a federation in Germany could not work properly if one of the states within the federation was markedly more powerful than the rest. Prussia had to be abolished in order to create a decentralised, federal Germany. As a submission to the War Cabinet on confederation, federation and decentralisation of the German state summarised this: the elimination of Prussia was a necessary part of creating a decentralised German state. This served as the intellectual basis for Allied Directive No. 46.[33]

28. 'On What to Do with Germany', 31 May 1943. PRO C6883/279/18.
29. 'The Dismemberment of Germany', 5 Aug. 1943. PRO C9040/279/18.
30. 'The German Reich', 15 Dec. 1943. PRO C15375/279/18.
31. *Ibid.*
32. 'The Dismemberment of Germany', 20 Sep. 1944. PRO C12806/146/18.
33. 'Confederation, Federation and Decentralisation of the German State and the Dismemberment of Prussia', Annex II PRO C16550/146/18.

The heroes of this short story are thus the bureaucrats.[34] They seem to have remained uninfected by the rhetoric of the politicians and the pamphleteers. Together with Eden and Attlee, they managed to circumvent Churchill's romantic wish to re-instate (and punish) Prussia while dismembering Germany. The bureaucrats' reasons for abolishing Prussia had little to do with any popular wish for revenge, though this no doubt helped obtain political support for their approach. Instead their plans were based on a reasonable analysis on what will make a post-war Germany better: the advantages of genuine federalism and the impossibility of realising this while the size of Prussia unbalanced Germany. One can only say that their erudition and intelligence, and their success in ignoring the excesses of their political masters, remind one of the best traditions of Prussian bureaucracy.

What Is Left Today?

What of the myths of Prussia since then? It is tempting to see the Federal Republic as a kind of anti-Prussia. Mirabeau once remarked that Prussia was not a state at all but an army. In contrast to this, the Federal Republic insists that its soldiers are first and foremost citizens. Instead of the militarisation of the state, we have the civilianisation of the army. Bismarck's famous dictum, 'the great questions of the time will be decided not by speeches and majority decisions, but by blood and iron' is precisely reversed in the Federal Republic. The world is seen almost wholly in terms of speeches and majority decisions; blood and iron are anathema.

The GDR, by contrast, could be cast as a sort of disfigured successor to Prussia. Its location was partly coincident with Prussia; like Prussia the GDR was a non-national state, while its ethos as an authoritarian, rather puritan and militarised society, bears a passing resemblance to at least one part of the Prussian myth. The re-erection of a statue of Frederick the Great in East Berlin suggests a certain attraction.

After the fall of the Wall, there is perhaps some new nostalgia for Prussia – fortunately, not for the Prussia of militarism, but for the *Brandenburgische Toleranz*. The Federal Chancellor's attendance

34. Incidentally, several of the 'bureaucrats' praised here were historians by training. - *Editors' note.*

at the elaborate reburial of Frederick the Great at Potsdam was perhaps less a reference to any particular view of Prussia and more a Rhinelander's wish to demonstrate his commitment to a united Germany.

We conclude that the admirers and detractors of Prussia are usually talking about different Prussias. Countries change over time; only the myths remained constant. But myths of earlier ages of heroism and virtue can do good as much as harm. Perhaps it does not matter if we remember the future and invent the past. And as for Prussia: *de mortuis nihil nisi bonum.*

Chapter 16

RAPALLO

Sirens and Phantoms

Cyril Buffet

The directing line of German policy has always been:
static in the West, dynamic in the East.
Rudolf Nadolny, 9 January 1934[1]

A thunderclap echoed in the diplomatic skies on the Sunday of Easter, 1922, when in Rapallo, the Weimar Republic and Soviet Russia concluded an agreement to normalise their diplomatic relations. The signing of the treaty by the German and Russian ministers of foreign affairs, Walter Rathenau and Georgij Vassilevich Chicherin, created a tempest in Europe.

Ever since, every suggestion of a Russian-German rapprochement has immediately been perceived as a resurgence of Rapallo. This name has become a historical reference which serves equally as an evocation of danger and as a temptation. In 1922, a new myth of international relations was thus created, even if it drew on previous events. The myth of Rapallo, just as other myths, effectively blocks further reflection, simplifies facts and actions, and furnishes a simple interpretational pattern for new situations

1. Quoted in Peter Krüger, 'A Rainy Day, April 16, 1922: The Rapallo Treaty and the Cloudy Perspective for German Foreign Policy', in Carole Fink, Axel Frohn and Jürgen Heideking (eds), *Genoa, Rapallo, and European Reconstruction in 1922* (Cambridge: Cambridge University Press, 1991), p. 58.

by showing them as repetitions of the past.[2] Such myths resurface regularly, even though the conditions which created them in the first place have disappeared a long time ago. But the images remain alive, because they constitute historical points of reference in an uncertain present and future.

The circumstances of the birth of this as of any other myth are very important. Rapallo came at a very particular moment; it is this that gives it its great memorability. At a time when they were invited to an international conference at Genoa which was supposed to address the delicate question of reparations, Germany and Russia decided to break away and come to an agreement on their own, much to the surprise of everybody else. This shocked the Western Powers as it seemed to upset the peace-order of Versailles, threatening instability. But for Germany and Russia, they held out a different option of foreign policy-making. Thus, as we shall see, the myth of Rapallo assumed different natures, that of the repulsive phantom or the alluring siren, depending on the angle from which it was seen and the purpose for which it was invoked.

Red Cloud

For the Germans and the Soviets in 1922, Rapallo had at once the same and a differing significance. The two pariahs of the international system, humiliated by the Western Powers, at Rapallo recovered their freedom of action. As depicted on the cover of the German magazine *Simplicissimus*, Rapallo was the Easterly resurrection of the two countries, impoverished but proud, which helped each other mutually to climb out of the grave-like hole into which war and defeat had pushed them.[3] They saw themselves as victims of the iniquitous Versailles order. Their treaty, by contrast, was inspired by equality and reciprocity.

Germany was particularly concerned to show itself doubly righteous, on the one hand accusing the West of having obliged it to ally with the East, on the other hand posing as defender of the European balance of powers. Baron Ago von Maltzan, who, as head of the Eastern Department of the German Foreign Office, together with Chancellor Joseph Wirth, was one of the main initiators of the Rapallo Treaty (the realisation of the active *Ostpolitik*

2. See Roland Barthes, *Mythologies* (Paris: Ed. du Seuil, 1957), pp. 230–231; Roger Caillois, *Le mythe et l'homme* (Paris: Gallimard, 1938), pp. 26–29.

3. *Simplicissimus* No. 6 (10 May 1922).

which he had been building up over the past year[4]) explained that Germany, already under strong pressure from the British and the French, was in addition threatened by a possible understanding between the West and Russia.[5] Rapallo was thus a prevention of the complete encirclement of Germany. Therefore the Germans did not understand, or feigned surprise at, the uproar created by this agreement. Speaking to the Reichstag in May 1922, Wirth declared that the Rapallo agreement 'is an honest and serious work of peace', 'an exemplary peace treaty', which created 'neither victor nor vanquished', 'a bridge between East and West'.[6] Even though he showed himself more reserved with regard to Rapallo, Rathenau, two weeks before his assassination, talked about his country's calling to be the hinge between the two parts of the Continent, particularly as Germany and Russia had experienced the same fate – defeat.[7]

A strong minority of Germans opposed the treaty, including the extremists who proceeded to murder Rathenau, its signatory. Popularised by the German press on the eve of the conference of Genoa, the idea of a 'community of fate' between the two great defeated powers of the First World War was subsequently taken up by many German leaders, including Gustav Stresemann.[8] General Hans von Seeckt, chief of the *Reichswehr*, commented in April 1922 on a 'very noticeable strengthening of the German presence in the world'.[9] Thanks to Rapallo, Germany came out of its isolation and could once more act as a great power.[10] Rapallo was thus regarded as positive by certain circles in Germany, because the agreement allowed Germany to free itself (or to give the impression of freeing itself) from a burdened past and to regain its lost status. Germans who thought thus dismissed the accusation that the agreement was a betrayal of Western interest in the

4. Hermann Graml, 'Die Rapallo-Politik im Urteil der westdeutschen Forschung', *Vierteljahrshefte für Zeitgeschichte* No. 3 (July 1970), pp. 366–391.

5. Wipert von Blücher, *Deutschlands Weg nach Rapallo. Erinnerungen eines Mannes aus dem zweiten Gliede* (Wiesbaden: Limes Verlag, 1951), pp. 162–165.

6. Quoted by Ulrike Hörster-Philipps, Norman Paech, Erich Rossmann, Christoph Strässer, *Rapallo-Modelle für Europa?* (Cologne: Pahl-Rugenstein, 1987), p. 93.

7. Walther Rathenau, *Schriften* (Berlin-West: Berlin Verlag, 1965), pp. 360–361.

8. Theodor Schieder, *Die Probleme des Rapallo-Vertrages. Eine Studie über die deutsch-russischen Beziehungen 1922 bis 1926* (Cologne: Westdeutscher Verlag, 1956), p. 56.

9. Quoted by F. L. Carsten, *Reichswehr und Politik 1867–1933* (Cologne: Verlag Wissenschaft und Politik, 1965), p. 144.

10. Hans Wilderotter (ed.), *Walther Rathenau 1867–1922: Die Extreme berühren sich* (Berlin: Argon, 1994), p. 418.

name of *Realpolitik*, because they thought they had simply beaten the others to a treaty with Russia. They wanted to prevent the West from playing off the East against Germany, by seeking to play off the East against the West themselves, as Chancellor Wirth confided in March 1922 to his ministers: '[G]ood relations with Russia ... can reduce Western pressures.'[11] Stresemann shared this view, and, on the eve of his death, he continued to see in the USSR a 'trump against the West'.[12] Maltzan said in Genoa that 'we need the Russian cloud over Europe'.[13]

Despite this, the greater freedom of action which Germany had gained through Rapallo was precisely what worried the French, the British and also the Poles. Clemenceau said bitterly that Germany 'was resuming its independence before the eyes of the world'.[14] Even some German ministers opposed the treaty, fearful of Western reactions.[15] The treaty evoked hefty debates within the German government, but was finally ratified by the *Reichstag* in July 1922. The contradictory reactions to the treaty among public opinion and the German political elite determined the later view of Rapallo, so that no unanimity as to the meaning of this historical reference emerged within Germany, and Rapallo became the pawn of ideological controversies, particularly in the 1950s and 1980s.

For the diplomacy of young Bolshevik Russia, Rapallo was uncontestedly a great success. Russia derived substantial advantages from it: not only did the USSR, too, break out of its isolation and receive its international recognition, but it also managed to break the Capitalist front and to sharpen disagreement among the Allies. As a consequence, the image of Rapallo was, from the beginning, a thoroughly positive one for the Soviets, so much more so as the treaty was presented as a manifestation of peace, solidarity, fraternity, even if Moscow was trying at the same time to prevent the West from playing Germany off against the USSR. Taking up in turn the idea of a 'community of destiny', Chicherin

11. Quoted by Hartmut Pogge von Strandmann, 'Rapallo-Strategy in preventive diplomacy: New sources and new interpretations' in Volker Berghahn and Martin Kitchen (eds), *Germany in the Age of Total War* (London: Croom Helm, 1981), p. 130.

12. Quoted by Hans W. Gatzke, 'Von Rapallo nach Berlin. Stresemann und die deutsche Russlandpolitik', *Vierteljahrshefte für Zeitgeschichte* Vol. 4 No. 1 (January 1956), p. 27.

13. Quoted by Krüger, 'A Rainy Day', p. 59.

14. Quoted by André Fontaine, *Histoire de la guerre froide* Vol. I (Paris: Fayard, 1965), p. 71.

15. Horst Günther Linke, *Deutsch-sowjetische Beziehungen bis Rapallo* (Cologne: Verlag Wissenschaft und Politik, 1970), p. 212.

in August 1920 told a high-ranking German diplomat that 'two unfortunate nations are natural partners'.[16]

Seen thus as the antidote to Versailles, Rapallo became a positive myth for Russia. One month after the conclusion of the treaty, the Bolshevik leadership, at the instigation of Lenin, praised it as model for the establishment of relations with a capitalist state, and as the 'only good way of getting out of the difficulties, of chaos and the risk of war'.[17] A memorandum of June 1925 reiterated this appreciation: the Soviet government expressed its conviction that 'the treaty of Rapallo is and remains one of the most significant documents of international politics', as it had figured as 'model of a voluntary, pacific accord' between States of opposite political systems.[18] From this time onwards, Soviet propaganda began to use the theme of 'peaceful coexistence' (an expression used for the first time in February 1920 by Chicherin himself) to stress the Soviet wish for reconciliation.[19] During the Cold War, the USSR would develop this theme further.

The Reversal of Alliances

The shock of Rapallo was not equally strong on both sides of the Atlantic and the Channel. Trying to rationalise their fear, the Americans greeted Rapallo with a certain unease, but they mainly disliked German-Russian economic co-operation.[20]

The British were upset, but not anywhere near as hysterical as the French.[21] Admittedly, the British government wished for the reintegration of Russia into the international community, and a German-Russian rapprochement would not have been particularly terrifying to them, had it happened in a tripartite or quadripartite framework, including also one or more of the Western Powers. But the British Prime Minister, David Lloyd George, had since 1919 cautioned against the dangers of a Russo-German alliance. In his Fontainebleau Memorandum, he warned France against

16. Quoted by Gustav Hilger and A. G. Meyer, *The Incompatible Allies: A Memoir-History of German-Soviet Relations 1918–1941* (New York: Macmillan, 1953), p. 51.

17. Quoted by Linke, *Deutsch-sowjetische Beziehungen*, p. 213.

18. Quoted by Schieder, *Die Probleme*, p. 83.

19. Hörster-Philipps *et al.*, *Rapallo*, p. 145.

20. Krüger, 'A Rainy Day', p. 57.

21. Pierre Renouvin, *Histoire des Relations internationales* Vol. III (Paris: Hachette, 1994), pp. 526–527; See also Stephanie Salzmann, 'British reactions to the German-Soviet Treaty of Rapallo' (MS. Ph.D. Cantab., 1990).

the devastating effects on the European balance of a possible agreement between Berlin and Moscow.[22] He repeated this warning to Marshal Foch and the French President of the Council of Ministers, Millerand, in the summer of 1922, calling a German-Soviet accord the 'most formidable alliance'.[23] On the day after the announcement of the signing of the treaty, Lloyd George met with the other heads of the delegations present at the conference in Genoa. He complained about the agreement, while seeking to avoid an open breach. The British ambassador to Berlin tried to play down the affair.[24] But having realised what an outcry the treaty caused elsewhere, Lloyd George later accused Germany of being 'guilty of an act of base treachery and perfidy, which was typical of German perfidy and stupidity, perhaps even more of Germany's stupidity than of her perfidy'. Describing the situation as 'very dangerous', he called this a 'rapprochement between two of the potentially most formidable powers of Europe'. He was 'disgusted at the low cheating' of the Germans, whom he claimed the Allies had treated as equals.[25] In short, Mr Rathenau was not a gentleman, and did not respect conventions. Lord Curzon, Foreign Secretary, added later that Rapallo was a 'gratuitous insult by the Germans'[26] who on that occasion revealed their 'cynical duplicitousness'.[27] Rapallo confirmed traditional British views of the Germans.

In the French case, we see nothing less than a trauma. Rapallo became synonymous for nightmare. The French delegate at the Genoa Conference, Louis Barthou, was reportedly furious; he categorically condemned the treaty as 'an act of unqualified disloyalty'[28] which created a 'particularly grave situation', reminding him of the Treaty of Brest-Litovsk of 1918.[29] The President of the Council, Raymond Poincaré, did not hide his anguish, judging that Germany was beginning 'to prepare her revenge',[30] which

22. Francis Conte, 'Lloyd George et le traité de Rapallo', *Revue d'histoire moderne et contemporaine* Vol. XXIII (Jan.–Mar. 1976), pp. 44–67.

23. *Documents on British Foreign Policy* [henceforth *DOBFP*] 1919–1939, first series Vol. VIII (London: HMSO, 1958), p. 724.

24. *DOBFP*, first series Vol. XX (London: HMSO, 1976), p. 869. *Lord D'Abernon's Diary: An Ambassador of Peace* (London: Hodder and Stroughton, 1929), pp. 332–336.

25. *DOBFP*, first series Vol. XIX (London: HMSO, 1974), pp. 432–433.

26. Pogge von Strandmann, 'Rapallo', p. 142.

27. Graml, 'Die Rapallo-Politik', p. 388.

28. Quoted by Renata Bournazel, *Rapallo: naissance d'un mythe. La politique de la peur dans la France du Bloc National* (Paris: PFNSP-Colin, 1974), p. 170.

29. *DOBFP*, first series Vol. XIX, pp. 424–429.

30. *Documents relatifs aux négociations concernant les garanties de sécurité contre une agression de l'Allemagne (10 janvier 1919–7 décembre 1923)* (Paris: MAE, 1924), p. 141.

only (Western) military action against Germany could forestall. The press decried the 'perfidious manoeuvre' of the Germans who had not hesitated to break 'the solidarity of the civilised nations' by allying with the 'barbarians'.[31]

These reactions to Rapallo have to be explained by the psychological context in France, which was particularly ready for a such a myth that combined two enemy images: a revanchist Germany and the Bolsheviks, threatening fundamental Western values. Since 1918, France had lived in the fear of a Russo-German challenge of the European order created by the victorious Western allies. Versailles did not allay the visceral fears of the French with regard to their security *vis-à-vis* an intrinsically evil Germany. The instability of the young Weimar Republic only fuelled them.

The fear of a German-Russian entente which would inevitably be damaging to French interests went back beyond 1918: the Tauroggen agreement of 1812 was retrospectively interpreted as a precedent for Rapallo. That had been the brusque change of course by Prussia, allying with Russia against Napoleon. The great French historian Michelet nourished delirious thoughts of a 'monstrously strong alliance' between 'the Russian mass' and 'German technology',[32] translated by Lloyd George as 'Russian resources' and 'German skill'.[33] Another historian, Bainville, continued this tradition of the warning against 'the danger of a Germano-Russian linkage'.[34]

Indeed, Rapallo had been predicted. In October 1921, the French Ambassador to Berlin, Charles Laurent, reported that Germany 'is counting on close association with Russia in order to destroy the economic and political balance created by the victory of the Allies and turn the result to its own advantage'.[35] On the eve of the Genoa Conference, the Parisian press were already writing about the theme of the great menace to peace which the next German-Soviet understanding would undoubtedly represent. The fear of such an understanding thus existed in France even before the agreement was reached and indeed was feared greatly, although it was the actual manifestation of this nightmare which crystallised it into a myth. This treaty became to them a manifestation of revisionism which aimed at destroying the League of

31. Quoted by Bournazel, *Rapallo*, pp. 189, 208.

32. *Ibid.*, pp. 118–119.

33. *DOBFP*, first series Vol. XIX, p. 433.

34. Jacques Bainville, *Les conséquences politiques de la paix* (Paris: Nouvelle Librairie Nationale, 1920), p. 233.

35. Quoted by Bournazel, *Rapallo*, p. 124.

Nations and Western cohesion, and which marked the renaissance of the power politics and hegemonic ambitions of Wilhelmine Germany. Rapallo thus seemed to furnish proof that France had good reason to distrust her neighbour, and equally, to distrust alliances, both those directed against her and those of which she was a member: the commitment of others was demonstrably unreliable, provisional, tactical.

Rapallo further seemed to France mind-boggling as it was an alliance of opposites, and thus not 'natural'. A democratic Germany chose the adventure of the East instead of co-operation with the democratic West. The French thus concluded that even as a republic, Germany was a destabilising factor in the European order. They saw this as reason to fear that Germany would drift away from the West. Rapallo thus joined the myths of the *Sonderweg*[36] and of *Mitteleuropa* (Germany as natural hegemon of Central Europe). In any case, Rapallo emphasised the difficulty which France had with the country which claimed to have a geopolitical rôle to play between East and West, without wanting to choose its camp. Rapallo confirmed the French vision of the hostile world surrounding France, and her own rôle as guardian of the established order.

The separate Russian peace treaty of Brest-Litovsk in 1918 had been perceived in France as treason, as it brusquely terminated the Franco-Russian alliance. This turn-about was even more worrying as it went along with the establishment of a political system that was hostile to the Western democracies: Russia at once became a traitor and an ideological enemy. The Bolsheviks presented a dual menace for France, external and internal, due to the presence in France of a Communist Party taking its directives from Moscow. For this reason, Clemenceau sought to encircle Russia with a *cordon sanitaire*. In joining Russia, Germany was thus forging a pact with a common enemy, Bolshevism.

The Russo-Polish War of 1920 seemed to corroborate these apprehensions: Russia and Germany had a secret understanding at the expense of the Poles, breaking with the new order of Europe of which France was one of the guarantors.[37] For the Polish delegate at the Genoa Conference, there was no doubt that his country would be 'the first to suffer' because of Rapallo.[38] Polish historiography does not cease to condemn Rapallo. Even after the

36. See chapter 14 in this volume, A. J. Nicholls, 'The Myth of the German *Sonderweg*'.
37. Bournazel, *Rapallo*, pp. 12–13, 97–106, 118–123.
38. *DOBFP*, first series Vol. XIX, p. 437.

Second World War, official historians of the People's Republic of Poland refused to agree on this point with their Soviet colleagues. The Poles denounced the Rapallo Treaty as aggressive: in their view, it had threatened Russia as much as Poland, as through the Treaty Germany had aimed to dominate all of Eastern Europe. Janusz Pajewski concluded from this that any co-operation with Germany could not be anything other than nefarious, and Jerzy Krasuski traced a direct dialectic line running from Rapallo to Locarno and finally on to Munich.[39] Many years later, after the end of the Cold War, Janusz Stefanowicz, former Polish Ambassador to Paris, was still afraid of Germany's *Drang nach Osten* ('Eastward-Ho!'), which would 'be continued either through and with Poland, or over and without her, with the risk of a "short circuit" evoking the ghost of Rapallo'.[40]

Anti-Myth

Confronted with any Germano-Soviet rapprochement, France had the choice between two strategies, one defensive and traditional, the other dynamic and innovative. It tried both alternatively. On the one hand, it could try to strengthen the ties with Britain (as attempted, with little success, by Poincaré in 1922 and by Pompidou in 1970), or with Russia (attempted by Pierre-Étienne Flandin in 1935 and Charles de Gaulle in 1944 and 1966). On the other hand, France could try to tie Germany firmly into a West-European framework (as Aristide Briand attempted in 1925 and Robert Schuman in 1950).

Even though it was ever-present in Western minds, the fear of Soviet-German convergence receded somewhat in the immediate aftermath of Rapallo. The treaty of Berlin in April 1926 (in which Germany and the USSR committed themselves to remain neutral if one or the other were attacked) did not provoke any hysteria. Admittedly, it came after the Soviet Union had been recognised by Britain and France (in August and December 1924 respectively) and after Locarno, which seemed to have restored a Western orientation of Germany.[41] Paradoxically, the myth of Rapallo

39. Leonid Luks, 'Die Weimarer Republik im Spiegelbild der polnischen Geschichtsschreibung nach 1945', *Vierteljahrshefte für Zeitgeschichte* Vol. 28 No. 4 (1980), pp. 410–439.

40. Janusz Stefanowicz, 'Central Europe between Germany and Russia: A View from Poland', *Security Dialogue* Vol. 26 No. 1 (Mar. 1995), p. 57.

41. *DOBFP*, 2nd series Vol. I (London: HMSO, 1966), pp. 651–690.

returned a decade later, when Paris concluded a treaty with Moscow. The architect of the Franco-Soviet Pact of 2 May 1935, Flandin, wanted to pre-empt a repetition of an isolated USSR turning to Germany for comfort.[42] The Parisian press took this up: a right-wing daily newspaper pleaded in favour of a Franco-Soviet pact for fear of a repetition of Rapallo[43] and the influential journalist Geneviève Tabouis feared that the Kremlin would otherwise end up 'falling back onto the tracks leading to the treaty of Rapallo'.[44] The French military came to the same conclusion: the French alliance with Russia aimed at 'bringing into [their] camp the Russian power, which might otherwise turn back towards a policy of Rapallo'; yet they balked at tying themselves 'to a government that had betrayed [them] in the middle of a war'.[45]

Four years later, both the British Ambassador in Berlin who talked about the 'treacherous cynicism of Stalin and Co.', and the French Minister of Foreign Affairs, Georges Bonnet, declared that they were not surprised by the Molotov-Ribbentrop pact, Bonnet attributing it to 'Russian unreliability'. Bonnet added that he hoped the Russians would later be as unreliable towards Germany as they had now shown themselves towards the West.[46] On the other hand, a former minister of the Popular Front government, Pierre Cot, severely criticised the USSR, thinking of 'nothing but its treason'.[47] The agreement between Molotov and Ribbentrop reinforced the French in their view that Russia was base and culturally inferior. A report by the Quai d'Orsay thus traced 'the secular tradition' of German-Russian relations back to Ivan the Terrible: the Germans brought to 'the Russian mass ... qualities deeply alien to it: seriousness, the love of order and discipline, technology'.[48]

For its part, the USSR proclaimed that the Moscow pact was a return to Rapallo, and Molotov denounced those who saw an advantage to themselves if relations between Moscow and Berlin were poor.[49] After the Second World War, German Communists tried,

42. Renouvin, *Histoire*, p. 662. See also Henri Azeau, *Le pacte franco-soviétique (2 mai 1935)* (Paris: Presses de la Cité, 1969).

43. *L'Echo de Paris* (10 July and 13 Sept. 1934).

44. *L'Oeuvre* (4 Sept. 1934).

45. *Documents Diplomatiques Français* [henceforth *DDF*], 1923–1935 Vol. X (Paris: Imprimerie Nationale, 1981), pp. 401–402.

46. *DOBFP*, third series Vol. VII (London: HMSO, 1954), pp. 131, 138.

47. Quoted by Jean-Baptiste Duroselle, *La décadence 1932–1939* (Paris: Imprimerie Nationale, 1979), p. 474.

48. *DDF*, 1936–1939 Vol. XIX (Paris: Imprimerie Nationale, 1986), pp. 40–41.

49. Fontaine, *Histoire de la guerre froide*, p. 72.

with varying degrees of coherence, to justify the pact: SED leader Hermann Matern thus explained that 'the conclusion of the German-Soviet Treaty of 1939 showed once more that the Russians had the wish to remain the friends of Germany'.[50]

Walking in the footsteps of Poincaré and Flandin, General de Gaulle tried to avoid a repetition of Rapallo, even before the end of the Second World War. With this in mind, he travelled to Moscow in December 1944 in order to seal what he called 'the beautiful and good alliance' with Moscow,[51] just as before in 1914. In his mind, this had to be done in order to assure the security of the Continent through Franco-Russian control of its central part.[52] He later stated: 'France is always an ally of Russia in case of a German threat.'[53]

Stalin, however, while agreeing to play de Gaulle's game in 1944, during the Cold War preferred to play the German card. He could count on sympathy on the part of some West Germans: the Christian Democrat leader Jakob Kaiser wanted to protect his defeated country from becoming the pawn of territorial rivalries between East and West. Consequently, he argued for a 'bridge-building policy' founded on Germany's neutrality and its understanding with its large neighbours. Early in 1947, he therefore rejected the 'either-or' policy of the blocks, which he wanted to see replaced with an 'as-well-as' policy.[54] In order to bring such men under their influence, Communists throughout Europe from December 1945 were given permission to follow their own 'particular path to Socialism'. In Germany, Anton Ackerman made himself spokesman of such a course, claiming to resume the policies of Rathenau and Stresemann.[55] Ackermann's new version of the *Sonderweg* for Germany was quite explicitly aimed at persuading the public to support it by focusing on national sentiments. This large-scale strategy was reinforced in 1947 when the

50. 'La politique soviétique d'occupation en Allemagne (1945–1947)', *Notes Documentaires et Etudes* No. 598, 14 April 1947, p. 15.

51. Quoted by Ernst Weisenfeld, *Quelle Allemagne pour la France?* (Paris: Colin, 1989), p. 23.

52. See Charles de Gaulle, *Discours et Messages, janvier 1940–janvier 1946* (Paris: Plon, 1972), p. 435, speech of 25 July 1944.

53. Weisenfeld, *Quelle Allemagne*, p. 66.

54. Waldemar Besson, *Die Aussenpolitik der Bundesrepublik. Erfahrungen und Maßstäbe*. (Munich: Piper, 1970), p. 35; see also W. Conze, *Jakob Kaiser*. Vol. III: *Politiker zwischen Ost und West 1945–1949* (Stuttgart: Kohlhammer, 1969), pp. 185–198.

55. Renata Fritsch-Bournazel, *L'Union soviétique et les Allemagnes* (Paris: Presses de la FNSP, 1979), pp. 47–50.

division of Germany became more accentuated, something which Stalin had tried to prevent, as this meant that the USSR lost control of the larger part of the country.

It is at this moment that the myth of Rapallo reappeared. Soviets and German Communists used it to demonstrate that there existed between the two peoples a convergence of interests and that it was in the nature of things for the two nations to support each other. In 1948, a Soviet historian, N. L. Rubinstain, wrote a book on the Treaty of Rapallo.[56] On the occasion of the twenty-fifth anniversary of the signing of the agreement, the East German Socialist Unity Party's (SED) ideology journal dedicated a long article to Rapallo, describing it as an 'important chapter in Soviet-German relations'.[57] Shortly thereafter, the Party commemorated Rathenau's assassination. But this propaganda campaign, aimed at defending German unity and relayed as such by the East German *Volkskongress* (popular assembly), met with muted enthusiasm. It was nevertheless relaunched in the spring of 1949, causing much concern in France. The French press talked about Rapallo as 'the new secret weapon of Stalin',[58] and the Gaullist weekly, having opened the 'file on German-Soviet collaboration', warned against the 'lit-up lanterns of Rapallo', as 'Prussian nationalism traditionally leans on Russia'.[59]

This Communist offensive in favour of a return to Rapallo took two forms: an intense press campaign and the establishment of personal contacts. For example, a Communist newspaper in Berlin claimed that there was 'a current of opinion which was favourable to the renewal of the policy of Rapallo', particularly as the past and the present now came together: '[A]s in 1922, the Capitalist world, in the clutches of economic difficulties, is seeking to cure itself at the expense of Germany and the USSR. As in 1922, the friendship of the Soviet Union is for Germany a vital necessity.'[60] This message was also relayed by politicians of varying influence, who were 'considered as moderates',[61] such as the historian Ulrich Noack, leader of the Nauheim circle whose programme aimed to guarantee 'peace through the neutralisation of

56. Alfred Anderle (ed.), *Rapallo und die friedliche Koexistenz* (East Berlin: Akademie Verlag, 1963), pp. 160–193.

57. *Einheit* No. 4 (Apr. 1947), pp. 496–498.

58. *Le Monde* No. 1288 (18 March 1949).

59. *Le Rassemblement* No. 103, 105–106 (23, 30 April 1949).

60. *Berliner Zeitung* (10 Mar., 15 Apr. 1949).

61. Ministère des Affaires Etrangères [henceforth MAE], Série Z Vol. 42, François Seydoux, Berlin, 28 March 1949, No. 230–238.

Germany'.[62] Otto Nuschke, President of the CDU in the Soviet Occupation Zone, toured the Western Zones with the aim of convincing his sister party under Adenauer of the justice of the plans for German unity proposed by the East.[63] While this journey was no success, the démarche of Rudolf Nadolny, former German Ambassador to Moscow, provoked (according to a French diplomat) an 'unleashing of emotions': some accused him of being 'an agent of the Soviets', others defended him as a patriot 'who is still haunted by the memories of Rapallo'.[64] Neither of these last-ditch attempts to prevent the creation of a separate Federal Republic of Germany bore fruits. The invocation of the myth of Rapallo did not provoke the expected reaction in West Germany, where public opinion remained deaf to the siren song, refusing to allow national unity to depend solely on the good will of the USSR.

German Uncertainties

The debate about Rapallo was nevertheless not silenced;[65] if anything, it became more intense, fed by the reminiscences of German diplomats[66] and by historical studies, conducted particularly by Americans.[67] During the following Cold War decades, the myth was invoked whenever there were any Soviet-German contacts or any Soviet proposals aiming specifically at Bonn: the Stalin note of 10 March 1952 proposing German reunification as a *quid pro quo* for continuing German disarmament,[68] the Rapacki Plan and Adenauer's journey to Moscow in 1957, during the second Berlin crisis

62. *Neues Deutschland* (27 Feb. 1949).

63. MAE Vol. 55, Jean Laloy, Frankfurt, 3 Mar. 1949, No. 200–201.

64. MAE Vol. 42, Saint-Hardouin, Baden-Baden, 12 Apr. 1949, No. 439.

65. *Der Rapallo-Vertrag und die deutsche Sozialdemokratie* (Berlin-East: SED/Agitation, 1950).

66. H. von Dirksen, *Moskau, Tokyo, London: Erinnerungen und Betrachtungen zu zwanzig Jahren deutscher Aussenpolitik 1919–1939* (Stuttgart: Kohlhammer, 1949). Wipert von Blücher, *Deutschlands Weg nach Rapallo*. Gustav Hilger, *Wir und der Kreml. Deutsch-sowjetische Beziehungen 1918–1941. Erinnerungen eines Diplomaten* (Frankfurt: Metzner, 1955). Max von Stockhausen, *Sechs Jahre Reichskanzlei. Von Rapallo bis Locarno. Erinnerungen und Tagebuchnotizen 1922–1927* (Bonn: Athenäum-Verlag, 1954).

67. Lionel Kochan, 'The Russian Road to Rapallo' *Soviet Studies* (Oct. 1950), pp. 109–122. *Idem, Russland und die Weimarer Republik* (Düsseldorf: Müller-Albrechts, 1955). E. H. Carr, *German-Soviet Relations between the two World Wars 1919–1939* (Baltimore: Johns Hopkins Press, 1951).

68. Boris Meissner, *Russland, die Westmächte und Deutschland. Die sowjetische Deutschlandpolitik 1943–1953* (Hamburg: Nölke, 1954), pp. 290–293.

(1958–1962),[69] throughout the development of *Ostpolitik* (1966–1973), and finally again, with a vengeance, towards the end of the Cold War and in the context of German reunification with Gorbachev's support.

In 1952, the German Democratic Republic (GDR) supported the Stalin note of 1952 *nolens volens*,[70] proclaiming the need for a return to Rapallo. Wilhelm Pieck, President of the GDR, wrote that after the First World War, the USSR was the first country to have recognised the defeated Germany as an equal, and that thirty years later, it was still the best guarantor 'of a united, pacific and independent Germany'.[71] Equally, on the thirtieth anniversary of Rapallo, Otto Winzer declared before the Berlin section of the SED that, however much international circumstances had evolved, the lessons of 1922 continued to apply.[72]

The Stalin note resulted in some debate in the West and deepened disagreements on the separate existence of the FRG within it.[73] The former Chancellor Wirth, who since his return from exile had been campaigning against German rearmament, involuntarily propagated the Russian theses by reminding the German public of the advantages which Germany had derived from the Rapallo Treaty.[74] But on balance, West Germans rejected the idea of a comparison between the situations of 1922 and 1952, calling Rapallo 'nothing but a memory without the least political actuality';[75] or arguing that 'the *Realpolitik* of the day before yesterday is today an illusion'.[76] While Jakob Kaiser, Minister for German Questions, favoured a positive reply to the Stalin note, Adenauer

69. Paul Noack, 'Rapallo, Wunsch und Wirklichkeit', *Politische Studien* No. 117 (1960), pp. 31–38.

70. Fritz Klein, *Die diplomatischen Beziehungen Deutschlands zur Sowjetunion 1917–1922* (Berlin-East: Dietz, 1952).

71. Quoted by Ivan K. Kobljakov, *Von Brest bis Rapallo. Geschichtliches Abriss der sowjetisch-deutschen Beziehungen 1918–1922* (Berlin-East: Verlag Kultur und Fortschritt, 1956), pp. 25, 282.

72. Otto Winzer, *Der Rapallo-Vertrag und seine nationale Bedeutung für Deutschland* (Berlin-East: Dietz, 1952).

73. Felix Stössinger, 'Die Wahrheit über Rapallo', *Deutsche Rundschau* No. 6 (June 1952), pp. 550–560. Margret Boveri, 'Rapallo, Geheimnisse, Wunschtraum, Gespenst', *Merkur* No. 9 (1952). pp. 880–892; Andreas Hillgruber, 'Bericht über eine Tagung', *Frankfurter Allgemeine Zeitung*, 4 Apr. 1981.

74. Fritsch-Bournazel, *L'Union soviétique*, p. 71. 'Die Reise hinter den Eisernen Vorhang', *Dokumentation der Zeit* (1952), pp. 1166–1174.

75. Hans von Raumer, 'Dreissig Jahre nach Rapallo', *Deutsche Rundschau* No. 4, Apr. 1952, p. 330.

76. F. R. Allemann, 'Zurück zu Rapallo? Möglichkeiten und Grenzen der deutschen Aussenpolitik', *Der Monat* No. 73 (Oct. 1954), p. 49.

vetoed it, determined not to undermine the process of building up trust in him and his government among the Western Powers, whose 'Rapallo Complex' he knew all too well. Judging that any arrangement with Moscow was impossible anyway, he was unwilling to give up the West-integration of the FRG for the uncertain hope of German reunification. Later, when establishing diplomatic relations with the USSR, he took good care not to arouse the spectres of Rapallo.[77] Before leaving office, he said that his policy had aimed at preventing a new Rapallo and a new anti-Rapallo reaction, i.e. both a German-Soviet rapprochement and a Franco-Soviet rapprochement directed against Germany.[78]

France, as usual, was particularly prone to Rapalloesque fantasies. In the debate about the European Defence Community (EDC), certain French deputies feared that the FRG would acquire greater sovereignty, which would tempt it to settle the issue of reunification directly with the USSR, thus betraying the interests of its European partners. Edouard Herriot claimed that 'the EDC Treaty, which supposedly pulls Germany away from Russia, in reality throws it into its arms'. In order to contain this danger, he recommended a rapprochement with the USSR, such as he himself had instigated in 1924.[79] Molotov did incidentally make advances towards Pierre Mendès France at the Geneva Conference of June 1954. Paris rejected this offer, and Moscow renounced the Franco-Soviet Treaty of 1944 when the FRG was incorporated into NATO.

Meanwhile, in Soviet diplomacy, two tendencies contended with each other. The 'Rapalloists' favoured a rapprochement with Germany; the 'Yaltaists', with the USA. The 'Rapalloists' presented the Rapacki plan (proposing a denuclearised zone in Central Europe) and then Adenauer's visit to Moscow 1957, in the spirit of Rapallo.[80] At the time, a Soviet specialist on Germany, Daniel Melnikov, published a series of articles praising the merits of Rapallo.[81] These writings were published in the context of a new historiographical offensive, jointly conducted by Soviet and East-German historians which even provoked replies from Western

77. Besson, *Die Aussenpolitik*, pp. 61–62, 195–196.

78. André Fontaine, *Histoire de la guerre froide* Vol. II (Paris: Fayard, 1964), p. 56.

79. Weisenfeld, *Quelle Allemagne*, p. 74.

80. Ernst Kux, 'Moskaus Konfrontation mit Washington: Kontroversen im Kreml?', *Neue Zürcher Zeitung* (4/5 Aug. 1984).

81. Daniel Melnikov, 'Rapallo. Then and Now', *New Times* (Moscow) No. 20 (1957); Gerda Koch, *Die deutsche Arbeiterklasse und der Rapallo-Vertrag* (East-Berlin: Gesellschaft für deutsch-sowjetische Freundschaft, 1957), 59 pages.

authors.[82] Particularly noteworthy are the works of Günter Rosenfeld[83] and Ivan Kobljakov who both produced analyses of the evolution of relations between Berlin and Moscow from the time of Brest-Litovsk until the Treaty of Rapallo. In the preface to the German edition of his book (published two years earlier in Moscow), the Soviet historian Kobljakov reaffirmed that 'peace and friendship with the USSR are the indispensable condition ... for the national existence of the German people and State'. He described Rapallo as the 'model', 'the foundation of a pacific co-operation between two opposed systems'.[84]

During the second Berlin crisis, de Gaulle adopted an attitude of apparent firmness, while declaring himself favourable to re-unification, so as not to let the Germans despair of Western support for this possibility, something which might have tempted them to conclude a separate agreement with Russia.[85] French fears seemed to become more concrete after the construction of the Berlin Wall. The Ambassador of the FRG in Moscow, Hans Kroll, tried to prepare a meeting between Khrushchev and Adenauer with the aim of preventing the Soviets from coming to an agreement directly with the Americans at the expense of the Germans. The Federal Chancellor even thought of inviting Khrushchev to Bonn. The Kremlin exploited the crisis of confidence between FRG and the United States by pointing out the advantages which Western Germany could draw from a new Rapallo: the USSR proposed bilateral discussions to the FRG. On 27 December 1961, the Soviet foreign minister handed a memorandum to Ambassador Kroll, the existence of which was leaked, resulting immediately in suspicions in the West, driven (according to Kroll) by a 'Rapallo complex'.[86] This document in a friendly manner advised the FRG not to sacrifice its national interests on the altar of anti-Communism.[87] Just as in 1922, the USSR advanced economic arguments, claiming that their country was 'an ocean of outlets' for the products of the FRG which the Western competitors sought

82. Adalbert Worliczek, 'Rapallo: Drohung und Wirklichkeit', *Die politische Meinung* No. 5 (1956), pp. 22–30. Herbert Helbig, *Die Träger der Rapallo-Politik* (Göttingen: Vandenhoeck and Ruprecht, 1958).

83. Günter Rosenfeld, 'Das Zustandekommen des Rapallo-Vertrages', *Zeitschrift für Geschichtswissenschaften* No. 4 (1956), p. 680.

84. Kobljakov, *Von Brest bis Rapallo*, pp. 5, 11.

85. Stanley Hoffman, 'Verlobt, doch nicht verheiratet', *Die Zeit* No. 14 (29 Mar. 1985).

86. Hans Kroll, *Lebenserinnerungen eines Botschafters* (Berlin-West: Deutsche Buchgemeinschaft, 1967), p. 540.

87. Besson, *Die Aussenpolitik*, pp. 290–298.

to prevent from 'using its particularly advantageous geographic and economic position'.[88] This theory was developed in full by an East-German historian.[89] Nevertheless, these efforts to seduce West Germany foundered on the almost unanimous hostility of the West German political elite;[90] eventually, Ambassador Kroll was recalled in 1962. Nevertheless, this story left its traces both in the East and in the West, where a historical interest in Rapallo was reawakened.[91]

In the East, Rapallo was sanctified as the obligatory point of reference for all Soviet policies towards Germany, and of all the GDR's contacts with the USSR. Both claimed for themselves 'the spirit of Rapallo', which continued to be used as a synonym for 'peaceful coexistence'.[92] The Soviet Union thus tried to sow discord in the Western camp, while the GDR used this theme to normalise its relations with the FRG. The fortieth anniversary of Rapallo was celebrated with great pomp by Soviet and East German academics and journalists. The Soviet-East German historical commission, founded in 1957, which had adopted as its mission the study 'of the application of Leninist principles of peaceful coexistence to international relations',[93] organised a large conference in April 1962 and subsequently published the conference papers on the events of 1922.[94] Published both in Russian and German, the papers emphasised the topicality of Rapallo, and vindicated the policies of the GDR.[95] The Director of the Historical Institute of the Soviet Academy of Sciences, V.M. Chvostov, explained that the profound significance of Rapallo lay in the

88. Quoted by Fritsch-Bournazel, *L'Union soviétique*, pp. 106–107.

89. Alfred Anderle, *Die deutsche Rapallo-Politik. Deutsch-sowjetische Beziehungen 1922–1929* (Berlin-East: Rütten and Loening, 1962).

90. Heinrich von Brentano (former FRG Foreign Minister), 'Der Vertrag von Rapallo. 40 Jahre danach', *Politisch-Soziale Korrespondenz* (11 Apr. 1962). 'Alleingänge und Sondertouren im Geist von Rapallo', *Vorwärts* (7 Feb. 1962).

91. Horst Lademacher, 'Von Brest-Litovsk nach Rapallo. Machtpolitik, Ideologie, Realpolitik', *Blätter für deutsche und internationale Politik* No. 11 (Nov. 1961), pp. 1037–1054. Walter Grottian, 'Genua und Rapallo 1922. Entstehung und Wirkung eines Vertrages', *Aus Politik und Zeitgeschichte* No. 25/26 (June 1962), pp. 305–328. Karl Dietrich Erdmann, 'Deutschland, Rapallo und der Westen', *Vierteljahrshefte für Zeitgeschichte* No. 2 (April 1963), pp. 105–165.

92. Wilhelm Orth, *Rathenau und der Geist von Rapallo* (Berlin-East: Buchverlag Der Morgen, 1962).

93. Anderle (ed.), *Friedliche Koexistenz*, p. viii.

94. Michael J. Sodaro, *Moscow, Germany and the West from Khrushchev to Gorbachev* (Ithaca: Cornell University Press, 1990), p. 50.

95. Anderle (ed.), *Friedliche Koexistenz*, p. vii.

recognition of the existing states.[96] Leo Stern, East-German president of this mixed commission, applied Rapallo to the particular situation of a divided Germany. Recalling that the theory of 'peaceful coexistence' between two states of different social order had come into existence with the Treaty of 1922, he recommended an agreement between the FRG and the GDR, the existence of which Bonn could not longer deny.[97]

Paradoxically, it was henceforth the turn of East German leaders to worry about the slightest hint of rapprochement between the USSR and the FRG, as this was likely to be at the expense of the GDR. This fear mounted in the summer of 1964, when Khrushchev, warning the Erhard-Schröder government against 'the repudiation of the spirit of Rapallo',[98] sought to test the mettle of the new team in power in Bonn through the mediation of his personal emissary and son-in-law Alexei Adjoubei, editor-in-chief of *Izvestia*, who did not hesitate to play on emotional strings in Bonn: lacking a 'soul', he explained, the Anglo-Saxons were not able to sympathise with the Germans, while 'we the Russians are the only ones who can understand you, the Germans'.[99] He concluded from his discussions in Bonn that the leaders of the FRG were disposed to renew the tradition of Rapallo, particularly as the Federal Government had revived Ambassador Kroll's project concerning Khrushchev's visit to Bonn. But, just as were the previous plans, these were aborted in view of the concerted opposition of a major section of the West German foreign policy making elite, as well as from within the SED and anti-Khrushchevians in the Kremlin.[100] Khrushchev himself was removed from office a few months later.

The Model and the Counter-weight

During the following years, de Gaulle played with the idea of the re-establishment of a European concert, founded on Franco-Russian control of the Continent *vis-à-vis* a united but less powerful Germany, the counter-weight to the danger of a new Rapallo. In

96. *Ibid.*, p. 32.
97. *Ibid.*, pp. 1–27.
98. 'Die deutsch-sowjetischen Beziehungen', *Deutsche Aussenpolitik* No. 5 (1964), pp. i–xiv.
99. Sodaro, *Moscow*, p. 61.
100. Fritsch-Bournazel, *L'Union soviétique*, pp. 126–127.

1966, he travelled to Moscow to proclaim 'the new alliance between France and Russia'.[101] In the following year, he pointed out to Willy Brandt (then the foreign minister of the grand coalition government in Bonn) that other than during the Napoleonic wars, France had never been the enemy of Russia.[102] This was a big hint at a time when the Federal government was undertaking the redefinition of its policy towards the East, the new *Ostpolitik*, dangerously coinciding, it seemed, with Moscow's policy of *détente*.[103] Aware of Western susceptibilities, Willy Brandt incessantly tried to reassure the FRG's allies. Admittedly, he referred to Rathenau and Stresemann, i.e. to Rapallo and Locarno:[104] he described Rathenau as the minister who had recognised 'the need of a harmonious equilibrium of the German policies towards the West and the East'.[105] But in 1967, on the occasion of the centenary of the birth of Rathenau, he asserted that 'there will be no more Rapallos', even if 'a normal and amicable relationship' between Germany and the USSR remains a 'duty', demanding 'patience and hard work'.[106] Three years later, he confirmed that the 'essential condition' of his *Ostpolitik* was the 'solid anchoring' of the FRG in the West.[107] Nevertheless, nightmares abounded in the West.[108]

They were shared in East Berlin. Fearful that the GDR would pay the cost of any rapprochement between Bonn and Moscow, Walter Ulbricht (the head of the SED and of the East German government) hurried to denounce the perfidious character of Brandt's policies, reminding the Kremlin that it had been bourgeois Germany which had finally betrayed Rapallo.[109] Even after the Erfurt meeting between Willy Brandt and Willy Stoph in March 1970, he reiterated his attacks, stressing the duplicity of

101. André Fontaine, *Un seul lit pour deux rêves. Histoire de la 'détente' 1962–1981* (Paris: Fayard, 1982), pp. 80–81.

102. Willy Brandt, *Begegnungen und Einsichten. Die Jahre 1960–1975* (Hamburg: Hoffmann and Campe, 1976), p. 152.

103. Hélène Carrère d'Encausse, 'De la coexistence pacifique à la détente. La politique extérieure de l'URSS au début des années 1970', *Etudes* (Feb. 1974), pp. 185–190.

104. See chapter 13 in this volume, Cyril Buffet and Beatrice Heuser, 'Marianne and Michel: The Franco-German Couple'.

105. Brandt, *Begegnungen*, p. 185.

106. Quoted by Ernst Schulin, *Walther Rathenau, Repräsentant, Kritiker und Opfer seiner Zeit* (Göttingen: Musterschmidt, 1979), pp. 130–131.

107. Brandt, *Begegnungen*, p. 456.

108. *Politique Etrangère* No. 6 (Autumn 1973), pp. 718–722.

109. Sodaro, *Moscow*, p. 99.

Germany which had been revealed at Locarno.[110] He found an unexpected ally in French President Georges Pompidou. Officially, de Gaulle's successor as President of the Fifth Republic supported *Ostpolitik*, but was suspicious of Brandt and even more of Leonid Brezhnev who tried to exploit German national sentiments in order to weaken its ties with the West. Like de Gaulle, Pompidou appreciated the political and strategic advantages of the division of Germany (emphasised by his diplomatic recognition of the GDR), but at the same time he feared destabilising effects of a German-Soviet rapprochement. Echoing Clemenceau, he stated bitterly that with the *Ostpolitik* of Brandt, 'Germany is now acting alone without asking anybody's permission', and worse still, 'the USSR has influence over it'.[111] In order to attempt to revert this tendency, Pompidou, too, succumbed to the old French reflex: he tried to counter-balance the Renaissance of German power by leaning on Britain (to which he opened the doors of the Common Market), on the US, and on Russia, which he visited in October 1970. A year later he told Brezhnev that the Germans are a 'shifty and changeable people' and, consequently, 'time has to pass before all danger has passed'.[112] This betrays Pompidou's deep unease after Brandt's surprise visit one month earlier to Brezhnev's summer-house in Oreanda near Yalta in the Crimea, which was not a good beginning in the eyes of the French. Not informed in advance of this visit, Paris suspected that Bonn and Moscow would secretly discuss military questions – an accusation that had also been made in 1922. An official of the Quai d'Orsay even called the German initiative 'treason'.[113] Willy Brandt tried to play the whole visit down, complaining of 'the latent distrust of the French the moment Germany and Russia consult together'.[114]

The USSR on the other hand adopted a resolutely benign attitude. Even in 1967, the Soviet political scientist Paul Naumov devoted a work to Brandt, considering the prospects of a renewal of Rapallo.[115] During the months which preceded the signing of the Moscow Treaty in August 1970, references to Rapallo abounded in the Soviet press, and both Eastern and Western historiography

110. *Neues Deutschland* (3, 5, 14, 18, 27 April 1970).
111. Quoted by Fontaine, *Un seul lit*, p. 248.
112. Quoted by Eric Roussel, *Georges Pompidou* (Paris: JC Lattès, 1994), pp. 455–456.
113. Weisenfeld, *Quelle Allemagne*, p. 126.
114. Willy Brandt, *Erinnerungen* (Frankfurt am Main: Ullstein, 1992), p. 208.
115. Sodaro, *Moscow*, p. 102.

once again developed an interest in this event.[116] Daniel Melnikov, now counsellor of Soviet foreign minister Kossygin on German affairs, in an interview with the West German magazine *Der Spiegel* declared peremptorily: 'I am for the principles of Rapallo', i.e. for the conclusion of bilateral pacts which would maintain order and security in Europe.[117]

Ostpolitik did not, in fact, change the European order radically. Western fears and Soviet hopes remained unfulfilled, until both were reawakened with the Euromissile crisis. This caused great reciprocal concerns, particularly in the 'Franco-German couple': the inherent disequilibrium in this relationship led both sides to seek contacts with Russia and to use it as leverage against the other.[118] This is the explanation for the 'race to Moscow' which the French President and the German Chancellor undertook in 1980.[119] In the same way, François Mitterrand judged Russia (and indeed the GDR) to be a 'useful counter-weight' to (West) German power,[120] as he proved at the time of reunification by rushing to Kiev and East-Berlin.

From 1987, Gorbachev's disarmament proposals, welcomed by the FRG's strong pacifist movement, was greeted with considerable suspicion by the governments of Britain, France, the United States (and the FRG).[121] Pierre Bérégovoy, former Finance Minister, asked himself whether Gorbachev did not intend to propose to the Germans 'their reunification through neutralisation'; Jacques Delors, President of the European Commission, observed that the FRG 'was distancing herself a little from Europe'; and Charles Hernu, former Defence Minister, used the unfortunate term 'national-neutralism'.[122] A collective work published at the time in the Federal Republic fuelled French anxieties. The Joseph Wirth Foundation, aiming at peace and disarmament, brought

116. G. Andreiev, 'Lenin and Peaceful Foreign Policy', *International Affairs* (Moscow) No. 5 (1970), pp. 3–14. Helmut Grieser, *Die Sowjetpresse über Deutschland in Europa 1922–1932. Revision von Versailles und Rapallo-Politik im sowjetischer Sicht* (Stuttgart: Klett, 1970). Venjamin M. Chvostov (ed.), *Deutsch-sowjetische Beziehungen von der Verhandlungen in Brest-Litovsk zum Abschluss des Rapallo-Vertrages*, 2 vol. (Berlin-East: Staatsverlag der DDR, 1967–1971). Ivan Kobljakov, '50 Jahre Rapallo', *Blätter für deutsche und internationale Politik* No. 5 (1972), pp. 45–453.

117. *Der Spiegel* No. 4 (19 Jan. 1970), pp. 90–100.

118. Michel Jobert, 'De l'Allemagne', *Politique Etrangère* No. 1 (1979).

119. Weisenfeld, *Quelle Allemagne*, pp. 134–135.

120. André Fontaine, 'Une autre crainte', *Le Monde* (27 June 1984).

121. Krüger, 'A Rainy Day', pp. 49–50.

122. Quoted in Weisenfeld, *Quelle Allemagne*, p. 198.

together a group of academics and politicians from the FRG, GDR and USSR to commemorate the sixty-fifth anniversary of the Treaty of 1922 and to debate the question: 'Rapallo: model for Europe'?[123] The group's reply was positive. They tried to demonstrate the continuity between Rapallo and the policy of *détente*, illustrating their theory with the Soviet-West German treaty of 1970. The East German historian Fritz Klein emphasised the pacific constancy of Soviet policy, which from Lenin's days to those of Gorbachev had wished to stabilise the international situation.[124] Taking up an argument put forward in the GDR, the West German Christian Democrat Alfons Siegel pleaded in favour of the updating of Rapallo in the sense of a 'pacific neighbourship' between the two German States; he even claimed that the division of Germany was an 'opportunity', as the FRG and the GDR could serve as a 'German-German bridge' helping 'East-West comprehension'.[125]

Particularly when German reunification became a real option, the myth of Rapallo asserted itself in Moscow as much as in Bonn, London, Paris and Warsaw, either in references to the treaty of 1922,[126] or worse, to a new Ribbentrop-Molotov Pact.[127] For several months, the British Prime Minister Margaret Thatcher tried to 'slow down the reunification' by playing on the Soviet Union, alone capable of 'counter-balancing the German predominance in Europe' manifested in the unilateral initiatives of the West German Chancellor Helmut Kohl.[128] Speaking to Gorbachev in Moscow, Kohl invoked 'the deep roots' which linked the Germans to the 'Russian soil': '[T]he entire history of Russia and of Germany proves that there has never existed between Russians and Germans a visceral animosity.' In November 1990, on the occasion of the treaty of friendship between the FRG and the USSR, Gorbachev in turn underlined the 'essential and specific rôle' of 'the

123. Hörster-Philipps *et al.*, *Rapallo – Modell für Europa?*

124. *Ibid.*, p. 148.

125. Alfons Siegel, 'Nachdenken über Rapallo als Impuls globaler Friedensgestaltung für heute. Von friedlicher Koexistenz und den Chancen der Entfeindung', in Hörster-Philipps *et al.*, *Rapallo – Modell für Europa?*, pp. 23–31.

126. Beate Gödde-Baumanns, 'Frankreich und die deutsche Einheit 1870/71–1989/90', in Klaus Schwabe and Francesca Schinzingen (ed.), *Deutschland und der Westen im 19. und 20. Jahrhundert*. Vol. 2, *Deutschland und Westeuropa* (Stuttgart: Franz Steiner Verlag, 1994), pp. 103–120.

127. Stefanowicz, 'Central Europe between Germany and Russia', p. 57.

128. Margaret Thatcher, *The Downing Street Years, 1979–1990* (London: Harper Collins, 1993), pp. 795–799.

Soviet-German factor' on the Continent.[129] A positive version of the Rapallo myth continued to thrive in the collective imagination of the Russians, in all its different colours and shades: the ultranationalist leader Zhirinovskij certainly developed anti-Western theses, but at the same time dreamt of carving up Europe between Russia and a Germany which he claimed to admire.[130]

The Force of Living Memory

In international relations, a myth of the sort we are dealing with here does not merely seduce or frighten; it can also become a policy instrument. It is with this in mind that one might look at the document of the CDU/CSU of 1 September 1994 which advocated both the enlargement and the deepening of European integration around a 'hard core'. Rejecting power politics and new adventures, seeking to 'save Germany from herself' (in the words of Chancellor Kohl), the Christian Democratic Party wished to tie the Federal Republic closely to its partners, while trying to transform its geographic position on the fault-line of East and West into a position of political mediation.[131] In order to persuade the West, and particularly France, of the benefits of such a policy, Wolfgang Schäuble (successor-designate of Helmut Kohl as head of the Christian Democrats) and Karl Lamers (foreign policy spokesman of this party) made subtle historical allusions with the aim of not only underpinning their arguments but also of preventing subsequent accusations of deviousness. In this context, they invoked the myth of Rapallo less as a threat than as a warning, asking the West to help strengthen Germany against previous errors and passing the responsibility of future nefarious developments to Germany's EU partners in case of a failure of further integration. They claimed that

> [t]he only solution which will prevent a return to the unstable prewar system, with Germany once again caught in the middle between East and West, is to integrate Germany's Central and Eastern European neighbours into the [West] European post-war system

129. Mikhail Gorbachev, *Avant-Mémoires* (Paris: Ed. Odile Jacob, 1993), pp. 161, 307.
130. See Graham Frazer, *Le cahier noir de Jirinovski* (Paris: Albin Michel, 1994).
131. Daniel Vernet, 'La France, l'Allemagne et l'Europe', *Le Monde* (13 Oct. 1994); Pierre Lellouche, 'Europe, le vrai dilemme franco-allemand', *Le Figaro* (13 Oct. 1994); Michel Korinman, 'L'axe Paris-Bonn, tabou de l'après-guerre', *Libération* (14 Oct. 1994).

> and to establish a wide-ranging partnership between this system and Russia. ...If [West] European integration were not to progress, Germany might be called upon, or be tempted by its own security constraints, to try to effect the stabilisation of Eastern Europe on its own and in the traditional way. However, this would far exceed its capacities and, at the same time, erode the cohesion of the European Union, especially since everywhere memories are still very much alive that historically German policy towards the East concentrated on closer co-operation with Russia at the expense of the countries between.[132]

This document demonstrates that it is not easy to imagine any reform of the European order without abandoning the constraining framework of historical references. It is not enough to want to get away from Rapallo; one would have to alter its perception in the imagination of people, and it is there that such myths and images are the most deeply ingrained.

132. CDU/CSU-Fraktion des Deutschen Bundestages, 'Reflextions on European Policy', distributed by the Konrad Adenauer Foundation, London (1 Sept. 1994).

CONCLUSIONS

Historical Myths and the Denial of Change

Beatrice Heuser and Cyril Buffet

> [T]hose who judge only from empirical evidence … maintain that something that hath once happened will happen again in a case that striketh them as similar [to one in the past], without, however, being able to judge whether the same causes exist. That is why it is so easy for such people to fall into error, from which those whom age and experience hath rendered clever are by no means exempt, as they are exceedingly proud of their past experience; it hath happened in this fashion to a number of those engaged in affairs of state and war, since they do not sufficiently consider that the world changeth …
>
> *Gottfried Wilhelm Leibniz,1703–1705*[1]

The preceding chapters allow us to draw some conclusions about the origins of myths in contemporary international relations, the circumstances of their creation, their nature and their function. While this will be the subject of this chapter, it is useful to begin with the patterns of myths we have found.

1. Gottfried Wilhelm Leibniz, *Philosophische Schriften* Vol. 6, *Nouveaux Essais* (Berlin: Akademie-Verlag, 1962), p. 50f. Translation by David Chuter.

Families of Myths

Considering both the myths discussed and those we have left out for reasons of space, a categorisation without considerable overlaps does not seem possible. What can be identified, however, is related families of myths.

For example, there are *myths of special relationships*. We have found those operating both in the positive and negative form, as especially good relationships (between France and Germany, Britain and the US), or as contrasting relationships (Britain as different from the Continent). The Franco-German and US-British relationships have in common that they are in fact relationships between states that are *not* equal, but which through this relationship create the illusion of equality. The FRG was not and is not a high-profile military power, indeed it was not and is not a nuclear power, but it is economically stronger than France. Its nuclear weapons, by contrast, are a central characteristic of de Gaulle's Fifth Republic and are often described as a counter-weight to Germany's economic strength. Since the Second World War, Britain has not been a superpower, but tried through its special relationship with the US to preserve a status greater than that which it could sustain on the strength of its own armed forces and economic power alone.

What is striking about both relationships is that the myth has developed a life of its own. In the British case, the special relationship, together with the myth of Britain's difference from the European continent, were consciously fostered to give Britain greater room for manoeuvre and more foreign policy options. But John Baylis and Antonio Varsori have shown how these myths have resulted in limiting Britain's options and making her a prisoner of her own belief-system. They can be seen to have prevented Britain from realising its own best economic interest, which could have been better met, as former Foreign Secretary Douglas Hurd has argued, if Britain had joined the European Economic Community (EEC) from the beginning thus allowing it to influence the EEC's development in Britain's interest.[2] Britain has become a prisoner of a myth of her own making.

Similarly, the Franco-German relationship has developed its own momentum, in this case operating in a benign way to drive both states to ever more compromises despite the radical divergence

2. Douglas Hurd's readings on Radio 4 of his – as yet unpublished – diplomatic memoirs on Monday mornings in the summer of 1996.

between the defence principles of de Gaulle's Fifth Republic and those of the FRG. Moreover, despite the underlying divergences, the myth of the relationship is believed outside France and Germany, so much so than people in other countries believe in the existence of a Franco-German axis, almost to the point in fearing a conspiracy among the two. *The Sunday Times* of 8 September 1996 thus actually employed the term 'Franco-Germans'. Similarly, de Gaulle strengthened the mystique of the British-American Special Relationship by referring to Britain and the US collectively as the 'Anglo-Saxons' (even though with this term de Gaulle wanted to describe Britain as a mere appendage of the US). The result is that however little substance they have to begin with, myths are strong factors in policy-making.

A sub-group of these myths are the Social-Darwinist myths: these find their expression in terms such as the 'hereditary enemy', the 'natural ally' or 'natural enemy'. Facetiously, one might also argue that the 'British way of war' (supposedly impervious to technological and political changes) is at least in part such a myth, just as is the American 'manifest destiny'. A related area is of course that of geopolitical myths, which invariably are based on a dose of half-digested historical 'evidence' and only in part on immutable geographic realities (always assuming that these cannot be offset by technological innovations such as the advent of air-power and missiles, or satellites, or information technology).

Closely related to myths of special relationships are *personified myths*, that is myths that are symbolised by individual human beings. For European integration, it is the great patron saint Jean Monnet, who, together with lesser saints such as Robert Schuman, are invoked on all suitable occasions. Then there are mythical couples, with the obvious examples of Churchill and Roosevelt, again Churchill and Eisenhower, Thatcher and Reagan; or Briand and Stresemann, de Gaulle and Adenauer, Schmidt and Giscard, Kohl and Mitterrand, or Begin and Sadat.

It is striking how important the cultivation of intimacy is in these bilateral relationships, evoking memories of the kinship between the princes of old. The media (and no doubt the government publicity apparatus) dwell on mutual visits to the private houses of these statesmen, on the fact that they call each other by their first names, in other words, they signal that there is a personal, human friendship between them besides a closeness in pursuing political aims. John Baylis has referred to the famous story of Churchill's sojourn in the White House. The Special Relationship was in serious doubt when Bill Clinton became President of the United States, and rumours were circulating in Washington that he continued to hold it against Britain that parts of the British government had campaigned against him and supported a re-election of President Bush. To counter these rumours, he is said to have insisted that John Major, like Churchill before him, sleep in the White House on a subsequent visit to Washington.

The counterparts of these myths of special friendship are myths of contrast or eternal enmity: Britain as different from (and united against) Europe, Europe as different from (and united against) Islam, and, going back to the Napoleonic Wars, the birth of German national identity as against French occupation. These forms of myth tend to act as sources of political unity at home, but invariably amplify conflicts with the outside world, and for this reason can hardly be described as benign. Nor are they admirable in any other way. If it is really only the solidarity against some (really or supposedly) hostile foreign power that unites a people, then it seems that other factors of internal cohesion (such as the success of its social or economic system, the attractiveness of its culture) are too weak to provide this cohesion on their own. Appeals to such myths of contrast are thus invariably signs of internal weakness and political and cultural poverty, and where they are not malignant, they are still pathetic.

Another family are the *myths of events*. These include Versailles, Rapallo, Locarno, the Ribbentrop-Molotov Pact, Dunkirk, Mers el Kébir, Yalta, Diên Biên Phu, Suez, Reykjavik and so on. These events, although they serve extremely well as shorthands for 'lessons', fall into quite different sub-groups. There are the *myths of betrayal and perfidy*. What more needs to be said than 'Dunkirk', 'Diên Biên Phu' and 'Suez' to 'prove' to any Frenchman that the perfidious Albion or the US cannot be trusted? Equally, 'Brest-Litovsk', 'Rapallo', the 'Ribbentrop-Molotov Pact' are myths of betrayal. Practically the only positive Western association with an event is that with 'Locarno' – but even that can be interpreted either as a late manifestation of the concert of Europe or, negatively, as a betrayal of the East as only Germany's Western frontiers were agreed, or as the weakness of the inter-war political system.

This brings us to the possibility of interpreting events in different ways, depending on different national perspectives. Rapallo has been associated in the East with peaceful co-existence and thus has a positive connotation. Dunkirk, of course, is seen as a pure logistic success in Britain, and Britons are blithely unaware of the grudge harboured against them by Frenchmen in view of their behaviour at Suez. Aline Angoustures has explored the Spanish Civil War as a myth of betrayal of the Republican coalition in Spain by the Western Democracies; British intellectuals from Orwell to Huxley (and most recently, Ken Loach with his 1995 film *Land and Freedom*) tend to see it primarily as a betrayal of the Left by Stalin and the Comintern, leading to a wave of defections of British intellectuals from the Communist Party.

Most of the myths of events are connected in one way or another with war or the coming of war, and are seen as turning points which led to war or to defeat in war. But there are also *myths of politico-military disaster* in war. The Spanish Civil War is a clear case, but so is one neglected in this collection, that of 'Vietnam or the quagmire' (Vietnam, the war that really was not America's business, and yet resulted in deplorable, unnecessary casualties). France is haunted by her collapse in 1940, by her experience of Algeria, while the peace-movement in Britain in the late 1950s, 1960s and the early 1980s cannot be understood fully without reference to the First World War.[3] With the exception of the Spanish Civil War, these myths tend to be specific to one country at a time. For example, 1940 is for France the symbol of ignominious defeat, while for Britain it is the glorious reference for the Battle of Britain and *Britannia contra mundum*, Britain alone facing an expansionist great power dominating all of continental Europe.

Connected with all these myths of doom and gloom is the *myth of inevitable disaster*, once a bad policy decision is made. Munich is bad because the Second World War followed, because Hitler reneged on his commitment. Yalta is bad because it led to the division of the world and the betrayal of the East. These myths presuppose in stark monocausality that it is one thing that led to another, without permitting any causal complexity. This assumption is also made in the 'domino theory' of the US in Asia (the basis of involvement in the Vietnam war), preceded by Dean Acheson's apple-cart theory (one rotten – Communist – apple in the cart would result in all apples rotting). These myths thus serve as oracles, as prophecies, always assuming that the decision that is to be made could still prevent disaster by 'learning from history'.

By contrast to myths of disaster, there are *myths of order* and forms of co-operation. These include the rule of international law,

3. See Beatrice Heuser, *Nuclear Mentalities? Strategies and Beliefs in Britain, France and the FRG* (London: Macmillan, 1998).

the Concert of Europe (with 'Locarno' as a sub-reference), the equilibrium and European integration. Known mainly to specialists, there is also the myth of the Holy Roman Empire as a precedent of European integration,[4] a myth with positive connotations in Germany, the Benelux countries, the Czech Republic, Austria and Italy (but emphatically not in France). Among these myths of order, the myth of the balance of power is not always benign or peace-engendering: it is founded on the need to offset any powerful state on the European continent (or even in the world), but is totally detached from any considerations as to whether such a power is expansionist and oppressive or peaceful and democratic, in other words, whether it is National Socialist Germany or the FRG, whether it is the USSR or the United States. This can artificially introduce conflict where there are no ideological or other political grounds for such conflict, merely out of a reflex of resisting *any* power merely because it is powerful.

We have also encountered *myths passed on through visual images*. These are particularly impressive through the 'immediacy' of the medium, which tends to be either photography (with its pretence of 'objectivity', as Marcellin Hodeir has demonstrated) or cartoons. The handshake between Soviet and American soldiers at the Elbe, American soldiers raising the stars and stripes on Iwo Jima, the 'Big Three' at Yalta, the American soldier being shot in Vietnam (usually with the caption, 'Why?', inspired in turn by Capa's Spanish soldier), Willy Brandt kneeling before the war memorial in Warsaw, the Kurdish mother and child gassed by Saddam Hussein, all carry their own mythical message, more impressively, more emotionally than words, and at least some of them have in turn inspired cartoonists in their work. Cartoons can also by the simple use of the mythical term as a label choose quite different images – for example, a lamb (with the caption 'Bosnia-Herzegovina' about to be devoured by two wolves, with the word 'Balkan Yalta' written below the picture) does not make any allusion to the photographs of the Yalta conference, but uses the imagery of animal fables.[5]

Finally, we have encountered myths in one of their most primeval functions, namely *myths as rites*. Freud and Jung[6] would

4. An idea reflected in the writings of German historians like Karl Othmar Freiherr von Aretin, Hartmut Bookmann, Heinz Schilling.

5. 'Balkanska Yalta', caricature in *Zunanja Politika* (1992).

6. See, for example, Carl Gustav Jung, 'Über die zwei Arten des Denkens', and 'Mythendeutung', in Karl Kerenyi (ed.), *Die Eröffnung des Zugangs zum Mythos –*

have had something to say about the need symbolically to slay the German dragon by wiping the state of Prussia, its heartland and the mythical incarnation of all that was evil in Germany, off the face of Europe. This not only satisfied French and British dislikes of Prussia, but also gratified the Catholic Rhenish and South German resentments harboured since 1871 against the Protestant upstarts in the East who had come to dominate the entire Empire. This also gave all the Germans (East and West), and the Austrians, a scapegoat on to which they could project all responsibility for the German catastrophe and the crimes of the National Socialists – there was a tendency to forget that Hitler was an Austrian and that Prussia was a stronghold of Social Democracy during the Weimar Republic. Adenauer greatly played on the West-orientated, Romano-Catholic history of West Germany which served as a basis of commonality and hence friendship with France, Belgium, the Netherlands and Italy. Also within the GDR, the Prussian past was firmly condemned until the early 1980s, when both the FRG and the GDR rediscovered positive elements in Prussian history, thenceforth competing for its heritage.

One could also see Franco-German friendship and reconciliation as a ritual symbolising German redemption and reintegration into the community of the righteous. This takes on a particular dimension (incidentally, together with Polish-German and Israeli-German relations) in times of moral crisis within Germany, when invariably it is prominent Frenchmen like François Mitterrand, Alfred Grosser or Joseph Rovan, or Americans like Fritz Stern, Gordon Craig, Elie Wiesel or whoever is US ambassador in Bonn at the time, who are invited by Germans to give their verdict on what is right and wrong.

Myths As Political Instruments

In all these cases, these historical myths in a split-second conjure up in the minds of audiences and readers certain associations, which the writer or orator wants to evoke. They are consequently a swift and effective way of communicating an idea, the shorthand for an argument. It is thus not surprising that they are used

---

ein Lesebuch, 5th edn (Darmstadt: Wissenschaftiche Buchgesellschaft, 1967, 1996), pp. 161–169.

particularly by people trying to persuade quickly: journalists and politicians.

This quick appeal makes historical myths attractive as instruments of journalism and political rhetoric. They catalyse consensus where the slow and difficult process of persuasion through rational argument might not produce the same result. They deliberately, through their elliptic quality, forestall logical questioning of the supposed historical parallel. Moreover they bring emotions and moral appeal to support the good cause into play where the issue really requires a careful and dispassionate balancing of different courses of action, all of them painful, none of them fully satisfactory or fully 'good', none of them promising clear success. They cast the speaker or writer in the rôle of the sage who has a clear vision of deep moral principles under all the overgrowth of complications and details.

Additionally, it deceives the audience or readership into a false sense of agreement with the author or orator. This use of myth for the building of consensus can also strengthen or create group solidarity, through shared beliefs, shared (historical) points of reference – myths can be the underpinnings of a political religion. We have encountered here rallying myths, designed to forge internal consensus: the myth of an Islamic threat to Europe, the myth of neutrality as the essence of Swedish identity, the myth of independence as the essence of French identity, Britain's splendid isolation or difference from the European Continent, the influence which the Dutch believe they can wield through righteousness and the defence of international law, the faith the Germans have after their Sin and Fall in the Third Reich in their redemption through Franco-German friendship and European integration.

In all of these cases, historical precedent is invoked to bestow legitimacy, and history is applied to an actual contemporary situation or to a possible development as an interpretational pattern.

Historical Analogy

A particular use is thus made of history, or to be more precise, of what is considered to be historical precedent. In a very complex environment, people seek simple explanations, using historical analogies to establish (supposedly) rules which help decide on a certain course of action. By invoking these historical experiences, with the implication that there is one (and only one) 'lesson' to be drawn from each, and that this in turn is generally known to the audience or readership addressed, a pseudo-consensus is created in the minds of readers or listeners on the 'lesson learnt'. It is thus very useful for politicians in particular to be the first to define the terms of any contemporary policy debate by invoking particular interpretations of the past.

The historical experience and its 'lesson' invoked thus form a shorthand (or symbol) that takes the place of a rational justification of a policy recommendation in a new situation. The way consensus is built through the allusion to a 'lesson of the past', shortcuts in the minds of an audience the critical, balanced examination of parallels (and differences) between a given, present situation and the historical analogy. The agreement which is triggered in the listener or reader usually refers merely to the recognition of the shorthand ('yes, I have heard of Yalta, that's the division of the world, a *bad thing*', or 'yes, balance of power, that's a *good thing* for Britain'). The agreement does not refer to a detailed examination of whether a new situation can indeed be compared with a past event, or whether a policy principle of the past is usefully applied here also. But these two reasons for agreement are confused in the minds of the audience or readers. The result is that of a feeling of agreement with the speaker or author, but for the wrong reason: one does not agree that the analogy is *valid* (after a detailed, informed assessment of similarities and differences), but that it is *familiar*. Rational argument is thus bypassed by a mere appeal to familiarity. The analogy, whether good or inadequate, takes on the guise of evidence; the 'lesson' of the historical event which is then used to suggest a particular policy appears as 'truth', rather than as one possible interpretation of the past event, which may or may not have significant, rather than superficial, parallels with the new event. In the working of this myth, it is crucial that critical reflection is bypassed.

Historical Teleology As 'Ersatz'-Religion

Why is it then that one can get an audience or readership to agree that something is likely to happen again, merely because it happened before? Today most historians would agree with Karl Popper that every historical event is unique, and that history, while not constituting a general development towards ever greater progress and happiness, nevertheless does not 'repeat itself' in the popular sense. Why is there nonetheless a temptation to seek a prophetic rôle for History with a capital 'H'?

Humans have, since the origins of recorded thought available to us, sought to bring order to chaos through a set of concepts helping them to interpret the world. They turned to myth – Schelling's 'primitive explanation of the world' – and to religions, to give some metaphysical meaning to all the madness and misery around them. The great religions have tended to identify Man's sins as reasons for punishment (catastrophe, plague, war) inflicted by some divine judge. The two religions which have formed European culture and political thought, Judaism and Christianity, have looked upon history as a long development. Beginning with the Fall from Paradise through Man's sin (to use Biblical language), history is described as repeated trials which give Man the opportunity to redeem himself, step by step, or to sin again: finally he will be redeemed at least in part through his own righteous deeds and reunited to God or condemned to eternal punishment.[7]

This teleological interpretation combines the notion of a more or less linear progress towards the goal of redemption (or a cyclical progress which will bring Man back to the Golden Age of initial innocence) with intermittently recurrent trials offering the opportunity of redemption. These ideas have become so deeply ingrained in European cultures that they also imprinted themselves upon the 'religions without God', the ideologies of the post-religious age, nationalism, Social Darwinism, racism, Marxism, but also Liberalism.[8]

Thus, although in a largely post-religious age the metaphysical meaning of life is sought outside religion, the tendency to look for trial and error, for metaphysical tests of a nation's valour or the strength of democratic values, has been inherited from the previous ages. Where in ancient and medieval times, history was the handmaiden of mythology and religion,[9] nationalism and racism have used history as a quarry to prove the fitness of this nation or that race, and Marxist-Leninists deduced from historical precedent

7. Although Protestantism puts greater emphasis on God's grace, all Christian Churches emphasise the need for self-sacrifice, good actions and the resistance to temptation and sin.

8. This is held by the Whig interpretation of history as a steady progress towards improvement in human society; see Arthur Marwick, *The Nature of History* 3rd edn (London: Macmillan, 1989), pp. 52–56, 91–93, 334.

9. M. I. Finley, 'Myth, History and Memory', in M. I. Finley, *The Use and Abuse of History* 2nd edn (1975, Harmondsworth: Penguin Paperback, 1995), pp. 11–33.

the patterns to be sought in the present and future which would elicit certain actions according to 'scientific' precedent.

Even in European belief-systems which are neither Marxist nor narrowly nationalist, history is drawn upon to provide interpretational patterns for the present.[10] But if it is used to forecast the future, one is in danger of slipping from drawing parallels to predicting repetition. Used in this way, history can become not a hermeneutic explanation of unique past events and their causes and consequences, but a framework of reference credited with the ability not only to explain past and present but to prescribe rules for action in present and future contexts. The historical analogy becomes oracle.[11]

Thus historical events, which in themselves are unique and the result of millions of actions and developments, assume the character of myths: of blueprints, or events that will or could repeat themselves, losing their uniqueness, becoming precedents, setting patterns. By referring to historical analogy in this way, the impression is given (explicitly or implicitly) that if a historical 'lesson' is not applied, if the policy prescribed is not adopted, then inevitably some past catastrophe will repeat itself. History thus once again becomes the ancillary of myth: it is simplified to the point where it is no longer unique reality, but distortion of reality. Complex situations are simplified into a choice between black and white; complex developments are reduced to monocausality.

What has also been passed on to us from the age of classical myths and old religions is the moral dimension. The use of historical analogies goes along with an implied value system of guilt and punishment, or of redemption through sacrifice the next time a trial comes around. In comparing Bosnia with the Spanish Civil War or Munich, there is the moral imperative of not repeating the past error or indeed sin, and to exculpate the past shortcoming by taking the right course of action this time. By emphasising the need for the Franco-German couple, there is the imperative of avoiding a return to centuries of fratricidal rivalry and war. The appeal to myths thus also suggests a distinction between a morally good decision and a morally bad decision. Through this moral appeal, the invocation of the myth does not solely warn of catastrophe if a different policy is chosen from the one recommended. The policy

10. For a most stimulating treatment of this subject, see Jacques Le Goff, *Histoire et mémoire* (Paris: Gallimard, 1988).

11. André Jolles, 'Mythe', orig. 1930, reprinted in Kerémyi (ed.), *Die Eröffnung des Zugangs*, pp. 199–201.

suggested is legitimated, justified by the myth, but is also given a gloss of moral superiority.

Hermeneutics and Heuristics, Hotplates and History

This is perhaps still not enough to explain why it is history – or given the very special, selective use that it made of the past, one should say 'History' with a capital 'H' – that is used in this mythogenous way. It is not only the quest for simple explanations or order in chaos, but also the desire to shield oneself and others from harm. If a correlation is made between past suffering and one's own actions which brought this about, then one can see the suffering in terms of past mistakes (which often include an underestimation of a past danger) which must in future be avoided by learning 'lessons' from the past and applying them to new situations. It is not surprising that the great wars that ravaged Europe, particularly in the past two centuries, have, like natural disasters, driven people to seek ways of predicting and even deflecting future catastrophes of the kind.

Human beings do not deal with the complex world around them solely as their genes dictate. They have the capability to learn, either through their own experience, or through behaviour and reactions taught to them by others. For example, most parents teach their children not to touch a hotplate. The 'lesson' conveyed is that hotplates are dangerous. But it is of course not true that hotplates are dangerous when they are switched off. Yet the more complex and accurate explanation – hotplates may or may not be switched on, and if they are not, you can safely put your hand on them – tends to be eschewed by caring parents. The simple message is the safest: don't ever touch a hotplate, because if you do, you will hurt yourself. For the purposes of protecting the child from pain, the simple, unambiguous prescription makes good sense, as few disadvantages are imaginable that might derive from following this prescription. Faced with this simple problem, the reduction of the problem to this simple formula is adequate, even if reality is distorted in the process. For it is not scientifically *true* to say that any hotplate is *always* dangerous to touch, as it cannot be found to be true every time the experiment is repeated. For any less simple problem, the distortion required to arrive at this simple formula is likely to be inadequate.

In international relations, can one learn from historic precedent in a way that makes it possible to 'teach' and 'learn' the lesson that one must never appease a dictator, or that any agreement between Germany and Russia will always be harmful to the 'West', or that a balance-of-power policy is always the right answer to Britain's 'national' interest? Let us return to the way in which 'lessons' are arrived at. The deduction of rules and 'prognoses' from repeated experiments is useful for the engineer or the physicist, for the surgeon or the sociologist. They are likely to apply to all situations which can be reconstructed in every detail, and that can then be repeated in every detail. Such evidence forms the experimental basis of all 'generalising sciences' (in the words of Karl Popper) such as physics or even sociology. These heuristic sciences can predict that whenever X occurs, Y will be the inevitable consequence, given the same circumstances. But as the historical event can neither be reconstructed nor repeated in every detail, history cannot serve as 'prognosis'.[12]

Repetition and repeatability are crucial in this context. These two characteristics *seem* shared by the 'generalising sciences' and by historical myths. All myths discussed in this book have a crucial element of repetition, or continual application. Repetition lies already in the fact that the myth itself crystallises around a moment of crisis that is half-expected, and is invoked once again during a superficially similar crisis. To be recognised as blueprints for further repetition, an event has to recall a previous event, a previous statement. Thus Rapallo is preceded by Tauroggen and the peace of Brest-Litovsk, Suez by Dunkirk and Mers el Kébir, Munich followed acquiescence in the German occupation of the Rhineland and the *Anschluss* of Austria, it followed the betrayal of the Spanish Republic and of Haile Selassie's Abyssinia. The myth of Yalta was inspired by the fear of a return of American isolationism (which after the First World War had *de facto* resulted in the ceding of Europe as a sphere of influence to whoever was prepared to make the effort to seize it) and the real spheres of influence agreement between Churchill and Stalin in December 1944, and preceded the *de facto* partition of Germany at Potsdam. The Adenauer-de Gaulle 'couple' was preceded by the Stresemann-Briand 'couple', the 'special relationship' between Churchill and F.D. Roosevelt was preceded by Theodore Roosevelt's admiration for Britain.

This repetition suggests to the superficial observer that there is a 'force of History' at work, that History can somehow repeat itself, given similar circumstances. It is this which leads to the assumption

12. Karl Popper, *The Open Society and Its Enemies* Vol. 2, *Heel and Marx* (London: Routledge & Kegan Paul, 1945, fifth edition 1966, repr. 1993), pp. 261–269.

that one is dealing not with unique events, but with a pattern, with a scientific law.[13] This, however, denies individuality, uniqueness, change. Predicting the behaviour of Saddam Hussein from the record of the behaviour of Hitler implies that there is a category of human beings (dictators) who all think alike and act alike in similar situations, or more daring still, that all human beings, given a particular situation, would act in a particular way. It denies the freedom of choice of such a dictator, which is claimed for one's own side for which an alternative to 'appeasement' is prescribed.

Moreover, the invoking of historical myths, by pretending that there is a law of historical repetition, serves as a pseudo-rationalisation, furnishing bogus scientific evidence for a decidedly unscientific argument. To claim that there is some eternal law of History that makes France vulnerable to a betrayal by Germany and Russia, or (singly or jointly) by Britain and the United States, denies the uniqueness of all these circumstances, the change of value systems in Germany since 1945 and in Russia since 1990, and abstracts from the particular political circumstances and risks of any given event (do Frenchmen retrospectively, really wish that the United States had used nuclear weapons in Indochina in 1954?). In other words, while there are parallels between Rapallo and the Ribbentrop-Molotov pact in that they were concluded between German and Soviet governments, and that both treaties upset the French, that is where the parallels end. In 1956, the US government thought the Suez expedition foolhardy, but some Frenchmen and Britons thought likewise. The 'consequences' drawn by de Gaulle from the 'lessons' of Dunkirk and Suez, namely France's withdrawal from NATO's military integration, cannot be 'scientifically' proven to be the only rational ones.

It would be more absurd still to argue that Suez was an identical repetition of the experiment of relying on the US in Indochina (Diên Biên Phu), or that the betrayal of Czechoslovakia at Munich was the identical repetition of the experiment of abandoning Manchuria, Abyssinia and the Spanish Republic to their respective fates. The interpretational pattern provided by the myth can never fully match the particular situation to which it is applied: no historical situation is ever as completely identical to another historical situation as a physical experiment with a limited number of variables can be, where the same result can measurably be reproduced. Mostly, the historical 'precedent' does not even come close enough to make it *reasonable* (as in our hotplate

13. *Ibid.*, p. 269.

example), let alone scientific, to use it as an interpretational aid for a new situation.

Usually, the invocation of the historical precedent, or of the 'myth', the rule derived from historical experience, blurs the view for the full understanding of the new (or developing) situation to the point where the latter becomes dangerously distorted. It is here that findings about human reluctance to contemplate an interpretation of a situation that departs from the expected norm must be stressed. Thomas Kuhn has shown us that even in the natural sciences,

> ... novelty emerges only with difficulty, manifested by resistance, against a background provided by expectation. Initially, only the anticipated and usual are experienced even under circumstances where anomaly is later to be observed.[14]

One could say that in international relations, there is a reluctance to focus on what is new, as interpretational patterns for it are lacking, and there are, instead, expectations as to how other nations might act, which are informed by their past behaviour. There is the pretence here that 'nations' have a single identity comparable to one human being, rather than being composites of millions of people who gradually undergo changes of leadership, generational renewal, and with this, may acquire new values, new experiences and new common points of historical reference. Even more so than with science, there is a reluctance in international relations to revise images of other nations. In the context of dangerous or even catastrophic experiences of the past, this is thoroughly understandable ('never touch a hotplate ...'), but it makes necessary 'paradigm shifts', or even simply the dispassionate analysis of a given situation, difficult. The problem arising from this is that in international relations, the imagination and the myth in themselves become real political factors, assuming power and affecting reality. This is done in a spirit of negating change; the prophecy of the recurrence of disaster is thus more likely to become self-fulfilling.

Myths vs. Change

This volume demonstrates the importance of myths in interstate relations. Myths are present in the minds of many, from historians

14. Thomas S. Kuhn, *The Structure of Scientific Revolutions* 2nd edition (Chicago: University of Chicago Press, 1970), p. 64.

themselves to decision-makers, journalists, commentators and the public in general. They determine how a situation is seen, to the extent that new situation can be misinterpreted dangerously. Public reactions, indeed policy decisions are then made not in relation to an actual situation or development, but to the myth which is projected onto reality. In this sense, 'imagination acts upon man as really as does gravitation, and may kill him as certainly as does prussic acid'.[15] The influence of such myths must be taken into account in attempts to understand interstate relations and foreign policy making. Historical myths in particular are of considerable importance. It would be vain today to explain Britain's attitude towards the European Union without recourse to the myth of British difference, or to interpret Franco-German relations without the myth of a special Franco-German friendship, or equally to analyse US policies in the Yugoslav war since 1991 without the myth of Vietnam, the fear of the quagmire. Any analysis of foreign and military policy is incomplete, indeed deeply inadequate, if these metaphysical dimensions of each culture, its subjective views of the past and its beliefs about the present are not taken into consideration.[16]

This volume thus cautions against facile historical comparisons which point to similarities without noting the differences. One should be careful not to conjure up spectres of the past which will overshadow and blur the analysis of the present, and as such are likely artificially to create darkness and misunderstanding. It would be wise to take recourse to historical comparisons only in a logical, rational way, remembering, with Leibniz, 'that the world changeth'. The scientific comparison points out similarities as well as crucial differences – only, the majority of one's students, readers and listeners will have switched off mentally before one comes around to discussing the differences. What they will remember is not the careful analysis, but the simplicity and appeal of the myth. 'Audiences', wrote Tom Stoppard, 'know what to expect, and that is all that they are prepared to believe in.'[17]

15. Sir James George Frazer, *The Golden Bough: A Study in Magic and Religion*, abridged version (London: Macmillan, 1924), p. 223.

16. Heuser, *Nuclear Mentalities?*, ch. 5.

17. Tom Stoppard, *Rosencrantz & Guildenstern Are Dead*, Act II, King of the Players.

APPENDIX: THE BERLIN MYTH

A Curse in Ten Cantos

Uwe Prell

Where a myth is invented, images are made great by objects, if it becomes mythology, objects are made great by images.
Goethe, Diary, *5 April 1777*

Neither mythology nor legends should be tolerated by science. These should be left to the poets, whose vocation it is to deal with them for the world's use and pleasure. Let the scientist restrict himself to the most immediate and clearest present. If, however, he does on occasion want to appear as rhetorician, this should not be denied him.
Goethe, Wilhelm Meister's Apprenticeship

This is the curse of evil deeds: That they spawn further deeds and always evil ones.
Schiller, Wallenstein: A Historical Drama in Three Parts

Canto 1

Released from the double cage of a divided Europe, Germany's only metropolis faces the future in bewilderment. Even half a decade after unification, debates about the future are

---

Translated by Christine Giese-Pretzlik and David Shaw
The author would like to thank Heinz Werner for valuable suggestions.

shrill, lamenting. Metropolis between West and East, capital of the Federal Republic, region of the future – familiar slogans to some, and yet they are like distant stars. While one half of the population complains that their new world is unexpectedly rough, to the other half also, almost everything has changed, as can be seen from the building-sites everywhere, and in particular, their wage slips.

Forced for one-and-a-half generations into a straight-jacket which guaranteed not only safety for Berlin but also safety from Berlin, Germany's largest city seemed squeezed into a size tolerable for all. 'The Berlin Myth' was a gentle fire for 'reveries at a Prussian hearth'.

Already the divided coexistence, conjured up one last time in the obituaries on the departure of the Allies in 1994, seems strangely foreign, outdated over night and unfit to be used for coping with an obscure present. What was the past, what lies ahead?

Canto 2

The 'Two Berlins' (Uwe Johnson) took almost two decades to grasp fully the consequences of the Second World War. Only after the Wall was built did it become impossible to deny that Berlin had lost not only its supra-regional political functions, but also its economic strength and its cultural charisma.

Exhausted by the struggle against the Communist threat, West Berlin nestled down behind the Wall, dozing on the intravenous West German drip of subsidies. Two major crises (the Soviet Blockade of 1948/1949 and the Khrushchev Ultimatum, with the building of the Wall, of 1958–1961) and then the achievements of the *détente* policies of the 1970s (in spite of which the Cold War might have turned 'hot') led to the conviction that the best way to avoid pain was to sit still. Remaining motionless, one gradually no longer feels one's chains, becomes accustomed to them, forgets them even.

Annually, on the now almost forgotten 'Day of German Unity', the political elite of West Germany jetted off to Berlin for a programme of commemorative events. The Reichstag, moored for eternity at the furthest edge of the western world like a rusting tanker, was brought back to life for a couple of hours: solemn music, exhortatory speeches, oaths of allegiance to the walled-in front-line city. Remember? There was a feeling that this building from another world could be more than just an irksome memory. Over the years the lament degenerated into a ritual, reinforced by the assurance that one day, if the Wall were to fall, everything would be like old times – without the negative tinge. But on the next day, the ladies and gentlemen would fly home to Hamburg, Frankfurt am Main or Munich, the new leading cities that had long overtaken the city with a future in which hardly anyone believed anymore.

East Berlin seemed different. Ideologically speaking, the 'Capital of the GDR' had a future to offer: 'Vanguard of the Working Class', 'Justice', 'World Peace'. It was the capital of the star pupil among the socialist apprentices, but at the same time it was a 'city on the front-line' besieged by the 'enemies'. Within, some were indifferent, resigned to the situation; others left the country, still others protested until they gave up, co-operated or were thrown out, and yet others tried to negotiate official channels. Those who believed in Socialism *à la* GDR were a minority.

West Berlin, the ideological enemy, in the GDR's own front garden was a permanent provocation to which only two responses were possible: either to 'eliminate' or to 'contain' the provocateur. The latter solution, the 'Wall', symbolised a war waged on several fronts against both the West and the people at home. Thus East Berlin degenerated into a fortress swarming with guards and with much clattering tiddly-om-pom-pom. A fortress with some cracks; but these were carefully guarded and almost always infiltrated. While West Berlin was on the intravenous drip of West German prosperity, the SED siphoned off capital as well as materials, workers and experts from throughout the GDR. Therefore East Berlin was not particularly popular among the citizens of the GDR. At best they shopped there, spent an evening at the theatre, visited a museum or the Palace of the Republic. Or they had business in the city, had been summoned by the 'competent authorities' to 'clarify a matter'.

Berliners had adjusted, both over here and over there. They accepted the absurd as a given, indefinitely. Politicians and officials found this situation tolerable, more so in West Germany than in the two Berlins and in the GDR. Cheeky, coarse and rebellious Berlin kept its mouth shut.

Canto 3

On 9 November 1989, all this changed. The peaceful revolution swept through the city like a storm, blew the dust out of the musty nooks and crannies of East Berlin and aired out the fustiness of the cliques of West Berlin. Their eyes were no longer held: suddenly the Emperor was naked. Marx-Engels-Platz and the Kurfürstendamm showed themselves in their true light: a deliberate, at best tolerated destruction of the old city, unimaginative buildings on one side, on the other a suburban boulevard of toy lanterns. Artificiality, surrogates, making do in difficult circumstances, but nothing like real, living boulevards like the Champs-Elysées, Fifth Avenue, Regent's Street or Karl-Johan-Gata in Oslo.

Despite the sobering winter and spring of 1989–1990, the bewilderment continued. The leaden times were past, but the 'golden' future seemed doubtful. Two internally divided societies collided, revealing themselves as pitifully fragile. The East: a community born out of necessity which merely paid lip-service to its basic values, unsustainable on a permanent basis. The West: a drudging alliance of convenience which craved distraction, a vanishing repertoire of common bonds. Consensus without substance *versus* substance without consensus.

For a moment, it all seemed perfectly simple. Socialism had failed and languid Western democracy had been given the unique opportunity to reinvent itself. But a divided society cannot grow together in a few nights of euphoria and embraces. The day after the storming of the Wall people went to work as usual. East Berliners did not unite with West Berlin, and it took West Berliners a while to understand that what happened on Alexanderplatz concerned them, too.

Canto 4

In this moment of breathless bewilderment the familiar and blaring fanfare struck up: the Berlin Myth – Potsdamer Platz in the 1920s, five o'clock tea in the Hotel Adlon, Fontane and Tucholsky, six-day bike races and Albert Einstein opening the Berlin radio exhibition. The Berlin Myth glitters like a Christmas bauble. The 'Düsseldorf Myth', the 'Hamburg Myth', or even the 'Stuttgart Myth' would sound silly by comparison.

A myth, word, speech, tale, fable, an 'absolute utterance which therefore need no longer be substantiated'[1] – of all German cities, only Berlin conjures up such a pyrotechnical display of images.

1. *Meyer's Comprehensive Paperback Encyclopaedia* Vol. 15 (Mannheim, 1992), p. 126.

Frederick the Great playing his flute; 'dropping the pilot', Bismarck; demonstrators holding placards reading 'Don't Shoot, Brothers'; torch-lit processions through the Brandenburg Gate; the Reichstag in flames; Goebbels in the Sports Palace – 'Do you want total war?' answered by a fanatical crowd's 'Sieg Heil'; 'raisin bombers' dropping CARE parcels; Ulbricht's 'No one is going to build a wall'; Kennedy's 'Ich bin ein Berliner'; and finally the mad night when the Wall 'came down'. Where madness is rife, the divine, heaven and hell are never far. The myth imposes itself; in 'contrast to logical cognition, [the myth] ...seeks to represent reality for which it needs to provide no rational proof'.[2]

Canto 5

We, however, will seek to represent reality, provide rational proof, form judgements. Thesis – substantiation – example.

The scenes invoked, from the flute-playing Frederick the Great to the fall of the Wall, all took place in Berlin. All are undoubtedly part of Berlin's history, but they are more than that: part of Prussian, German, European history. Indeed, the war provoked by Hitler and the Cold War had repercussions spanning two generations and half the globe.

Any attempt to distil one city's history from this would be meaningless. Here is the first peculiarity: Berlin's history was never just Berlin's history. Ever since the city acquired a political role as a royal residence, Berlin has always been more than a regional centre. And yet it has only been the hub of the country for a short time, unlike Paris or London. Although Berlin has often been important for national and international politics, the nature of this importance is difficult to define. No one epithet sums up the character of Berlin as it does for other German cities, the 'Hanseatic city' Hamburg, the 'financial centre' Frankfurt, the 'Swabian metropolis' Stuttgart, the 'home of justice' Karlsruhe. Berlin's role was seldom constant over more than one generation. The search for a permanent position on a regional, national and international basis, is the second peculiarity of this city's history.

This quest for a sustainable self-image has always been marked by fundamental contradictions, as has all of Germany's past. On the one hand Berlin has nearly always reflected the prevailing order of the time. On the other, the city has always been a stronghold of

2. *Ibid.*

opposition forces seeking reform, restoration, or even revolution. Even when official policy attempted to impose its stamp on the city, this could never be done entirely or permanently. Berlin has always been:

- Both the stage upon which the Monarchy unfolded its splendour and the stronghold of Social Democracy (despite Bismarck's attempts to suppress it)
- Both the mercurial centre of the Weimar Republic and also the target of the extremes fighting it;
- Both the centre of terror and also the site of the most nearly successful attempt to free the country of its murderers;
- And finally, both a Communist capital and the shop-window of Democracy.

There have always been several Berlins in one and the same city – this is the third peculiarity.

Thus, on closer inspection, the myth turns out to be a simplification of a number of complicated processes, a true myth, which seems to sum it all up.

Canto 6

This observation would be banal if it were not so distressingly relevant today. With the fall of the Wall in 1989, history seemed to honour the promise held out for so long – Berlin on the way to German, if not European summits, rushing spectacularly from one major event to the next.

During the revolutionary winter of 1989–1990 few in the city doubted that the 'days of greatness', or what people thought of as such, would return soon. The fall of the Wall seemed a portent of divine providence, a mythical vision, a completely different 'seizure of power' outshining, at least temporarily, the memory of its hateful counterpart of 1933. New superlatives sprouted – the largest urban fallow fields in the world! The greatest competitions for construction contracts of all time!!

But reality had other things in store – those who banked on the Berlin Myth had a lot to learn, as the Virgin Megastore and the fnac bookshop showed. The list of abandoned projects grew. Of course, it is nothing special for projects to fail, but for so many of them to fail in such a short time is remarkable. Handicapped by its own distorted growth, the city prepared for a great leap. But anyone who has been fettered for decades has to learn to walk before he tries to run. Or, to quote Gottfried Benn: 'See the situation for what it is.'

Canto 7

Since 1990, Berlin has been technically unified. Despite the grumblings of officials, the city's parliament and the city's government moved from the district of Schöneberg to the district of Mitte, in order to demonstrate unity in their own practice. This was the right decision. Administrative reforms, the renewal of the infrastructure, from the sewers to the electricity cables, the reorganisation of the city's theatres and museums, were achieved within two to four years, by and large with an unusual efficiency, the greatest modernisation of the city since the formation of Greater Berlin in 1920. And yet, it failed to reassure the Berliners: it had its origins less in an analysis of the needs of society and more in the expansion of the West's administration into the 'acceding territory'. This alone cannot create a community. A society is more than a set of regulations, infrastructure, commerce and a little distraction. Despite all the bustling thoroughness, 'inner unity' was not addressed, which may explain the successes of the Communist successor party in the elections of 1990 and 1994.

Let us remember: when the Wall came down, both German societies were ailing. East and West were tormented, paradoxically, by both upheaval and apathy. The economic miracle of the West was at its end, international competition had become severe. The government of the old Federal Republic, with Helmut Kohl at its helm, was administering the bitter medicine of welfare cuts in order to make the West German economy more competitive; where this worked, it was at the price of harsher working conditions here, unemployment and exclusion there, social friction in the middle, upheaval and new mobility *versus* apathy and resignation.

The situation in the GDR was worse. The poverty of the East was there for all to see. A society so blatantly founded on illusion could not completely repress all questions. Despite the many entanglements with the state security system, sections of the church, youth and intellectuals, and even leading figures in the institutions, became increasingly rebellious in the 1980s. It is they who brought down the Wall.

From this stems the dilemma of unity: although West German democracy was able technically to absorb the consequences of the GDR's collapse, the mentality of each society lives on. Thus unification was treated in West Germany as if it were a problem to be overcome by administrative crisis management, while the East German revolutionaries were never given the chance to create a new society for themselves. Berlin was at the epicentre of the earthquake, yet it was left to its own devices or else exposed to tough competition with major national and international cities. Retrospectively, the Wall was not only a physical construction, it was above all a mind-set.

Canto 8

What is to be done? For Heaven's sake, no new institutions, no committees, no programmes. But rather a few questions and suggestions, an outline of a process, yet to be defined, of a tool which could help to break the Berlin Myth, which obstructs the view of reality, and helps to break new ground.

Take for example Berlin's publishing houses. One thing the city does not need is more coffee-table books in the uniform style of the Nikolai publishing house. Or another warmed-over feature supplement on the grand masters of the Weimar era. Nor does the publicly financed *Short History of Berlin*, with its official seal of approval, contribute substantially to the advancement of the city. All this is too much, and yet not enough.

We must accept Berlin as an arena of transition, not only with sobriety and pertinence, but also with the courage to face the controversial, a willingness to enter into debate and discussion, running the risk of being proved wrong, as long as we have faced the real, material and spiritual problems. An image of the new city must be created, slowly and clearly as if it were being spelled out letter by letter, with extremely simple questions. What, for example, is the significance of the fact that Berlin is now a Federal State? What does the new proximity of Eastern Europe (for those in the West) mean? What does the new proximity of Western Europe (for those in the East) mean? What will the city live on? How can the service metropolis Berlin function, when hardly anybody needs these services, let alone can afford them? Why are we witnessing an artistic crisis in the theatre, literature and the arts? Who has what interests at heart? Simple questions, fundamental and straight to the point.

The editorials and headlines of 1990, 1991 and 1992 extrapolated Berlin's future from the 'Berlin Myth'. The consequences are already visible: buildings after the latest fashions. But what is important is what is on the inside, not the outside. Will they be empty shells, or will they one day accommodate real people? For whom is this city being rebuilt? Publicity brochures promise slick facades, elegant shops, quality products; soon the city's major shopping centres will include not only the Kurfürstendamm and Alexanderplatz but also Friedrichstraße and Potsdamer Platz, the commercialised Berlin Myth. But is there a large enough market for them? Wouldn't a glance at income statistics have formed a more solid basis for all this development?

Canto 9

So, to hell with the Berlin Myth! The devil take all the blather about a pulsating cityscape, shining tarmac, frantic life, the romanticism of Potsdamer Platz and nostalgia of the Roaring Twenties. Berlin is constipated with too much future. Down the drain, then, with the sugary-sweet sticky toffee of empty talk about visions for the future. Berlin is an impoverished city. The current capital of the jobless is broke. In reality it can at best afford only bread and water: it has *real* problems to contend with.

Canto 10

Perhaps new answers can be found in a different way, in a different place. Take a stroll in one of Berlin's neighbourhoods, for example Walther-Schreiber-Platz in Steglitz. You will find unarguably one of the most unattractive buildings in the city: the Forum Steglitz, an aluminium eye-sore, designed by the architects Finn Bartels, Georg Heinrich and Christoph Schmid-Ott and opened in 1970. But it works and it's worth a visit. On the ground floor, hiding at the back, is the Bornmarkt, recently done up in the new German market style – glass, mirrors, the exquisite beauty of wood presented in easy-to-clean Formica. But never fear, the people here are genuine. Take a look around. Go to one of the stalls, perhaps to 'Eva's'. Eva is a Filipina who runs a breakfast bar with Freddy. A large coffee costs DM 1.60, a small one, DM 1.50. There is beer, too, of course, or vodka, and the filled rolls are of the best, the usual Berlin repertoire. But Eva has smuggled some exotic touches into her menu: avocado spread, tropical drinks, and these novelties are selling like hot cakes.

The way people use buildings matters, the way they make ultra-modern architecture their own. Fortunately, no one can plan this. And it pays to listen, for example, to those more than well-built German men with their petite little wives from the Philippines or Thailand. An hour spent sitting on one of the bar-stools there, and the listeners will find it difficult to reconcile what they hear there with all the official speeches, brochures and statements. The Berlin Myth – Eva's regulars just shrug their shoulders, chew on their raw mince sandwiches or take a drag on their cigarettes. It's a scene worthy of Heinrich Böll. No, this is not a romantic sociological eulogy on the 'healthy instincts' of the so-called 'simple folk', who are actually far from simple. This is an attempt to remind ourselves of the people who will have to use what is now being built.

It is not the Reichstag or the Brandenburg Gate, it is not Unter den Linden or the Kurfürstendamm – it is these people who *are* Berlin. Those who listen only to the wooden language of politics have long since forgotten that these people exist. Citizens, the electorate, the 'herd of voters'. Those who claim that the problems are too complicated to explain to these people obviously just can't be bothered. What they get in return is the torn city and the fractured society we have today.

Perhaps the 'Berlin Myth' is a divertissement, creates a superficial consensus and a backward-looking future. But it is not a sustainable foundation on which to build a living, human city.

NOTES ON CONTRIBUTORS

Aline Angoustures, who holds a Ph.D. in History from the Institut de Sciences Politiques (Sciences Po'), is researcher at the Commission for Refugee Appeals (Commission des recours des réfugiés) and associate research fellow at the Centre for Twentieth-Century European Studies (CHEVS – National Foundation for Political Sciences). She is the author of *History of Spain in the Twentieth Century* (in French: Eds. Complexe; in Spanish: Ariel, 1993), and of numerous articles on Spain and its image in France.

John Baylis is Professor of International Politics at the University of Wales, Aberystwyth. He is also a Fellow of the Royal Historical Society. He was an Academic Consultant at the National Defence College and a Visiting Professor at Brigham Young University, Utah, USA. He has published widely on twentieth-century British history, International Relations and nuclear strategy. His most recent publications include *Ambiguity and Deterrence: British Nuclear Strategy, 1945–64* (Oxford: Oxford University Press, 1995); *Anglo-American Relations since 1939: The Enduring Alliance* (Manchester: Manchester University Press, 1997) and *The Globalization of World Politics: An Introduction to International Relations* (Oxford: Oxford University Press, 1997), edited with Steven Smith.

Cyril Buffet holds a doctorate in History from the Sorbonne (Université de Paris IV). He was a Fellow of the German Alexander von Humboldt Foundation and a Fellow at the Centre Marc Bloch in Berlin. He teaches at the graduate School of Journalism in Lille and is foreign policy adviser to the French National Assembly. His books include *La France et l'Allemagne, 1945–1949: Mourir pour Berlin?* (Paris: Colin, 1991), *Berlin: A History of the City of Berlin, from its Origins until German Reunification* (Paris: Fayard, 1993), and (with Rémy Hardoutzel) *La Collaboration…* (Paris: Perrin, 1989), and he is the author of a television documentary, *Fremde Freunde* (Arte: 1997) on Franco-German relations. He is an expert on twentieth-century French and German history and the history of Brandenburg and Prussia.

David Chuter holds a doctorate in English Literature from the University of London (King's College), which examined Shakespeare's *Merchant of Venice* from the point of view of Renaissance *mentalité* and economic culture. He is now an official in the British Ministry of Defence (MOD). He has been a Research Fellow seconded from the MOD at the Centre for Defence Studies of the University of London, where he wrote *Humanity's Soldier: France and International Security, 1919–2000* (Providence and Oxford: Berghahn, 1996). He is currently also working on a book on civil-military relations.

Robert Cooper is a career member of Her Majesty's Diplomatic Service. He is currently Minister in the British Embassy, Bonn. He is a former head of the Policy Planning Staff in the Foreign and Commonwealth Office in London. His publications include *The Post-Modern State and the World Order* (Demos, 1996).

Ann-Sofie Dahl, née Nilsson, holds a doctorate in Political Science from the University of Lund. Before becoming a senior security analyst at the Swedish National Defence Research Establishment (FOA), she was a Visiting Fellow at the Center of International Studies at Princeton University and a Visiting Researcher/Resident Scholar at the Department of Government at Georgetown University. Since 1994, she has been the Head of the Security Policy Division of the Swedish War College. She is the Secretary General of the Swedish Atlantic Council. Her publications include *Political Uses of International Law* (Lund: Dialogos, 1987), *Den Moraliska* Stormakten (Stockholm: Timbro, 1991), with Eusebio Mujal-León *Die Sozialistische Internationale in den 80er Jahren* (Bonn: Schöningh, 1995), and she is the editor of *Sveriges säkerhetspolitiska vägval* (Stockholm: Folk och försvar, 1994).

Beatrice Heuser is a Senior Lecturer in War Studies at King's College London, and holds a D. Phil. from Oxford and a Habilitation in Modern History from the Philipps-University of Marburg an der Lahn. She is the author of *Western Containment Policies in the Cold War* (London: Routledge, 1989), *Transatlantic Relations* (London: Pinter, 1996), *Nuclear Strategies and Forces in Europe, 1949–2000* (London: Macmillan, 1997), and *Nuclear Mentalities? Strategies and Beliefs in Britain, France and the FRG* (London: Macmillan, 1998). She has worked as a consultant for the British government, the European Commission and NATO.

Marcellin Hodeir holds a degree in History and International Relations. Since 1980, he has been archivist of the photographic archive of the Historical Service of the French Air Forces (SHAA) at the Château de Vincennes. On behalf of the French Ministry of Defence, he has organised numerous photographic exhibitions and published as well as edited publications on subjects such as the Air Forces in the First World War.

Jan Willem Honig is a Senior Lecturer in War Studies at King's College, London. He was educated at the Universities of Amsterdam and London

(King's College). He joined the Department of War Studies in 1993, after having taught at the University of Utrecht and New York University. He was also a Research Associate at the Institute for East-West Security Studies in New York. His publications include *NATO: An Alliance under Treaty?* (New York: 1991) and *Defence Policy in the North Atlantic Alliance: The Case of the Netherlands* (Westport, Ct.: 1993). His latest book, written with Norbert Both, *Srebrenica: Record of a War Crime* (Penguin, 1996) was short-listed for the 1997 George Orwell Prize. His research interests also include warfare in the Middle Ages.

Peter Krüger holds the Chair of the History of the nineteenth and twentieth centuries and is Dean of the Faculty of History at the Philipps-University Marburg an der Lahn. He is a member of the Collegium Carolinum of the Charles University, Prague. He has published widely on nineteenth- and twentieth-century European history, and his publications include: *The Foreign Policy of the Weimar Republic* (*Die Außenpolitik der Weimarer Republik,* 1985), *Versailles* (1986). He has edited several volumes on Germany and the interstate system in Modern History (*Kontinuität und Wandel in der Staatenordnung der Neuzeit,* 1991; *Deutschland, deutscher Staat, deutsche Nation,* 1993; *Ethnicity and Nationalism,* 1993). His research interests include the history of international relations and constitutional history.

Rémy Leveau is Senior Research Fellow of the Conseil National de Recherches Scientifiques (CNRS) in France. He has been a visiting fellow at the Faculty of Law at the University of Rabat, the University of Ann Arbor, St Joseph's University in Beyrouth, and has worked at the Fondation Nationale des Science Politiques and taught at the Institut d'Etudes Politiques in Paris. He was most recently Vice-Director of the Centre Marc Bloch in Berlin. He has written two books: *Le Fellah marocain, défenseur du Thrône* (Paris: Presses de la FNSP, 1976) and *Le sabre et le turban: l'avenir du Maghreb* (Paris: Burin, 1993).

Reiner Marcowitz is Assistant to the Professor of Modern and Contemporary History at the Technical University, Dresden. He holds a doctorate from the University of Cologne (Department of Philosophy). He is the author of *Option für Paris? Unionsparteien, SPD und Charles de Gaulle, 1958–1969* (Munich: Oldenbourg, 1996) and of several articles on international relations in the Cold War. He is currently working on a Habilitation in nineteenth-century German history.

A.J. Nicholls directs the European Studies Centre of St Antony's College, University of Oxford, where he is an Official Fellow. He is also a lecturer in Modern History at the University of Oxford. He is a leading specialist on modern German history. His two most recent books are *Freedom with Responsibility: The Social Market Economy in Germany, 1918–1963* (Oxford: Clarendon Press, 1994), and *The Bonn Republic: West German Democracy 1945–1990* (London and New York: Longman, 1997). He is also the editor of many recent collective works on aspects of German history, resulting from the Volkswagen programme of Visiting Fellowships to St Antony's College.

Uwe Prell is a political scientist who works as an editor for NISHEN communications. He has published many articles and essays for academic periodicals as well as for the press (including *Die Welt, Süddeutsche Zeitung*), and has organised several exhibitions, one on the history of the Berlin airlift. He has co-authored several books, including *Blockade und Luftbrücke 1948–1949* (West Berlin: Stiftung 'Luftbrückendank', 1988); *Berlin Handbuch* (1991); *Museums in Berlin and Brandenbourg* (1996).

Marc Trachtenberg is Professor of History at the University of Pennsylvania. He is the author of *Reparation in World Politics: France and European Economic Diplomacy, 1916–1923* (New York: Columbia University Press, 1985) and *History and Strategy* (Princeton, N.J.: Princeton University Press, 1991), and is the editor of the six-volume *The Development of American Strategic Thought* (Garland: 1985–1990). His most recent book, *Europe in the Cold War, 1945–1963*, draws on newly available documentation from US, British, French and German archives and edited government documents.

Antonio Varsori is Associate Professor of the History of International Relations and holds the Jean Monnet Chair of the History of European Integration at the Faculty of Political Sciences of the University of Florence. He has been a Research Fellow at the University of Reading and a Visiting Fellow at the University of Southampton. He is member of the editorial board of the *Journal of European Integration History* and deputy-editor of *Storia delle relazioni internazionali*. His publications include *Il diverso declino di due potenze coloniali* (Rome: 1981), *Gli Alleati e l'emigrazione democratica antifascista, 1940–1943* (Rome: 1988); and he is the editor of *La politica estera italiana nel secondo dopo-guerra, 1943–1957* (Milan: 1993) and *Europe 1945–1990s: The End of an Era?* (London: 1995).

Index